Sharing Sacred Spaces in
the Mediterranean

NEW ANTHROPOLOGIES OF EUROPE

Matti Bunzl and Michael Herzfeld, editors

Founding editors
Daphne Berdahl
Matti Bunzl
Michael Herzfeld

Sharing Sacred Spaces in the Mediterranean

*Christians, Muslims, and Jews at
Shrines and Sanctuaries*

EDITED BY
DIONIGI ALBERA AND
MARIA COUROUCLI

Indiana University Press
Bloomington & Indianapolis

First published in French as *Religions traversées: Lieux saints partagés entre chrétiens, musulmans et juifs en Méditerranée*, 2009 Actes Sud.

This book is a publication of
Indiana University Press
601 North Morton Street
Bloomington, Indiana 47404-3797 USA

iupress.indiana.edu

Telephone orders   800-842-6796
Fax orders   812-855-7931

© 2012 by Indiana University Press and Maison Méditerranéenne des Sciences de l'Homme (MMSH)

♾ The paper used in this publication meets the minimum requirements of the American National Standard for Information Sciences—Permanence of Paper for Printed Library Materials, ANSI Z39.48-1992.

Manufactured in the United States of America

Library of Congress Cataloging-in-Publication Data

Religions traversées. English.
  Sharing sacred spaces in the Mediterranean : Christians, Muslims, and Jews at shrines and sanctuaries / edited by Dionigi Albera and Maria Couroucli.
     p. cm. — (New anthropologies of Europe)
  Includes bibliographical references and index.
  ISBN 978-0-253-35633-8 (cloth : alk. paper) — ISBN 978-0-253-22317-3 (pbk. : alk. paper)
  1. Religious pluralism—Mediterranean Region. 2. Mediterranean Region—Religion. 3. Christianity—Mediterranean Region. 4. Judaism—Mediterranean Region. 5. Islam—Mediterranean Region. I. Albera, Dionigi. II. Couroucli, Maria. III. Title.
  BL687.R46713 2012
  201'.5091822—dc23   2011020226

1 2 3 4 5 17 16 15 14 13 12

This volume is published with the support of the Directorate General for Research of the European Commission, in the framework of the RAMSES² Network of Excellence, funded by the 6th Framework Programme (contract CIT3-CT-2005-513366), under the coordination of the National Book Centre of Greece. This volume is solely the responsibility of the publisher and the authors; the European Commission cannot be held responsible for its content or for any use which may be made of it.

CONTENTS

Sharing Sacred Spaces in the Mediterranean

Sharing Sacred Places—
A Mediterranean Tradition

MARIA COUROUCLI

The presence of shared or mixed sanctuaries, sacred places where several re-ligious groups perform devotional practices, often within the same space and at the same time, is a well-established phenomenon in the Mediterranean. This book outlines a comparative anthropology of these pious traditions from the *longue durée* perspective, combining ethnographic and historical analysis. Eastern Mediterranean societies have experienced a revival of the religious domain in recent years: in many places, religion, often accompanied by the rise of religious fundamentalism, has invaded everyday social and political life—all relatively recent phenomena of the postcolonial era. The present context is thus marked by the ultimate separation of ethnoreligious communities within most circum-Mediterranean nation-states, a victorious outcome of a long strife that began in the nineteenth century: Christians, Jews, and Muslims have finally achieved religious homogeneity within political territories, putting an end to a long history of living side by side. This happened progressively, as independent countries adopted the model of a homogeneous nation-state (one language, one religion, one—collective—identity) imported from Western Europe. We tend to forget that this was a monochrome model: photographs from Paris, London, Amsterdam, or Berlin in the 1950s still remind us that not so long ago Western European capitals were inhabited almost exclusively by white Euro-peans. Less than three generations later, the model is obsolete: globalization and massive migration to the metropolitan cities have transformed Western democracies into multicultural spaces.

Not so in the southeastern Mediterranean, where nation building is more recent and where memories of ethnic and religious wars have been revived by recent—or ongoing—conflicts. In this post-Ottoman space, ethnoreligious minorities have been banned from national territories many times over the last hundred years: for example, memories of three important events, the Balkan wars (1912 and 1913) and exodus of the Muslim population from the Balkans, the Armenian massacre in Ottoman Anatolia (1915), and the massive exodus of the Greek orthodox population from Kemalist Turkey (1924) were still recalled during the most recent wars and ethnoreligious "cleansing" in the former Yugoslavia (1990s). During such conflicts, entire communities were forced to abandon their homes and holy sanctuaries, to leave room as it were for the construction of homogeneous national territories. In the Balkans, the Muslim population almost disappeared at the beginning of the twentieth century (except in Bosnia, in the Albanian central and western regions, and in Greek Thrace). At the same time, Near Eastern Christian minorities in Muslim countries (from Turkey through Syria to Egypt) kept declining. All through the twentieth century, as nationalisms were rising in the Middle East and North Africa, Western European powers became less efficient at protecting Christian communities, now minorities often fearing persecutions.

The weakening of the Christian communities and power in the Arab and Muslim modern world has been described as the reverse of the *Reconquista* (when Christian Catholic power gradually reestablished itself in the Iberian Peninsula between the tenth and the fourteenth centuries). Toward the end of the Middle Ages, it had become impossible for a Muslim to settle in the Western Christian kingdoms and territories. Thus, as Western Christianity lived confined in monocultural and monochromatic societies, the culture of sharing, multiculturalism, and coexistence, once pan-Mediterranean, survived only on its eastern shores.

Sharing and Mixing as Common Mediterranean Experience

Both the Byzantine (4th–15th centuries) and Ottoman (14th–19th) Empires were multiconfessional political constructs, and were culturally less homogeneous than their Western counterparts. From Morocco to the Middle East and from the Balkans to Anatolia, local communities often consisted of more than one religious group. Here the "Other" was the neighbor with whom one exchanged, not always peacefully and never on an egalitarian basis (Lory 1985; Anagnostopoulou 1997; Weyl Carr 2002). Ottoman religious plurality or "tolerance" was related to a specific political system, sometimes called "ottoman despotism," a reference to Wittfogel's "oriental despotism," a model of agrarian empires that combined absolutist political organization and strong state structures. Within these societies, ethnicity and religion constitute social markers defining different social status for each group, while minorities, excluded from both power and honor, form specialized groups, socially mobile and politically privileged (Gellner 1983:103). In other words, social segregation and modes of cohabitation between majority and minorities were related to the presence or absence of privileges and implied important differences in social status; a situation quite far from modern Western conceptions of human rights, which stem from traditions related to individual freedom, such as the Habeas Corpus Act (1679). Historical case studies provide wonderful insights into the different ways of dealing with individual and social liberties in pre-national societies. In seventeenth-century Crete, for example, the three religious communities, Latin Christians (Roman Catholics), Oriental Christians, and Muslims, lived side by side (Greene 2000:5). The ways in which the two Christian communities coexisted during the first five centuries of Venetian domination were neither forgotten nor abandoned. When the Latins left, the urban orthodox population continued to interact with the "Other" in much the same ways, only this time these were Muslim settlers or Christians converted to Islam. Urban merchants from all these groups intermarried and sometimes lived as mixed families, where the parent/child bond cut across different religious communities. These porous religious frontiers characterized Ottoman Crete during the seventeenth and eighteenth centuries. But when the French merchants and diplomats arrived, they upset the balance, and under their influence local society was divided into well-defined religious communities, foreshadowing the era of nationalism (Greene 2000:207–208). Traditions of mixing and sharing began to disappear, and notions of mutually exclusive identities gradually became the new norm. During the nineteenth and twentieth centuries, within most circum-Mediterranean nation-states, Christians, Jews, and Muslims strived to achieve religious homogeneity within political territories, putting an end to a long history of cohabitation. The present configuration is marked by the ultimate separation of ethnoreligious communities.

A Tradition of Cohabitation

Most of the shared shrines of the Mediterranean that are still visited today are situated on its eastern shores; their presence reflects a common past, a long co-existence of culturally mixed populations, often expressed by notions of "tolerance" vis-à-vis the religious "Other" in daily interaction. A controversial term, "tolerance" needs to be contextualized whenever used, as it can convey more than one meaning. Hayden (2002a:205–231) distinguished between "passive" tolerance, meaning noninterference, and "positive" tolerance, an active term implying the acceptance of the other as different. The debate is far from being closed (Bowman ch. 1 in this volume).

Shared shrines within the larger Byzantine and Ottoman lands are traditionally situated on frontiers, on territorial boundaries where conversions and conflict have taken place. They flourish far from cities and central authority, where soldiers and church officials rarely venture—in other words, where local populations managed to live peacefully side by side. "Eastern" local configurations and customs are quite different from what takes place in nineteenth-century colonial lands, as in French Algeria for example, where local ecclesiastical authorities, despite the official prohibition against missionary activity, tolerated some form of proselytism, making it difficult to draw a line between evangelism and mixed practices (Baussant 2002:199–210).

What kind of patterns of interaction are implied between individuals and groups by the term "cohabitation"? This volume offers an ethnographic look at a number of ways of sharing and living together, different configurations that can be traced back to long and profound historical sequences. Mixing or sharing is not a simple affair. It does not imply an equivalence between groups or an absence of hierarchy; on the contrary, religious groups interact in a highly regulated space, where social status and rights are conferred on an individual as member of a particular religious community. In the broader Ottoman area, the most common form of sharing sacra is the one involving pilgrims and visitors of sanctuaries who belong to the two largest groups in this region, Muslims and Oriental Christians, and the most common configuration is Muslims visiting Christian shrines. The same pattern—Muslims visiting the Others' sacra—has been observed in Jewish holy places in North Africa. This pattern is present in later sanctuaries, for example, Catholic holy places built on Muslim lands: mixed pilgrimage practices take place in and around sanctuaries dedicated to Christian saints. Thus far, shared ritual practices involving the coming together of Jews and Christians (Oriental or Latin) have very seldom been described. Why? We are just beginning to understand these phenomena. Comparative studies in anthropology and history could provide some leads, but we need more ethnographic facts and comparative analysis on symbolic patterns and actual ritual practices among the clergy, pilgrims, and visitors to these different shrines.

The *Longue Durée* Perspective

The present volume, based on ethnographic and historical research across time and cultures from the *longue durée* perspective, aims to be a first comparative study of mixed religious practices. As we compared notes during our seminars and conferences it became clear that, unlike contemporary Western European migration policies, traditional practices of sharing sacra were not informed by any top-down multicultural policy or ideology. They belonged to the historical heritage of Eastern Mediterranean societies, where the coexistence of more than one religious group within one territory, under one authority, represents a legacy of the Byzantine and Ottoman systems. The special ways in which this life together was experienced and practiced in what Western Europeans still call the Near and Middle East reveal a great deal about the social and symbolic organization of these traditional societies; religious practices of both Muslims and Oriental Christians are an important part of this common cultural heritage. Another aspect of our comparative research was to question the use and validity of terms and categories employed by historians and anthropologists in relation to the variety of the phenomena observed, by our insisting on the micro scale: contributors to this volume came to question notions such as "sharing," "faith," or "pilgrimage," for example (Baskar, Couroucli, Driessen, de Rapper, Valtchinova). These considerations relate to wider questions in the anthropology of religion within literate/historical societies; for example, how useful is it for our analysis to distinguish between "popular practices" and "official religion"? Another interesting common element concerns religious institutions per se: they cannot—and do not—allow for mixing or hybridism; members of the high clergy know very well that pollution is above all "matter out of place" (Douglas 1970:194). *Hubris,* the ancient Greek term for defying the gods and provoking Nemesis, punishment for defiance, and *hybrid,* a creature resulting from mixing, share the same etymology. In the case studies presented here, representatives of the higher clergy—from all religious denominations—behave in a traditional, and predictable, way with respect to shared shrines, prohibiting "mixed" practices whenever these go beyond local frames, becoming "visible" from afar.

Mixed practices do not constitute a single model; they are symbolically and practically complex activities, and their variations can be traced to political, demographic, and social conditions prevailing at the time of observation, as the relative importance of the religious communities concerned is changing over time. In all configurations examined in this volume, the degree of "tolerance" toward these practices on the part of the authorities or on the part of the local population is directly related to the prevailing political context. As we begin to comprehend the general political patterns consistent with greater or lesser tolerance toward sharing sacra, we need more ethnographic knowledge, thick descriptions of the many forms these practices take today in distinct but nevertheless similar, or parallel, configurations.

Local Ways, Marginal Ways

Locality and marginality are two common characteristics of mixed religious practices, as many of these activities seem to take place at the margins of religious institutions, in specific holy spaces, associated with a saintly figure, usually named, who inhabits or occupies the place (Couroucli, de Rapper, Poujeau, Valtchinova). Mixed practices are indeed local phenomena organized along margins and interstices, where other types of relations between people also have a chance of being established (Brown 1981:22). In the Balkan and Anatolian landscape of the nineteenth and twentieth centuries, these holy places are more likely to be found outside towns and villages, beyond the reach of central religious and political authorities. Whenever such shrines are situated inside cities, as in Constantinople/Istanbul for example, they are usually outside spaces directly controlled by the higher clergy: the fountains or sanctuaries people visit do not lie *inside* a parish church or a mosque, but are situated in their vicinity (garden, courtyard, minor chapel). Churches and mosques are places of worship for the religious community as a whole; but those seeking healing and grace are pilgrims, who need to displace themselves, visit other places: tombs (*türbe*) of Muslim saints or chapels of Christian saints, but also caves, fountains, or sacred trees where the spirits of holy men can manifest themselves, chthonian spirits living in the underworld.

Another common characteristic that runs through the following chapters is that sharing is not an everyday practice: it is an exceptional modality, inscribed in local tradition, and as such is related to borders and margins (of institutions, village territories, or even customs). Sharing implies the blurring of religious frontiers and the opening up of specific spaces (limited in time and place) where the human community sharing common knowledge on ancestral holy places gets together. Baskar (ch. 3) points out the importance of human bonds within the local community in Bosnia, where help between neighbors extends to taking care of the other's shrines in their absence, even when they have been displaced by state authorities. In Egypt and Syria, sanctuaries become spaces of social interaction: during festivals and saints' days celebrations in the Orthodox and Catholic monasteries of the Syrian countryside (Poujeau, ch. 10) and outside villages in Egypt (Mayeur-Jaouen, ch. 8); de Rapper also underlines the marginal character of these practices in Albania today. Fliche and Albera show how the Catholic church of St. Anthony in Istiklal (Istanbul) also attracts visitors by playing on its marginal status. Unlike normal times in towns and villages, sacred time and space transcend frontiers and social barriers, facilitating—and legitimating—contacts between individuals who would otherwise not meet in the public sphere. For example, Coptic festivals (*mouled*) in Egypt are also occasions for boys and girls, Christian and Muslim, to meet, being at once within and without community boundaries. In the same kind of spirit, monasteries in Syria offer services that parish churches (who follow ecclesiastical regulations more strictly) cannot fulfill, such as celebrating marriage ceremonies during a mourning period (Poujeau).

Historians and folklorists have associated mixed religious phenomena with collective memories of conflicts, conquests, and conversions, quite frequent in peripheral frontier zones, the *marches* of the empire, where Christianity and Islam met and confronted each other. Hasluck (1929), who studied mixed shrines in the Balkans and Anatolia at the beginning of the twentieth century, described these phenomena as part of the long process of the Ottoman conquest of Byzantine provinces, involving conversions of local populations and the transmission—and sharing—of sanctuaries from Christian monastic heterodox communities to Muslim orders such as the Bektashi. For Hasluck, massive conversions took place as the Ottoman armies conquered these western lands: many monasteries built around sanctuaries, which used to form networks of Christianity in the countryside, lost their monks and became dwelling places for dervishes, holy men belonging to the religion of the new lords (Hasluck 1929:521). These isolated sacred places continued to be visited by the local population, as they still fulfilled important functions: people kept going there to seek healing, pray for a good harvest, or celebrate the changing of seasons. Most ethnographic examples from sanctuaries renowned for their healing power attracting both Christian and Muslim pilgrims are situated in the larger post-Ottoman space. This tradition goes as far back as Byzantine times: one of the earliest testimonies of similar practices (from the thirteenth century) is the miraculous healing of the emir of Sivas's wife in St. Phocas sanctuary in Trebizond (Foss 2002).

Mixing in Practice

Are mixed practices standard practices within pre-national societies? Stewart has suggested that "an anthropology of syncretism must comprehend how zones of purity and hybridism come into being. . . . This can be achieved through a combination of historical and ethnographic case studies where syncretism or antisyncretism are at issue." When culture is not viewed as a stable structure but as the result of historical and social processes, "then syncretism can be used . . . to focus attention precisely on accommodation, context, appropriation, indigenization and a host of other dynamic intercultural and intracultural transactions" (Stewart 1999:55). In the chapters of this volume the reader will find out how the religious frontier is being crossed in both directions: first, and most frequent, Muslims cross into Christian territory by occasionally visiting their shrines. These one-way crossings are the most frequent configurations in the Eastern Mediterranean: in Turkey, in the Balkans, in Syria, Lebanon, or Egypt. Local narratives and discourses address this inequality by referring to religious majorities and minorities and their corresponding separate territories where boundaries are set to avoid pollution, separating pure from impure (Mayeur-Jaouen, ch. 8). Crossing in the opposite direction is done in a different mode: Christians and Muslims do not usually mix within a Muslim holy place at the same time. Thus, in the Balkans and the Black Sea area (at the beginning of the twentieth century) where sanctuaries have become Muslim holy places, Christians gather to celebrate a saint's day once a year, for a limited time, as guests of the *tekke* keepers (Baskar, Bowman, Couroucli, de Rapper).

It should be recalled that mixed practices concern two types of activities: individual devotional practices, related to a personal wish or demand (healing, or success in business, marriage, or school), can take place any day of the year (Albera and Fliche); on the other hand, taking part in a pilgrimage or mixed celebration is not such a strong act of devotion and does not always involve a formal exchange between pilgrim and the guardians of the holy place. Local terms distinguish these two kinds of activities: *ziyârât* (in Arabic) or *proskenesis* (in Greek) corresponds to individual acts of devotion, to be distinguished from being a visitor to a festival, *mouled,* or *panygeris.*

Cultural and religious modes of sharing are informed by specific time and space contexts: after having listed a number of "common" practices, one realizes that the "mixed" pilgrim corresponds to no single *habitus.* He is a person adapting to local custom, following a specific path, reproducing gestures or repeating words or prayers of those who have preceded him. He becomes a *bricoleur,* manipulating objects and signs within a symbolic territory and combining these with his own cultural and religious singularities.

ONE

Identification and Identity Formations around Shared Shrines in West Bank Palestine and Western Macedonia

GLENN BOWMAN

The recent wars in Yugoslavia, in which religious identities were foregrounded in ethnonationalist confrontations, fixed the region's reputation as a "fracture zone" between East and West (Islam and Christianity, Orthodoxy and Catholicism). Analogously, the "Holy Land"—already viewed as a setting for religious warfare—has become, with the establishment of a Jewish state in a demographically mixed territory, an icon of interreligious antagonism enduring since "time immemorial." These developments support popular discourse, already legitimated by some academics, contending that persons' religious identities are fundamental and fundamentally antagonistic to other religions. However, both regions, in living memory (and at some sites until the present day) have seen intensive intercommunal activities around both urban and rural religious sites. Such commingling was opposed by the religious authorities that "owned" some of these sites; it was encouraged at others by, for instance, the Sufic Bektashi. Although both regions were part of the Ottoman Empire, the different systems of religious and secular authority in the two areas during the Ottoman Empire, the different forms of religious activity fostered or suppressed by post-Ottoman states, and the development of ethnoreligious nationalisms provide grounds for comparative analysis of the development of religious communalisms in different contexts. This chapter will present beliefs and practices related to sites in southwestern regions of former Yugoslavia and along Israel-Palestine's Jerusalem–Bethlehem–Hebron axis to assess the impact of such "cohabitation" on cultural and political identities and understand the forces that work to undermine it.

Syncretism and Anti-syncretism: Teleologies of Culture Contact

It is impossible to avoid the term "syncretism" in discussing intercommunal mixing at shrines. Syncretism is defined by the *Oxford English Dictionary* as the "attempted union or reconciliation of diverse or opposite sets of tenets or practices" (the *OED* furthermore notes that its usage is "usually derogatory"). As Stewart and Shaw point out in their introduction to *Syncretism/ Anti-Syncretism: The Politics of Religious Synthesis* (1994), "'syncretism' is a contentious term, often taken to imply 'inauthenticity' or contamination, the infiltration of a supposedly 'pure' tradition by symbols and meanings seen as belonging to other, incompatible traditions" (Stewart and Shaw 1994:1). They locate the roots of this pejorative usage of the term in the reaction of both Catholic and Protestant theologians to seventeenth-century efforts to reconcile Lutheran, Catholic, and Reformed denominations. Such ecclesiastical reactions were themselves examples of "anti-syncretism," defined as "antagonism to religious synthesis shown by agents concerned with defence of religious boundaries" (Stewart and Shaw 1994:7). Stewart and Shaw and their contributors demonstrate how anti-syncretism—and the charges of "inauthenticity" and "pollution" it mobilizes—has opposed syncretism in academic, political, and popular debate to the present day. Nonetheless, Stewart and Shaw also discern a laudatory approach to syncretism in modern anthropology, initially emerging in Herskovits's portrayal of syncretism in *The Myth of the Negro Past* (1941) as a mode of assimilation in "melting pot" America, and visible today in postmodern celebrations of "the invention of tradition" and "cultural hybridity" (see Stewart and Shaw 1994:5–6 and 1).[1]

This "war of words" between syncretists and anti-syncretists tends to efface the original sense of syncretism and, when extended to the analysis of "shared shrines," distracts attention from what actually happens at those sites. Is a shared shrine necessarily "syncretistic"? Robert Hayden certainly does not believe it is; for him sharing serves—since the presence of the other appears to threaten the integrity of self—to fortify further the frontiers between sectarian communities. He writes that "processes of competition between groups that distinguish themselves from each other may be manifested as syncretism yet still result, ultimately, in the exclusion of the symbols of one group or another from a religious shrine" (Hayden 2002a:228). Thus apparent syncretism serves, for Hayden, to strengthen communalist identities rather than to dilute or meld them. If, however, we take up Herskovits's assessment of syncretism as instrumental in the progressive "acculturative continuum" (Herskovits 1941, cited in Stewart and Shaw 1994:6) proceeding from culture contact to full cultural integration, then syncretistic "sharing" at holy places forges new and irremediable "hybrid" or "creole" identities. For the anti-syncretists, and Hayden, there is, despite appearances, no sharing; for assimilationists such as Herskovits there is, after sharing, no going back. Identities are either fixed or irrevocably transformed.

"Syncretism" as a term first appears in *Peri Philadelphias* (On Brotherly Love), one of the seventy-eight essays of various dates that make up Plutarch's *Moralia*. Here the Roman historian (46–120 CE) described "the practice of the Cretans, who, though they often quarrelled with and warred against each other, made up their differences and united when outside enemies attacked; and this it was which they called 'syncretism'" (cited in Stewart and Shaw 1994:3). This definition, which Stewart and Shaw note "anticipated Evans-Pritchard's concept of segmentation" (ibid.:4), circumvents the issue of identity transformation that renders incommensurate the two approaches to mixed shrines discussed above. Plutarch describes a situational assumption of a shared identity that, subsuming those that preceded it, can nonetheless be shed when the assault that brought it about has been overcome. Although Plutarch's usage does not explicitly pertain to religious practice or refer to sites constituted as "syncretistic" by shared practices, his definition easily extends to sites where common interests give rise to shared practices and even shared identities. Identities are mobile without being either fixed or amorphous; amity is possible, but neither necessary nor binding. Here issues of agency, and of those things that restrain or impel it, come to the fore. Unbinding the discussion of mixed shrines from the constraints of particularly "loaded" definitions of syncretism enables us to navigate between the Scylla of fixed, conflictual identities and the Charybdis of "evolutionary" transformations of blended identities. Shared practices at mixed sites may entail antagonism and may forge novel identities, but neither is necessary; sharing may just as well be the practice of a moment engaged by persons who return, after that "communion," to their traditional selves and ways.

That passage through definitional straits does not, however, simplify, but rather complicates the approach to mixed shrines. If syncretistic shrines cease to be exclusively either arenas for "competitive sharing" or sites of a "mechanical mixing" (Stewart and Shaw 1994:6), then we need to know much more of what goes on in them if we are to characterize them at all. Once commonality is disentangled from the "politics" of syncretism and anti-syncretism, generic discussions of mixed shrines become problematic and we are forced to pay close attention to the particularities of the field. What is the character of that mixing or sharing if engaging in common practices at the same site neither necessarily solidifies identities antagonistically nor opens them to transformation? To ascertain this we are forced to pay close attention to what people are doing—and saying they are doing—while they are in the process of doing it. It is vital to attend to *who* is saying *what* to *whom* and *who* is listening; long-term historical processes may bring about observable and documentable effects, but what actually occurs in reaching those ends and what sorts of silencings and debates take place in the process are important to note if we want to really know what goes on in "sharing."

Hayden's study (2002a) examines historical accounts as well as court records of an extended struggle over a shrine at Madhi in Maharashtra revered by Muslims and Hindus alike, and compares this case with the historical and ethnographic record of struggles between Muslims, Catholics, and Orthodox Christians in the Balkans leading up to the frenzy of expulsions and destructions that marked the Yugoslav "Wars of Secession." In all the cases he discusses he extrapolates the character of previous in situ intercommunal interaction around the respective shrines from processes taking place well after legal or literal conflict had become the sole form of interaction. If, however, we are not to assume "end results" are predetermined by the initial moments of mixing at shrines, then we must attempt to see what happens on the ground *while* syncretic practices are occurring. Ex post facto descriptions, even when they are not themselves extensions of the struggles, are always shaped by what preceded them; we all know what happens when the victors tell the story, but even when recounted by victims it rarely accords with what preceded the crime. Furthermore, once we assume the role of agents and agency in activities around mixed shrines, we must also consider questions of power and resistance. It is likely that some persons or groups will work against sharing, while others engage in, if not actively promote, it; only close attention to the discourses operating around shared or mixed sites will allow us to know which of the multiple positions around the issue of sharing were occupied and how one of those, if that is the case, overcomes others and becomes hegemonic.

Mar Elyas and Bir es-Saiyideh: West Bank Communalisms

My original interest in the topic of "mixed shrines" was generated by observations in August 1984 at the Mar Elyas monastery located between Bethlehem and Jerusalem in the Israeli Occupied Territory of the West Bank (Bowman

1993). Muslims and Christians (both Orthodox and Latin), not only from the nearby cities of Bethlehem and Jerusalem but as well from surrounding towns and villages, gathered on the grounds of the monastery on the day preceding the feast of the Prophet Elijah to picnic with friends and family. In the midst of barbecuing, playing musical instruments, and socializing, small groups would leave the olive groves bordering the monastic buildings to join a queue culminating at a large icon of St. George at the right front of the main chapel. The attraction seemed less the icon—although some (usually Christians) would kiss or touch the icon and leave small gifts in front of it—than the length of chain looped before it. This would be lifted by one member of an approaching group and passed three times over the heads of others in that group—adults and children alike—and down the length of their bodies so that the enchained had finally to step out of the loop.

What interested me were the very different explanations given by the various groups present at the monastery (priests, Boy Scouts, foreign visitors, Christian and Muslim Palestinians) of why they themselves were there, why members of other groups were in attendance, what the ritual of passing through the chain meant to them, and what they thought it signified to others (Bowman 1993:433–439). While explanations of *why* the chain was efficacious differed between lay visitors of different religious affiliations (Christians said that Elias or St. George acted protectively *through* the chain, while Muslims tended to argue that the chain simply worked to ward off madness, other illnesses, and bad fortune), all agreed that they had come—aside from for the good company of a summer feast—to take a prophylactic blessing from the chain on one of the rare days when liturgical celebrations opened the church and offered them access to it.

Members of the Brotherhood of the Holy Sepulchre, the elite of the Greek Orthodox Church in the Holy Land, variously explained attendance by local Palestinians and their "binding" with the chain either as manifest testimony of dedication to the Church and to God (those who rendered that explanation refused to acknowledge that Muslims were among those gathered) or as evidence of the pernicious superstition of uneducated "Arabs" among whom even the Christians were "no better than Muslims." Although the priesthood and the laity had little if any contact other than bumping into each other in pursuit of their respective rituals, the interaction of local Muslims and Christians was friendly and open both in the vicinity of the chain and in the fields around. Lay members of respective religions freely asserted their differences, while simultaneously affirming their community around the holy place: "the religious difference doesn't matter, we all come. It is for friendship and community as much as for religion" (Bowman 1993:438).

Five years later, during the early days of the first intifada, I was taken to an underground cistern in the center of the nearby mixed Muslim-Christian town of Beit Sahour, where, in 1983, locals had reported sightings of the Virgin Mary in its shadowed depths. The Beit Sahour municipality, which was to play a significant role in organizing nonviolent resistance to Israeli occupation (Bowman 1990 and 1993), had subsequently built a shrine, Bir es-Saiyideh, over the cistern expressly for the use of both Muslims and Christians of all denominations. This was operated by a committee made up of representatives of all the significant religious communities in the town (Orthodox, Muslim, Catholic, and Greek Catholic). The exterior of the shrine appeared distinctly modern, and, aside from the cross surmounting it, bore less resemblance to a church than it did to a traditional Islamic *makÿm* (a building with a domed chamber characterizing a Muslim shrine). Inside, the walls were covered with icons and paintings of Christian subjects given by worshipers, but profusely and randomly scattered among these were a significant number of gifts, paintings and pictures that, in their avoidance of pictorial representation, appeared Muslim. The cross and the predominance of a Christian tone was not surprising; the site was, after all, dedicated to a figure highly revered in Christian worship (although also venerated in Islam). What seemed more important than a more thoroughgoing syncretism was the appearance of the devotional objects of other religions (objects that would be rigorously excluded in a church or mosque owned and operated by the religious institutions), and that no one visiting the shrine (and there was a constant flow of local people passing through it both individually and in groups) seemed offended by evident signs that a community wider than that of their own religious community used the place.

I was told by both the caretaker and the Greek Catholic priest who accompanied me on one visit to the site that religious practices at the shrine reflected this heterogeneity. As the shrine belonged to the municipality, representatives of all local religious communities were able to book time in it. Since the stories surrounding the Nativity of Jesus are celebrated by Muslims and Christians throughout the Bethlehem region as founding myths of the local communities, Muslims and Christians alike gathered at the shrine to celebrate their traditions in a place where the sacred had interacted with their locality. Sometimes these were shared celebrations, nominally organized according to the calendar of one of the religious communities (such as the Orthodox

Ascension of the Virgin celebrated on the 15th of August), while at other times local Christian and Muslim officiants carried out ceremonies specific to their congregations. Moreover, as with the blessings available to all at Mar Elyas, water from the cistern in the back of the shrine was taken by both Muslim and Christian Beit Sahourans as a sacred substance for healing, blessing, and providing good luck. I asked the caretaker why the Marian shrine was owned by the municipality and not, as one would expect, by one of the Christian churches. He indignantly replied: "We are here Muslim and Christian, and there are two Christian groups. The municipality builds for all the people, and the people all own and use the well."

There was already, at Mar Elyas in 1984, sporadic evidence of a political logic of solidarity that, by the time Bir es-Saiyideh and Beit Sahour were caught up in the first intifada, came to subsume communitarian identities within an overarching, albeit temporary, nationalist discourse.[2] At Mar Elyas national identification had come to the fore only in response to aggression toward "Arabs" expressed by the foreign priests and to the violent harassment by Israeli border police of Palestinian merchants who had set up booths to sell toys to children (Bowman 1993:457). In Beit Sahour by 1989 religious identity had, in the face of repeated Israeli aggressions against the community, become—at least in public discourse—relegated to a secondary position behind national identity. In a context in which the existence of the entire community and the lives of all its members were perceived as being at mortal risk, differences between individuals, families, religious communities, and political groupings were, at least in public fora, underemphasized: "The bullets do not differentiate between Christian and Muslim, P.L.O., DFLP, etc. . . . If I want to throw a stone [at a soldier] I will not call to my neighbour to say 'become a Muslim and then we will throw stones together.' We forget our religion; we forget our political groups" (Bowman 1993:447). The shared character of the shrine of Bir es-Saiyideh both reflected the common everyday experience of a mixed community with shared traditions and expressed the political program of a local leadership committed to defeating sectarian fragmentation. Subsequent developments, whereby formal Muslim participation in the Bir es-Saiyideh committee was terminated and moves were set in play to build a large Orthodox church over the site (Bowman 2007), reflected the collapse of that program, although I, in the spring of 2007, witnessed substantial popular Muslim participation in both praying at and maintaining the shrine.

Macedonian Mixing

Within Macedonia I chose to look at three sites, two in western Macedonia and one in the northeast. The first is Sveti Bogoroditsa Prechista (Holy Mother of God Most Innocent) outside of Kicevo (a mixed city in a region with a profoundly mixed Muslim-Christian population). Sveti Bogoroditsa Prechista is a large active Orthodox monastery whose spectacular nineteenth-century church contains within it a well over which is a pierced stone through which both Muslim and Christian visitors crawl prior to taking away water from the well. The second, Sveti Nikola (St. Nicholas), is a tiny Macedonian Orthodox church on the outskirts of Makedonski Brod, a rural municipality of approximately six thousand inhabitants (all Christian). What designated the church for selection was the presence *within* the church of a *türbe* (tomb) of a Bektashi saint, Hadir Bābā, visited by Bektashi and members of other Sufi orders as well as by Macedonian Albanian Sunni Muslims not only from neighboring mixed villages but also from more distant sites. Finally, the Husamedin Pasha mosque is an empty early-sixteenth-century mosque overlooking the city of Stïp, a city with an Orthodox majority that nonetheless contains significant populations of Sufi Roma as well as Macedonian-speaking Sunni Muslims. The mosque contains within its grounds a Halveti Sufi *türbe* where Ashura celebrations are carried out by the town's Sunni and Halveti Muslims, and the mosque itself is opened on the 2nd of August for a priest-led celebration of the Orthodox feast of the Prophet Elijah. The three sites, respectively, represent a Christian church in which Muslims and Christians alike engage in rituals that appear to be markedly Christian, a popular mixed shrine with evidence of both Christian and Muslim objects of reverence, and a Muslim place of worship that both Christians and Muslims seek to expropriate, ritually and physically, as their own. The three allow for observations of what at least formally seem to be "sharing of practices," "mixing of practices," and "antagonistic tolerance."

Sveti Bogoroditsa Prechista

There is no doubt that Sveti Bogoroditsa Prechista is an Orthodox monastery, but this does not prevent a continuous flow of Muslims—Sufi and Sunni alike—from coming into its chapel, circumnavigating its icon-dense interior, crawling three times through the small passageway beneath the icons of Mary and Jesus, and collecting water from the well beneath it to take back to their homes. Muslim and Christian visitors to Sveti Bogoroditsa Prechista claim to come explicitly for healing; the shrine, in large part through the medium of the well water, is renowned for inducing fertility in the sterile, returning sanity to the mad, straightening bent limbs, and other thaumaturgic cures. Even the imam in the central mosque of nearby Kicevo sends members of his congregation to Sveti Bogoroditsa Prechista when he feels they are afflicted by "Christian demons" that can be driven out only by beneficent Christian powers.

In Sveti Bogoroditsa Prechista Muslim visitors appear to carry out the same sorts of ritual activities as do the many Christian visitors to the site. Like Christians, Muslims light candles and approach the icons throughout the interior of the church, particularly those lining the iconostasis, and leave before them small gifts (sometimes money, often towels or new, packaged articles of clothing such as socks or shirts). Then, as do the Christians, they go to the rear left of the church, where an east-facing icon of the introduction of the Holy Virgin to the Temple and a west-facing icon of Jesus' healing of the paralytic at the Pools of Siloam (Jn 5:8–10) surmount an artificial hole through a wall. On the left of the east-facing icon is hung a long string of cross-inscribed beads that are passed over supplicants three times before they crawl, again three times, through the hole in the direction of the west wall of the church. Having done this, they collect for themselves, or have given to them, water that has been drawn from the well below which they first splash on their faces three times and then take to their homes to drink or give to others who are ill ("when the water runs out the sickness returns, and people come back for more"). Some visitors, Muslim and Christian, decide to stay in the monastery, where they do work to support the church and are healed by that residence.[3]

Closer observation of Muslim visitors, as well as interviews with them, reveals that although they appear to follow the same practices of approach and deportment as do Christians, they succeed, by holding back from Christian groups while moving through the church, in masking small but significant differences. In approaching icons they do not kiss them and they do not cross themselves, and in praying they silently mouth Muslim prayers and hold their hands open and palm up rather than clasped in Christian praying mode. Nonetheless they have no hesitation in acknowledging that the powers they approach are Christian; this is a healing place that is known to work, and therefore when one is ill or needful of help it is one of the preeminent places to approach (many of those interviewed—Muslim and Christian alike—said they had visited several places, both Muslim and Christian, in search of cures, fertility, etc.).

There is here an intriguing practical logic in operation; people visiting sites whose powers are renowned as efficacious (particularly for healing) will, at those sites, carry out the rituals appropriate to those powers as far as is possible without explicitly violating the dictates of their own religions (Muslims, for instance, will not cross themselves). Knowing that certain visits and the rituals involved therein have worked for neighbors of other religions, they mimic those activities as far as possible without "self-harming," in the hope that such copying will produce the same effects for them, despite confessional differences. This is not a syncretism insofar as identities are not transformed, but it is a sharing. It is also a sharing acknowledged and legitimated (perhaps because they know people will do it regardless of whether or not they approve) by religious leaders, such as the imam of the Kicevo mosque, who themselves would never think of entering the holy places of another religion.

In the Church of the Apostles Peter and Paul in Kicevo we were told by the priest that many local Muslims (Kicevo is half Orthodox and half Muslim) come to the church not only to get holy water and to ask for blessings, but also, to provide specific examples, when a Christian man has converted to marry a Muslim woman but nonetheless wants their child baptized[4] or when Muslims want priest-blessed icons to keep in their houses.[5] The priest prays over Muslims with a special prayer—that designated in the prayer books for the unbaptized—and instead of laying his cope over their heads raises it before them.

This "space" for the unbaptized, and the non-Orthodox, is interestingly paralleled in the legendry and architecture of Sveti Bogoroditsa Prechista. The mother superior of the monastery told us that "in the past" the superior of the monastery and a pasha were discussing the respective virtues of Christianity and Islam. They decided to test whose faith was the right one by filling two glasses with water and dropping them some five meters off a balcony, whereupon the glass of the pasha broke while that of the superior remained intact and its water did not spill. The pasha consequently decided to donate 120 hectares of land in the vicinity of Brod to the monastery, and the superior, in appreciation, promised that part of the church would be built for Muslim use.[6] Although the current superior stressed that the narthex was not "intended" for Muslims, she also stressed that it is the part of the church "they can come to." It is not clear what the superior meant by this insofar as it was clear that Muslims frequented the whole of the church, but this part of the church, like the analogous part of the prayer book, was evidently deemed "appropriate" to those who were neither Orthodox nor Christian.

The "sharing" occurring in the church is, however, vulnerable precisely because of that space which is designated as open to the other. While none of the Muslims we interviewed at Sveti Bogoroditsa Prechista mentioned this, one of the nuns—a novice recently graduated from university in Skopje—stressed vehemently that "Muslims" claim that the undecorated part of the church belongs to them and asserted that they are organizing to "steal" it from the church. She, when asked for water by Muslim visitors, would tell them either that there was none or that they could get it themselves from the fountain outside.

Sveti Nikola

Sveti Nikola hides within a grove of trees overlooking the town of Makedonski Brod. One approaches up a long flight of stone steps that carries the visitor from the old Ottoman-period houses at the base of the hill, past concrete communist-period housing blocs, to a gateway flanked on the left by a niche containing a simple painting of St. Nicholas—worn around the mouth from continuously being touched—and surmounted (at least on our initial approach) by an eight-inch-high cross surrounded by simple iron scrollwork. The church itself is a small square building (six and a half meters on each side) with an apse on the northeastern wall that, from the difference in roofing materials, appears a later addition. There is no cross on the roof of the church, although a small indented cross is worked into plaster above the narrow window of the apse.

The interior of the church is simple, with a stone slab floor covered with a multitude of diverse and overlapping pieces of carpet. The wooden iconostasis is covered with pictures of saints, apparently locally done. On the right of the church, running parallel to the southeastern wall, is a flat-topped platform approximately two meters long by three-quarters of a meter wide, raised about forty centimeters above the floor level and covered with multiple layers of cloth (the top covering green, with a gold piece beneath it). Closer observation shows that, particularly in the vicinity of this platform, the carpets and the pictures on and leaning against the wall are Muslim and represent Mecca, Ali and Hussein, and moments of what is in effect Shia history.

There are two ways to approach the Sveti Nikola church and its function as a mixed shrine. The first is to perform an archaeology of its history. This is not something that can easily be done from the shrine, or even the town, itself. Local Christians, asked about the shrine, related stories of how an old bearded man "in the past" saved the townspeople from plague by having them kill an ox, cut its hide into strips, link them together, and mark out as much land as could be contained within the resultant rope for dedication to a monastery (see Stahl 1986:178 on magical boundaries). People, when asked, often said that the old man—Sveti Nikola—is buried beneath the raised platform within the church. Visiting Muslims told exactly the same story, except that in their version the old man was Hadir Bābā, a Bektashi saint who had disguised himself as a Christian and who was subsequently buried within the *türbe* (tomb) in the church.

Makedonski Brod today is completely Christian, and local people, talking in and around the church, speak as though it has always been. A local historian, formerly a communist and still a secularist, said, however, that until the early-twentieth-century Balkan wars Makedonski Brod was a hub of Ottoman administration known as Tekkiya because of the Bektashi monastery built above the town. This version of history, suggesting that the Sveti Nikola church is in fact the *türbe* of the founder of the Bektashi *tekke*, is supported by an archaeological note in a Skopje museum newsletter asserting that "on that place today can only be seen the *türbe*, in which, according to the stories of the local population, was buried the founder of the *tekke, Haydar Bābā*" (Stojanovski 1979:53). Other conversations brought up mention of the 1994 consecration of the building as a church by the local bishop and the removal, "sometime a while ago," of a triangular frame that had for years sat on top of the tomb of St. Nicholas. From this approach it seems evident that Sveti Nikola church was, at one time, the central feature—the founder's tomb—of a Bektashi monastery and that it, in the wake of the flight of "Turks" from the town after the Balkan Wars and then through the long period of post-1945 state disapprobation of formal religion, had sat—"disenfranchised"—above the town, approached by different communities who remembered it in different ways until, in the nationalistic fervor following the collapse of Yugoslavia and the formation of "Orthodox" Macedonia, the church expropriated it.

The diachronic analytic suggests an inexorable movement toward expropriation of the site by one of the communities that currently seem to "share" it. Another way of examining Sveti Nikola is to look synchronically at the relations taking place at the present time within the shrine, and that perspective, while not denying the trajectory indicated by the historical view, offers insights into forms of interaction between communities around a mixed site that a "teleological" interpretation would render invisible.

Dragina is the Orthodox caretaker of the Sveti Nikola shrine, and, as she is getting old, she is assisted in keeping the place clean and functional by her son

Boge, who works as a schoolteacher in the town, as well as by a number of men who make up the "Church Committee." On the fifth of May, the day preceding the Orthodox Feast of St. George, Dragina, Boge, and those with time to help work to prepare the church for the "pilgrimage" to the site that local people will enact for the feast. Preparation involves rendering the site much less like a mosque and more like an Orthodox church, and thus the carpets are taken up from the floor and the various Muslim images and objects are hidden from the view of visitors. Green "Muslim" ox-tallow candles and the Muslim prayer beads (*sibhah*) that visitors step through for blessings (similar to those at Mar Elyas and at Sveti Bogoroditsa) are removed from the "tomb" of St. Nicholas and replaced with white "Christian" candles and a smaller rosary.[7] The site, thus "Christianized," is ready for the hundreds of visitors, nearly all Orthodox, who visit that evening and throughout the following day. At dawn on the seventh, however, Dragina and Boge are busy in the church "returning" the site to its normal mixed state. Carpets are carefully relaid, and intense discussion takes place around where exactly the image of Ali with his sword, Zulfiqar, should be placed and how to arrange the cloth that partially covers it. Prayer rugs are laid around the *türbe,* the *sibhah* are replaced, and the tallow candles are lit because "they" are coming and must be made to feel at home.

There is, of course, an issue of economics involved in this; "the others" leave generous gifts, and, Dragina says, "we benefit from it." Nonetheless the affection she shows for visitors and the easy generosity with which she and others, including the priest, give red "St. George" eggs to, and fill the water bottles of, Muslim visitors belie a purely economistic reading. Women Muslims ask Dragina to pass the *sibhah* over them for blessings, and when a respected Sufi *dervish* from Kicevo comes to the shrine (praying with his wife in the direction of the iconostasis rather than toward the *türbe*[8]), Dragina—concerned about her son's continuing failure to find a wife—asks the man to pass the beads over Boge so as to read his fortune.

Whereas the description above suggests an easy sharing of the site, and an institutional and personal openness by Orthodox keepers toward the presence of Muslim "others," the following suggests ways that, without even being provoked by "higher" powers, such sharing might disintegrate. When we visited Sveti Nikola a week before St. George's Day, the gate to the grounds of the church was surmounted by a small metal cross surrounded by ornamental scrollwork. While interviewing people who were gathered in the grounds I asked about the absence of a cross on the roof of the church itself. One man responded aggressively, "I'll show you the cross," and left the grounds, returning twenty minutes later with a six-foot-high gold-colored anodized cross. This, it turned out, was a gift he, a *Gasterbeiter* returned to his hometown for a vacation, was presenting to the church.[9] A week later the small cross had been angle-ground off and thrown aside, while the gold cross had been welded in its place, overwhelming the entryway and the icon of St. Nicholas.

On the day following St. George's Day an Albanian-speaking man spoke to me about the "insult" of the cross over the gateway, claiming that local people have no right to erect a cross over a place that has "been Muslim for centuries." Asked what form of Islam he followed he responded, "It doesn't matter; I am a Muslim." He then approached members of the Church Committee gathered nearby, saying, "This cross separates us; no Muslims will feel comfortable coming to this big and historical place which we used to come to visit. We have been here for years and have felt good to come here, but this is a barrier to us. . . . How would you feel if I came to your church, to your home, and put a minaret there?" The men responded apologetically, saying that they understood the problem and that they would talk with the man who paid for the cross, who, they claimed, was absent even though he was in fact present as a member of the group. The committee was clearly discomfited, acknowledging after the Muslim left that there was a problem but seeming uncertain how to address it.

Husamedin Pasha Mosque

The mosque, now fairly derelict, is an early-sixteenth-century "central" mosque that was seriously damaged during the Balkan Wars yet functioned as a mosque for the minority Muslim population until 1945, when it was closed. At that time the local Halveti Sufi community, an order quite close to Orthodox Sunni Islam, began to celebrate the feast of Ashura on the grounds of the mosque where a *türbe* (that of Medin Bābā) stands. In 1953 the mosque was reopened as a secular building and used as a gallery space for the Stïp Museum. In 1956 that closed, and the mosque has generally been unused since that time, although for a while the "Children's Embassy," a Macedonian NGO established in 1992, held events in and around the building.

At the same time (1992), allegedly because of the intervention of the nationalist Christian Democratic VMRO (Democratic Party for Macedonian National Unity) government, access to the mosque was given to the local Orthodox Church that began celebrating the Feast of the Prophet Elijah *inside* the mosque. This celebration, based on the idea—for which there is no firm evidence—that the original mosque was built over an Orthodox church, uses the mosque's interior both for a liturgy with icons set in the *mihrab* and for a subsequent communal meal. Since then and throughout the year Christians inscribe crosses on the exterior of the mosque and burn candles on its porch. Until very recently local Halveti Muslims referred to the mosque as "St. Elijah's Church."

In the past three years the Islamic community, strengthened by substantial financial contributions coming into it from diasporic Štip Muslims in Turkey as well as other Islamic sources, has been revitalized, restoring the only operative mosque in the town and building an Islamic school. A number of its members have been discussing the desirability of restoring the Husamedin Pasha as the central mosque, have gained access to a document issued by the Macedonian Institute for the Protection of Cultural Monuments announcing that the mosque is a protected monument (which they interpret as indicating that the mosque belongs to them as the appropriate cultural minority), and have stopped calling it St. Elijah's Church and begun referring to it as the Husamedin Pasha mosque. One man we interviewed in April 2006, an activist in this movement, told us that the Christian celebrations as they were currently being carried out were "inappropriate for a place of worship." The year before he and a friend had walked by during the feast and, afraid to enter the mosque, had seen through the door "Christians eating and drinking *rakia* (a distilled fruit alcohol) around a table they'd set up in the middle." Despite their sense of the mosque's desecration, he asserted that when the mosque is turned back to "what it should be" he "will share it with Christians on the day they want to use it."

We spoke as well with a priest from the Church of St. Nikola, the town's main church, who told us that Sveti Elia (the mosque) was built over the foundations of a destroyed church. The priest told us that

> according to the ground-plan, this is a church, but when the Osmanli Turks came, they turned it into a mosque. The foundation is still a church. We want to make it a church again, but from Skopje they would not give us permission. Otherwise, it would have been a church by now. Now we don't know what it is any longer: neither one nor the other. We want it to be a church, and we will make it a church. We are asking for a permission to dig inside and see what will be revealed, but they know it is a church in the foundations, and that's why they deny us the permission. It will be a church. Why should it be a mosque? They have one already.

For him the mosque is no more than a historical excrescence occluding access to the real holy site that lies beneath it.[10] According to his description the Christian worship that takes place there proceeds as though that Muslim intervention were invisible: "During the ceremony a prayer is sung, a bread *Panagia*[11] is raised in the air, and everything takes place inside. . . . Outside the anointment takes place." The Orthodox priesthood, powerful in Štip, intends, when it convinces the government to allow it to carry out the archaeological survey which will, in its eyes, legitimate its "restoration" of the church, to tear the *Husamedin Pasha* mosque down and build over it "a new and more beautiful ancient church."[12]

In February 2006 members of the Macedonian Roma community, for the most part Halveti Sufis, had unofficially gained temporary access to the mosque during preparations for the Ashura feast at the neighboring *türbe* of Medin Bābā. These Muslims, who as a community had not had access to the mosque since its closure in 1945, removed accreted rubble from the mosque (leaving the Orthodox ritual materials, including icons of Elijah, in place in the niche in which they were stored between feasts), swept and washed it, and laid carpets on the floor. They then, with members of the Islamic Religious Community of Štip, held a *namaz* (prayer) inside the mosque. Afterward the Halveti had their Ashura feast inside the mosque. Subsequently the key to the mosque, normally kept by the curator of the Štip Museum, was found to have gone missing.

Little was thought of this until the eve of the feast of the Prophet Elijah (2 August 2006) when, as local Christians gathered for the two-day celebrations and began setting up on the grounds their booths for selling food stuffs and candles, it was discovered that a second lock was welded to the doors of the mosque. Late in the afternoon, as the priests from the Church of St. Nikola arrived to prepare the interior of the mosque for the *Panagia* and the saint's day liturgy, it became evident that that lock had been mounted by the Islamic Religious Community organization and that no one present had a key. The Muslim organization, when contacted, refused to remove the lock, claiming that the site was a mosque and theirs. Amidst muted muttering and assertions that the site had been used for the feast since time immemorial, the *Panagia* and the anointing were held on the portico while local people leaned candles against the doors and piled small gifts of cloth and flowers in front of it. Throughout the evening and over the following day locals came, prayed before the locked door, and left angry.

Conclusion: Multiconfessionalism and
Mixing in Orthodox Contexts

In the cases set out above I have attended to the boundaries between Orthodox Christians and their Muslim neighbors, and have considered the ways in
which—in multiconfessional societies—these boundaries are variously reinforced, opened, and transgressed. I would emphasize the multiconfessional
context insofar as in Macedonia—as in Palestine and in contradistinction to
Greece—the close proximity of communities that are not Orthodox strongly
influences the ways in which Orthodox Christians and Orthodox institutions
deal with heterodoxy. Not only are laypersons here, used to interacting in various contexts with others who are not of their religious persuasion, less prone
to xenophobia (in the literal sense of "fear of strangers or foreigners"), but
also religious authorities find it more difficult to impose conceptions of ritual
purity on sites traversed by the beliefs and practices of heterogeneous peoples.

Nonetheless, the trajectory evident in the scenarios drawn from both Palestine and Macedonia indicates that mixing and sharing are at increasing risk
of being replaced by separation and antagonism. The contemporary tendency,
promoted by discourses of both nationalism and resurgent scripturalism, is to
mark intercommunal activities as at best unorthodox and at worst blasphemous; there is a strong possibility that in bringing them to wider attention
by describing them I will expose them to forces analogous to those that have
worked to extinguish similar manifestations elsewhere. However, insofar as
both intercommunal amity and intercommunal antagonism are discursively
constructed, it seems vital, in the midst of the war of words evident in debates
over the "clash of civilizations" and "antagonistic tolerance," to show that there
is nothing natural or necessary in hating your neighbor, and that people, when
they perceive interaction and amicability as working for rather than against
them, are fully capable of mixing with, and embracing, the other.

Notes

Originally published as "Processus identitaires autour de quelques sanctuaires Par-
tages en Palestine et en Macedoine" in *Religions traversées: Lieux saints partagés entre
chrétiens, musulmans et juifs en Méditerranée,* ed. D. Albera and M. Couroucli (Arles:
Actes Sud., 2009), 27–52. I am grateful to the British Academy and to the Arts and
Humanities Research Council for grants that enabled field research in both Palestine
and Macedonia, and to Elizabeta Koneska, who assisted me in my Macedonian field
research.

1. This polarization around "syncretism" appears to be conjunct with larger "culture wars" (see Rena Lederman's comments on "the fault line, which cleaves contextualist and essentializing ways of knowing, [which] runs through American culture," Lederman 2005:50, see also 74n2); the rhetorics of "anti-syncretists" often seem to share ground with those of ethnic nationalists and religious fundamentalists, while those who see syncretism as a good thing tend to sound like advocates of federalism, globalization, and secularism.

2. This intercommunal solidarity was, as I show in my study of a political murder in Beit Sahour (Bowman 2001) and in an updating (Bowman 2007) of my earlier *Nationalising the Sacred,* context dependent and faltered as, after Oslo, the political situation came to seem to favor sectarian interests over joint resistance to the occupation.

3. An unused room near the monastery's main gate was formerly used for holding mad persons who were thought to be healed by that incarceration (a practice identical to that described by Taufik Canaan at the monastery of St. George at Khadr near Bethlehem [Canaan 1927:79–80]).

4. The priest indicated that by church law both parents must be baptized but that local priests baptize such children anyway "so as not to damage the marriage community of the couple."

5. There is an echo here of the practices of "Crypto-Christians" previously carried out in the Balkans under Ottoman rule (see Skendi 1967:234 and passim), although the presence of Crypto-Christianity was neither implied by the priest nor would have been necessary in Macedonia since the collapse of the Ottoman Empire.

6. Whether there was truth to the legend, or whether the legend was generated to explain the architectural anomaly, the narthex at the western end of the church is undecorated and is the only part of the church not ornamented with splendid frescoes.

7. Initially these objects and images were "hidden" behind the iconostasis on the floor of the apse, but I noticed, in the period leading up to the feast day, that someone (perhaps a Bektashi visitor) had later hung them on the apse's northeastern wall amidst the icons surrounding the altar (and had placed the green ninety-nine beaded *sibhah* on the altar). These remained there until the town priest (who had seemingly ignored them while in the apse on the previous day), coming to the church on the morning of the feast day to perform the liturgy, removed them, placing them again on the floor with the images turned to the wall.

8. There is, however, little uniformity in the Muslim practices; some pray toward the iconostasis of the church, others toward the *türbe* from its "foot," while others perform *zikir* (a devotional choral chanting of Islamic texts) between persons kneeling at each corner of the platform. Most Muslim visitors, like most Christians, circle the *türbe* between one and three times.

9. Another wealthier economic migrant, who returned from Australia annually with his family for summer vacations, had given the town a ten-meter-high cross to be mounted, like those being erected all over Macedonia, on the mountain above the town.

10. Insofar as Islam historically follows Christianity and, in Islamic thought, corrects and clarifies Christian interpretations of revelation, Muslims are able to attend Christian sites that, although manifesting an imperfectly understood divine

revelation, are nonetheless informed by revelation. For Christians Islam is a heresy or deviancy, and attendance at a Muslim site is effectively blasphemous. As Hasluck points out, "a mosque, unless it has been (or is thought to have been) a church is rarely, if ever, taken over as a church by the Orthodox" (Hasluck 2000:104).

11. A small loaf of bread (*prosphora*) when stamped with an image of Mary as Mother of God becomes the *Panagia* that is blessed over the altar during the divine liturgy.

12. My translation of the priest's phrase effects an echo of another quote in a story told me by a UN peacekeeper in Visegrad, Republika Srpska, who recalled a Serb militiaman who, when berated for taking part in the destruction of "the beautiful and ancient Old City" of one of the mixed Muslim-Christian Bosnian towns, responded "but we will build a new and more beautiful ancient Old City in its place" (Bowman 1994:159).

TWO

The *Vakëf*: Sharing Religious Space in Albania

GILLES DE RAPPER

Translated by David Macey

The phenomenon of joint Muslim-Christian attendance at the same places of worship has been widely reported in Albania. The annual pilgrimage from the city of Laç to the church of St. Anthony of Padua in the north of the country attracts thousands of Catholic worshipers, but it also attracts Muslims and Orthodox Christians. Widely covered by the media, it allows the religious dignitaries of different confessions to demonstrate that they are on good terms. The fact that they can share places of worship is used as an argument to prove that the different religions present in Albania are tolerant and can coexist peacefully. Important shrines such as Laç or Mount Tomor are not, however, the only places where Muslims and Christians worship together at the same time. In a country where most regions are inhabited by mixed populations, religious practices in shared spaces are also to be observed at a much more local level. The phenomenon is particularly obvious in what we can, with some qualifications, call the "religious revival" of the postcommunist period. After the period between 1967 and 1990, when religion was banned, a large number of different sites—churches, mosques, and monasteries, but also tombs, ruins, springs, and stones—began to be visited by growing numbers of people. The vernacular notion of *vakëf* then began to take on a particular meaning. The term is used to refer to most of these places that, despite their diversity, share certain characteristics. They are usually peripheral and marginal places (in terms of their relationship with churches or mosques, the clergy, and the national territory), but they are also places where devotional practices enjoy a relative freedom.

The reemergence of the notion of *vakëf* in this context raises two questions. The first is the close relationship that can be observed between the *vakëf* and the coexistence of Muslims and Christians. According to some informants, a *vakëf*, is, unlike a church or a mosque, "for all religions." This raises the issue of how the Muslim or Christian character of such places relates to the fact that they are visited by followers of both religions, and of the ways in which they are attended. The second question is historical: the Albanian word *vakëf* obviously derives from the Arabic *waqf*, which entered the Balkan languages via the Turkish *vakıf*. The term *waqf* belongs to the religious register. In Muslim law, it refers primarily to a legal deed that allows the owner of a piece of real estate to make it inalienable. The income it yields is used for charitable purposes. The term refers, in other words, to the foundation of a charitable institution and, by extension, to the institution itself. The institution of *waqf* was very widespread in the Ottoman Empire, and was therefore recorded in the Empire's Balkan provinces (Deguilhem 2003). As we shall see, in Albania the word was still used to refer to a category of real estate the income from which was used to finance and maintain both Muslim and Christian institutions until they were nationalized and collectivized by the communists after the Second World War. This raises the question of what this semantic shift means and why it occurred.

I will begin by attempting to define the notion of *vakëf* as a category of religious activity in postcommunist Albania. I will then look at the ways in which Muslims and Christians interact within these shared places. The ethnographic data comes from two regions in southern Albania in the Devoll and Gjirokastër districts. It was collected in 1995–1996 and between 2001 and 2005.

A Category of Religious Activity in Postcommunist Albania

My first contact with the *vakëf* category was in late 1995, between Christmas and New Year's, when I was staying with a Muslim family in Bilisht (Devoll). The festive atmosphere—both in the town and on television—seemed to lead our conversations to folklore and religion. One evening, the conversation turned to certain places in the region that were still seen as noteworthy, even though most of them had disappeared during the communist period: the church in the village of Poloskë,[1] which is mainly Muslim, and the healing powers of its icon ("No matter where you looked at it from, it seemed to be staring you in the eye"); the monastery of Saint-Elie in the mixed village of Hoçisht, with its forty rooms ("one for each village in Devoll"); and the church of St. Nicholas in the same village, which was built with money remitted by emigrants and turned into a cooperative building by the communists. The same village is home to the *vakëf* of Satrivaç, "the holiest [*i shenjtë*] place in the region," and the most famous: I was told that people came to it from as far away as Korçë and even Tirana.

"Satrivaç is a *vakef*[2] for all religions," explained Kujtim, who was the head of the household; "Orthodox Christians, Catholics, and Muslims go there, and so do Gypsies [*evgjit*] . . ."

"Especially Gypsies," his wife, Drita, interrupted. "People who are sick spend a night there, and are cured. There is a kitchen annex, with cooking utensils. People bring their own ingredients and make their own meals. There is no priest, but there are three domestic servants [*shërbëtor*]. . . .

"Inside, there is a magic mirror. When a true believer places a coin on it, it remains stuck to the mirror. They make a sacrifice [*kurban*] of a sheep, and leave its head and skin."

Shortly afterward, Drita explained to me that the framed family photograph hanging by the door had been taken in Satrivaç the previous year. They went there every summer for a picnic that brought the whole family together. A few months later, I actually went to Satrivaç with my hosts for a family picnic, and discovered the *vakëf*. It was a single-story whitewashed building, with a small cross on its tiled roof. Inside, three rooms opened on to a vestibule. One of the rooms was being visited by people who seemed to have had the same idea as we did on the morning of 30 June. To the back of a room, there was an icon of Saints Cosmas and Damian surrounded by smaller icons on a table covered with a cloth.[3] The warden of the *vakëf*, who was himself an Orthodox Christian, confirmed my "discovery": Satrivaç, the holy place venerated by my Muslim friends, was a church dedicated to Saints Cosmas and Damian that had been taken over and turned into offices by the army under communism, and then restored to the faithful at the beginning of the 1990s. The faithful go there especially to celebrate on the saints' feast day on 1 July. Yet when I told Kujtim about my discovery, he smiled and calmly replied, "No, it's not a church. It's a *vakëf*." Which means, among other things, that the presence of Muslims is not inappropriate because a *vakëf* is "for all religions."

In the meantime, I had come across enough *vakëfe* (the plural of *vakëf*) in the villages of Devoll not to be surprised by his answer: I had become used to translating the word as "holy place" without making any distinction between Muslim and Christian, in keeping with the local usage that makes *vakëf* synonymous with *vend i shenjtë*.[4] But this was the first time I had heard it being applied to a Christian church, rather than to all sorts of "holy places" ranging from mausoleums and chapels to isolated altars and pierced stones. Referring to another major holy place in Devoll—Inonisht in the Muslim village of Kuç—Drita had shown me how the existence of a *vakëf* blurs the line that divides Muslims and Christians: "A *vakef*," she explained to me, "is like a mosque, but smaller. There is only one room, but there is everything that is in a mosque: icons, and all those things. There is no priest [*hoxhë*] and people go there whenever they like, in the same way that they go to church [*si në kishë*]." A mosque with icons . . . you go there in the same way that you go to church. That is how Drita described a Bektashi[5] mausoleum some distance away from the *tekke* in Kuç.[6] Both were demolished under communism (to make way for a barracks in one case); since the 1990s, both Muslims and Christians have been able to visit them freely.[7] As the inhabitants of the Muslim village of Menku-las (Devoll), which has four *vakëfe*, said, "*vakëf* can be used by all religions." They are religious places, but they are not associated with any one religion. They are also places that can be visited at any time, without any need for the mediation of a religious specialist. This form of practice was well adapted to the communist period, and is still well adapted, now that there are almost no clergy in the villages.

The frequent use of the word *vakëf* in Devoll and the other regions of southern Albania that I have visited contrasts so sharply with the word's few appearances in the ethnological literature that one wonders about the status of both the no-tion and the places to which it relates. It appears that we are dealing with a local category that has to do with religion "from below" and that disappears once we adopt a more institutional viewpoint. The *Albanian Encyclopaedic Dictionary* gives only one meaning, defined as "properties owned by Muslim religious institutions" (Buda 1985:150). This is the historical meaning of the word, which derives from the Arabic *waqf* (pious foundation). The dictionary adds that the word is also used to describe properties owned by Christian institutions such as churches and monasteries.[8] The *Dictionary of the Modern Albanian Language* (1980), for its part, mentions another meaning of the word: "holy place" (*vend i shenjtë*), defined as having to do with "the mystical religious imagination," but does not go into further detail.[9] The same is true of the field of ethnologi-cal knowledge, where the word is not recognized by specialists in the study of religion, even though it is widely used in southern Albania.[10] Mark Tirta, who has written widely on "folk" practices and beliefs, scarcely uses the word. He records only a few local instances of its use, especially in toponyms, and claims that it is not always understood by the population. Certain woods and forests (in, for instance, Tirana's Malësi) are said to be *vakëfe*, though they have nothing to do with religious institutions, past or present. They are described as "heavy" (*i rëndë*) places, or places where fairies and djinns rest (Tirta 2004:58). Tirta himself does not establish any link between the places known as *vakëfe* and the properties in mortmain that are owned by religious institutions. When there is concordance between a "holy place" and a property owned by a religious institution it is, in his view, because the institution has appropriated an existing pagan holy place (Tirta 2004:58). He prefers to use the expression *vend i shenjtë* (holy place). It seems that while "folk" can be used in a positive sense as a synonym for "authentic" and "national," as in most ethnographic accounts of Balkan Europe, the same is not true of a word whose obvious Muslim origins are not in keeping with the idea of a folk religion with obvious pagan roots. The ethnologists' expression *vend i shenjtë* is, however, and as we have seen, used locally as a synonym for *vakëf,* as is the expression *vend i mirë* (good spot). The latter expression appears to be older, and is the only one recorded by Georg von Hahn in the mid-nineteenth century. The Austrian consul defines a "good spot" as a *heiliger Ort, in der Moschee der Ort um die heilige Nische, aber auch im Freien, wo z.B. jemand geschlafen und stumm oder traub aufgestanden ist* (Hahn 1854: vol. 3:7; see also vol. 1:159). This definition is interesting in that the same expression is applied both to official places of worship and to places that stand out because of their special relationship with the sacred. In his book on the "customs and traditions" of Zagori, a mountainous region inhabited by a Christian population that lies between Gjirokastër and Përmet, Evien Peri gives us an idea of the transition from one meaning of *vakëf* (property held in mortmain) to the other (holy place), or of the links between the two:

> [*Vakëf* was] part of the real estate or personal property belonging to both village churches and monasteries. This type of property was inviolable. These properties were also called *vakëf.* No one could lay a hand on a branch, or even a leaf, of a tree, not only because this was the property of a sacred institution, but also because of the tradition that had grown up, and which still exists today. Even today the villagers of Zagori will not take either wood or fodder from land belonging to churches and monasteries, or which once belonged to them. The tradition survived even during the period of collectivization, when the property of these institutions was taken into collective ownership; the villagers said nothing but would not exploit them for their personal use or for the use of their families.[11]

Whilst it is conceivable that the property of religious institutions was regarded as inviolable—which would explain the metaphorical use of *vakëf* to mean "shrine" when referring, for example, to the national territory from the first half of the twentieth century onward—the author seems to accept that this did not exhaust the special relationship between the villages and the *vakëf.* That relationship was based upon avoidance, and the author relates it to "tradition." The "tradition" in question is a reminder of what ethnologists describe as traces of a "plant cult." It is in keeping with a tendency, which has been observed elsewhere in Albania, to regard certain woods or isolated trees as sacred. In a short essay on the protection of forests,[12] a forestry official from the Ministry of Agriculture asks, "Why is it that, in holy places, people have always regarded the ban on cutting down trees as a sign of the sacred and inviolable nature of such places?" He goes on to express what is a widespread feeling in Albania: "Wherever there are big old trees, they suggest the existence of a holy place. In our country, this gives rise to some astonishing and incredible situations, as when Muslims show their respect for a wood that once belonged to a church by calling it a *vakëf.*" He gives an example of this kind of situation from the Dibër region, where all the forests of the village of Selishtë have been cut down, with the exception of the one known as "the church's *vakëf,*" even though no one remembers the existence of the church in question. "When, ten years ago, the state decided to fell some of the trees in this forest, all the Muslims in the local community refused to allow the forestry service to desecrate the sacred trees." As we can see from this example,[13] not all the places that are now described as *vakëfe* were once held in mortmain (in the sense of *waqf*), and the relationship between the Ottoman institution and the contemporary category is not based upon any continuity. Do we have to conclude that the idea of a *vakëf* comes within a "folk" category of religious activity that is absent from ethnological studies, and even from studies of the folklore of postcommunist Albania? From the viewpoint of certain Muslim informants, there is indeed a difference between *vakëfe* and mosques, which are more "official" places of worship. One Muslim in Bilisht, a former math teacher who was now involved in the trade with Greece, said in 1996 that the town's mosque, which was damaged during the Second World War, was never repaired before it was completely destroyed in 1967, because no one saw any point in repairing it. He explained this by adding that "Muslims go to the *vakëf* rather than the mosque. Mosques are reserved for important ceremonies. The only mosques Muslims attend are the ones that are next to a *vakëf.*" Muslim informants in Menkulas also report that "as a rule, people say that the *vakëf* is more efficacious, more powerful, than the mosque."

Before it took on its modern meaning of "places of the sacred," the word *vakëf* was used in Albanian to refer to a type of property. That meaning derives from "pious foundation," a term used under the Ottoman Empire (Deguilhem

2003). The word is still used in the old sense, which is close to Muslim law, in Albanian toponyms. The district of Berat known as Vakuf, for example, owes its name (which has been in use since at least 1757) to the fact that it stands on *waqf* land, and not to the presence of a sacred site (Sulo 1997:47, 49). Similarly, the region known as "the *Vakëfe*," which is on the outskirts of the district of Korçë, now consists of seven villages. The oldest, which were given by Sultan Bayezid to a locally born bey at the end of the fifteenth century as a reward for his services during the capture of Constantinople, were turned into *waqf* by the bey as early as 1503. The name still survives, but does not imply that there is anything holy about the region.[14]

Until the Second World War and communist collectivization, the word was used to describe, among other things, lands owned by religious institutions, both Muslim (mosques and *tekke*) and Christian (churches and monasteries), as well as other pieces of real estate (mills, bridges, shops). These properties were either exploited by the religious institutions themselves or leased to villagers on an annual basis in exchange for part (usually one-third) of the harvest or income. Some were either sold or rented out on behalf of the institution.[15] An informant in Sul (Devoll) recalls that until the years after the Second World War, the upper part of the old cemetery, which was by the entrance to the village, was left as pasture (*mera*): "At the time of year when the grass grows, the space was divided into several plots that anyone could rent. The money went to the mosque."

Defined in the old sense of real estate belonging to a religious institution, the word belongs mainly to the past. It is not simply that the object it referred to disappeared during the collectivization of the 1950s and 1960s, but that it became unthinkable when the religious institutions themselves vanished and when all places of worship were closed in 1967. It has now reappeared in a context in which the land has been decollectivized and in which some real estate has been restored to religious institutions (this was authorized from 1990 onward). There are, however, limits to this return to the old meaning, as the lands in question tend to be described as *pronat e xhamisë/e kishës/e teqesë* (property of the mosque/church/*tekke*), rather as though the word *vakëf* no longer applied in the present context. A visit to a *vakëf* in Libohovë in the district of Gjirokastër in 2005 illustrates the semantic shift that occurred when the Ottoman juridical category ceased to exist. The tomb (*dylbe*) of Demiri Baba is on the edge of the Teqe-Fushë (*tekke* of the plain) district, which is the lowest quarter of the town that stands on the slopes of Mount Bureto. It is alternately referred to as a *teqe*, *vakëf*, or *dylbe*. The mausoleum is surrounded by a wood of hackberry trees (*çerçem*). Some of the trees were cut down during the crisis of the early 1990s, before the people of the area insisted that their links with the *vakëf* made them inviolable. Beyond the wood, the closest meadows are rented out, and the money is used to maintain the *vakëf*. According to my guide, who lived in the neighborhood, the land was not, however, *vakëf* land in the old sense, but "land of the *vakëf*" (*pronat e vakëfit*). It belonged, that is, to the tomb, defined as a holy place, rather than to a religious institution. In this case, the word no longer refers to a form of property—land—but to a sacred place marked by a mausoleum. To illustrate this semantic shift, it might be noted that a village such as Vithkuq (Korçë) was described from the sixteenth century onward as *vakëf* property (Mile 1984:91–92). The word no longer applies to the village and its lands as a whole, but only to certain sacred places within its territory, such as the former Monastery of St. Peter, which will be discussed below.

Without going into the word's history in greater detail, one wonders to what extent current usage has to do with the disappearance of the juridical object (the property of religious institutions) as a result of the secularization of Albanian society and the collectivization of the land, which meant that the word was available for other purposes. In a sense, and as we shall see, the fact that places of worship that have been destroyed are referred to as *vakëfe* suggests that the more recent usage implies that *vakëf* is a quality those places acquired when they fell into disuse.

A survey of the various types of place that are described as *vakëf* shows that an initial distinction has to be made between the ways in which Christians and Muslims use the term, as the latter seem to use it more frequently. If we look at the term's general usage, we find that it is often applied to places that are associated with death or destruction. As we have seen, Muslims often use the word to refer to tombs or mausoleums that preserve the remains of men who were famed for their religious and humane virtues.[16] Such tombs can be found in many villages, as well as in towns. Simpler models are called *varr* (tombs). These are isolated tombs surrounded by a fence or low wall with a niche where candles can be lit and where, in some cases, a little money is left. The identity of the man buried there is not always known. In such cases, the name of the *vakëf* derives from its location, physical environment, or powers, as every *vakëf* has its own "power" (*fuqi*), and especially its power to heal. As a rule and as we shall see, houses are not usually built near these tombs. There are also mausoleums, which are known in southern Albania as *dylbe* (a corruption of the Turkish *türbe*, which also appears in the Albanian *tyrbe*) or, more rarely, *mekam*. These are roofed constructions built over one or more tombs (and sometimes cenotaphs) called *mezar*. The identity of those who are buried there is usually known, even though little may be known about their origins or history. They were often the founders of or leading figures in a local community. In Lazarat (Gjirokastër), the Bektashi caretaker described the mausoleum in the cemetery as "the *dylbe* of the dervish Hyseni."[17] He describes the simple tomb farther down the slope and by an oak as "the *varr* of the dervish." This illustrates the difference between a mausoleum with a name and an anonymous tomb. According to certain informants, *dylbe* is a synonym for *vakëf*, and many mausoleums are indeed described as *vakëfe*. That they are also *dylbe* is of secondary importance. Under communism, many of these tombs were demolished or closed down, and some were used for other purposes.[18] Some have now been rebuilt, like the tomb of Zeneli Baba in Lazarat (rebuilt in 1991). It was demolished during the communist period "by some people from the village, people in the Party who died shortly afterward," adds the caretaker. Bektashi *tekke* are also often described as *vakëfe*, partly because they are often associated with such tombs, which can be either inside the enclosure or at some distance from the *tekke*. Conversely, some *dylbe* are referred to as *tekke*, though the term is now inappropriate, given that the *tekke* no longer exists; the *dylbe* is all that remains. In the village of Lazarat, for example, what is described as the Bektashi *tekke* in fact consist of a *dylbe*—that of Zeneli Baba, which was rebuilt in 1991—and a building used for meetings, which was still under reconstruction in 2005. It is this building that the *vakëf*'s caretaker described as the *vakëf*. Muslims, finally, use the word *vakëf* to describe some Christian places of worship, and especially those that are famed for their healing powers (they are often monasteries or former monasteries). Christian chapels or oratories come into the same category, especially when, as we shall see, they are associated with ruins. In Libohovë, on the site of a settlement that has been abandoned, there is a little chapel that a Muslim shepherd described to me as a *vakëf*. "It was built four or five years ago by someone who lived nearby and who went to Greece or America. He built it because the place was known to be a *vakëf*; there used to be a fig tree there, and some old stones." He thought that the place was called Spiro.[19] In this case, the chapel signals the existence of the *vakëf* and makes it a physical reality. He adds that there is another *vakëf* not far away. It is a former church that was converted into a large dwelling house under communism.

In all these cases, Muslims make a distinction between *vakëfe* and mosques, which are places of worship, and may even contrast the two: a mosque is not in itself a *vakëf*. Christian usage makes the same distinction. The word is never applied to the village's central church, which is always called *kishë* (church). It is, on the other hand, applied to the chapels or small churches (*parakishë, kishkë, vakëfkë*) that are usually found on the edge of the village's territory and that, unlike the central church, are associated with particular families or events. The word *vakëf* is also applied to churches or former monasteries[20] that are the object of pilgrimages or that are famed for their healing properties, especially if they are also attended by Muslims. In a sense, a *vakëf* is, from a Christian point of view, often associated with Muslim practices or Muslim attendance. It is significant that one Christian author who describes the churches and monasteries that once existed, or still exist, in Voskopojë (Korçë) uses the word *vakëf,* sometimes in quotation marks, to describe those that are known to be attended by Muslims from neighboring villages (Falo 2003:29, 123, 182, 205). Once again, the word is used to describe places that are not churches, or peripheral places that are associated with other practices. The monastery of St. John Prodromos, to which we will return, is one example. It is outside the village, beyond the river and surrounded by pines, but it also stands out from Voskopojë's other places or worship because of those who attend it: "The buildings that surround the charming church on three sides, the many chambers, the cellars, the stables, the fountains, the kitchen and the oven are visited by many worshipers [*besimtarët*] but also, astonishingly by Mahometan infidels [*të pabesët muhamedanë*]. The *vakëf* welcomes them as though they were its sons" (Falo 2003:29). Evoking the "inter-confessional [*ndërfetar*] nature" of the place in terms that could be applied to many other *vakëfe* in the region, the author writes: "A little world up there in the mountains, cut off from the world and peaceful, acknowledges only one power, God . . . and serves all men, no matter who they are" (Falo 2003:29).

There is also a tendency to apply the term *vakëf* to places that are not peripheral in the spatial sense but from which "official" religion, either Muslim or Christian, has retreated, or that have been either abandoned or demolished. The distinction between a *vakëf* and a mosque does not, in other words, always hold. The mosque in Bilisht may well have been poorly attended before it was destroyed in 1967, as people now say, but that did not prevent its site from being marked and recognized as a *vakëf* in the 1990s. No one took it over in order to build a house, and a niche was created at ground level to take candles or offerings of money. This is not an isolated case: any ruin or site of a place of worship that has been demolished is likely to be described as a *vakëf.* Muslims apply the term to mosques that were demolished under communism, and especially in 1967, regardless of whether or not anything remains of them. In the Bejler area of Libohovë, offerings of flowers and branches are left by the lower part of the minaret, which is still standing. In the so-called mosque area of Vidohovë (Devoll), a pile of stones marks the site of a mosque that was demolished in 1967. A small construction has been built in the middle of a fenced space, and people light candles and leave flowers there. They say that it is a *vakëf*. The same is true of certain *tekke* that, even though they have been abandoned or are in ruins, are regarded as *vakëfe*. This also applies, finally, to Christian places of worship that were in many cases demolished long ago, as when, for example, a village was Islamized. In Muslim villages, it is not unusual for the inhabitants to remember where a church built in Christian times stood, to go on referring to it as a "church," and to regard it as *vakëf*. For the same reason, disused cemeteries are also regarded as *vakëfe,* and any trace of construction is believed to mark the site of a church.[21] In Miras (Devoll), for example, the cemetery, which is on the heights to the west of the village, is close to the place called "at the church" (*te kisha*), and traces of a building can be seen there. Candles and offerings are left on a small altar, which is said to be a *vakëf.* In Libohovë, Muslims say that on 15 August, they honor what they call Stojan's *vakëf;* the church of a Christian village destroyed by a landslip in the late nineteenth century once stood here. Christians also regard ruined churches as *vakëfe*. In Voskopojë, the St. Paraskevi's church, which was destroyed by fire in 1976 (at which time it was used to store maize), is a *vakëf*. The site where it once stood on the way out of the village is marked by a small building containing an icon and surrounded by grass and stones. In what was once the village of Dhambel (Devoll) on the Greek-Albanian border, the ruins of the church are regarded as a *vakëf*. Albanians who cross the frontier illegally leave offerings as they pass through the old village. Many villages were displaced at a relatively recent date. Their abandoned sites are still known, and the places where their churches once stood are marked by small constructions known as *konizmë*[22] to mark the sacred nature of the spot even though no trace of the churches themselves remains. This is, for example, the case with an old village called Manastir, which the inhabitants of Selckë (Gjirokastër) regard as the original site of their village.

Once they have been named and categorized as *vakëfe,* certain of these ruins are given a new and local interpretation. Because they are *vakëfe,* they may, for instance, be believed to have powers that they did not originally have. The people of the village of Sul speak of a *vakëf* that has been built on the site of the neighboring abandoned village of Llaban (Devoll). It consists of three stones that form a table some thirty centimeters high; sickly children are made to crawl under it in the hope that it will make them grow. The practice recalls that associated with the pierced stones described by Frederick Hasluck (2000 [1929]:178–180), which has also been recorded in the same region. The very name given to the *vakëf*—Sallatash—reveals a different origin. *Sallatash* is in fact the word for the stone table in the courtyard of a mosque where the coffin rests during the funerary rite. It can therefore be assumed that the old village's mosque became a *vakëf* when it was abandoned. A holy place that is believed to have certain powers has survived the demolition of the institutional place of worship, and now marks the site of a village that no longer exists.

In all these cases, the word *vakëf* refers to places that are peripheral with respect to the village's main place of worship, which could be either a church or a mosque, or a place of worship that has been abandoned. They are places from which a certain form of religious activity has retreated. In more general terms, they are often places associated with death and destruction.

Shared Places

There are recent examples of the metaphorical use of the word that makes a *vakëf* a place that welcomes people of various groups. Outside that sacred place, relations between them may not be friendly, but they all find sanctuary inside it.[23] And one of the features of a visit to a *vakëf* is that day-to-day hostilities are suspended. As a lady from Korçë remarked on a visit to the *vakëf* in Satrivaç on the feast of St. Cosmas in 2003, "Here, people have to respect one another." In order to understand why both Muslims and Christians can visit most *vakëfe*, and the ways in which they do so, we have to begin by describing the different types of practice that are associated with them.

These practices help to explain what a *vakëf* is. Three types of practice can be identified: avoidance, ordinary worship, and extraordinary worship.

"*Larg vakëfit, larg të vdekurit,*" recalled an informant in Libohovë as he deplored the fact that people in the area had used blocks of stone from old tombs to build houses: "Far from the *vakëf,* far from death." *Vakëfe* and the things in their vicinity, such as graves, are not meant to be places for the normal activities of the living. And building a house on the site of a *vakëf,* or using stones from it to do so, is something to be avoided because it will bring bad luck (Tirtja 1976:59–60). Bekim reports that there is a holy place (*vakëf, vend i shenjtë*) in the courtyard of his house in the Muslim village of Menkulas. He knows nothing about its origins. He says that in 1978, or under communism, he needed some land to build a house. As the land was unoccupied and did not belong to anyone, someone suggested that he should take it over. He at first refused because he knew that the place was holy (*i shenjtë*), but then agreed because he had no choice. Even though religion had been banned, people still lit candles there and left ears of corn (*grurë*) there. He planted a rosebush (*trendafil*) on what he believed to be the site of the *vakëf*. A woman from Tirana who had married into Bekim's lineage (*soj*) in Menkulas had a dream in which she saw the exact spot where it once stood. One day, she went to the house with a stick (*shkop*) and planted it in the ground near the rosebush. In the summer of 1995, Bekim built a small structure on the site. In accordance with the Greek custom, there was a niche for an icon, and a cross on top of the roof. This is a further illustration of how the notion of a *vakëf* blurs the boundaries between different confessions. People go there to light candles, and leave money. Bekim uses the money to keep the *vakëf* in good repair. When we visited it in March 1996, he said that he was going to build a fence to keep out the children and chickens. It is dangerous to go near or enter a *vakëf* unless you have good intentions, or if you have no reason to be there. As we entered the courtyard of Bekim's house in Menkulas, one of his friends observed that the act of lighting a candle must be performed *me shpirt* (with sincerity); otherwise it would have unfortunate consequences. The village's mosque had been demolished in 1967, and a school had been built on the site. It was next to a *dylbe*. This sometimes serves as a reminder to those who might otherwise forget that this is a holy place. "Four men, including my grandfather, and a woman are buried there. They were important people in the village. Under communism, the *mezar* were demolished by the party, and their bones were moved to the cemetery. But the woman appears to her husband every night; she asks for them to be freed." One of the school's classrooms is still regarded as *vakëf* today. A father recalls that one day in 1994, his son, who had arrived early at school, went into the room to study. "Two men, dressed completely in white, rose up out of the ground and told him that the place was sacred and that he had to leave it immediately. He ran home, and did not go back to school for three weeks." In Bilisht, Drita went on: "In all *vakëf* there are stories to frighten the children, to stop them going into them or taking away offerings [*peshqesh, të falura*]. In Inonisht, the *vakëf* in Kuç, they used to say that if anyone stole the offering, God would close the door to stop the thief from getting out. A barracks was built of the site of the *vakëf*; people said that any soldiers who cut down the poplar trees would immediately die." There are in fact many tales about ill-intentioned people who died after entering a *vakëf*. In Lazarat, for example, the Bektashi caretaker says that three Greek soldiers entered Zeneli Baba's mausoleum in 1940: "The first to go in fell to the ground, and the others had to carry him out. They made no attempt to go back in." Animals too have to be kept away from *vakëfe*. In Libo-hovë, a former old *tekke* was turned into a "cultural center" under communism, but fell into ruins and was abandoned. "Three or four years ago," someone living in the area recalls, "a guy tethered his cow and a bull to the door of the *tekke*. His son told him not to do it, because cows should not be in a *vakëf*. A stone with a Turkish or Arabic inscription fell from the door and cut off his toes."

The second type of practice—ordinary worship—is a sign of respect for the holy place and the powers attributed to it. In some cases, no particular request is made, except for a vaguely defined protection. In other cases, go-ing to the *vakëf* is associated with a particular situation or request: illness, sterility, a decision to emigrate, exams at school, birthdays, and so on. The site of the old village of Selcë, on the road between Bilisht and Vërnik, is marked by a *vakëf* known as Kristofori. The name derives from the name of a chapel dedicated to St. Christopher, which stands beneath a big walnut tree. A man from Vërnik recalls that, as he drove past it one day, he saw the driver of a vehicle go out of his way to stop at the *vakëf* and leave a ten-*lek* note there. When he asked him if he did that every time he went by, and why, the driver said that he had gone past it with his wife some time ago. She asked him to stop and leave some money in the *vakëf*. He refused to do so, saying that it was not worthwhile. As they were coming back from Vërnik the next day, the car's suspension went. Ever since, he always stopped at the *vakëf*: it was cheaper than replacing the suspension.

At certain times of the year, some *vakëfe* are the setting for extraordinary devotions. Christian holy places are visited on the feast days of the saint to whom they are dedicated and Bektashi *tekke* are visited on Sultan Nevruz's day (22 March). In August 2006, Bilisht's literary society, the Friends of Dritëro, cel-ebrated both its second anniversary and the seventy-fifth birthday of the writer Dritëro Agolli, who was born in Menkulas. According to the society's president: "The ceremony took place in the holy place [*vend i shenjtë*] of the village of Kuç in Devoll where, seventy-five years ago, Ahmeti Baba gave our great Dritëro his name in the village's *tekke*. Sadije [Dritëro's wife] brought three sacks filled with earth. It was the first time she had been to this holy place."[24] As we shall see, people often take earth to the *vakëf* they visit, and then take it home with them.

The feast days of Christian saints are called *festë* (feast) or *panair* (fair) and are celebrated in similar ways. Worshipers begin to arrive on the afternoon of the day before the feast, visit the saint's icon, and may attend Mass in the evening, but spend most of their time preparing to spend the night inside the church or around campfires near it. The following morning, the crowds are

even bigger. Mass is celebrated, and people continue to visit the church, while
the majority have family picnics. They begin to leave in the early afternoon,
and everyone has gone by the end of the day. This was the pattern of the feasts
we attended at three *vakëfe* in the villages of Voskopojë (monastery of St. John
Prodromos, 24 June), Vithkuq (Monastery of St. Peter, 29 June), and Hoçisht
(Satrivaç, church of Saints Cosmas and Damian, 1 July). It should be noted that
in most cases, people go to a *vakëf* that is famous for its feast for nonreligious
reasons. They go mainly for pleasure, and because they enjoy the rural or
mountain setting, the pure air, and the cool water of their springs. Some have
long been known as "places for tourists" (*pikë turistike*). It was not without
reason that, under communism, a pioneers' camp (*kampi i pionerëve*) was
established very close to the monastery of St. John Prodromos in Voskopojë.
Now that communism is a thing of the past, it has become a hotel complex
that attracts a lot of visitors in summer. Under communism, Satrivaç was the
site of the Feast of the Battalion (7 August), which commemorated the formation of a partisan battalion during the Second World War. The ceremony was
subsequently transferred to a bigger site in the neighboring village of Poloskë.
A contemporary eyewitness recalls that in the 1930s people went to *vakëfe* not
only because they were holy places or had magical powers. Recalling how he
met Koçi Xoxe (a future communist minister of the interior who was executed
in 1949) in the early 1930s, Pandi Kristo (1914–1994), another former minister
who was jailed in 1948, writes:

> We met by chance at one of the picnics young people from Korçë used to
> organize at the region's tourist attractions. Koçi regularly organized picnics
> in Dardhë in Moravë, in Shën Naum, Voskopojë, Shën Marenë in Pogradec
> and Shën Trivac [Satrivaç] in Hoçisht. Young workers and students from
> Korçë met there to discuss patriotic issues, put on little plays and organize
> concerts at which patriotic songs were sung. I recall that, at the end of these
> picnics, pamphlets about progressive and communist ideas were handed
> out to the students, who regularly took part in these activities.[25]

Most of the tourist destinations frequented by these young "progressives" were
obviously Christian sites. The feasts held there now attract visitors of both
religions, but they also attract tourists.

At first glance, these feasts are not notable for their devotional intensity,
and it seems difficult to differentiate between those who come as "believers"
(*besimtar*) and those who come as "tourists" (*turist*). One also has the impression that there is little difference between them in terms of their geographical

origins, religious affiliation, or nationality, rather as though the boundaries between the different groups had become blurred. If we look more closely, we find that Christians and Muslims do visit the three *vakëfe* for different reasons, and that their devotional practices are different. There are also processes of differentiation at work, and they preserve the alterity of the other even though all join in the feast. In a sense, the presence of the other does not go unnoticed: it is known and recognized as such. In many cases, the large numbers who attend these places of worship, be they Muslim or Christian, actually stress that members of the other religion are there. When I attended the inauguration of the mosque in Bilisht in June 1995, my Muslim friends said more than once, both during and after the ceremony, that "half the people [there were] Christians." This was their way of saying both that they had relatively little interest in religion (the Christians were more devout) and that they were "tolerant" of the many Christians who had come to attend a Muslim ceremony. The same applies to the three feasts under discussion. It is usually those with whom the holy place is associated who point out that followers of the other religion are present. In all three cases, it was mainly Christians who noticed the presence of Muslims, who were more discreet. Encounters between Christians and Muslims are asymmetrical: it is the Christians who welcome Muslims into Christian holy places. The same lack of symmetry is apparent at the linguistic level; no one speaks of "shared" or "mixed" sanctuaries or of "joint participation." Christians tend to say of Muslims that "They come, they come too" (*vijnë, edhe ata vijnë*). The fact that these places are shared, therefore, does not completely abolish the hierarchical relationship between the two groups.

This lack of symmetry raises two questions. The first is that of the visibility of confessional affiliations: to what extent are they on display or concealed? While the presence of Muslims is acknowledged and noticed, it is in fact quite inconspicuous, compared with the other, more official occasions that bring together representatives of the four confessions (Sunni and Bektashi Islam, Orthodox and Catholic Christianity).[26] It is as though all the talk about Muslim involvement placed the emphasis not on confessional diversity, but on the underlying unity between Christians and Muslims: Muslims frequent Christian holy places because they are former Christians who have converted to Islam. Several factors help to create this impression. First, there are no religious vestimentary markers: Christians and Muslims dress the same way, both in everyday life and when they visit Christian holy places. Wearing a cross is not always a distinctive sign, as many Muslims, especially if they are young or migrants, are quite happy to do so. Some behaviors do, however, give Muslims away. In

Satrivaç, in June 1996, the caretaker of the *vakëf* reminded visitors where they were if, on entering the church, they simply turned their caps around so that the peaks covered their necks rather than taking them off, and if they betrayed their Muslim origins by beginning to take off their shoes. Muslims seem to be accepted only to the extent that they behave as though they were Christians. Most devotional gestures are in fact common to both religions, even though it is not always easy to determine their origins. Visitors to the church touch or kiss the icons, the uprights of the iconostasis, and the church doors, leave offerings of money or in kind, light candles in front of the church (Voskopojë, Hoçisht) or on the porch (Vithkuq). Both Christians and Muslims practice incubation,[27] sleeping either in annexes or against the outside wall of the chancel. So far as we were able to observe, not everyone crossed themselves before the icons. And according to my Christian informants in Vithkuq, Muslims do not join in the Mass, which is reserved for those who have been baptized.

It should be pointed out that, in these Christian holy places, the Christian nature of the ritual, and sometimes of the places themselves, is limited. There are few clergy, and they are discreet. The saint's icon is not taken out of the church on the feast day, and there is no procession around the church or through the village, unlike what is reported for other places (Duizings 2000). In Hoçisht, morning Mass on St. Cosmas's Day is celebrated in a different church on the way into the village because the Satrivaç church has no apse. When Mass is over, both the popes (priests) go back to the church of Saints Cosmas and Damian by car, while the faithful who have been to Mass mingle with the crowds who come by coach from Bilisht or Korçë. Relatively few people take part in the services; many visitors, even if they are Christians, have not come for that purpose.

The main exception to this nondifferentiation between practices has to do with sacrifices (*kurban, gjak*).[28] In Hoçisht in June 1996, the caretaker of the *vakëf* told me that only Muslims make sacrifices; Christians, he said, know nothing of that "custom" (*zakon*). A portico has been built by the stream where Muslims can cut up and prepare the lambs that have been slaughtered beneath the two oaks behind the church. When I visited Hoçisht with a Muslim family from Bilisht on St. Cosmas's Eve, we killed and ate a sheep we had bought in the market in Bilisht that morning. The purpose of our visit to the *vakëf* was to have a picnic (*piknik*) that brought together the "lineage" (*fis*). Even when it takes place outside a religious context, this practice often involves eating lamb kebabs.[29] Because of the festive atmosphere in Voskopojë, some families bring a lamb with them, but it is always slaughtered and prepared outside the precincts of the monastery—where they picnic on cold meat or the ready meals they have brought with them—either in the pine woods or somewhere in the vicinity. This does not mean that sacrifice is an exclusively Muslim practice. Christians make sacrifices, in a family context at Easter and on St. Constantine's day (21 May or 3 June). The atmosphere is similar to that surrounding the feast of St. John, and the celebrations sometimes take place in a mountain woodland setting, as they do near the village of Bradvicë in the Devoll. There is no clear difference between Muslims and Christians when it comes to such practices, principally because they are mainly associated with the *vakëf*. The blood sacrifice itself is one of a series of practices involving the distribution of food. Both Muslims and Christians observe them, even when they do not make sacrifices on these feast days. Christians share some foodstuffs, such as cakes, with Muslims, and are given portions of meat.

The second question relates to the explanations Muslims give for their presence in Christian holy places. The first explanation makes reference to the *vakëf* category. Muslims visit Christian churches and monasteries because they are *vakëfe* rather than because they are Christian places of worship. They go there because they have the powers of a *vakëf*. They also go because they enjoy it, and because the visit is a break from their daily routine. On several occasions, my Muslim friends described the Christian religion as a religion of pleasure, as the religion of people who know how to have a good time, and contrasted it with the austerity of the Muslim religion. As we have seen, the fact that many *vakëfe* are high up in the hills, in woods, near streams, and, as a rule, away from the towns means that they are "tourist destinations" and that people go there for a day out. When they are discussing religious practices and beliefs, Muslims often play down the differences between Muslims and Christians: it is, they say, belief in God that matters, and the ways in which we worship God are of secondary importance. The same point is made by some Christians and especially the local clergy: "We all came from the same mud," said the pope of Voskopojë when asked about the Muslims who take part in the feast of St. John; "worshipping God is what matters." The pope uses the same argument when asked about pilgrims who observe practices, such as taking away earth, that are not recognized by the Church: "[Women] love this place, which is a holy place, and their love for it encourages them to take part of it away with them, so as to enjoy the benefits of its holiness. Christianity does not tell them to do so, but given that they do so because they love the saint and believe in his power . . . After all, if God lets them . . ."

The other side to the Christian attitude is the belief that Muslim participation is an admission that the Christian religion is superior because it is obvious and natural. From that point of view, it is only natural that Muslims visit Christian holy places, because that is where the true religion is to be found. "Christianity is the natural religion all over the world," said a Christian from Korçë. "That Mahomet should have appeared in the desert and found followers there is only natural because people over there had no religion. But here? Why?" This idea is reinforced by the idea that Albanian Muslims are former Christians who converted, and who have therefore retained something of their old religion and inevitably want to revert to it. The converse is not strictly true in this domain: some of the Christians I met in Vithkuq said that they "respected" (*respektoj*) Muslim festivals, just as Muslims respected Christian festivals, but that taking part in them seemed incongruous to them.[30] In contrast, they say, the Muslims who come to St. Peter's observe all the religious rites just as we do. They are believers, and have great respect for the religious rites of the Orthodox. That is possible because Muslims inevitably try to learn those rites by imitating Christians ("They learned to cross themselves by imitating us") and by reading the literature that is on display.

This does not mean that individual Christians do not worship in Muslim holy places, at least when the two groups are able to interact. In June 1996, I visited the new Halveti *tekke* in the village of Eçmenik (Devoll),[31] which was still under construction, with a small group of colleagues from the Department of Education (both the caretaker of the *tekke* and his wife are teachers). In the course of our visit, the caretaker asked a lady from the department for advice because her husband had been involved in building the new church in their village of Ziçisht. He wanted to know how the *vakëf* should be laid out and how it should be decorated. A small building by the roadside indicated where the *tekke* was going to stand. Its window was barred. When we visited it, everyone—Muslims and Christians alike—left a little money there, and the lady from Ziçisht lifted up her son, who was four or five, to let him kiss the window bars, just as she would have in a Christian holy place.

The notion of the *vakëf* appears to express the idea of a place of worship whose confessional affiliation, though it is never completely forgotten, is less important than its sacred nature. In the communist and postcommunist context, in which confessional loyalties could not always be openly displayed, visiting places whose confessional identity was vague (ruins) or ill-defined (graves and monasteries), either in secret under communism or openly in the present climate, may have looked like a religious practice that was less shameful or less demanding than attending a church or mosque. We can conclude that the contemporary notion of the *vakëf* is a reaction to a retreat on the part of religious institutions under communism. The nationalization and collectivization of the land and real estate, together with the secularization of society, destroyed the realities to which the juridical sense of the word once referred. Some of its religious connotations (inviolability, sanctity, respect) then led a population that had been deprived of its religious institutions to recuperate the term, and to apply it to all sorts of places associated with the old religions, but in such a way as to blur confessional boundaries. As a result of this process, it seems that any place that has been abandoned or demolished is likely to be interpreted as being a former place of worship, as though the systematic demolition of religious buildings during the communist period had had the effect of extending the sacred values that are still associated with former places of worship to all ruins.[32]

Notes

1. According to the "anthropological statistics on Northern Epirus" established by the Hellenic administration in 1913, the village of Poloskë was home to 79 "Hellenes" (Orthodox Christians) and a total population of 625. The map of Christian schools in the *vilayet* of Monastir published in 1909 by the Instituto geografico di Agostini (Rome) shows a "Greek" church in the village of Poloskë. The census undertaken by the French army in 1918 recorded it as having 566 inhabitants, most of them Muslim. See Bourcart 1922:295.

2. I retain the local pronunciation (*vakef*) for conversations recorded in Devoll; elsewhere in the text, I use the standard form (*vakëf*). The form *vakuf* is found in central Albania.

3. The very name of the place is testimony to its origins: Satrivaç is a corruption of the Bulgarian *sveti vraçi* (the saints who heal). The term is commonly applied to Saints Cosmas and Damian, and the name is also found elsewhere in the toponymy.

4. The translation adopted here is a reminder that the Albanian *i shentjë* and the French *saint* have the same etymology and derive from the Latin *sanctus,* but they tend to be "sacred" places in the sense that Alphonse Dupront, for example, uses that term (Dupront 1987).

5. The Bektashiyye is a mystical Muslim brotherhood that is well established in southern Albania.

6. A *tekke* is a building belonging to a mystical Muslim brotherhood; the Albanian form of the word is *teqe.*

7. On Kuç's *türbe* and *tekke¸* which attracted lots of visitors in the interwar period, see Clayer 1990:340–341.

8. The Ottoman administration appears to have begun to apply the word to Christian institutions at a very early stage; it was applied to the monasteries on Mount Athos as long ago as the late fifteenth century. See Balta 1995, especially 39–47.

9. Kostallari 1980: entry on *vakëf.*

10. Elsie 2001 does not mention it.

11. Peri 2001:119.

12. H. Kola, "Shenjtori i gjelbër," *Aldreams,* n.d. (http://www.albdreams.com/portal/content/view/557/59, consulted in March 2007).

13. Older examples are reported by Ippen 2002 (1908):90. They are from the Mat region, whose inhabitants, who have been Muslim for two hundred fifty years, respect woods that shelter the ruins of Catholic churches. The author does not record any use of the word *vakëf.*

14. Dhima 1989:248. The reference is to Ilias bey Mirahor, who was born in Panarit (one of the villages in the *waqf*) and who founded the town of Korçë on lands that he owned.

15. For an ideologically biased but well-documented account of the institution of *waqf* in Albania, see Mile 1984.

16. Some tombs of Christian priests can also be described by Muslims as *vakëfe.*

17. According to the same informant this is Hysen Gjini, who was born in Lazarat. He was the dervish at the *tekke* in Gjirokastër, and came back to Lazarat to die in about 1970.

18. One former victim of communist persecution describes how his family was sent into internal exile (*internim*) in Kaninë (Vlorë) in the 1960s. "My brother Skënder, together with his four young children, was housed in the Sheh's *türbe,* without electricity and without water. The rest of us had to live in a tumble-down hen house" (Sulo 1999:30–31).

19. He meant St. Spyridon.

20. It should be pointed out that, in the regions in question, the word *monastir* is always applied to monasteries that are no longer in use. In most cases, the church is all that remains.

21. When no trace of the building remains, the graves may be described as "unknown." In the (Muslim) village of Vinçan, which is between Korçë and Voskopojë, the pieces of land known as *vakëfe* are the sites of what are described as "unmarked graves" (*varret e paditura*), and the villagers know nothing about their origins. Hoxha and Hobdari 2005:127.

22. From the Greek εικόνισμα (icon).

23. In the commentary on Gjergj Xhuvani's film *Dear Enemy* (2004), which is set in a small town in Albania during the Second World War, the house in which representatives of the various sides meet (a demobilized Italian soldier, a partisan, an Albanian collaborator, a Jewish watchmaker, and a German Kommandant who pays courtesy visits) is described as a *vakëf.* Such a gathering could not have taken place outside the sacred space of the house, whose owner accepts them all (http://skenderluarasi.shqiperia.com/shqiparet_spanje36.php, consulted in March 2007). In an interview, a colonel in the Albanian army describes how his brother was expelled from his military school for political reasons in 1952, and recalls how its head justified his expulsion: "Our army is not a *vakëf,* and it is not its job to take in the sons of the enemy" ("Souvenirs du colonel Xhemal Imeri," *Panorama,* 3 August 2004, 12–13 [http://www.panorama.com.al/20040803/faqe12/2.dhtm, consulted in March 2007]).

24. Bashkim Gjoza, interviewed in *Nositi* magazine (http://www.poradeci.com/gazetanositi/1377.aspx, consulted in March 2007).

25. "Pandi Kristo deshmon për historinë" (http://www.forumishqiptar.com/ archive/index.php/t-28723.html, consulted in November 2006).

26. The pilgrimage to the church of St. Anthony in Laç on 12 June is one example. In the 1990s, it became a showcase for religious "tolerance." So too did the ceremonies and televised reports that followed the death of Pope John Paul II in March 2005.

27. Incubation or dream oracle is a healing ritual: the practice of sleeping in a temple or sacred area in the hope of being visited in dream by the saint and thus be cured. See Alice-Mary Talbot, "Pilgrimage to Healing Shrines: The Evidence of Miracle Accounts," *Dumbarton Oaks Papers* 56 (2002), 153–173.

28. There are two words for "sacrifice." The first is the Turkish term *kurban,* which is also used by Christians. The primary meaning of the Albanian word *gjak* is "blood," but it can also mean "sacrifice." As a rule, the two words are synonymous, but a distinction is sometimes made between the two. A *kurban* must not be eaten by those who offer up the sacrifice, and all of it must be distributed. They can eat part of a *gjak* after most of it has been distributed.

29. The term used on such occasions is the verb *ther* (to cut the throat of).

30. As we have seen, this does not prevent Christians from joining in some Muslim ceremonies, such as the inauguration of the mosque in Bilisht in 1995.

31. The Halvetis are another mystical Muslim brotherhood.

32. My thanks to Dionigi Albera, Nathalie Clayer, and Galia Valtchinova for reading and commenting on this article.

THREE

Komšiluk and Taking Care of the Neighbor's Shrine in Bosnia-Herzegovina

BOJAN BASKAR

In the novel *Lodgers* by the Sarajevo writer Nenad Veličković (2005), the (Bosnian Muslim) curator of the City Museum who, during the siege of the city, lives with his family and some other incomers in the basement of the museum, is taking care of a collection of Orthodox icons; the narrator (his daughter) comments wryly that he is saving Serb icons from the Serbs who would like to destroy them in order to save them from the Muslims.

While saving cultural heritage of other ethnoreligious communities is not a very reliable indicator of the level of tolerance, it has an obvious relationship with taking care of others' shrines. In this chapter, I focus on these latter practices, which I view as an aspect of a more general attitude toward the "familiar other" characteristic of a number of Bosnian contexts. Maintaining shrines belonging to neighbors of other religions when they are away, or offering help in building them, is viewed as a largely self-conscious act of recognition and valuation of their religion and their way of life. Several concepts used in anthropology come to mind here as a possible basis for a theoretically informed description of this attitude, among them culture (or cultural) and habitus. Both concepts, however, imply an overrating of the preconscious or unconscious dimension of behavior.

Presuming that a fair analytical treatment of this matter can hardly be disentangled from previous studies by numerous other scholars, I pay considerable attention to the examination of predominant approaches to the sharing of religious practices and shrines. I therefore look at the two paradigmatic notions that underpin the usual explanations: syncretism and imperial legacy.

The "Nature" of Bosnian Tolerance

In Bosnia, the interdependence of ethnoreligious communities and the mutual acknowledgment of the cultural differences that developed over the centuries of the Ottoman rule long preceded the modern discourse of tolerance and peaceful coexistence. The latter hardly emerged before the Austrian rule starting in 1878, and even then remained of rather limited scope. The idea that the discovery of ethnocultural mixing (*Vermischungen*) and hybridity (*Hibridismus*) by Austrian ethnographers at the turn of the nineteenth century may be related to the discovery of ethnically mixed regions such as Istria (Nikočević 2006; Johler 1999:95) is more difficult to substantiate in the case of Bosnia. The notion of (religious) *syncretism* that imperial scholars found more appropriate to characterize the Bosnian variety of religious plurality, which now for the first time included Islam, is more relevant. Witness, among others, Kosta Hörmann (1888), the Austrian student of Bosnian Muslim folklore, who claimed that Bosnian Muslims were descendants of the medieval Bosnian nobility who embraced the Islamic religion without changing their national feeling and without forgetting their ancient customs. These, he maintained, were simply adapted to the requirements of the new religion. (This notion of syncretism is further discussed below.) The notion of syncretism was eventually extended from the religious to the cultural sphere, where it referred to cultural merging, hybridity, and multiculturalism. As Peter van der Veer (1994:196) observes, the role played by the term "syncretism" in societies with religious cultures is equivalent to that played by the term "multiculturalism" in societies with secular cultures. The broader notion of syncretism is still usual in current discussions in the region (e.g., Moranjak-Bamburać 2001).

While the feeling that Bosnia was a land of religious and cultural tolerance began to crystallize during the Austrian period, we should not disregard its later developments. One later event that significantly affected it was the holocaust of Bosnian Sephardic Jewry. Prior to World War II, when Bosnia-Herzegovina was swallowed up by the Croatian *ustaša* puppet state, Bosnian Jews hardly had any experience of anti-Semitism.[1] In the beginning of 1941, Derviš M. Korkut, the curator-librarian of the Provincial Museum in Sarajevo, published a short article titled "Anti-Semitism Is Foreign to the Muslims of Bosnia and Herzegovina," where he argued that Bosnia-Herzegovina was a classic case of religious tolerance and that the Jewish cemetery in Sarajevo, one of the oldest in Europe, was proof of that since it had never been desecrated. The "most beautiful" proof of the tolerance, however, was the fact that four domestic religious places of worship were built exactly one beside the other (quoted in Bakaršić 2001:279–280). This argument eventually became a topos in discourse on Bosnian tolerance. Derviš Korkut (Bosnian Muslim), together with the director of the museum, Jozo Petrović (Bosnian Croat), later became the key protagonist in the affair of saving Sarajevo's famous *Haggada Codex* from the Nazi general Hans Fortner when, in late 1942, Fortner visited the museum with the intention to seize this richly illuminated medieval Jewish manuscript, which had been brought to Sarajevo by Sephardic Jews expelled from Spain (Bakaršić 2001). Other cases of saving the cultural heritage of neighboring ethnoreligious communities have been reported for Bosnia.

The idea of syncretism, which has long been invoked by scholars from the region, was obviously bound up with various projects for nation building (Yugoslav, Bosniak, Serb), although in a more complex way than in, for instance, the case of Greece (see Stewart 1994). Having said that, I will nonetheless argue that their work does reveal a genuinely scholarly interest in cultural alterity: the discourse of syncretism cannot be reduced to that of nationalism. Despite the obvious fact that the humanist and social science disciplines (or at least those most involved in nationalist projects) in the region typically developed a monoethnic perspective, I maintain, first, that other scholarly traditions— albeit more marginal and therefore the object of less attention—did explore contexts of cultural pluralism, and second, that in a sense Bosnia represents an exceptional case. This naturally implies that much more attention must be paid to scholarly contributions from the region. If, or when, a distinction has to be made between the regional (or local) and foreign scholars, the respective contributions of the two categories and their interaction must also be assessed more carefully. The notion of *komšiluk* (neighborhood) that has been recently brought to the fore within the paradigm of imperial legacies, for instance, was initially introduced by scholars from the region. With the war in Bosnia, *komšiluk,* now usually viewed as an element of the Ottoman legacy, has become a matter of considerable interest to those scholars who either believe that it can represent a model of multiethnic tolerance and peaceful cohabitation, or explore its potential to resist or prevent the violent destruction of the multiethnic social fabric. Recent characterizations of *komšiluk* relations by Western scholars as "cultural pluralism [as] intrinsic to the [Bosnian] social order" (Bringa 1995:83), "radical interdependence" (Campbell 2003:240), or "the long tradition of benevolence toward each other and toward different sacral legacies" (Doubt 2000:47) might seem to introduce a brand-new perspective made possible by most recent theoretical developments in the social sciences in the West. However, these descriptions are little better than those offered by local scholars in earlier decades, when the homegrown discourse of peaceful cohabitation served primarily as a prophylactic. Taking regional scholarly traditions seriously therefore implies recognizing that the views of foreign scholars on Bosnia might have been more informed by local scholarly traditions than is usually acknowledged.

Among outside anthropologists who have recently studied Bosnia and turned attention to shared religious practices, Tone Bringa no doubt deserves special consideration. Bringa's local mentor was the ethnologist Miroslav Niškanović, who had published a decade earlier an article on the shared Muslim and Orthodox festival of *Aliđun* or *Ilindan* (St. Eliah's Day), which used to take place beside the *türbe* of Gerzovo in Northern Bosnia (Niškanović 1978; see also Niškanović 1985). Niškanović maintained that the afternoon celebrations, when the Orthodox joined in beside the *türbe* for the *dernek* (a fair with music, dance, and sport contests), were in reality *two separate* but *parallel* festivals. Bringa did not adopt his view. Having referred to the *dernek* of Gerzovo in the first chapter of her book (Bringa 1995:17–18), she apparently avoids challenging Niškanović openly. She seems to have preferred to formally acknowledge his argument, adding also that "differences arise but people continue to coexist, albeit in competition" (1995:18). Yet in the next sentence she turns Niškanović's exclusivist argument into a recognition of an ambivalent reality characterized by *both* shared and separate places (or events or practices), by *both* inclusion and exclusion, *both* "two" and "one." Recognizing this fundamental simultaneity, Bringa actually joins a wide chorus of local and foreign scholars whose position on this question was, and is, that the controversial topic of the nature of the Bosnian tolerance cannot be resolved within the either/or alternative.

The disagreement between Bringa and Niškanović further epitomizes a wider difference between two prevailing views not only of shared practices but also of the "nature" of the Bosnian tolerance and the future prospects of living together. Niškanović denied that the Gerzovo *dernek* was shared by the two communities. He therefore declined to see it as one event, regardless of the fact that the two groups would congregate in the same place and even engage in a series of contests. An ethnographer who paid attention to intercommunal exchanges would probably have noted that much more than this was going on there. However, what might have seemed in 1978 no more than a slightly odd judgment on the part of an ethnologist began in the 1990s to look like a denial of the reality of the *zajednički život,* or coexistence of different communities. But it was perfectly consistent with the central tenets of the Bosnian Serb and Croat nationalist ideology, which insisted that the peoples of Bosnia-Herzegovina cannot live together. Among those who responded favorably to these calls for separation along ethnic lines were a number of foreign anthropologists. Andrei Simić, for instance, criticized those scholars who were spreading myths of Bosnian tolerance and coexistence and proposed instead a variant of the ancient-ethnic-hatreds thesis by claiming that peoples of Bosnia were "deeply divided and steeped for generations in tales of heroism and imbued with a quasi-religious ethos of revenge and retribution" (Simić 2000:115). When he attempted to produce evidence to support that claim, all he could do was cite a couple of passages from various books on Bosnia by authors who sometimes shared his view and argued that these ethnoreligious and class divisions were long-established. The only "ethnographic" evidence he supplied came from his Serbian grand-uncle from Herzegovina, who already in 1961 warned him about the Muslims and the Croats from the other side of the Neretva River and even showed him his cache of arms. The more influential Robert Hayden went one step further and solved the problem of the lack of evidence of the impossibility of living together and of inexistent positive tolerance in Bosnia by simply dismissing it. He bluntly asserted that the only kind of tolerance to be found in Bosnia was negative (or Lockean) tolerance, that the only sharing of religious sites was competitive sharing, and that the ethics of responsibility demanded the partition of Bosnia along ethnic lines. The plentiful evidence to the contrary has been superbly ignored (e.g., Hayden 2002a, 2002b).[2] The foreign anthropologists' denial of the reality of Bosnian tolerance therefore seems to have precedents in the regional scholarship.

A Few Examples

Taking care of others' shrines involves practices that may be characterized as largely nonreligious. They are therefore not part of shared religious practices, at least not in the strict sense of the term, yet they are nevertheless continuous with them.

There were cases when the local Christian population would look after the *türbe* of the *šehit* when there were no Muslims left in the village. One such case is the already mentioned *türbe* in Gerzovo, where *binational dernek*—as Niškanović termed it—used to take place for the Aliđun/Ilindan. The tomb was quite important since it was believed that the *šehit* buried in it was Alija Đerzelez in person, the main hero of the Bosnian Muslim epic ballads, who is considered by most scholars to have been a real historical figure. When the last Muslim family maintaining the *türbe* moved out of the village, the *türbe* fell into decay. After World War I, the *türbe* was restored by the villagers, all Orthodox Serbs. Even the priest contributed a sum of money. After that the *dernek*s could take place again. After the Second World War the *dernek*s stopped and the *türbe* burned down. In the 1970s, one Muslim from the neighboring village restored it and maintained it. In November 1991, during the siege of the Croatian town of Vukovar, "četniks" from a neighboring town dynamited it (Žanić 1998:229). The case of the *türbe* of Smail-Aga Čengić from Herzegovina, who was killed in the nineteenth century in a campaign against the Montenegrin tribe of Drobnjaci, is similar. When all Čengići moved out from the place (Lipnik in Gacko), the *türbe* was looked after by a neighboring Orthodox family. It was demolished by the četniks during the Second World War (Žanić 1998:290).

Neighbors looked after each other's shrines, but there is also some evidence to indicate that they actually helped to build them. Tone Bringa has reported that in the mixed Muslim-Catholic village she studied, villagers of both confessions emphasized "that Catholics had also contributed money to the building of a new mosque, while Muslims had contributed money to the building of a new church" (Bringa 1995:75). Another example of intercommunal help in building the sanctuary comes from the mixed Muslim-Orthodox village of Baljvine. This village is now famed for its concord; the concord is epitomized by the village minaret, allegedly the only one in Republika Srpska not to be torn down. There are two accounts of Baljvine intercommunal help by two different witnesses. The first one is given by Bosnian Croat essayist and publicist Ivan Lovrenović. In his book *Bosnian Croats: Essay on the Agony of a European-Oriental Micro-Culture* (Lovrenović 2002a) he describes, with a certain ethnographic sensitivity, several examples of sharing, of mutual help and mutual respect. One example is the building (it was actually a reconstruction) of the mosque in Baljvine that he witnessed as a youth in the early 1970s. In order to rebuild it, the Serb villagers, whom he observed carrying water and sand from the riverbed up the steep hill on their small horses, had to take time off work in the factories of neighboring towns (2002a:126). He also claims that, during the Second World War, the Baljvine Muslims and Orthodox took such care of each other that not one villager perished.

The same claim is made in the second account, which comes from the Baljvine villager Salih Delić. His testimony was collected by Svetlana Broz, a cardiologist from Belgrade who served as a volunteer doctor during the war in Bosnia. Svetlana Broz soon found out that many of her patients were indifferent about their health problems but felt an urgent need to tell someone that it was because of a few good people from the other side, either neighbors or perfect strangers, that they were still alive. (She also realized that she was an ideal person to play that role: not only was she a volunteer doctor; she was also the granddaughter of Marshal Tito, which may have been more significant.) So she started to systematically collect testimonies among all national groups and eventually published a voluminous selection of these testimonies (Broz 1999).[3] In his testimony titled "Can You Count on Your Neighbors?" Salih Delić told of the great solidarity between Muslims and Serbs that he witnessed in Baljvine during the Second World War and also during the last war. Both Muslim and Serb villagers came off fairly well as a result. The village itself emerges from the Second World War intact, but during the last war it was badly damaged, this time by Croatian units who left only the mosque untouched. He also talked about the mosque. It was built before he was born, but he often heard the stories about how Serbs donated money to the project and helped to build it. Then, in 1990, a Muslim delegation from the village asked the council of the neighboring town (Mrkonjić Grad) for permission to build an Orthodox church. The permit was issued quickly, but construction was eventually interrupted by the war. After the war the church had to be rebuilt and was finished the year of Salih's testimony, that is, 1998 (Broz 2004:4–5).

Was taking care of others' sanctuaries a common practice in places with mixed populations? To judge by the relative scarcity of discussions of this topic in ethnographic and other related literature, one is inclined to say that it was not. It has to be recalled, however, that these practices have not become an established ethnographic topic. Local opinion, on the contrary, largely holds that it was ubiquitous. The fact that Tone Bringa came across it in her village surely suggests that it was not unusual. The case of Baljvine, on the other hand, seems more of an exception.

This notwithstanding, some caution is appropriate when judging local claims that mutual help in building sanctuaries was the norm. These claims reveal an idealizing tendency and should probably be interpreted as a category of claims that assert local solidarity and amity toward outsiders, in the same vein as the claim, which is well known to Mediterranean anthropologists, that *Here we are all equal.* Tone Bringa was obviously cautious, as she persisted with questions as to who precisely contributed and who did not. She admitted she never managed to establish how many Muslims or Catholics actually contributed. She also said that she suspected that not everyone did contribute; however, enough people did so for this idealized solidarity model to be perpetually reinforced and thus effectively sustained (Bringa 1995:75).

Explaining Syncretism. From Survivals . . .

From the point of view of the Muslim villagers of Dolina, helping to build a church was *sevap,* a religious merit (Bringa 1995:75). One Bosniak scholar considered this help to be an example of *moba:* when villagers announce that they are embarking on a project that requires help, their fellow villagers give it on a cooperative basis (Mirza Hasan Ćeman, personal communication). This traditional arrangement was mainly used for major agricultural tasks that needed to be done quickly, and especially mowing and harvesting. The *moba* was based on reciprocity, but it was also fun as it implied sociability and ended with a feast. The host had to give his workers plenty of good food and drink. This custom received a lot of attention by Yugoslav ethnologists. One of the reasons for its popularity, especially during the socialist period, was its putative Slavonic origin.[4] Lending a neighbor a hand in building the house was also considered *moba,* yet helping to build a shrine proves a somewhat different case since there is no individual host or family.

Studies of Bosnian religious syncretism by local scholars traditionally relied on the notion of survivals. From this evolutionist perspective the merging phenomena of syncretism were basically seen as a consequence of the common (South) Slav origin of different religious communities in different historical periods. Modern syncretic Christian religious practices, such as belief in the curative power of tombs and practices of tomb-visiting of Bosnian Serbs and Croats, attracted little attention (see, for example Radmila Filipović-Fabijanić [1978]). These beliefs were regarded as elements of earlier religious systems that had survived because they were absorbed into the Christian religion. Filipović-Fabijanić also recognized the existence of interconfessional tombs (meaning Muslim tombs that are also visited by the Orthodox and the Catholics), yet she decided that they demanded a separate study. Such a decision may be seen as motivated by methodological nationalism that separates things that should be dealt with together. It might, however, also have been prompted by the feeling that the first topic was marginal while the second, that is, interconfessional, aspect was central. The real issue was actually Islam, or more precisely, conversion to Islam.

The traditional Bosnian Muslim (or Bosniak) narrative of Islamization maintains that at the very beginning of the Ottoman takeover of Bosnia a mass conversion of Bogomil nobility (or followers of the Bosnian Church) took place. They converted, first, because they were persecuted as heretics by the pope and a few other Catholic rulers, and second, because their Bogomil (or Patarin) doctrine had more in common with Islam than with the two Christian churches present in medieval Bosnia. Amazed by their willingness to convert, sultan Fatih allowed them to keep their estates and granted them the title of beys. In earlier centuries, the skeleton of this story was invented by Bosnian landed nobility (begs and agas) who needed a myth of the continuity of Bogomil-Bosniak landowner elite in order to legitimize their possessions. By the end of the nineteenth century, the story had evolved into one of the central myths of Bosniak historiography and gained special importance in the process of construction of the Bosniak identity. Austrian authorities in Bosnia encouraged its further promotion since they found it highly convenient for their policy of promoting the Bosniak identity against the claims of Serb and Croat nationalism. Slightly modified variants of this argument still dominate the accounts of conversion given in current Bosniak textbooks.

The sequence *Ancient (pre-Christian) South Slavs → (Christian) Bogomils → (Muslim) Bosniaks* that is established by this narrative can be seen as a variant of a more abstract sequence *Pre-Christian South Slavs → Christian South Slavs → Muslim South Slavs.* The latter has served as a matrix out of which other variants have been generated and employed in other national ideologies. "Survivalist" studies of Bosnian syncretism have as a rule taken up one or another of these variants, thus proposing various answers to questions such as Who were the Ancient Slavs in Bosnia? Who were the Bogomils? Who are the Bosnian Muslims? Common to all, however, has been the assumption that Bosnian religious syncretism is an outcome of the sequence itself. In the dominant "Bosniak" variant, Bosnian Muslims are Ancient Slavs and heretic medieval Bogomils. Some still survive in Bosnian Islam and make it syncretic. In one "Serb" variant, they are medieval Orthodox Christians (i.e., Serbs) who survived under Bosnian Islam. This variant suggests that Bosnian Muslims are the descendents of (forcibly) converted medieval Serbs. Hence their syncretism. Such was the thesis developed by the Serb scholar Tihomir Đorđević in the 1930s. After six decades, it was criticized by the Bosniak scholar Muhamed Hadžijahić (1990:102–103) whose main complaint was that Đorđević elided the Ancient Slavs from the sequence. This criticism is of peculiar interest here since Hadžijahić, in order to thwart Serb and Croat attempts at appropriation, argued radically against any possible presence of Christian elements in Bosnian Islam. By Christian he meant Orthodox and Catholic, while he tacitly exempted putatively the heretical Christianity of the Bosnian Church. While Đorđević, having strongly emphasized the medieval/Christian part of the sequence, virtually eliminated pre-Christian Ancient Slav survivals, Hadžijahić did (only apparently) the opposite. This led him to claim boldly that festivals of Đurđevdan (St. George's Day) and Ilindan (St. Eliah's Day) were not Christian at all, but pre-Christian; Ilindan was originally a Manichean cult of the sun, and so forth. Hadžijahić thus denied that Catholic and Orthodox festivals were syncretic at all, while he implicitly exempted Muslim festivals from the same qualification. The reason why both Muslims and Christians celebrated *Aliđun/Ilindan* is that they share the same common (South) Slav heritage. Considering the Catholics and the Orthodox, Hadžijahić radicalized to an extreme the common "survivalist" assumption that real causes were hidden in the origins.

From this common perspective, saints, shared by Muslims and Christians, were seen as transformations or mergers: St. Eliah, the Christian saint, eventually became Alija (i.e., merged with Ali, the Prophet's son-in-law). By the same token, shared places of devotion were shared because they were all built on the same spot. For instance, Muslims prayed for rain at old Muslim cemeteries because these grew out of Bogomil cemeteries where the Bogomils used to pray for rain earlier. To give another example: the Muslim *mevlud* prayers that were said on the mountaintops were said in the same places where pagan Slavs, and later Bogomils, had once worshiped.

The assumption that the truth of things reveals itself in their origins demands a long-term diachronic perspective. All essential events had taken place long ago, and what unfolds after them is a somewhat blurred repetition of the same quintessential identity that is there from the beginning. Critical events that from time to time strike this linear sequence are the result of an exogenous collision (e.g., "Christianization," "Islamization"), yet they are actually taken for endogenous. Syncretisms that result from interaction, on the other hand, may be, for instance, relegated to the category of "Turkish-Oriental influences." What pertains to such a category is considered of minor importance; it may be, for instance, represented as a recent layer, a thin veneer that strives in vain to hide the essential identity. Syncretism becomes strata, and these are implicitly hierarchized. Ethnography becomes a hunt for survivals, and the art of distinguishing between the essential and the nonessential.

Reducing processes of interaction across communal and regional boundaries to the notion of influences makes it possible to ignore most of these processes and their actors, or to describe them as autochthonous developments. Thus the issue of agency—such as the various dervish orders that encouraged these practices—has remained virtually unexplored in the local scholarship. The question of outside agency remained beyond its epistemic horizon. As such, it could have been considered unworthy of scholarly attention. At the same time, the impact of the outside agency was minimized and autochthonous developments were postulated.

. . . to the Ottoman Legacy

While the implicitly nationalistic perspective[5] tends to minimize the Ottoman impact and locate all decisive causes, without identifying them, in the pre-Islamic or rather pre-Christian period, the notion that the legacy of the Ottoman Empire might help to explain the phenomena of sharing seems to be gaining ground in local scholarship too. Ivan Lovrenović (2000), for example, recently deplored the present state of local scholarship that he held responsible for the continuing reproduction of myths about the Ottoman period. Its interpretation, he lamented, was always dependent on the ethnoreligious affiliations of the scholar: the Ottoman legacy was either celebrated for its tolerance or denigrated as the "dark night of tyranny" (2000:114). While Lovrenović laid stress on the double face of the *millet* legacy (isolated ethnoreligious communities with a mentality of segregation, but also transcommunal interaction and convergence), historian Drago Roksandić (2003) focused on imperial legacies in the *Triplex confiniuum* (the military borders of the Ottoman, the Habsburg, and the Venetian empires). Despite the centuries of cross-border incursions, wars, hostilities, and displacements of populations that allowed him to conceptualize these imperial legacies as a history of shifting borders and populations, he also saw this mountainous peripheral area as a unified border area with an intense and richly diversified network of cross-border communications (2003:120–121).

While the *millet* system has been shown to be an essential aspect of the Ottoman legacy, there emerged a new interest in the institution of *komšiluk* (the neighborhood) as a basic unit of shared life. In regional scholarly traditions, the interest in the neighborhood stemmed from their links with the German *Volkskunde*, which established the neighborhood as one of the types of organic community it studied. According to this tradition the neighborhood represented a developmental sequence in the evolution from family to tribe (Bausinger 1971). By the 1960s, there appeared another strand of studying urban neighborhoods, which originated in urban sociology. This approach had a significant impact on the development of Yugoslav sociology, while it also affected Yugoslav ethnology and resulted in some interesting cross-fertilizations between ethnography and urban sociology. These developments are perhaps best epitomized by certain developments within Croatian ethnology, where this scholarly tradition was established by early ethnographers for whom "neighborhood" (they did not use the Turkish term for it) was an essential category in questionnaires. Under this heading they studied primarily mutual obligations and norms, such as paying ritual visits to neighbors or the *moba*. The neighborhood was conceived as a tight frame that ordered everyday relations between villagers. Anthropologist Dunja Rihtman-Auguštin (1984), who studied a series of monographs on Croat folklife from the turn of the nineteenth century that used this questionnaire, found that in most cases the ethnographers had selectively looked at monoethnic Croat villages. There were a few exceptions, however, such as one monograph on a mixed Croat-Serb village in the *Triplex confiniuum* area of the Dalmatian hinterland. This study, based mainly on data supplied by a Serb villager, contains interesting data on intercommunal relations in the *komšiluk*, suggesting that they were based upon a combination of friendship and intolerance, concord and conflict, as well as ritualized mechanisms for maintaining good neighborly relations (Rihtman-Auguštin 2000:202–203). To some extent, the focus on the social life of neighborhoods remained characteristic of later developments within Croatian anthropology. Vera St. Erlich (1966), who wrote her important monograph on Yugoslav families under the supervision of Kroeber, is a case in point.

In Bosnia, the notion of *komšiluk* has a more specific meaning, and refers to everyday relationships between different ethnoreligious groups living in proximity to one another. As a result, those Bosnian scholars who studied it were more likely to focus on intercommunal relations and cultural pluralism. During the period of socialist Yugoslavia, Bosnia-Herzegovina was, together with other ethnically mixed regions, intensely exposed to the official Titoist rhetoric of *brotherhood-and-unity* that regularly included a chapter on peaceful coexistence, praising the ethnocultural diversity as an important resource of the fortunate Yugoslavs. Discourse on tolerance and cohabitation was also cultivated as a preventive measure against the rise of nationalist tensions. Its use was no doubt politically opportune, but it could also have been an expression of genuine fears and hopes.[6]

One academic field that deserves special mention here is the local scholarship on the Bosnian oral epic. This solidly developed scholarly tradition has had to deal with diverse issues of intercommunal cultural practices, social life, and tolerance in the borderland of the three empires. Here, the notion of the *komšiluk* assumes a peculiar meaning that is virtually synonymous with the notion of the *krajina* (military border) itself. This meaning is well attested in the cross-border exchanges that took place over the centuries. A corpus of letters written between the sixteenth and the eighteenth centuries by Bosnian Muslim military commanders to their counterparts on the Austrian and Venetian side of the border, but also to *uskok* leaders in Venetian service, to Venetian and Ragusan authorities, and to Montenegrin tribal chiefs, was aptly studied by the literary historian Muhsin Rizvić (1980, 1994). The expressions *na susistvu* or *na komšiluku* (in the neighborhood) and *na krajini* (in the [military] borderland) appear both in formulaic sentences (mostly greetings) and in the body of the text. Requests for various favors, invitations to a wedding, discussions of terms for ransoming or exchanging slaves or settling minor border disputes, and gifts were often accompanied with wishes for good neighborly relations. Correspondents addressed each other as neighbors, but also friends, relatives, and ritual brothers. The most curious example is probably a letter from 1684 sent by Mustafaga Hurakalović, the *kapetan* of Udbina and Lika, to the *uskok* commander (*harambaša*) Petar Smiljanić. Mustafaga (who eventually became the epic hero Mustay-beg of Lika) asked his "brother and friend" Petar, whom he regarded as a hero equal to himself, for several favors: first, some intelligence; then (his mother's wish), the ransom of an enslaved Turkish girl; and, finally, a request for a bottle of *rakija*. He also sent greetings to Petar's son Ilija, "of whom we heard that he became a hero in this *krajina*," together with a falcon's feather for Ilija's cap.

These cross-border exchanges took place during periods of peace. To be more specific, their content had a lot to do with the implications of war. In contrast to the epic ballads, heroic exploits seldom appear in the letters, while the general atmosphere, social relations, and values of the borderland society were more or less the same. Oral epics were themselves a shared cultural form and practice; "singers of tales" from different communities mainly sang about the same heroes and the same events, and sang them in the same language, with the important exception of Albanian singers, who nevertheless shared with the rest certain heroes and events from the *krajina*. Their audiences were often mixed; sometimes they were homogeneous, but the singer who sang to them belonged to the other community. A mixed audience could comment on the exploits of the heroes of both sides, compare the singer's tale with their own notions of what was historically true, make jokes, and laugh. Singing about the deeds of one's own heroes too passionately or allowing them to kill too many opponents from the community present among the audience could have been offensive to the latter (Murko 1951).

Local studies of oral epics in a way mirrored the characteristics of their object of study. On one hand, the scholarship was shared. Scholars from all communities recognized the shared nature of the phenomenon and, to some extent, studied it from a comparative and holistic perspective. On the other hand, however, each nationality tended to nationalize its own epic tradition, to differentiate it from that of other national traditions, and to institutionalize it as a national heritage and the foundation of the national identity. This obviously involved a sustained attempt to appropriate the tradition (of songs, heroes, musical instruments . . .) for nationalistic purposes, and gave rise to both claims and counterclaims. The question of how to correctly denominate the whole phenomenon (was it South-Slav? Serbo-Croat? Dinaric? or just Serb? or Bosniak?) was always open to dispute. As scholars of the Titoist period were aware that they were tackling highly incendiary material, they would often take precautionary measures such as ritually emphasizing the need for tolerance or proposing the *krajina* cross-communal communication, sharing, and cohabitation as an exemplar for the present Bosnian society. For various reasons this defensive discourse was especially characteristic of Bosnian Muslim scholars. Rašid Durić (1983), who studied the songs about the Bosniak hero Budalina Tale, typically referred to common South Slav ancestors who had been regrettably divided by force and religion, and emphasized that besides unavoidable conflicts there was a shared life of the three communities interwoven with numerous threads of mutual respect and spiritual proximity. He naturally did not miss the opportunity to represent Muslim Budalina Tale and his Orthodox ritual brother Little Radojica as exemplary friends who were strong enough to overcome religious divisions and challenge their historical destiny.

Crossing Communal Borders

In times of war, friends from the other community turned into foes, yet special interpersonal relations established across communal borders, in particular ritual brotherhood, could protect individuals, or even save their lives. As political scientist Xavier Bougarel (2004:122–123) contends, the *komšiluk* installs itself in a space of everyday life and interpersonal proximity whence the state is absent. In this space it crystallizes a hierarchized pluralism, characteristic of the Ottoman communitarian order, thus contributing to its stable and peaceful character at the everyday level. This certainly implies a fragility of the *komšiluk,* yet Bougarel seems to go too far because he takes it for granted that the peace and stability of the *komšiluk* turns into its opposite when the state withdraws its control. He actually forces the absence of the state control and the state's active instigation of intercommunal violence into the same category, and therefore fails to see the *komšiluk*'s attempts to maintain peace and stability and to resist outside attempts to destroy intercommunal ties.

Outside the *krajina,* and in urban environments, the proximity of everyday intercommunal relations was not very different. Here, spatial proximity was more important than religious and ethnic divisions, but obviously could not overcome them. In some Bosnian neighborhoods Muslim women did not need to be veiled in front of their male Christian neighbors (Hadžijahić, Traljić, and Šukrić 1977:101).[7] In the *bezistan* of the Sarajevo *čaršija,* merchants from different communities trusted one another. When a Muslim merchant had to go away for a while, say in order to fulfill his religious duties, his Jewish neighbor would take care of his stall, and vice versa (Ćeman 2006).[8]

We now require a thorough analysis of apparently systematic relations between diverse practices that cross communal borders, to find out whether they make a coherent picture. The coherence of these practices has been widely taken for granted, whereas the practices themselves have as a rule been described, or simply recorded, separately; for example, intercommunal godfatherhood (*šišano kumstvo,* or "haircut" godparenthood); ritual brotherhood and sisterhood; milk kinship; shared *krsna slava* rituals (celebration of the family's patron saint, widely believed to be exclusively Orthodox); mutual exchange visits; marriage and divorce of Christians by a *kadi;* shared oral epic traditions (together with shared modalities and places of their performance); and, naturally, shared sanctuaries and pilgrimages. Some of these practices were typically intercommunal; others allowed for an extension across communal boundaries.

More attention should also be devoted to evidence of intercommunal solidarity that was overlooked because it did not fit into any established rubric; for example, the Franciscan friars in Olovo, whose church of Virgin Mary used to be a major pilgrimage center, wrote down that at the eve of the pilgrimage Muslim women would sweep the streets leading to the church and hang lamps outside their doors (Lovrenović 2002a:127; see also Hadžijahić 1978–1979). Lovrenović also noted that in Baljvine Muslims would lay in supplies of bacon and *raki* for their Orthodox guests, but naturally, kept them apart from their own food (2002a:126).

The revival of interest in *komšiluk* interrelations is obviously a product of the war in Bosnia and a reaction to much-publicized horror stories about evil neighbors who suddenly started killing neighbors. In this kind of cover-age by the mass media, the notion of "neighbors killing neighbors" became a catchword that supposedly revealed something essential about Bosnia, that is, its fatal entanglement in ancient ethnic hatreds. Revisiting the notion of the *komšiluk* by several scholars of Bosnia or former Yugoslavia attempted to refute this essentialist vision. In tackling the *komšiluk* they were inevitably faced with questions regarding its nature, its relation with tolerance and cultural pluralism (were they rooted in the *komšiluk* as a traditional fabric of social life?), and its efficiency in resisting ethnic violence. The *komšiluk*'s ability to actively prevent ethnic violence was virtually never considered absolute or strong enough to be relied upon, yet opinions as to its power to do so vary considerably. As mentioned earlier, Xavier Bougarel (2004) described *komšiluk* relations as es-sentially ambiguous, fragile, and inherently prone to turn into their opposite when the state collapsed. By contrast, Dunja Rihtman-Auguštin was cautiously optimistic. In her chapter titled "Neighbors between the Two 'if'" (Rihtman-Auguštin 2000) she argued that the traditional society from the imperial border developed institutions that, although unable to prevent the eruption of violence, worked toward tolerance. In Rihtman-Auguštin's view, the efficiency of the *komšiluk* is not to be neglected, while for Bougarel it seems to be null. But this difference is linked to a difference in the conception of the nature of the *komšiluk*. For Bougarel the *komšiluk* is fundamentally an expression of the Ottoman *communitarian* order consisting of hierarchically ordered and essentially closed religious communities, while Rihtman-Auguštin finds these communities less close and the closeness itself less critical. Behind her discus-sion of the neighborhood, another question, apparently more fundamental to her, is concealed, that of how scholars do (or should) deal with such questions as the "nature" of the ordinary people, their inherent goodness or evilness, their manipulability and its limits, their conformism, or also their potential to swing to a nonconformist action such as saving lives of neighbors or even strangers. That's the reason why she finds convincing evidence of nonconformist acts on the part of "good people," such as that collected by Svetlana Broz, so important. Perhaps surprisingly, Bougarel is also well aware that this kind of evidence of people helping or saving others during the war has been seriously neglected by scholars of ethnic cleansing in Bosnia-Herzegovina and Croatia.[9]

Cases of ordinary people saving their neighbors (or others) of different ethnic affiliation may be related to the ethics of *komšiluk* in different ways. Scholars of genocide (e.g., Carmichael 2002; Sémelin 2005) have argued that individuals who unpredictably opt either to become perpetrators of mass violence or to oppose it (by saving lives of their targets, by fighting them . . .) do not reveal anything particular about their society or culture. Yet the fact remains that the number of perpetrators—and even more so of "good people in evil times"—varies significantly from place to place. In Bosnia-Herzegovina, there were many examples of people helping victims and thereby exposing themselves to extreme danger, although this is largely unknown, also thanks to the scholarly underestimation or ignorance of this evidence. By contrast, from the "classical" anthropological perspective, in which variability of behavior has been explained in cultural terms, the decisions of individuals to help their victimized neighbors would be seen as consonant with their *komšiluk* culture, which values not negative but positive tolerance, that is, an active care for the "neighbors" of other ethnoreligious affiliations. These two views are not contradictory inasmuch as behavior is not seen as determined by culture but as related to it either congruously or incongruously. From the anthropological perspective, persisting expressions of a will of living together that is being efficiently proved by resumption of "common life" in some parts of present-day Bosnia (Bringa 2002, Donia 2006) can be seen as an essentially cultural phenomenon, that is, cultural in the sense that it persists amidst upheaval. Similar resumption of "living together" and sharing after the violence of the civil war has been reported for mixed places in Lebanon (Kanafani-Zahar 2004b). This insistence on living together, on interacting across communal boundaries, and on paying attention and respect to others is something very different from the picture suggested by anthropologists such as Andrei Simić and Robert Hayden, whose claims that peoples of Bosnia-Herzegovina clearly do not want and have never wanted to live together embarrassingly echo the mantra of Bosnian Serb and Bosnian Croat nationalist propagandists. While no one denies that there were cases of animosity, as indicated by Simić, these should not be irresponsibly generalized, but the variety of situations should be ethnographically observed and accurately described in their complexity.

Notes

1. An interesting account of a lack of any apprehension in a Sarajevo Jewish family as late as in the mid-1930s is memoirs by Moïse Abinun (1988).

2. A heated polemic provoked by relativistic accounts of genocide and ethnic cleansing in former Yugoslavia recently took place in the journal *Anthropological Theory*; see, among others, Cushman 2004 and Hayden 2005.

3. The book was afterward translated into English under the title *Good People in an Evil Time: Portraits of Complicity and Resistance in the Bosnian War* (Broz 2004). It contains an apt introduction by anthropologist Laurie Kain Hart.

4. The interest in *moba* seems to have been reflected in monographs of foreign ethnographers. Both Lockwood (1975) and Bringa (1995) dedicated a few pages to its discussion.

5. This could have been at the same time a Yugoslavist perspective.

6. A relevant sociological study of the Bosnian urban *komšiluk* that pays attention to intercommunal relations is Mujačić 1972 and 1973. (I thank Xavier Bougarel for this reference.) An interesting essay on the Serbian urban *komšiluk* is Žunić 1998.

7. If Muslim women have to be veiled in front of those men who are marriageable to them, Christian men obviously don't fit this category, and if they are familiar and trusted on the basis of local proximity, they may be in a sense assimilated to the category of non-marriageable relatives (*mahram*).

8. Such a mixture of Muslim, Christian, and Jewish merchants within the *čaršija* area was also observed in the 1920s by the British traveler Lester Hornby (1927; in Jezernik 1998:275).

9. Among publications providing such evidence he refers to Broz 1999 and Maček 2000 (Bougarel 2004:140).

FOUR

The Mount of the Cross:
Sharing and Contesting Barriers
on a Balkan Pilgrimage Site

GALIA VALTCHINOVA

Since the seminal work of Frederick Hasluck, *Islam and Christianity under the Sultans* (1929), research on religious mixing in holy places has been mainly oriented toward identifying practices of coexistence (Albera 2005b:350–352, 2008; Shankland 2004:26–32). With the processes of "nationalizing the sacred" (Bowman 1993) in places such as Palestine and the adjacent region, where great religions have been intermingled for centuries,[1] there is an increasing attention to violence that makes the management of religious mixing increasingly problematic. Against the all-pervasive discourses and images of "the violence of religion," ethnographic work helps depict a rich and multifaceted reality of the current upsurge of religion. Following the logic of anthropological practice, this chapter aims to match historical research to fine-grained ethnography in order to raise broader theoretical issues about religious mixing.

The study that is at the core here pursues two goals. First, it aims at delineating the *practical modalities* of religious mixing identified through research on historical context combined with ethnographic fieldwork. It is also intended to address a few questions underlying fieldwork. Should observed cases of religious mixing be seen as invariable facts (in the sense historians give to the latter term), as a constant characteristic of a particular religious landscape that other, more "monolithic," religious landscapes are devoid of—or, by contrast, as a process and a particular phase in the existence of a sacred place that may occur everywhere, and whose shape and duration depend on the contexts and circumstances? Embracing the vision of religious mixing as a context-dependent process raises other questions: should we imagine it as a move in one direction, toward more and more (or less and less) mixing—or as a permanent negotiation between actors endowed with power and constantly changing interests? The attention anthropologists pay to "shared" holy and pilgrimage sites that become places of "conflict" suggests that thinking of religious tolerance or intolerance as a status quo leads to the risk of essentialism. To take but one of the best-studied examples, the conflict around Ayodhya in India (van der Veer 1988) demonstrated to what extent religious mixing in modern and contemporary times is a sociopolitical variable. Closer to our Balkan field, Ger Duijzings (2000) has shown the same logic at work on Christian pilgrimage sites in Kosovo, where places of "traditional" mixing of Christians and Muslims became monoconfessional spaces with the implosion of the Yugoslav tlineFederation. These and other studies suggest the need for identifying what I would call the "elementary structures" of religious mixing, in order to understand the mechanisms of sharing a devotional site. What follows is a study of the acts and gestures of shared devotion at a holy place as embedded in their particular contexts in order to capture the changing process of religious mixing.

Attention to context points to another cluster of questions: can one isolate *contexts* that make possible religious coexistence, or that allow that a shared devotion takes place on the same place and in the same time? Or, to put it more generally, should not one explore the interrelation of *structure* (of religious devotion at a particular holy place) and *agency*[2] in loci where "divine" or "supernatural" presence is held to manifest itself?[3] As Albera (2005b:358) suggests with regard to Jerusalem, it is difficult to find religious mixing in places where religious hierarchies are well embedded and powerful, and religious institution is almost part of the "sacred landscape." Does the same hold for places of divine grace established not by long tradition but by a more recent visionary event or a revelation, the "lieux où souffle l'esprit" (Albert 2000)? In holy places of the latter kind, the progressive way in which the institutional machine takes hold leaves room for the initiative of individual and collective actors. At the holy places revealed through a vision or in a divine apparition, one can observe the dynamics and constant negotiation that characterize religious mixing. Studying the process from such a holy place could be all the more fruitful when one takes time into account and pays particular attention to contexts of sociopolitical rupture or change. Building on the case of a holy place in Bulgaria revealed in recent times (1930s), and the pilgrimage that has taken there since the end of communism (1989),[4] I will deal with two aspects of the topic at hand. One of them is identifying the setting and "configuration of events"[5] conducive to shared devotional practice at a holy place, or to separation and unmixing—for example, what "structures of context"[6] are more or less conducive to mixing?

The other is studying in the field the ways in which religious mixing works. How should we define "sharing" of a sacred place and space or a devotional practice by people of different religions: by agency, intention, or claims to the confessional ownership of the holy place? Are religious actors conscious about mixing? And who should be considered religious actors? Is "mixing" synonymous with interaction, or does it include the mere presence at the same place and in the same time of people who ignore each other, what Hayden (2002a) calls an "antagonistic tolerance"? I look for answers to these questions by considering structures of devotion over the long term and in precise historical contexts, with a focus on local and supralocal religious actors.

The Field Site in the *Longue Durée*: Boundaries and Mixing in the Rhodopes Mountains

Located in the heart of the Rhodopes, in the southeast of the Balkan Peninsula, the pilgrimage site of Krăstova Gora (Mount of the Cross) is in the midst of a region of intense religious tension—and one in which populations and cultures mixed for centuries. The centuries-long Greek presence based on the city of Philippopolis/Plovdiv and the town of Stenimachos/Stanimaka had a deep cultural impact on the area, providing the reference for a model Christian piety. At the end of the nineteenth century, a "little Hellas" flourished around the latter town[7] even though the countryside was populated mainly by Slav-speaking Bulgarians. The latter, scattered in small villages, were associated with rustic Orthodoxy, consisting more in cultural markers than in regular church-bound practice. Already before the nineteenth century, large parts of this rural Bulgarian-speaking population were converted to Islam, thus forming the group later known as the Pomaks. Other groups identified as primarily Orthodox Christians were the Valachians (Vlasi), Romanian-speaking semi-nomadic pastoralists, and the Greek-speaking Karakačani, or Sarakatsans.[8] Back in Byzantine times, Monophysit Armenians were settled by force in the then border area, and their peculiar Christianity left a deep mark on the local religious life.[9] Under Ottoman control (which for most of the area lasted between the 1360s and 1912), substantial layers of Bulgarian-speaking and Turkish-speaking Muslims, as well as various Roma groups, added to the mix of Christian populations. It is not by chance that the former (the Pomaks) are the most numerous population in the villages surrounding the Christian holy place, a coincidence interpreted by recourse to popular historical knowledge and a largely invented "memory" of their origins.

The immediate area that is the focus of the pilgrimage is a border zone in two ways. Located in the band of transition from predominantly Christian to predominantly Muslim populations,[10] it was progressively (1878–1912) incorporated into the modern Bulgarian state. Nevertheless it remained a "critical juncture" in the Bulgarian political project, and after the Russian-Turkish war of 1877–1878 (which led to the birth of the modern Bulgarian State), it was a zone of high political tensions, especially with the annexation (September 1885) of Eastern Roumelia by the Bulgarian Principality.[11] From 1886 to 1912, the border between the Ottoman Empire and the new State—which used to be thought of as a front line between Christian and Muslim land—ran close to the future Mount of the Cross. The memory of this border is embedded in landmarks, local names, and people's memories.[12] The Balkan Wars (1912–1913) deeply changed the political configuration and demographic characteristics in the region, from then on divided between Bulgaria and Greece. After minor shifts the Bulgarian-Greek border was definitively established in 1920, some fifty kilometers south of Krăstova Gora.

Each border shift resulted in expulsions and displacements of local populations. With the retreat of the Ottoman Empire, groups of local Muslims left their places of birth for Turkey.[13] These displacements peaked during and after the First World War; in the 1920s the last groups of Turks left the villages surrounding what would become a Christian holy place. However, most of the Bulgarian-speaking Muslims remained, their new neighbors being the Christian Bulgarians who moved into the depopulated places.[14] Thus Krăstova Gora emerged in the 1930s—the decade that saw the deployment of the politics of national homogeneity[15]—at the boundary between two Pomak villages and a place deserted by Turks and freshly repopulated by Christian Orthodox Bulgarians. At the same moment, the Greek population of Stanimaka and the rural "Little Hellas" emigrated to "motherland Greece" in the framework of the Greek-Bulgarian voluntary exchange of population (1923).[16] Their places were taken by Bulgarian peasants from the mountainous villages or Bulgarian refugees from the historical regions of Thrace in Turkey and Greece, as well as from Greek and Serbian Macedonia. Twenty years later, in the first decade of the Cold War, the Muslim populations dwelling near the Greek-Bulgarian border were displaced forcibly (Gruev 2003). Several groups of displaced Pomaks and Turks were settled in Stanimaka and the villages formerly known as "Little Hellas."[17] Muslims continued to settle in the town and the surrounding villages throughout the socialist period, attracted by the opportunities to work in booming industries. All these movements of population obscure the structure of religious life, blur networks, and impede the clear identifications of confessional cleavages. In the 1990s, the ancient "Little Hellas" offered to the observer the view of both mosques and churches, and only at closer scrutiny could one see the thin line separating museum-like "church religion" from ongoing religious life.

Moving Religious Boundaries

As we have seen, the Mount of the Cross sits at the juncture of three different traditions of Eastern Christianity and a varied Islam. Christian tradition is sustained through the centuries by the Petritzon/Bachkovo monastery and the town of Stanimaka, a stronghold of Greek Orthodoxy and Greek culture with several dozen churches, chapels, and rural monasteries. The Petritzon monastery, founded in 1081, possessed many villages, pastures, and meadows: the Mount of the Cross is located on the margin of its extensive domain.[18] Founded to serve as a center of Georgian (in Byzantium also called Iberian) Christianity,[19] in the first centuries of its existence it was the local arena of competition between Georgian and Greek monks,[20] to finally become the stronghold of Greek Orthodoxy, the largest *stauropege* in the southeastern Balkans.[21] Dedicated to the Mother of God (Assumption of the Virgin), by the eighteenth century the monastery of Bachkovo had become a center of an important Marian pilgrimage, where the Mother of God was revered following the Athonite model (Hristemova 2005). Located close to Stanimaka and possessing numerous orchards, vineyards, and houses, the abbey was associated with the town's reputation under the Ottomans as a pious stronghold of Orthodoxy. In the mid-nineteenth century the town's nickname "Little Jerusalem" was a mark of pride for the local inhabitants, as it distinguished their Church-regulated religious practice from the diffuse Christianity of peasants in the outlying villages.

Indeed, the "rural Christianity" of the villagers in the mountains had little to do with the elaborate formal devotion and piety in Stanimaka. In the countryside the care of souls depended on occasional visits of priests, and chiefly on the itinerant monks known as *taxidiotes,* whom the big monasteries, especially those of Mount Athos, used to send out into "the world" to raise funds in exchange for basic pastoral care.[22] Thus only the basic sacraments were observed, with a priority on the last rites; marriages and baptisms could accumulate for months. Given the relative absence of clergy, laymen and -women among the villagers functioned as religious specialists in case of death or a potentially fatal illness.[23] The inventiveness of village specialists points to resources within an aural culture, and a culture of memory.[24] The first village shrines, locally called "chapels" (*pareklisi*), were small constructions where the itinerant monks or visiting priests could stay, and in which the religious objects and books were kept. Village parishes in the strict sense of the word were nonexistent until the early nineteenth century. The first churches of the villages in this area were erected in the 1830s, in the beginning of the Ottoman Tanzimat (Reform) era and shortly before local voices claimed the "Bulgarian-ness" of this rural Christianity.[25] It is in this context that we first hear of the "Mount of the Cross" to designate an area densely populated with Pomaks and Christian Bulgarians, where "pope Grigorios," a *taxidiotes* from Mount Athos, had provided pastoral care, preaching and teaching for more than two decades.[26]

However, in the vast countryside to the south of Stanimaka and more generally throughout the central Rhodopes it is Islam that dominates. In the area of Krăstova Gora, Sunni Islam is traditionally embraced by the Pomaks. In a way similar to what was noted for the Christian villages, Muslim villages did not have mosques until quite late: the material structure of devotion was articulated around shrines built *extra muros:* the *türbes* (tombs of Muslim saints) and *tekkes*—dwelling places of living saints, or revered religious virtuosi, where religious brotherhoods could meet.[27] When the retreat of the Ottoman state from the region in 1912 substantially weakened local Islam, these shrines were the last refuge of local Islamic practice. In the neighborhood of Krăstova Gora are two such *türbes*, one to Sarı Baba, located at the junction of the territories of one Christian and two Pomak villages, and the other to Yenihan Baba, the mythical *ghāzī* of the Rhodopes.[28] Built on one of the highest peaks of the central Rhodopes (which was named Yenihan for the *ghāzī*), the latter is located on the former Bulgarian-Ottoman frontier, and marked the religious landscape as a Muslim one. These *türbes* attracted popular devotion of Pomak and Turkish villagers from far away, and thus contributed to building ties of solidarity rooted in religion. Little is known of how they functioned during the interwar period, but their importance as boundary and identity markers must have drawn the attention of the activists of the "Pomak revival."[29] It is in this context that the "Mount of the Cross" emerged in the late thirties on a peak opposite Mount Yenihan.

Another kind of quasi-religious structure was common in the rural area marked by Islam: fountains or springs constructed to commemorate the deceased. As a rule, they were built by the descendants (occasionally by friends or a person from the same generation), and the pious inscriptions make clear that we have a peculiar form of religion-cum-memory, rooted in the practice of *sedaka* (the Muslim category of public charity). It is probably this emphasis on family ties and memory—the "primordial" bond cherished by all religious groups—that explains the generalization of this practice across religious boundaries. Today, such fountains are part of the landscape of both Christian and Muslim villages. Visualized through a Muslim practice, this culture of memory helps bridge the gap between the two communities.

Between Dialogue and Retrenchment: Religious (In)Tolerances

The visibility of churches and Christian piety in the area of Stanimaka when the Ottoman Empire was at its height called for a kind of religious "response." Around the mid-seventeenth century a pious Muslim center with a school, richly endowed with land (under *vakıf* regime), was established near the former village of Papazli (from *papas*, priest). The village was promptly transformed into a *kasaba* (small town) and renamed as Islamlı.[30] Clearly an effort "to promote Islam in an area of combative Orthodoxy" (Ivanova 2005:48), this episode points to the limits of Ottoman tolerance. However, as Marc Baer (2004:191–192) suggests, it should also be placed in the context of confrontation between conflicting trends within Ottoman Islam. The Muslim religious center did not survive: two centuries later, the travelers passing by report its buildings in ruins.

Around the mid-nineteenth century the "combative Orthodoxy" in and around Stanimaka was in the grip of two nationalisms. The struggle for Bulgarian national emancipation took the shape of religious rivalry with "Greeks" and against the Patriarchy of Constantinople.[31] The symbiosis of the town and the abbey, two strongholds of Greek culture and what was seen as religious Hellenism, made this rivalry especially harsh. It was expressed in an "ethnic" appropriation of parish churches, in the nationalist marking of Christian holy places that were usually revered by Orthodox people with different languages and cultures, and in the overall tendency to exclude the confessional other. The "Greek" churches became closed to "Bulgarians," and the "Bulgarian" churches became closed to "Greeks" while opening their doors to Muslims.[32] Greek and Bulgarian nationalism infused pilgrimages and pious processions, especially those related to the cult of the Mother of God (Greek Theotokos, Bulgarian Bogorodica). In the first years of the twentieth century the cult of Mary, here traditionally a mark of Greek culture and ethnicity, was increasingly appropriated by Bulgarians. This intraconfessional rivalry played out in the symbolic language of visions and messages, which the Mother of God delivered to local women, both Greek and Bulgarian.[33] It was in this context that Stanimaka became renowned as Little Jerusalem, a nickname claimed in particular by the local Greeks. At the end of the twentieth century, it is Krăstova Gora that was referred to as Little Jerusalem, but this time in Bulgarian nationalist perspective.

Whatever the excesses of the Bulgarian-Greek religious competition, the major problems for the Bulgarian State in this area were nevertheless due to the presence of substantial Muslim populations. The Pomaks held a peculiar place in the Bulgarian nationalist vision: while their attachment to Islam made them "traitors" to their "ethnic roots" and national "spirit," they could still be "retrieved" for the Bulgarian national idea, provided that they abandoned Islamic practice and agreed to modernize their culture, marked by "fanaticism" and backwardness.[34] In this vein, the first step of the Bulgarian state in the territories "liberated" during the first Balkan War was to evangelize the Pomaks in late 1912 and early 1913. This initial campaign, in which army and Church joined forces, was a failure (Eldarov 2004). Another, better organized attempt was made starting in the mid-1930s. Placing the emphasis on culture, its promoters paid particular attention to shared devotions and everyday forms of religious syncretism. This campaign was under way by the time visionary events took place near Krăstova Gora. After an interlude of relative tolerance, starting from 1960 the Bulgarian communist regime launched regular campaigns aimed at the cultural assimilation or the expulsion of the Muslim populations.[35] The culmination of this policy was the campaign launched in 1984 for the assimilation of Turks; its failure and the massive exodus of Bulgarian Turks to Turkey in the summer of 1989 was a prelude to democratization and the change of regime.[36] These events have been echoed in the Pomak areas of the Rhodopes and have influenced the context in which the reinvention of the Mount of the Cross took place.

Therefore, religious mixing could be negotiated, maintained, or reduced within systems that allowed it, with the Ottoman Empire structured by *millets* (religious communities). It is important to acknowledge the possibility of such negotiation even in state-national systems in which the structural tendency to unify and homogenize their populations allows little room for religious difference. In both cases, inter- and intrareligious tolerance depends on sociocultural contexts and political stakes. In both environments, religious mixing recedes in the face of politics of identity construction.

An Ethic of Togetherness: The *Komşuluk* from
Implicit Knowledge to Explicit Ideology

The oscillations observed in the actual practice of religious tolerance are embedded in a *modus vivendi* of everyday cohabitation that privileges flexibility and arrangement with the *other*. This art of cohabitation is supported by a discourse of tolerance to the religious other. In the Ottoman Balkans both are known by the term of *komşuluk* or *komşiluk* (from Turkish *komşu*, neighbor), which is still part of the local and national vocabularies.[37] Beyond the reference to "neighborhood," it has become a cultural category embracing the complex of rules and implicit knowledge about how to live together, side by side, without losing one's religious identity, in a context where religious mixing used to be everywhere in the same way as boundary was omnipresent. Rooted in the cohabitation of *millets*, the nonterritorialized structural units of the Ottoman Empire, the good neighborhood proved to be an effective local sociocultural mechanism to regulate the everyday life of overlapping religious communities, one that helped to reduce tensions and settle vexing issues. If this ensemble of conventional attitudes and forms of sociability was supposed to ensure peaceful cohabitation in everyday life, it also allowed a safe distance between them.[38] Often regarded as a "traditional" guarantee of religious peace, the *komşuluk* works through informal codes that are not well adapted to the modern categories of identity, belonging, or citizenship. It was already suggested that societal modernization and the deep sociopolitical changes that many Balkan societies have experienced in the last decades make the *komşuluk* less and less effective, or, as the recent war in Bosnia has shown, a double-edged sword.[39]

Bulgarian claims of the persistence of "good neighborhood" as a local art of living together are based on a different premise, even if they rose in a similar context. The multivocal symbolism of the *komşuluk* was used in the aftermaths of the campaign of "Revival process" against the Turks, whose mass emigration to Turkey opened the "ethnic crisis" that was the prelude to the end of Communist regime in November 1989. Beginning in 1990, the notion of the *komşuluk* was manipulated in political discourse and academic writing, which fused to build the concept of a "Bulgarian ethnic model." Supposedly rooted in the local experience of togetherness that would resist all pressures from above, this "model" is presented as having made possible the peaceful transition from communism to democracy. Historical data, but also fieldwork done in the central Rhodopes, were used as proof for this theory.[40] In the course of a long-term project of field research on Krăstova Gora and its area (1993–1995), a subtle and complex interaction took place between ethnographers and their "informants" (most of them pilgrims), in the course of which the latter were at once asked about the local practice of religious mixing and shared devotion, and conveyed the implicit message to adhere to a politically correct vision of the *komşuluk*.[41] For the external observer, such political appropriations of "the field" increase the probability of facing local strategies of encryption, by which people tell the "truths" they perceive as being to their advantage;[42] hence the necessity of a particularly "thick" ethnography.

The Invention of the Mount of the Cross: between Apocalyptic Symbolism and Political Action

In the course of the 1930s, visionaries and peasant prophets were increasingly visible and vocal in Bulgaria, a country in crisis associated with revanchist nationalism. As the region most marked by religious otherness, the Rhodopes were a favorite area for religious entrepreneurs. The earliest hints at a devotion to the Holy Cross in a place located in the mountains were reported in the mid-1930s in newspapers of ultra-Orthodox organizations. The master narrative about the devotion, springing as early as 1933 or 1936 from mystic visions of Jordan, a deeply faithful but marginalized young man, took shape quite late.[43] The core of what came to be known as "the legend of Krăstova Gora"—a pure instance of Lévi-Straussian bricolage—is composed of sequences of dreams and visions he allegedly had over a period of several years, while constantly moving between Stanimaka, the abbey of Bachkovo, and Borovo, the nearest village to the holy site. The most important revelation was that after the fall of Constantinople the True Cross was brought into the area by Orthodox monks who, pursued by the Ottomans, buried it under the hill called Krăstov [of the Cross]. The hidden Cross was supposed to come out "when the time comes." In the post-1989 process of telling and retelling, the legend borrows from the sorrowful mode of the Bulgarian national narrative about the Rhodopes and its Muslim population, a land of martyrs to the Ottoman sword or converts to Islam. The Holy Cross was allegedly saved by monks of the local monastery of Holy Trinity (affiliated to the Bachkovo abbey), which was imagined as having predated the Ottoman invasion. The monks succeeded in recovering the holy relic by cunning, but pursued by the sultan's troops, they perished in a general massacre, and the holy shrine itself was erased from the earth.[44] Among the first miracles reported, the alleged "healing" of a member of the royal family, Princess Evdokia, in the late thirties, was crucial for setting up the pilgrimage.[45] In the same period Jordan had other visions that led him to reveal the foundations of churches allegedly destroyed by "the Turks" near a Pomak and a mixed village. His efforts culminated in 1939, when a big iron cross was erected on the highest point of Krăstov. Done in alliance with an ultra-Orthodox association, the Good Samaritan, this initiative was discreetly supported by the Bulgarian King Boris III (1918–1943).[46] Pomaks allegedly participated, carrying the cross on their backs. Clearly aimed at demonstrating the latter's integration in the Bulgarian nation, such stories are today part of the legend as told in the pilgrims' booklets. A decade after the iron cross was erected, the Mount was already represented as central to the religious landscape of the Christian Rhodopes, in a map drawn up by Jordan himself showing the spread of Christianity from Stanimaka and the abbey of Bachkovo to the mountain's heart.[47] From mystic revelations to the production of pious images—and by the symbolism of his proper name (derived from the river Jordan, a powerful association to Christ's baptism)—this fervently Orthodox visionary appears to have carried out a lifelong mission of bringing the Cross to the infidel, that is, to the Bulgarian-speaking Muslims, thus bringing them "back to their roots."

After the communists come to power (1944), the spread of Christian faith in the Rhodopes was slowed but not stopped. "Brother" Jordan was able to pursue his activities through the mid-fifties. A chapel was built on the hilltop as late as 1956, and Masses were regularly held until around 1960. The devotion declined after its driving force, the visionary man, was arrested and sent to a communist prison camp.[48] The devotional practices persisted, mainly by townspeople from Stanimaka, even after the formal prohibition of the pilgrimage in the late sixties. In a manner similar to Jordan's action half a century before, the first step in the revival of the pilgrimage in the late eighties (1988) was the claim of the parish priest of the nearest town, Father Vasili, that he had had a dream revelation to care for the holy place. In Balkan Orthodox cultures, dream revelation is the most common way to legitimize a religious undertaking as Divine Will, a symbolic language spoken and understood by both religious and laypeople, the faithful and the unbeliever, available even under communism.

The massive renewal of the pilgrimage in the summer of 1989 coincided with the "ethnic crisis" that paved the way for the democratization of the country. Subsequently, following a true devotional explosion, Krăstova Gora has become the symbol of a "return to religion" and the postcommunist religious revival. At a closer look, it appears, however, that devotion to the Cross is run as a well-organized enterprise, its promoters coming chiefly from Assenovgrad (formerly Stanimaka) and the abbey of Bachkovo. Among them we find side by side priests and monks, but also laypeople (including journalists) recently converted from "unbelief" to fervent Orthodoxy. They work together to write down from oral testimony and reinvent the legend of Krăstova Gora, fitting it to the master historical narrative and to the new political and cultural context. This reworked legend mixes old and new protagonists of local history, both collective (the "three hundred slaughtered monks") and individual (Jordan) actors. By emphasizing their martyrs' fate—martyrs of Ottoman Islam for the former, of communism for the latter—both are part of the same eschatological vision.

Despite the fact that the pilgrimage was reactivated by a priest, the Bulgarian Orthodox Church has been rather slow to take control of the site and the devotional movement. Since 1992 and until at least 1998,[49] the Church is deeply divided. The new shrine erected in 1994–1995 was sponsored mainly by donations and the income from the annual pilgrimages. Halfway between a monastery and a parish church, the shrine is intended to provide a place for divine liturgy during pilgrimages. The rest of the time it also serves as a place for celebrating rites of passage, mainly baptism and marriage. It is also the cornerstone of the newly invented tradition: according to the local Orthodox clergy, its building is the first step to the "reconstruction of the monastery whose three hundred monks were burned by the Turks." In the first years its management was entrusted to the charismatic Father Vasili, who thus became "*higoumenos* [abbot] of the monastery of Holy Trinity." Already famous as a channel of Divine Will, he pursued his dialogue with Heaven in order to explain, among other thing, the erection of a dozen chapels along the road from the new shrine to the iron cross. "Serving the Cross" was Father Vasili's mission, and telling the history of the holy place in informal conversation or sermons was an integral part of his mission. Asserting the importance of personal experience of faith in the establishment and the "reinvention" of the holy place, he gave much importance to visions and divine revelations, both Jordan's and his own. Thus visionary experience becomes part of the ethos of Krăstova Gora, a kind of certificate of the authenticity of one's pilgrimage. Believers tried to conform to it by pretending to have spontaneously experienced something to which they were intentionally guided.[50]

The massive production of visions *about* the holy place, and *at* the site itself, offers a clue to the popularity of the Mount of the Cross in the first postcommunist decade. We have already singled out the importance of unresolved issues of national identity for the "invention" of the Cross Mount and its transformation from a peripheral place to a sacred center. Focus on memory and commemoration of martyrs, be they of "the Turks" or "the communists," can also account for its impact. However, the unusual popularity of this holy place throughout Bulgaria—a popularity that in the first years spread across confessional boundaries—points to an explanation that privileges bonds and togetherness over difference. Due to its internal but also informal character, visionary experience—especially if shared by others on the site—provided a feeling of commonality, the insurance that one's pious attitude was not considered erroneous or inappropriate.[51] One publicized way to experience the magic of *that* place, "seeing lights" (not necessarily a cross) was a kind of minimal condition of being there. Furthermore, it offered a pattern of experience available not just to the faithful but also to the "unbeliever" (the non-Christian as well as the skeptic), without implying conformity to a particular ritual grammar, something that could be embarrassing in the public show of piety. So seemingly spontaneous but in fact provoked or imitative visions of light were agreed to be and welcomed as religious experience specific to the place. It offered a kind of "religiousness" specific to the place and relatively neutral in respect to confession and belief.

Thus we come closer to the central dimension of the holy site of Krăstova Gora, which is social and religious mixing. Making the pilgrimage helps suppress most of the established boundaries. The attraction of the place owes much to the combination of unusual physical effort required to reach the place and free, unrestricted forms of the devotion. In the first postsocialist years the "organized" trip ended some six kilometers before the hill; from there pilgrims climbed by foot to the hilltop. The difficult walk up the mountain, the help given to the elderly, the search for a suitable place to spend the night in the open (the site lacking any facilities), the spotting of the rare points of water and food supply, and finally, the physical appropriation of the holy site, without a guide, through word of mouth—all contributed to the atmosphere of the annual pilgrimage held on September 14 (Invention of the Holy Cross).

Even now there is no "entry" into the pilgrimage, no obligatory itinerary: one may start one's tour by visiting the old chapel, the new church, or the iron cross. Myriads of individual paths cross and intersect in these points, as well as in the search for small crosses imprinted on stones or trees. The largest crowds form in front of the shrine during the night liturgy, as well as at points from where the iron cross may be watched at midnight, when "the heaven opens" and miracles are most likely to occur. As a rule, the heaven opens only for the believer. This quest for the small personal miracle merges with a more general expectation tending to the future, namely, the fulfilling of the promise that "the Cross will come out by itself" from the hill: an eschatological expectation par excellence.

Religious Revival and Sharing the Holy Place

On the Mount of the Cross, an Orthodox Christian holy place, the mixing of Christians, Muslims, and adepts of various religious movements or spiritualities took place chiefly in the first postcommunist decade. How did these *others* conceive the holy place; did they appropriate the sacred space, mapping it according to their own ritual's needs, or did they limit themselves to the minimal interaction, without leaving any peculiar mark of their presence?

In the early 1990s, the eschatological expectation was fostered and reinforced by the hopes related to democratization and well-being associated with the ongoing radical sociopolitical change. It was probably the meeting of the two types of expectation that produced the diffuse religiosity combined with the quest of personal well-being, which some Bulgarian ethnographers called "the useful sacred." Its distinctive mark, namely great diversity of religious practices, Christian and non-Christian, was presumably best observed on Krăstova Gora, throughout the 1990s. Indeed, the earliest ethnographic reports (1992–1994) notice the presence of Muslims and Protestants (of different denominations) at the annual pilgrimages, as well as the visits apart from the big ceremonies.[52] They also noted the occasional presence of Yoga practitioners, as well as of individuals and small groups of New-Agers. The presence of these groups was rather discreet, in interstitial time (outside the pilgrimage) and space (on marginal locations of the holy site).

Sometimes, the *confessional other* ventured into the heart of the sacred space in order to perform a ritual bricolage in the shrine or around the key devotional symbol: the cross. Such an instance was observed in May 1994, when, after the sacrifice of a lamb (the *kurban*), a Pomak woman dipped her hands into the blood and then embraced the cross, leaving bloody marks on it.[53] What might seem a strange and inappropriate act was a sequence of a healing practice centered on *kurban.* Here as in most regions of the Balkans, this elaborated ritual and its polyphony of meanings (including "for health") are shared by Muslims and Orthodox Christians.[54] Its sense was immediately accessible to the Orthodox, and those passing by or watching did not seem surprised or offended.

The tolerance manifest in this and similar cases has much to do with implicit knowledge of a society.[55] More specifically, it is rooted in the conviction that illness and suffering could justify recourse to the *other*'s sacred place even outside the conventional forms and limits. This was well understood also by Father Vasili, himself a native of the Rhodopes who had the intimate knowledge of the local uses of religious mixing. As the only clergyman on Krăstova Gora until 1997, almost ten years after having received the divine call to this duty, Father Vasili encouraged the sharing of the holy place and advocated tolerance toward the non-Orthodox, especially toward Muslims. Inspired by his long experience of the holy place, he expressed his vision for religious mixing: "God is like this peak: he is unique and One but many paths lead to Him. There are three paths to reach the hilltop: one starting from [the village of] Borovo, another from [the village of] Belitza, a third one from [the village of] Mostovo. In a similar way, there are various paths to God: that of the Christians, that of the Muslims and that of the Buddhists. All these routes converge and lead to the peak."[56]

This manifest opening to the *other* rests on a less visible, tacit assumption about the discretion of the other's religious practice. It is part of the social knowledge shared by Christians and Muslims in a similar way as the norm of proper religious conduct. First and foremost, it concerns practices that are especially marked by religious difference, such as the *kurban*. For, even if the latter is practiced by both communities, the way of performing it is highly specific to each one. When Muslims make their *kurban* in the Christian holy place, the proper conduct of sharing requires them to immolate the lamb away from routes and paths, in the shadow of trees, to draw water elsewhere than from the "holy spring" crowded by the pilgrims, and in general, not to perform their rites at important moments of the Orthodox pilgrimage. Depending on the point of view in context,[57] these small adjustments might be considered either proofs of tolerance or strategies of avoidance.

Ethnographies carried on Krăstova Gora in the longer term point to two important variables that orient religious mixing from the viewpoint of the confessional other. One of them is availability of a shrine or a material devotional network identified as one's own religious tradition; the other is belief about the greater effectiveness of the *other*'s shrine. For Muslim people, visiting ("visit," perceived as neutral, is preferred to "pilgrimage") the holy places of the confessional other depends on these places' presumed or believed effectiveness "for health," on media-relayed devotional fashions, as well as on the accessibility of similar Muslim places. In the moving reality of the postsocialist religious revival, the latter is an especially changeable variable.[58] In other words, research on religious competition requires us to approach the field site in terms of networks, both in space (the available holy places within a restricted area in their relationship) and in time (active and inactive devotions).[59] The revival or reactivation of a devotion, and the multiplication of sacred places within the area under research may lead to big shifts in a religious landscape. More importantly, the emergence of a new sacred place, one related to the "own" tradition of the confessional other, or better corresponding to the latter's expectations in terms of facilities or accessibility, may quickly redirect the flow of pilgrims.

Exactly that is happening at Krăstova Gora: the gradual withdrawal of the confessional other from the Christian holy place. Field research from the early 1990s suggests that during the postsocialist boom of the pilgrimage Krăstova Gora attracted a substantial number of Pomaks. These Muslim visitors came from the same pool of devotees that used to revere the district *tekke*s and *türbe*s. Ethnographic reports mention remarks like "Jesus or Allah, God is the same,"[60] as well as more sophisticated constructs in which Jesus is related to the saints of the Muslim shrines: "Yenihan baba, Sarı baba and Jesus Christ were brothers."[61] Such statements supported the idea that peaceful cohabitation of Christians and Muslims in Bulgaria was possible, there and then. The instances of religious mixing happily matched the *komşuluk* that was believed to exist in its purest state in the Rhodopes. There are good reasons to think that, similarly to the positive discourse of "good neighborhood relations" that was held by the local authorities throughout the Rhodopes, religious mixing was tolerated, even encouraged there, especially when a Christian holy site hosted Muslim "guests." But what mostly mattered in the early 1990s was the "postcommunist religious revival," a revival seen in manifestations of religiosity in the widest sense of the word, and reinforced by scholars and the media. The academics, as well as common people, were convinced that after decades of communism, the need for religion suppressed for decades by the aggressive atheism came to be powerfully expressed. The general assumption about the "freezing" of religion under communism offered a convenient scheme for reading the mix of Christian pilgrims and Muslim visitors as a celebration of the freedom for religious identity in general, whether Muslim or Christian.

Toward a Monoconfessional Mount of the Cross

Since the beginning of the new millennium, the expectations about an idyllic mixing of different confessional groups and religious movements on the same holy place have been contradicted by the pilgrimage's evolution. Changes were already perceptible in 1997 when the author started doing fieldwork there.

"Going to Krăstova Gora" was gradually losing the facet of a physical and spiritual liberation—not necessarily a pious one—by spending a night on an open
hilltop.[62] A progressive "Orthodoxization" of the holy site was evident: small
or larger chapels were built to mark the important point of the pilgrimage as
well as to frame a sort of "sacred route" with a concentration of the most spiritual and holiest places. The informal attitudes of the "visitors" became more
and more influenced by a stricter code of conduct, and acts and postures seen
as disrespectful were publicly reprimanded. Observations regarding proper
conduct previously had come from laypeople: pious men, elderly women,
or recent converts from atheism, who took the opportunity to comment or
criticize. Such claims to religious authority based on tradition or recently
acquired knowledge seemed called for because of the lack of clergy. The rare
priests were busy with services, and it was only after 2005 that the newly built
monastery of Holy Trinity was home for several monks on a permanent basis.
In fact, what attracted criticism in the late nineties were pilgrims who lacked
an elementary religious culture, not the intrusion of the religious *other*. The
latter would become a problem only if proselytizing, which was never the case
of local Muslims; proselytism was blamed on adherents of "sects." The enthu-
siastic nighttime vigil so amenable to visionary experience drew from a mix
of, on the one hand, the kind of mountain excursionism typical of socialism,[63]
and on the other, a diffuse, inarticulate religiosity in which everybody was
free to join. Therefore, the initial efforts for disciplining the diffuse religiosity
and channeling its excesses were aimed more at the joyful festive mood than
the religious mixing and the intermingling with less-structured spiritualities.

Between 1997 and 2000, there is every evidence that the place continues
to change. On the one hand, the Christian pilgrimage is increasingly institutionalized. If in the first years one could hardly find a priest accompanying a
group of pilgrims, by 1997 Orthodox priests were already part of the religious
landscape of Krăstova Gora, their black robes distinguishing them within pilgrims' groups as well as around the new shrine. Parish priests coming with their
flocks from all over the country to take part in the Divine Liturgy at midnight
in front of the church helped to create a feeling of unity of the truly Christian,
and separateness vis-à-vis those coming without spiritual guides. The massive
presence of Orthodox clergy is especially visible during the annual pilgrimage
and the major religious feasts, when religious services are staged with more
magnificence and tend to last longer. During the 1997 annual pilgrimage to the
Holy Cross, the carrying out of the Divine Liturgy at midnight required the
joint participation of all Orthodox priests present at the site, those coming with

pilgrims' groups along with the local clergy. Priests from the two opposing syn-ods of the Bulgarian Orthodox Church served together, which was exceptional at this time. A subtle relationship can be observed between religious fervor and learning the proper conduct of the faithful, on the one hand, and group solidar-ity centered on one's own Orthodox priest, on the other. All these evolutions slowly but inevitably coalesce the many "small" solidarities—those of formal and informal groups coming each with its own logic and vaguely religious pur-pose—into a "community of creed"[64] whose members communicate through the liturgy. Last but not least, in the first years of the twenty-first century one can note a hardening of the Church vis-à-vis the pilgrims and mere visitors. The growing numbers of monks residing on Krăstova Gora facilitate this at-tempt to introduce more discipline: in an increasing number of cases, they react to improper conduct or to rituals that are not immediately identifiable as Orthodox. This trend became dominant after Father Vasili's death in 2004.

Ethnographers who concentrate on the *other's* practices suggest that the presence of Muslims on Krăstova Gora started declining already after 1995, and by 2000 was barely visible. The Pomak pilgrims turned to other sacred places, chiefly their own. The religious dynamics proper to the group, especially in the Rhodopes, led to the reactivation of old Muslim shrines. Even if the network of traditional shrines has not been fully reconstructed, new powerful impulses come from Yenihan Baba. By 2000, the still-modest shrine of the *ga'zi* attracted Pomaks and Turks from all over the Rhodopes, Sunni as well as Alevi. From these meetings, a new feeling of a confessional *continuum* emerged, and a new all-Muslim solidarity was established. At the turn of the millennium, the cult of Yenihan Baba and the pilgrimage to the hilltop—opposite to Krăstova Gora and higher—has become the main religious reference of the Muslim popu-lation of the Rhodopes, even for those who (for practical or other reasons) preferred to visit the Mount of the Cross. With the construction of a new shrine in 2004, the cult of Yenihan Baba has been manipulated for political goals, while "Yenihan" has become the center of a national pilgrimage rallying all Bulgarian Muslims.[65]

Conclusions

By way of conclusion, let me suggest a few elements of the "structure of context" that enables religious mixing. The case of the Mount of the Cross convinc-ingly shows that holy places that emerge in modern times at the borders of big confessional ensembles—especially at the intersection of Christianity and

Islam—are loci where religious mixing and sharing go hand in hand with the building of more or less rigid boundaries. This is all the more the case of sacred loci identified through divine revelation: human channels, visionary men or women, have always been receptive to social (and often to political) influence, and the messages they receive have been subject to constant reinterpretation. The ambiguous character of a Christian or Muslim sacred place established under these conditions is largely due to the rise of politicized confessional belonging, of religion-as-memory and religion-as-identity. Far from being a purely religious experience, the devotion manifested in such places is at once a spiritual quest and an arena for affirming and negotiating identity.

The Mount of the Cross illustrates the subtle economy of tolerance that is specific to the revealed *loci sanctae*. Given that such holy places usually emerge in landscapes previously untouched by the divine grace, social pressure and special political context are important, even required, for providing legitimacy and having their holiness accepted. The struggle for the recognition of the new holy place within one's own religious tradition may not favor religious mixing. Similarly, the eschatological expectations that are more pressing in such places are meaningful within one religious tradition, and therefore tend to emphasize their monoconfessional aspect. On another hand, the pilgrimage to a revealed sacred place is largely a search for the unmediated contact with God, and this contact structurally enables confessional mixing. As long as the unmediated contact with the divine prevails and is experienced as an inclusive moment, a place of devotion may be shared with the religious other. But the place's regularization—and especially the introduction or multiplication of institutional intermediaries—is a step toward the exclusion of the other.

Not surprisingly, gender and social characteristics, as well as political orientation, are important variables when trying to distinguish between social actors who privilege tolerance and the living-together and those who advocate exclusion or the building of boundaries. One is tempted to place women in the first category, and men, and more specifically the clergy, in the latter. However, as the case of Krăstova Gora shows, religious specialists from the lower clergy may work in either direction. Expressing the complexity of the sociopolitical contexts, these figures of local stakeholders articulate the interplay of local and supralocal levels. In a similar manner the visionary men and women, acting as depositories of the divine word, may influence things in both directions. What matters *in fine* is the delicate equilibrium between earthly powers and divine order, an equilibrium that is permanently negotiated by humans and redefined within a society.

Acknowledgments

This paper is a revised and expanded version of the French text published in the volume *Religions traversées*. I am grateful to my Bulgarian colleagues, ethnologists Margarita Karamihova, Elka Mincheva, and Evgenia Troeva, who shared with me impressions and data from their early fieldwork (1993–1995) on Krăstova Gora. Discussions with Emma Aubin-Boltanski, Maria Couroucli, and Bernard Lory helped strengthen and sharpen the argument. My warm gratitude goes to William A. Christian Jr., who helped me to substantially improve the English version and deeply influenced my understanding of religion. I take sole responsibility for the data and the interpretations.

Notes

1. Behind Bowman 1993, see also Aubin-Boltanski 2007, 2008, for fine-grained studies of this area.

2. The tension between structure and agency is explored by Bensa and Fassin 2002, especially 9–10.

3. Originally *mise en présence,* a concept borrowed from E. Claverie (2003).

4. Between 1997 and 2002, I participated in three annual pilgrimages to Krăstova Gora and separately did a dozen shorter visits, mainly accompanying groups or individuals (candidates for "miracles") during separate pilgrimages. Access to archival field materials of Bulgarian ethnographers who participated in the vast research program "Krăstova Gora" (1993–1995) helped to improve my understanding of the pilgrimage at its earlier stage.

5. Originally *configuration d'événements,* an analytical category in French sociology (Claverie 1991:159–164).

6. A *calque* from Sahlins's (1985:136–156) concept of "structure of conjuncture."

7. On these "islands" of Hellenism north of Greece properly speaking, see X. Kotzageorgi 1999 and hints in Filipov 1996.

8. I rely on the data about early populations in the area of Stanimaka reported by C. Asdracha (1976:58–75).

9. Cf. Asdracha 1976:56; some scholars seek an Armenian input in the local Christian patchwork also through the major religious foundation, the Petritzon or Bachkovo monastery; see below.

10. For a historical-anthropological study of this area, with an emphasis on the Muslims, see Brunnbauer 2004.

11. On the events see Crampton 1997:81–83. Russian military presence in the Rhodopes in early 1878 was met with fierce reactions by the local Muslim population, the Bulgarian-speaking even more than the Turkish one: a "Pomak Republic" was proclaimed over twenty-two villages located west of Krăstova Gora. Rejecting the national project of a Christian constitutional Bulgarian monarchy and claiming to return back to the Ottoman Empire, this "republic," based on traditional Islam, was revived after the annexation of Eastern Roumelia: see Lory 1989.

12. The Bulgarian-Ottoman border was "modern" with its checkpoints, patrols, and customs; it was nevertheless more permeable, and in a sense negotiable, than the Bulgarian-Greek border established in the same region after WWI and especially following the Second World War. This permeable character of ancient borders compared to the more recent ones is strongly emphasized in both collective memory and personal recollections about life in the past. Large parts of the local Christian populations lived from seasonal migration: see Kanev 1975:75–104, 233–272, 360–412. Narratives illustrating the easy border crossing, and exchange with people "from the other side" almost on a daily basis are part of many family histories I have collected in this area since 1999.

13. It is hard to qualify in modern terms of deportation or exile what Brubaker (1996:152–156) called "the *unmixing of peoples* in the aftermaths of Empire." Except for the exchange of populations adjacent to the Bulgarian-Turkish border established in 1913 in Thrace (the region of Edirne) and on the mountain of Strandzha/Istranca, there was no exchange of population between Bulgaria and Turkey after the First World War, as there was in the case of Greece (1923).

14. It was typically the case of people from Momchilovtsi, the largest Bulgarian Christian village in the area of the pilgrimage, which had remained in Ottoman territory until 1912. In the interwar period, the natives of this huge and overpopulated village were the main agents of the "re-evangelization" of the Rhodopes.

15. See Crampton 1997:161–162 for a succinct review; Neuburger 2004: chs. 2, 3, for more details.

16. The best-documented work on the Bulgarian-Greek exchange of populations remains Ladas (1932:101–263).

17. "Town of Assen" renamed by the name of tsar Ivan Asen II (1218–1241), the most glorious figure of the Second Bulgarian Tsardom, mentioned as the commissioner of a commemorative inscription found in 1866 in the ruins of a local fortress. This inscription from 1230 fueled the Bulgarian-Greek nationalist confrontation, which was especially harsh in Stanimaka, and was destroyed at the beginning of the twentieth century.

18. For the boundaries of this domain see V. Tapkova-Zaimova (1989:429–30).

19. The monastery was founded by two brothers of Georgian background, the Pakourianos or Bakouriani, who were ennobled and rose to high positions of the Byzantine Empire under the first Comneni: the elder, Gregorios, was a successful army general of Emperor Alexis I Comnenus (1081–1118). Being a native of the area of Taik—where by this time Georgians were mixed with Armenians and the name of Iberians was often used to refer to the Monophysit creed common to both, and not to a Georgian descent—the "ethnic origin" of the Bakouriani has become the subject of identity claims from Georgian and Armenian scholars: see Arutjunova-Fidanjan 1978 and Lomouri 1981.

20. The Typicon (founding rule) conceived by its founder contains a clause forbidding the recruitment of Greeks into the monastic community: see P. Lemerle 1977:149–150.

21. In Greek Orthodoxy, a *stauropege* is a monastery independent from the local diocesan authorities—a sort of abbey—which is placed under the immediate control of the patriarch of Constantinople. Hereafter, the term "abbey" will be used alternatively for the monastery.

22. The function of *taxidiotes* for controlling the countryside is outlined by Bryer (1979).

23. For instance, these village ritual specialists used to bring some earth of the village cemetery into one of the parish churches of Stanimaka or into the abbey, asking the clergy to sing the Mass over it: this consecrated earth was put inside or over the fresh tomb (Kanev 1975:107).

24. For the strong memorial dimension of rural Orthodoxy and its "the church was in the house," see Hart (1992:17–21, 147–150, and passim). For the aural culture— or "le règne de l'écriture pour oreilles averties," to borrow from the title of A. Gokalp's (1992) article—in Greek Orthodox context, see Couroucli (1992:268–270).

25. For the details I rely on Kanev (1975:106–109).

26. The monk Grigorios (before 1835–circa 1880), locally known as *Pop Gligorko*, is a personage whose real existence is contested by some historians. What is known of him depicts a figure highly untypical compared to the Bulgarian stereotype of the "Greek monk": enduring every hardship, he shared the peasants' life and learned the local idiom enough to deliver to them elementary teaching, both religious (the catechism) and secular. Since the 1930s, this semilegendary figure has been subject to Bulgarian nationalist revision, mostly through the historical novel *Vreme razdelno* [Time Departing] (1964), which depicts in a particularly emotional way the conversion to Islam of the Bulgarian-speaking population of the Rhodopes (cf. Todorova 2004:148–152).

27. The *türbes* and *tekkes* are associated chiefly with Alevi of Bektashi cults: see Ivanova 2001, and also Gruev 2000, who points at the curious fact that the shrines the most revered by Pomaks are related to heterodox Islam, while this group is overwhelmingly Sunni.

28. The figure of the *ghāzī*, a sort of Ottoman conquistador acting by sword and preaching and thus contributing to the conversion of the infidels to Islam, is common to Balkans Muslim populations and often manipulated (Clayer and Popovic 1995:340–342, 353–356).

29. Led by the organization *Rodina* (Motherland), the Bulgarian-oriented "Pomak revival" launched in 1937 had some success in the central Rhodopes: see Gruev 2003:33–35; Neuburger 2004; Todorova 2004:139–140.

30. See Sv. Ivanova 2005:46–47, a *vakıfname* of 1663.

31. Starting from the 1820s, Bulgarian elite (lay and religious) embarked on a struggle for separating Bulgarians from the community of the Greek Orthodox populations—the Ottoman *Rum millet*—which was administered by the patriarch of Constantinople. An autocephalous Bulgarian Orthodox Church ruled by an exarch was created after the sultan's recognition of a separate Bulgarian *millet* (February 1870), but not recognized by the patriarch of Constantinople, who accused it of "phyletism" (ethnicism) and ruled out the Bulgarian schism (1872); for the events see Crampton 1997:66–76. Indeed, the Bulgarian claims were premised on the Ottoman concept of *millet* and had a clearly political aim; "Bulgarian" Orthodoxy remained fully conformed to the Greek rite.

32. In the area of Stanimaka, even the Orthodox churches most affected by this religious competition remained open to Muslims coming in "for health" purposes: cf. Ivanova 2001:543–544.

33. On the Greek-Bulgarian "battle" through religious symbols, see Dobreva 2005; Baeva and Valtchinova 2009.

34. For the Bulgarian discourse on the Pomaks and the practices aimed at their integration, see Konstantinov 1992, 1997; Neuburger 2004; Todorova 2004.

35. For details, see Konstantinov 1992 and Lory 1993.

36. Of the many studies dedicated to this campaign, popularly known as "the Rebirth process," the "change of names," or "baptizing the Turks," see for instance Poulton 1991:129–161 and Bell 1999.

37. The *komşuluk* is seen as a structural feature of the multireligious society in Bosnia: see Bringa 1995; Bougarel 1996:99–125; Sorabji 2007; for Bulgaria, see T. Georgieva 1995.

38. For a fine analysis of this double effect see C. Sorabji 2007 and the chapter of Bojan Baskar in this volume.

39. For instance, Bougarel (1996:114–125) criticizes the straightforward relationship between *komşuluk* and "religious tolerance" in Bosnia, relating the practice of living together to what he termed "intimate crime."

40. See A. Zhelyazkova 1995: more than half of the case studies come from the central Rhodopes. See also the contributions in G. Fotev 2000.

41. Such a double use of fieldwork on Krăstova Gora appears at careful reading of E. Ivanova 2000.

42. Cf. a similar observation in Bax 2000:331–332.

43. Widely known under the name of "Brother Jordan," this curious personage was never part of a religious order; living from charity, he was not welcome in the abbey of Bachkovo and was barely tolerated by the parish priests. For Jordan's activities and the networks that supported him, see G. Valtchinova 2005.

44. For the variants and sources of the legend, cf. Valtchinova 2000.

45. Here I draw on various histories published in the two pilgrims' booklets by the mid-1990s, and presented as "memories" of "firsthand witnesses"; Anonymous 1994:83–85, 101–102; Anonymous 1996:150–151.

46. The interest of King Boris III in prophecies and the occult was widely known; for the ideology and activities of the association see Valtchinova 2009.

47. This "map" is represented in pious images designed by Jordan between 1949 and 1953, in the style of the popular prints of the Mount Athos, and reproduced as postal cards.

48. Cf. Anonymous 1994:89–90; Anonymous 1996:112, 148–149, 151.

49. Provoked by accusations about collusion of the highest hierarchy with the communist regime, the Orthodox Church split into two synods (governing collective bodies): a presumably procommunist (the Red) one, and the anticommunist (the Blue) one: see Broun 1993, 2000. While this schism was officially settled in December 1998, resistance by priests in many places kept the tension high and impeded the normal functioning of services and parish life well after 2000.

50. The two booklets for pilgrims published and circulated by the mid-1990s (Anonymous 1994, 1996) report stories of luminous visions allegedly shared by pilgrims. The second one, suggestively titled *The Jerusalem of the Rhodopes*, hints at possible "glimmers from the celestial Jerusalem." These pious writings, some of which are relayed by local and regional media, are the charter of narratives of visions that have progressively become an authoritative "model" for talking about one's own

experience on Krăstova Gora. They provide a stock of images and formulae, as well as the authoritative "history of the place" to which pilgrims interviewed in 1997 and 1999 had recourse when asked to tell their personal feeling of the pilgrimage. Once introduced in the public space and becoming part of the shared knowledge about "the specificity of the Cross Mount," accounts of visionary experience are mostly circulated by word of mouth: during the annual pilgrimage of 1997, I was present at a short-lived visionary sequence that arose from a rumor about light seen in the sky during the nighttime celebration.

51. In the first decade of postsocialism in Bulgaria, an ethnographer could not fail to observe people hesitant to do the basic devotional acts or gestures (crossing oneself, the posture for praying) and to say basic prayer. In the absence of help from the clergy (due to the internal quarrels in the Church), the lack of religious culture imputed to communism led occasional church attenders to adopt various strategies of ritual mimicry in order to conceal their poor knowledge of the religious norm and of Christian teaching. As a rule, errors or inappropriate gestures were pinpointed by elderly women (the most regular church attendants, and also the most active in pilgrimage), who stood for the priests in admonishing piety and proper performance.

52. See E. Ivanova 2000:19–21, 38–39. I am indebted to E. Troeva for information about the presence of Pentecostal Roma on Krăstova Gora in July 1994.

53. Observed by M. Karamihova; for details see Karamihova and Valtchinova 2009:349.

54. For a generalizing view of a Balkan *kurban* see B. Sikimić and P. Hristov 2007. The same cultural reality is treated by M. Couroucli elsewhere in this volume.

55. The term of "implicit" or "social" knowledge is used according to the definition of Michael Taussig (1987:394), as "an essentially inarticulable and imageric non-discursive knowing of social relationality . . . acquired through practices rather than through conscious learning." Following in his steps while looking at the breakdown of Yugoslavia, van de Port (1998:97, 100) found that this "traditionalist" knowledge, "muted and marginalized," "rarely surfaced in public discourses" but conveyed the whole social and political dynamic. The culture of secrecy under communism, as well as the structural lack of transparency of the social world of state socialism, made central this type of knowledge even in the context of postsocialism.

56. Coined in the early 1990s, the metaphor of the three "paths to God" was employed by Father Vasili in a TV interview broadcast in September 1994. He regularly used it in speeches and included it in a booklet he wrote about the miracles (Arininski 2000:17).

57. Difference in appreciation may be due to confession (being Muslim or Christian), but also to the degree of belief (which varies greatly, after the "era of atheism"), to regularity of religious practice, and not least, to one's perception of a gap between expectation and real experience of the holy place. All these varieties of criticism or diverging opinions have been observed by the author during fieldwork.

58. The most visible features of the recent evolution of Islam in the villages and towns of the Rhodopes Mountains are the building of new and large mosques, the multiplication of imams trained in Saudi Arabia, and a general trend toward Arab-style Islam, which is seen as "pure": see Ghodsee 2009.

59. This approach owes much to the category of local religion as developed by W. A. Christian Jr. (1989b).

60. See Ivanova 2000:5, 17, 37; 2001:542–543.

61. Cf. Grigorov (1998:555); being the beloved subject of the local media, such "legends" also are circulated by historical writings oriented to the general public.

62. Reports from ethnographic fieldwork conducted in 1993–1994 insist on a widespread sociability and drinking among groups of friends, even during the nighttime service, by "visitors" coming to the annual pilgrimage (September 13–14).

63. For the peculiar sociability associated to the practice of "mountain tourism" in socialist Bulgaria, its codes and the representations related to it, see Benovska 2006:9–13.

64. Originally *communauté croyante,* a category for religious late modernity in French sociology of religion: see D. Hervieu-Leger 2000 (1993).

65. For a succinct history and the later developments of this holy place see Troeva-Grigorova 2010.

FIVE

Muslim Devotional Practices in Christian Shrines: The Case of Istanbul

DIONIGI ALBERA AND BENOÎT FLICHE
Translated by David Macey

This chapter presents the findings of ongoing research (begun in 2005) into Muslim attendance at Christian places of worship in Istanbul. Our work is ethnographic, and concentrates on contemporary configurations of these phenomena. It attempts to ascertain the extent to which it is still possible to detect signs of the devotional crossovers that were, until the establishment of the Republic, quite common in both Anatolia and the rest of the Ottoman Empire. F. Hasluck's pioneering work (2000) provides an extraordinarily rich catalogue of these religious crossovers. The book provides the last snapshot of a religious world that was to be turned upside down within a few years, and reveals to us a society in which many places of worship were shared for hundreds of years, and in which attending the other's sanctuary was a common modality of belief.

Phenomena of this kind were not uncommon in the capital, where, until the eve of the First World War, half the population was non-Muslim (Pérouse 2004:38). For instance, Henri Carnoy and Jean Nicolaïdes's description (1893) of the Church of the Fish in Istanbul provides convincing evidence of joint attendance. Famed for the healing powers of its *ayazma* (spring), the church was, at the end of the nineteenth century, the focus of a major pilgrimage that, according to a contemporary witness, attracted over forty thousand people, making it one of the best-attended religious sites in the city. It was visited not only by Greeks but also, our two folklorists tell us, by "Armenians, Turkish women and sometimes even Turkish men. And what is more, the Muslims are not fanatical" (Carnoy and Nicolaïdes 1893:67).

This was not a one-way traffic. At this time, Christian women also visited the tomb of Zümbül Efendi:

On the first three Fridays of the month, and especially of the lunar month of Mouharram, both Turkish and Christian women give handkerchiefs to the muezzins, who wave them from the top of the minarets as they read the *salâ*. After the *salâ*, the muezzins come down from the minarets holding large numbers of handkerchiefs, and return them to their owners. When fastened to the head or a belt, these handkerchiefs cure all sorts of illnesses. . . . on that day (the tenth day of the month of Mouharram), the water from the spring gushes to a considerable height. The caretaker distributes it to the women—including the Christians—who use it to cure all manners of illness. (Carnoy and Nicolaïdes 1893:117, 119)

And what of today? Is it still possible to observe such fluid devotional forms and practices? Several factors appear to suggest that we cannot. Paradoxically, the transition to the Republic gave the state greater control over the population's orthodoxy. The establishment of the Republic did not lead to the state's withdrawal from the religious field, and the abolition of the caliphate in 1924 did not lead to the separation of church and state. Mustafa Kemal established the Diyanet İşleri Reisliği and then the Diyanet İşleri Başkanlığı (DIB: Directorate of Religious Affairs), which reported directly to the prime minister's office. The institution is responsible for the regulation and administration of all questions pertaining to belief and ritual. It is a directorate and not a ministry, which makes it more immune to political changes. Its members are appointed and remain in post whatever the political color of the government. Within the framework of the new legislative and institutional provisions, religious matters were regarded as a public service to be provided by the state, mainly by defining the framework for religious education and worship. The Diyanet turns men of religion into agents of the state, controls the "clergy," and influences the content of the Friday sermons preached in the mosques. Far from breaking its links with religion, the secular Republic organizes and teaches religion, and controls it even more closely than the empire had done. The Turkish state lays down religious norms, tries to impose them on society, and aspires to being the supreme religious authority with exclusive control over religious affairs (Massicard 2004:57). In this context, a number of religious practices have been outlawed on the grounds that they are heterodox. They include *ziyârât* ("visits") to saints for therapeutic purposes and the use of *hocas* to ward off the evil eye. Such practices are deemed illegitimate because they do not conform to the *sunna,* and are described as "superstitions." And interfaith crossovers clearly come into this heterodox category.

More importantly, the history of the twentieth century resulted in a homogenization of the population. The "ethnic map" of Turkey was greatly simplified, even though it remained highly differentiated (Bazin 2005:394). The "religious map" became even more monochrome. The Greek and Armenian populations were considerably reduced, as were other non-Muslim minorities (Jews, Assyro-Chaldeans, Christian Arabs). Confessional otherness therefore became much less common than it once was.

Although they are few in number, non-Muslims have, as a result of a long and slow process of evolution, become part of Turkish society. But certain nationalist tendencies on both the right and the left still regard these Turkish citizens as foreigners and as the agents of a "fifth column" that poses a threat to the country's integrity. They are "enemies of the country," no matter whether they are Christians or Jews. This belief has given rise to many publications that attempt to demonstrate the existence of plots orchestrated by foreign powers. Arslan Bulut (2005) tries, for example, to argue that Greece is trying to use "missionaries" to "roumelize" the Black Sea region.

There is in fact an imaginary construct concerning "the missionary," and its roots lie in nineteenth-century history. At that time, missionary activity became a major feature of the West's claim to moral and physical superiority (Kieser 1999). After the declaration of religious freedom in 1856, the Ottomans officially had to tolerate such activities. Relations between the authorities and the missionaries remained tense, however, mainly because of Islam's negative image of them and because of the way they addressed themselves primarily to minorities. Although the Republic had introduced secularism, the fear of conversion persisted. Turkish citizenship was certainly equated with possession of an identity card, but religious affiliation was still closely associated with national affiliation, and apostasy was often equated with national betrayal (Bozarslan 2004:35). Fear of Christian proselytism is a recurrent theme in the nationalist press—in both its leftist and Islamist forms—which sees missionaries as a threat to the integrity of the national community by using money, job prospects, or the promise of visas to travel abroad as weapons in their struggle to convert Muslims (Pérouse 2004:39). For a Muslim, visiting a Christian place of worship is not something to be undertaken lightly. Far from being natural, it meant defying convention and putting oneself in danger of being converted.

Without entering into a discussion of the shortcomings of the international media, which often exaggerate the development of an anti-Christian climate, it has to be noted that our research takes place in the context of growing tensions around the issue of non-Muslims. The virulent polemics over the conference "about the Armenians" in 2005, the assassination of the Italian priest Andrea Santoro in Trabzon in 2006, the attack on his Slovene colleague Martin Kmetec in Izmir a few days later, the attack on Father Brunissen in Samsun in July 2006, the demonstrations against the pope's visit in the autumn of 2006, the murder of the Armenian journalist Hrant Dink on 19 January 2007, and, even more recently, the murder of three Protestants in Malatya on 18 April 2007 are all reminders that the question of non-Muslims is still a sensitive issue. Having said that, Turks interpret most of these events in terms of "political destabilization" rather than "religious conflict." When they attack Christians, the "extremists" are, they believe, trying to destabilize the country and to discredit it, especially in the eyes of the European Union, which puts such emphasis on religious freedom and the rights of non-Muslims.

Our ethnographic research shows that, despite this difficult context, interfaith crossovers are not uncommon in today's Istanbul. They survive despite the displacement of populations, the pressure to homogenize modalities of belief, and a climate that is not always exempt from tensions and fears. These interfaith crossovers take many different forms. In the pages that follow, we can provide no more than a preliminary survey, and it is inevitably summary.

Devotional Crossovers in Istanbul

The contemporary history of Istanbul's Christian populations has been painful, and punctuated by forced departures and harassment, and sometimes by real pogroms. According to the 1927 census, there were still some 200,000 Christians in the city. The census of 1965 recorded the presence of 127,000 Christians. It is now estimated that that number has fallen by half. Orthodox Christians have been particularly affected, with their numbers falling from about 100,000 in 1927 to fewer than 50,000 in 1965. There are now approximately 2,000 Greek Orthodox and 50,000 Armenian Orthodox Christians (the latter figure has remained broadly stable since the 1927 census), as well as greatly reduced numbers—they are difficult to quantify—of Catholics, Protestants, Syriacs, and Syro-Chaldeans. A lot of religious buildings have survived. Most are maintained and are open for worship. Some of these places of worship still attract a Muslim "clientele."

Holy springs (*ayazma*) have long been major sites for interfaith crossovers because they are visited by followers of different religions "without any distinction as to confession" (Pérouse 2005:281). Certain evocations of the recent past are reminders that, even in the twentieth century, several Christian *ayazma*

Table 5.1. Number of Christians in Istanbul according
to Turkish Census Data (1927 and 1965)

Religion	1927	1965
Gregorian	53,129	61,215
Catholic	23,930	11,559
Orthodox	100,214	47,207
Protestant	4,214	4,872
Other[1]	16,696	2,498
Total (Istanbul)	198,390	127,351
Total (Turkey)	257,814	206,825

Source: F. Dündar, 1999, Türkiye Nüfus Sayımlarında Azınlıklar [Minorities in Turkish
    Censuses] (Istanbul: Doz Yaylınları).
Note: 1. This category includes Syriacs, Syro-Chaldeans, and other Nestorians.

(most of them Orthodox) were also visited by Muslims. J.-F. Pérouse mentions the case of the Ayakapi *ayazma,* which "ten to fifteen years ago was still
visited by many Muslims" (Pérouse 2005:269). The phenomenon is now less
widespread. Many *ayazma* have been destroyed or are in ruins, even though
they often survive in the form of place-names. Some are still visited, but more
discreetly than in the past.

In several cases, the *ayazma* is inside a church, and helps to ensure its
fame. The Church of the Fish (Our Lady of Pygie),[1] which has already been
mentioned, is one example. The origins of the church, which is now inside an
Orthodox monastery, go back to the fifth century. The fish that give it its name
are associated with the memory of a miracle, and they still swim in the water
of the *ayazma.*[2] But what was once a major festival has now been reduced to a
minor event, and the number of Muslims who attend it seems to be declining.

The Armenian Church of the Archangels,[3] which is located between a
mosque and a synagogue, is another place of worship that is visited by worshipers of different denominations. It once belonged to the Orthodox Church, but
was granted to the Gregorians by a sultan of Armenian origin in the seventeenth century. A chapel dedicated to St. Gregory the Illuminator houses a very
famous *ayazma.* Believers come to fill small flasks with the water. Miracle cures
are said to have taken place, many of them as a result of incubation practices.

The church of Panaya Paramithias (Our Lady of Blachernae)[4] is also visited by Muslims. It has a distinguished history and houses the most venerated
Byzantine *ayazma.* The first church was reputedly built by Empress Pulcheria
(between 450 and 453) on the site of a holy spring in order to house the relics
of the Virgin, which, according to one version of the story, had been given

to her by her sister-in-law Eudoxia, who was living in Syria. The church was destroyed by fire in 1424. The chapel of the *ayazma* was the only thing left intact. It was incorporated into a new church built in the nineteenth century. Located in a poor neighborhood, it is now visited mainly by pilgrims from the Slav countries and Greece. But a few Muslims also come to it from Anatolia (from Bingöl, for example) to drink the miracle-working water after having had premonitory dreams. Local Muslims do not attend the church on a regular basis, but until a few years ago some Muslim women did visit it because of the "magical" practices that were performed there by an Orthodox priest.

The history of these places of plural worship has not always been one of decline. A number of shrines have seen their heterogeneous "clientele" remain stable or even increase in recent years. Such "fashionable" places, which attract growing numbers of worshipers, include the Orthodox church of Panayia Vefa, which is better known to the Muslims who attend it as Ayın Biri Kilisesi (Church of the First of the Month). The name is a direct reference to the pilgrimage that takes place on the first day of each month.

Built in 1800 in the Unkapanı neighborhood, the church is a small chapel dedicated to the Virgin, which is attended by many people of various religions. Most of the pilgrims are now Muslim. The place is familiar to Stamboulites of all social classes. Television starlets mingle with visitors from modest backgrounds. Its fame has been spread by the press, which regularly devotes a few articles to these devotional practices.

The church is famous for its spring, which is beneath the chapel. Pilgrims drink the water, wash their hands and faces, and then go to be blessed by the pope. The visit also revolves around the purchase of the small keys that are sold at the door. The keys are the object of special treatment: the pilgrims rub them against the glass protecting the icons and turn them backward and forward in the locks of the frames containing the holy pictures. Each key corresponds to a wish. When the wish has been granted, the key must be returned to the church.

The Christian shrine that attracts the largest numbers of Muslim worshipers is probably now the Orthodox monastery of St. George on Büyükada Island. Once visited by people of different religions, it has in recent years become extremely popular with Stamboulites. Huge crowds take boats to go there from Istanbul's ports, especially on 23 April, which is St. George's Day. Most of them climb the hill to the monastery, where they perform acts of devotion and enter the little chapel. Many offerings are given to the monastery. These visits are the occasion for many different devotional practices that will not be discussed here.[5]

We will focus on another case of interfaith crossover that, without experiencing the acme of the pilgrimage at Büyükada Island on St. George's Day, sees a huge flow of people of different religions converging every day toward the church of St. Anthony of Padua, situated in one of the liveliest districts of the town.

St. Anthony of Padua

There has long been a Catholic presence in Galata. When the Genoan trading post was surrendered to Mehmet II in 1453, its inhabitants were granted the right to retain their places of worship, even though the suburb gradually ceased to be a Catholic town after the Ottoman conquest. The existence of the cult of St. Anthony of Padua in Istanbul probably has to do with the activities of the Franciscans who settled there in the Middle Ages. The existence of a chapel dedicated to St. Anthony of Padua in Kasım Paşa was recorded in the seventeenth century (Borromeo 2005:232). At that time it was, however, the cult of his homonym St. Anthony the Abbot that facilitated contacts between Muslims and Christians. The church, which followed the Latin rite, was inside a complex that also included a hospital (in the lower part of the town, near the walls and not far from the Bosphorus) and was also attended by Greek Orthodox Christians and Armenians as well as by Muslims. The latter performed their ablutions in the hospital's piscina, whose water was famed for its healing powers, and "never failed to pray to St. Anthony at the same time; many of them actually took part in the Saturday evening ritual when the chaplain read the gospel and sprinkled the sick with oil before the altar" (Borromeo 2005:238–239).

A church dedicated to St. Anthony of Padua was built in 1724, close to the French ambassador's palace and attached to the monastery of the Conventual Franciscans. Destroyed by fire, the church was rebuilt in stone in 1763 (Comidas de Carbognano 1992:65). The plan to build today's great complex was drawn up at the very beginning of the twentieth century. The first stone was laid in 1906 and, after some difficulties and several interruptions, the church was finally opened for worship in 1912, and officially dedicated the following year. In 1932, Pope Pius XI conferred the title of "minor basilica" on St. Anthony's (Frei Eliseu 2007; Sammut 2006).

Istiklâl Caddesi, which became one of the busiest and most frequented arteries in Istanbul after its rehabilitation in the 1990s, runs through the old neighborhood of Pera (now Beyoğlu). The St. Anthony of Padua complex adjoins this avenue that is at the heart of life in Istanbul. The church does not stand on the avenue itself, and the entrance is marked by an imposing façade in red brick. A gate gives access to a large courtyard bounded by the building of the Franciscan monastery and the church itself. The red brick of these buildings contrasts with the gray tonalities of the other edifices.

Built in the neo-Gothic style, St. Anthony's is one of the largest Catholic churches in Turkey. In contrast with other Catholic places of worship in Istanbul, Mass is celebrated every day (in Italian, Turkish, Polish, and English). The vast crypt beneath it is used by the Chaldean community (which follows the Eastern rite and uses Aramaic for the liturgy). It is a real church, of the same dimensions as the one above it, and with separate access.

As we shall see below, St. Anthony's geographical position and visibility make it a tourist attraction. It is also a welfare center: on Tuesdays, Iraqi women from Tepebaşı—a poor district close to Istiklâl Caddesi—come for the bread that is distributed by the Conventual Franciscans.

St. Anthony's is, finally, a major place of worship and, on Sundays, a meeting place for populations that are almost invisible in Istanbul, such as the Filipino women who work as domestic servants and nursemaids, the many African migrants who have often ended up in Istanbul after traveling so far, and expatriates from the European Union.

The St. Anthony's complex has on several occasions been the setting for ecumenical services involving other Christian communities (Orthodox, Armenian, and Syriac), and for interfaith gatherings. As well as being the scene of official ceremonies, St. Anthony's attracts daily crowds of worshipers who come to perform various acts of devotion. The Catholics are joined by Orthodox Christians (both Greek and Armenian), and above all Muslims, both Sunni and Alevi.

These crossovers have been witnessed by some exceptional figures. Pope Paul VI celebrated a Mass at St. Anthony's during his apostolic visit to Turkey in 1967. In his homily, he recalled how fond his predecessor had been of the church, where he used to preach on the saint's feast day. As a matter of fact, the future John XXIII lived in Istanbul when he was a papal delegate to Turkey between 1935 and 1944 and often attended St. Anthony's, which was his favorite church (*sicut lucerna super candelabrum,* as he defined it). In order to emphasize the importance of this special connection, a statue of John XXIII was unveiled in the church's courtyard during Benedict XVI's visit to Turkey in 2006. Quite aside from John XXIII's fondness for the church, Paul VI added in his homily, one of its other claims to reputation was that the cult of St. Anthony extended beyond the circle of the Catholic community. The saint's cult, he said, touched all manner of souls, no matter where they came from or what they believed in. He therefore praised the Conventual Franciscans for their action.[6]

These circumspect references allude to phenomena of mixed worship that appear to have become more common in the decades that followed. We were present on one official occasion at which these crossovers were evoked. In June 2006, solemn ceremonies were organized to celebrate the centenary of the basilica's foundation. On the evening of 13 June, which is St. Anthony's day, a High Mass was jointly celebrated by Catholic ministers in the presence of representatives of the Orthodox clergy, who stood to the side of the altar. The apostolic nuncio to Istanbul, Msgr. Antonio Lucibello, used this as an opportunity to deliver a homily centered on the theme of religious dialogue. Having evoked the spirit of the Second Vatican Council—and identifying, with reference to a text by Paul VI, three modalities of dialogue (interdenominational, interreligious, and with atheists)—he emphasized the important role played by the church of St. Anthony in such matters. To make his point, he described his own experience. Visiting the church one Tuesday, he found a heterogeneous crowd of worshipers belonging to different religions—including a large number of Muslims—and was impressed by the way nuns and monks gave them a sympathetic hearing. Their role was all the more important, he added, given that the international context was marked by so many religious tensions and conflicts.

Reports of the devotional crossovers that have taken place in the church can even be found in the international Antonine press. In an interview published in the French edition of *Le Messager de Saint Antoine* of November 2006, which was devoted to Benedict XVI's visit to Turkey, Fr. Alfonso Sammut, who was the superior of the small community of the Brothers of the Convent of St. Anthony in Istanbul between 1983 and 1996 (he is now a priest at the Conventual monastery in Izmir), recalled his astonishment at discovering how many people attended the church when he first came to Istanbul. "I came here for three years in 1983. My first day in Istanbul was a Tuesday. I was astounded to see how many people had crowded into the church" (Saint-Pierre 2006a).

Another article in the same issue deals more specifically with the church itself:

> On Tuesdays, as on other days of the week, the great avenue of Pera, a broad pedestrianized street where signs advertising major international brands can be seen amongst the traditional Turkish shops, is swarming

with people. But on Tuesdays—more so than on other days—many of the passers-by enter the church of St. Anthony.

A group of veiled Muslim girls are here on a school trip. Book in hand, architecture students have come to look at the building, whose foundations consist of concrete pillars to compensate for the instability of the terrain. Men, either on their own or in twos, and women in the prime of life climb the steps, go into the church, and immediately turn right. They pause before the kiosk where a Little Sister of Father Foucauld is selling candles. Large candles cost five Turkish liras (2.50 euros), and small ones one Lira (0.5 euro). There is a constant coming and going as hands tender coins, choose candles and go to light them. Not everyone is a Christian; far from it, even though there used to be more Muslims before the hard-line ideologies of recent years became so entrenched.

This is because the church of St. Anthony is one of the best-known in Istanbul. And one of the most popular. The presence of minor conventual brothers has something to do with this. At the moment, there are five of them living in the monastery adjoining the church.[7]

The same phenomena are evoked in an article in a Portuguese issue of the same magazine (Frei Eliseu 2007), which devotes a paragraph to the Muslim presence:

> The Muslims. The most impressive phenomenon to have the church as a protagonist is the crowds that pass through the basilica every day, and especially on Tuesdays, as though it were a pilgrimage. They come to ask for the protection of St. Anthony, and for help and special favours for themselves and their families. There are simple people from all walks of life, educated people and artists, men and women, young and old. They all come to light a candle, and to recite a prayer with faith and devotion, each in their own way. They then write their supplications, or their thanks for prayers that have been answered, in a book.

These descriptions emphasize that the church is attended by a wide variety of people from different social and confessional backgrounds, and point out various aspects of the devotional practices that take place every day in the church, but especially on Tuesdays, such as the candles and the book in which people write their prayer intentions. As we shall attempt to show below, things are in fact even more complex and multifarious. Our research is based upon repeated observations of how people behave in the church, interviews with the clergy and their assistants, and an analysis of the prayers recorded in the book. This ethnographical work attempts to capture "interfaith in the making," to paraphrase Albert Piette.

A Plural Space

As we have already noted, the reason for St. Anthony's success seems to be that it has more to offer than other Catholic places of worship in Istanbul. Mass is said more often, and is celebrated in several languages, including Turkish. The church is open for worship every day, and from nine in the morning until eight in the evening. It should, of course, also be remembered that the basilica is very central and stands on the busiest pedestrianized street in Istanbul. As the newspaper of the Conventual Franciscans notes with satisfaction, "Everyone who lives in Istanbul had been inside it (or has at least heard of it)," and this makes St. Anthony's "the church in Istanbul by antonomasia."

How many people visit it every day? According to our estimates, the church had about three thousand visitors every day in 2005, and many more on Tuesdays. That is, of course, a rough estimate, as there are certain variations relating, for example, to the weather and other vagaries. We also found that visitor numbers fell by about one-third between 2005 and 2007, and this is confirmed by those in charge of the shrine.

The number of visitors varies depending on the time of day. While mornings are usually quiet, numbers rise between midday and 2 o'clock, and then peak from 3:30 onward. In June 2005, various sampling methods showed that between 600 and 750 people per hour visited the church at about that time. The crowds begin to drift away from 6 PM onward. On Tuesdays, visitor numbers are already much higher in the morning and continue to rise throughout the day. We also found, however, that there were also larger numbers of visitors in the early afternoon.

More visitors are women, but women are not in the overwhelming majority. On some days, there are only slightly more women than men, and as a rule women do not represent more than 60 percent of all visitors. It is difficult to determine how many are Christian and how many are Muslim, simply because the indicators of their religious identity are sometimes discreet. It is impossible to tell at a glance whether we are dealing with Muslims or Christians. Given that it is impossible to interview all worshipers about their faith, we have to rely on indices such as the "Islamic" headscarf in the case of women, the absence or presence of the sign of the cross, behavior at the stoup, posture during prayers, and so on. On the basis of these indicators—which are not, as we shall see, always unequivocal—we estimate that at least half the people who enter the basilica are Muslim. Our estimates concur with those given us by the priest in charge of St. Anthony's.

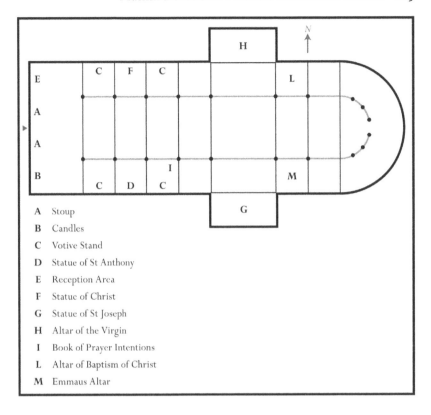

A   Stoup
B   Candles
C   Votive Stand
D   Statue of St Anthony
E   Reception Area
F   Statue of Christ
G   Statue of St Joseph
H   Altar of the Virgin
I   Book of Prayer Intentions
L   Altar of Baptism of Christ
M   Emmaus Altar

Before looking at the concrete ways in which this shared space is appropriated by followers of different religions, it may be helpful to provide a sketch of the setting in which the actors' practices take place. We will therefore try to describe the focal points that attract the attention and devotional activities of those who attend the church.

When we have crossed the courtyard, climbed the steps, and gone through the gate to the basilica, the first elements we encounter are the two stoups just inside the door, one on the left, the other on the right. A glance at the interior reveals a vast architectural complex: lofty columns line the naves, and a dim light filters through the stained-glass windows. If we look first at the central nave, we see two rows of pews with an aisle in the middle, stretching to the main altar, which is surmounted by a crucifix suspended from the high ceiling.

Inside the door, the space to the right welcomes the visitor with a display of candles, which are for sale. On Tuesdays, they are sold from a kiosk; on the other days of the week, visitors serve themselves and put the money in a slot. Religious magazines and books are displayed on the literature stand behind it.

If we go down the side-aisle to the right, we immediately encounter a votive stand propped up against the wall, and then glass-fronted cupboards displaying a few metal ex-votos. To the side, there is a statue of St. Anthony, protected by glass and flanked by a plaque engraved with a prayer to the saint. As we go on, we encounter another votive stand, again propped up against the wall. Every Tuesday, a book is left by the central pews for visitors to write down their prayer intentions. In the transept, we eventually come to the altar of St. Joseph on the right, surrounded by a marble balustrade, and a second altar with a fresco depicting the Meeting at Emmaus. There are prie-dieu in front of them. If we continue to the right, we come to a door that gives access to the sacristy.

If we turn left on entering the church, we immediately come to a door giving access to a space behind a glass partition; as we shall see, this is where the priest spends most of Tuesday, receiving visitors. If we continue down the left side-aisle, we see a statue of Christ, protected by glass and flanked by two votive stands leaning against the wall. In the transept, we find the altar of the Virgin, again surrounded by a marble balustrade. Close by, there is another altar with a fresco depicting the baptism of Christ. There are prie-dieux in front of it.

People move around the church in different ways. First, there are the tourists (European, American, and Japanese) who visit the church because it is a "sight," and possibly because they want a moment's break from their tour of the city. There are not very many of them, and they usually do not stay for long. Then there are the many Turks who have come on what might be called a "journey of discovery." Almost all of them are Muslims. For some of them, a visit to the church is a sort of extension to their visit to Istiklâl Caddesi. They are quite relaxed in terms of their physical posture (hand in pockets or behind their backs), but show their respect for the place (they usually whisper). Some simply come to get a general impression and leave after a quick look around. The majority take a much more detailed tour. They pause in front of the literature stand on the right, in front of the burning candles, read the prayer to St. Anthony, look at the statues, and contemplate the stained-glass windows. Some sit in the pews for a moment. The attendants who once stopped visitors from taking photographs inside the church have relaxed their vigilance since 2007. Lots of visitors can be seen immortalizing the whole church or a few details (the statues, the windows, the naves) with the help of their mobile phones. Visitors who are on a "journey of discovery" often come in small groups of several people, or in family groups. A few couples can also be seen walking down the side-aisles in ways that display their physical affection for one another (they walk hand in hand, or with the man's arm around the woman's shoulder). Some of the Muslims who come as "tourists" are accompanying someone who has a devotional attitude, and after wandering around, they may in their turn end by saying a prayer.

At the other extreme, there are visitors who really are taking part in what might be called "a Catholic routine." Visiting Catholics and Istanbul residents (Europeans, Africans, Filipinos, a few Turks) come to St. Anthony's to attend Mass (especially on Sundays) or to pray on their own. They stay for a moment, either kneeling or sitting in the pews. They are recognizable because they adopt a "pious" physical stance and regularly make certain gestures, such as crossing themselves as they enter or leave the church.

While some visitors merely walk around the church and while some behave like "ordinary" Catholics, a wide range of other practices can be observed, especially in the side-aisles, which are used as a place of worship by followers of different religions and denominations, who move around it in different ways and in accordance with different logics. "Routine" visits can be combined with the offering of candles or contemplation before St. Anthony's statue. But most of the practices that can be observed inside this space are autonomous, and are based upon the use that is made of the available material infrastructures. The side-aisles have a rhythm of their own, relatively independent of the liturgical time of the church as a whole—which tends to be focused more on the central space (the pews and the altar).

Most of these people are Muslims, but there are also significant numbers of Orthodox, Armenian, and Syriac Christians. Their social profiles vary considerably. Their vestimentary codes reveal that they are from different backgrounds. There are groups of school students, elegant women dressed in "European" style, and office workers carrying briefcases who have popped in for a moment, but there are also much more modest people and shabbily dressed women.

The amount of time they spend on their devotions varies, as does their intensity. At one extreme, there are those who make short visits and who in some cases stay for only a minute or two. "Regulars" can be seen entering the church, going to the candles, paying for them, and lighting them without the slightest hesitation. After a brief moment of contemplation in front of the statue of St. Anthony or the votive stands, they are ready to go back out into the bustle of Istiklâl. At the other extreme, some visits are very elaborate, last for hours, and involve a vast range of ritual gestures. They often involve a circumambulation in the church, usually from right to left. Some circumambulations involve minor variations, such as sitting in the pews for a moment or returning via the right-hand side-aisle. Although it is impossible to divide them into rigid categories, office workers and students tend to make quick visits, while most of those who stay longer are women from modest or humble social backgrounds.

Tuesday at St. Anthony's

On Tuesdays, all devotional structures are in place. Our description will therefore concentrate on that day, which represents the weekly high point of worship at St. Anthony's. The large numbers in attendance are quite in keeping with the old Catholic tradition that makes Tuesday "St. Anthony's day." The tradition appears to date back to the Middle Ages, as the saint was buried in Padua on Tuesday, 17 June 1231.[8]

Another tradition, which is quite widespread in certain regions of Italy, consists in visiting the church on thirteen successive Tuesdays. The tradition dates from the seventeenth century, and is thought to relate to a miracle performed by the saint in Bologna. We have seen no clear evidence to suggest that the custom is observed in the church in Istanbul. The priest did, on the other hand, tell us of people who visit it on seven successive Tuesdays and who walk seven times around the church on each visit. This is, in his view, an echo of the biblical episode in which Joshua marches seven times around the walls of Jericho.

On entering the church at almost any time on a Tuesday, we were struck by the large numbers of people in the lower part of the right-hand side-aisle. This is where the elements that attract the greatest numbers of visitors are concentrated. Queues can often be seen at the kiosk where a nun welcomes visitors. Some glance through the literature that is on display just behind it out of curiosity. Large numbers linger to pray before the votive stands or the statue of St. Anthony. They include several Muslims, as can be inferred from the number of women who have adopted an "Islamic" vestimentary semiotics (a headscarf covering the neck and a long, roomy coat) or from people who adopt the body language of a Muslim as they pray with the hands held out in front of them at the level of their stomach or their torso, and then passing in front of their faces as they say "amin." When we spent an hour recording devotional practices before the statue of St. Anthony, we noticed that only 20 percent of all devotional gestures corresponded to crossing oneself. That percentage, which has only an indicative value, should probably be revised downward, as it includes several clumsy and hesitant attempts to cross themselves.

How do visitors behave in front of the statue of St. Anthony? We observed their different attitudes and practices late in the afternoon on several Tuesdays. The most common practice (46% of cases observed) consisted in reading the

Gesture	Looking at ex-voto	Lighting candle	Praying	Reading	Making sign of the cross
Percentage	11%	31%	11%	45%	2%

Turkish inscription on the sign at the foot of the statue: "Almighty and eternal God who consoles all who suffer bitterly, who helps the poor, who brings the gospel of the truth to men thanks to St. Anthony, help us to follow the example he set us in our lives, and grant us your protection at difficult moments." Acts of devotion were observed in 54 percent of all cases. More than half of them took the form of praying while standing or, more rarely, kneeling. Twenty percent involved the sign of the cross, and 22 percent involved "touching" the glass. This could range from mere contact with the hands to writing with the help of a candle, or even kissing it. There is of course no correlation between the gestures we noted and the number of worshipers, as one person can make a number of gestures. Those who have come to pray mingle with people who have come simply to explore the church, and this explains why so many of them read the inscription.

The statue of St. Anthony is not the only focus for the devotional practices that can be observed in this part of the church. The statue is close to the two big votive stands, the glass cases containing the ex-votos, and the metal plaque engraved with the prayer to St. Anthony. Using the same technique, we counted the various gestures we observed. They break down as follows:

Even here, reading the text and looking at the ex-votos prove to be, at least in part, aspects of "exploratory" visits. The small number of people who cross themselves shows that most of them are Muslims. Some of them are familiar with the church and have visibly come to light candles. The candles can be heavily charged with meaning. Witness this sharp altercation between an attendant and a young woman. When she saw him extinguishing candles that had scarcely been consumed in order to put them in a bucket, she criticized him for putting them out too soon and relit them.

There are not many ex-votos in the glass cases. Most are small metal objects reproducing anatomical details (usually legs), tiny keys, or banknotes that have been pinned together. The priest told us that the church used to receive many more ex-votos. Some Muslims would even bring a sheep or a chicken. The friars wanted to put an end to this practice, or at least reduce its frequency. Their attempts to promote a less "concrete" relationship with the supernatural ("which is not in our own material interest," he added) appear to have been crowned with success. Even so, some people do sometimes leave offerings beside the candles. The staff have instructions to take these objects away and give them to other passing visitors.

Most Tuesday worship takes place near the statue of St. Anthony. The statue of Christ, which is opposite it in the other side-aisle, receives much less attention. Some light a candle for St. Anthony, and then repeat the same gesture in front of the statue of Christ. Others take a more complicated route around the church and return to the statue on the way back from their circumambulation. Their gestures are similar to those we have described in the case of the other statue.

Tuesday is also a day for being generous. Several worshipers, both Christian and Muslim, bring offerings of bread, rice, or clothes. At five, everything is distributed to the neighborhood's poor. Tens of women crowd into the courtyard to wait for it to be distributed by a monk at the door to one of the monastery buildings. Bread is probably the most common offering, and it is laden with symbolic connotations. Offering bread is a well-established Antonian tradition. The custom of giving bread to the poor in the name of St. Anthony probably dates back to the Middle Ages (and may be related to a miracle performed by the saint). It became very popular from the late nineteenth century onward, and has turned into a sort of defining feature of the charitable work of Conventual Franciscans.

In the case of the basilica in Istanbul, we find, however, that the practice has been reinterpreted. This seems to have been the work of the worshipers themselves, who appear to have overcome the clergy's reticence. Those who arrive with bags of bread deposit them at the kiosk, but usually keep one or two loaves and lay them at the feet of the statues of St. Anthony and Christ. Other worshipers who are walking past them or who have stopped to say a prayer immediately take a piece of bread and eat it. That habit was obviously curbed by the way the monks manage the space. The attendants used to pick up what remained of the bread that had been left by the statues to keep it out of the hands of the worshipers. In 2007, we noticed that they must have been given different instructions and that they had come to take a more kindly view of the practice. The bread is sometimes left for quite a long time at the foot of the statues, and worshipers are free to help themselves to it.

This innovation means that taking and eating a piece of bread has now become one of the sequence of ritual acts that are performed in front of the two statues. It can be assumed that we see here the influence of the Orthodox custom of distributing the bread that has been blessed to the faithful at the end of the Mass. But we also have here a real symbol of sharing that transcends differences. Religious boundaries are blurred by the collective breaking of the bread, which is immediately eaten by Christians and Muslims alike. The religious affiliations of those who give and those who consume the bread do not matter. We might almost say that we are seeing a sort of secular paraphrase of Eucharist, as a peripheral—and interfaith—transposition of the authorized rite, which is performed by the clergy in the central space, and in which only Catholics can, in theory, be full participants.

The use that is made of the stoups also marks a departure from their primary functions, though it is far from universal. The fact that many visitors take no notice of them on either entering or leaving the church is an indication that they are not Christians, especially if they also fail to cross themselves. Our data indicates that the stoups are in fact rarely used: on average, only two in ten visitors take any notice of them. If, however, we observe the practices of this minority, we find that they often behave in specific ways. Just over one-third, and no more, use the stoups to make the sign of the cross with holy water. Most of those who do stop to use them do so for purposes and practices that can be scarcely described as Catholic. Muslim visitors often use them to perform a sort of ablutions: they wash their hands or splash water onto their necks, hair, and faces. We have seen some women anointing themselves from head to foot with the holy water. Some even go so far as to fill mineral-water bottles after performing their "ablutions." In this case, the analogy with the practices associated with Orthodox *ayazma* is striking, and it might be said that the stoup has become a replacement of the *ayazma*.

Tuesday is also the "day of the book." Some years ago, the priest in charge decided to provide a book in which anyone who wished to do so could write whatever they wished. His initial design was to integrate it into the prayers said during Mass. His idea was that everyone would say prayers on behalf of the supplications written in the book. He told us that he had to put an end to the experiment after two months because everyone was rushing to write something down as Mass was being said. A queue would form, and he almost had to wrest the book away from the crowd. The book is now always available close to the statue of St. Anthony, but it is not part of the ritual of the Mass. Although its use is now marginal in terms of liturgical space and time, it keeps an important role.

What requests are written down? Our initial analysis looked at a sample for December 2003, including 107 messages. We found, first of all, that there are few explicit declarations of faith, either Muslim (1.8%) or Christian (3.7%). Most of those who pray address God, using three forms of address that make it difficult to tell if it is a Muslim or a Christian who is writing. "Allah" is the most common form of address (46%), followed by "Tanri" (22%)—a more neutral term used to address God that is also used by Catholics—and "Rabbi" (18%), a more mystical term that is employed by different denominations. Only 8 percent of all requests are addressed to St. Anthony, 5 percent to Jesus (Isa or Mesih [Messiah]), and 1 percent to Mary (Meryem). The frequent use of "Allah" and the relatively low number of specifically Christian forms of address are an indication that many of those who write in the prayers book are Muslim. It also shows that people prefer to address themselves directly to God rather than to a saint. Although the saint is an object of veneration, he is rarely mentioned in the prayers recorded in the book that is left at his feet.

The book is also an excellent source that allows us to understand why people come to pray in the church. According to our survey, their main concern is with their health. Most ask for an illness to be cured or for protection by performing an apotropaic act. The second-most frequent requests concern money and work. There is no mention of lost objects, even though helping people to find things they have lost is usually seen as one of St. Anthony's "specialities." The requests concern not only the petitioners themselves, and may be made on behalf of members of the immediate family (children, husbands and wives, parents). Brothers, sisters, aunts, and uncles, on the other hand, are rarely mentioned.

As we have already noted, some long visits involve the circumambulation in the church and include a visit to the cross-aisle. Both the transept altars—which are dedicated to St. Joseph and the Virgin respectively—become the support for other rites performed by a certain number of women, most of them Muslim. They throw candles into the space in front of the altars (which are behind balustrades), and many of them open and close the little gates that give access to the space several times (usually three times). These acts seem to reveal a logic similar to that governing the "key" rituals performed at Ayın Biri—and keys do figure in the ex-votos that are brought for St. Anthony. It is probable that some of St. Anthony's devotees also visit Ayın Biri. Be that as it may, one again has the impression of being in the presence of interfaith crossovers, with similar rituals being performed in different places.

Tuesday is also, finally, the day for audiences. Requests for help sometimes need the mediation of the clergy. In order to channel them, the priest in charge has organized a sort of "reception center" in the small space to the left, next to the door. In both the morning and the afternoon, he receives anyone who wishes to meet him, without any distinction as to religion: both Muslims and Christians are free to come to talk to him. The conversations take place face-to-face in a small private space. A few chairs are set against the wall for those who are waiting. The space is full throughout the day: four or five people can always be seen waiting.

We were able to discuss these aspects with the priest. Most of the people who come to speak to him are Muslims. They have different reasons for coming. According to the priest, the most humble, who are usually illiterate, ask him for help against attacks from the evil eye or, in more serious cases, *cin* (djins). The phenomenon is apparently quite common in Istanbul. Several priests confirmed that some *hoca* (*hodjas*) send them "patients" who have been attacked by Christian *cin*, against whom they are powerless. Although he refuses to become involved in what he describes as "magical" and "superstitious" practices, the Franciscan father does not send such "patients" away, and takes the time to listen to them.

People from the higher and more educated classes (the priest mentions teachers, doctors, artists, and journalists), on the other hand, ask him for spiritual guidance in times of distress or existential crisis. They open their hearts to him, and talk about their problems and their lives. We indirectly witnessed the intensity of these exchanges when we saw people emerging from them in tears and visibly moved. According to the priest, these are not confessions in the strict sense of that term, but he also stresses that they do have something in common with confession. Whatever the nature of the interaction, the meeting ends with a prayer being said by the priest, who also makes the sign of the cross.

The differences between the basilica's peripheral and central spaces become more obvious at Mass times. The ends of the space that is accessible to all are closed off: ropes at the level of the transepts make the circumambulation in the church impossible. The celebration of Mass gives a great cohesion to the central space in front of the altar, and practices involving the side-aisles are marginalized, even though people continue to wander around in front of the statues and votive stands. Some Muslims sit down in the pews, even during the Mass.

Once again, a variety of attitudes can be observed: some are just curious, while others are more involved in the ritual. Some appear to take little notice of what is going on around them, like the women we saw, while Mass was being celebrated, absorbed in reading suras from the Koran, which rested discreetly in their laps.

When the moment for Communion comes, the question of the delineation or dislocation of religious boundaries becomes more sensitive. Some of the Muslims sitting in the pews sometimes join the Christians to receive the host. Mechanisms have therefore been introduced to prevent what Christians see as a profanation of the Eucharist, which is in danger of being transformed into "bread that has been blessed." Before giving Communion, the celebrant reminds those present that the sacrament is reserved for Christians. The missal used during the celebrations marking the church's centenary in 2006 also reminds visitors (in both Turkish and English) that "Our non-Christian brothers and sisters cannot receive Holy Communion." These filters are not always really effective. When external signs raise doubts about the Christian faith of a worshiper who comes to receive the host, the celebrant may even ask him or her questions about religious affiliation. If his suspicions are confirmed, he refuses to give Communion and simply gives the worshiper his blessing.[9]

Conclusion

Although preliminary, the survey we have carried out does allow us to conclude that several phenomena of interfaith crossovers do still occur in contemporary Istanbul. The history of recent decades has certainly seen the decline of a number of Christian places of worship that were once frequented by Muslims, but other shrines have become more popular and now attract more non-Christian worshippers. In quantitative terms, such phenomena are far from negligible, and that seems to us to justify an in-depth general study.

For the moment, a closer analysis of the church of St. Anthony allows us to recognize a certain number of concrete manifestations of the religious coexistence that occurs in such shared shrines. Our investigations have shown that they can be visited in a wide variety of ways, and we have established a preliminary typology. Muslim involvement takes the form of both exploratory visits, which tend to look like tourism, and devotional visits, which can present a variety of profiles. While their goals are always the same, as are their votive intentions, the modalities of devotional actions vary considerably.

In general terms, St. Anthony's is a space in which individuals of different confessions mingle, and their behaviors are inventive and have little to do with any Catholic routine. As a matter of fact, everything is very flexible. Very different devotional manifestations coexist under the roof of the basilica, but appear not to interfere with one another. As a rule, no one takes any great notice of what anyone else is doing. Everyone performs their own rites—either on their own or in small groups—without paying much attention to what their neighbors are doing. Votive practices establish a sort of frontier around individual worshipers. They are fully absorbed in what they are doing and concentrate on the supernatural and the objects that mediate their relationship with it. They quietly wait their turn to touch the glass protecting the saint or to write in the prayers book. Even sharing St. Anthony's bread is a fairly atomized action that involves no verbal exchanges, and there is not really any choralism. The only people who remain vigilant throughout the day, the only careful observers, are those who remain so because that is their job: the attendants and, of course, the indiscreet professionals known as anthropologists.

Some devotional forms that are typical of a Catholic environment have been adopted, and to some extent distorted, by Muslims. They include the tradition of St. Anthony's "Tuesdays," the bread, the stoups, the prayers book, and Communion. We have here a creative "consumption" of devotions that is not restricted to the suggestions made by the clergy,[10] and obtains a lot of room for maneuver. The multivocal nature of the space allows for a delicate balance, but it never becomes a cacophony. The sequence of visits that punctuate the day is orchestrated by the priest and the attendants, who play a major role in the indirect management of worshipers of different religions. The daily life of the basilica is therefore the outcome of multiple negotiations, most of them tacit.

The tact and diplomacy with which the sanctuary is managed thus delineates a ritual territory within which both Muslims and Christians of other confessions can perform their devotions. The space of the basilica is crossed by frontiers, such as those between the central nave and the side naves, that are at first sight imperceptible. While they do tolerate highly heterodox practices, the members of the clergy try to channel them by placing the emphasis on their spiritual aspect and discourage what they regard as superstitious practices. There are therefore restrictions on certain practices (such as ex-votos in kind, and Muslims taking Communion), while others (such as using the water in the stoups for "ablutions," and opening and shutting the doors) are tolerated. In the latter cases, it is the Muslims who seem sometimes at the origin of interfaith circulation between Orthodox and Catholic shrines.

What is the role of the saint to whom the church is dedicated? Unlike the Virgin, St. George, or St. Nicholas, St. Anthony is not a figure who lends himself to an interplay between Islam and Christianity. And yet this eminently Catholic figure does attract the devotion of other Christians and Muslims. Similar interfaith crossovers can also be observed in shrines dedicated to the saint in Albania[11] and Sri Lanka. Such phenomena no doubt merit a comparative study, which would probably clarify the role played by the Franciscans in popularizing the saint among followers of other religions. And yet the figure of St. Anthony cannot account for all the various religious practices we have observed in the basilica in Istanbul. Although he is an important referent, it is significant that the saint does not figure greatly in prayer intentions. His powers, which explain why he attracts so many devotees, seem to have been projected onto the whole space of the basilica. One has the impression that the place—the basilica as a whole, and especially the statues, the candles, the stoups, and the doors—is more important than the saint.

The fact that the church is so readily accessible probably explains why it receives so many visitors. It is a space that can be reached without any great investment of time. It is a haven of silence—and of contact with the supernatural—in the heart of the city. It is only a short distance from Istiklâl. It is also a space that couples can visit, and where they can share the experience of being in contact with the sacred while remaining physically close to one another.

Although the church continues to attract large numbers of visitors, their numbers did fall, in relative terms, during the period under consideration. The number of candles sold is in that respect a good indicator. According to the staff, sales fell by some 40 percent between 2004 and 2007. The number of loaves of bread that were donated also fell. The most likely explanation for this is the difficult climate we described earlier. It is hard to predict what will happen in the future, as that will no doubt depend upon the sociopolitical situation. It is, however, significant that large numbers of Muslims still visit the church, despite the tense atmosphere and the fear of violence.

The elements we have identified with respect to St. Anthony's suggest possible lines of research into other places of worship in Istanbul. A synoptic look should make it possible to raise questions about how practices circulate between different religions, about how individuals learn about other religions, and about how they negotiate with the clergy. It would also be useful to analyze the historical context in further detail, as this would help us to understand the reasons why certain sites are losing their power to attract non-Christians while others are becoming more popular, as well as the mechanisms that allow interfaith crossovers to persist in what appears at first sight to be a very inhospitable climate.

Notes

Dionigi Albera has carried out this research in the framework of the program "IMASUD" (2007–2011), financed by the ANR. Benoît Fliche has carried out this research in the framework of the program "CONFLITS-TIP" (2006–2009), financed by the ANR.

    1. Balıklı Kilisesi ve Manastırı.

    2. When the Turks were besieging Istanbul, a priest was cooking fish by the spring. On learning that the Turks had entered the city, he said that he would believe

the news only if the fish, which were already half-grilled, jumped back into the water. They promptly did so.

3. Surp Hiresdagabet Gregoryen Ermeni Kilisesi.

4. Panaya Paramithias Rum Kilisesi ya da Meryman Ana Vlakerna Kiliesi.

5. Cf . Maria Couroucli's contribution to the present volume. Mathias Gokalp's film *Dilek* (2005) gives a good account of the pilgrimage.

6. The full text of his homily can be consulted on line at http://www.vatican.net/ holy_father_paul_vi/homilies/1967/documents/hf_pvi_hom_19670726_it.html.

7. Saint-Pierre 2006b.

8. St. Anthony's feast day is 13 June, which is the date of his death.

9. We have so far been unable to observe Christmas Mass, which also attracts large numbers of Muslims.

10. On this notion, see Torre 1995.

11. See Gilles de Rapper's contribution to the present volume.

SIX

Saint George the Anatolian: Master of Frontiers

MARIA COUROUCLI

Translated by David Macey

The Valiant Maid (Mother of Digenis) and the Saracen

There is fighting in the East and fighting in the West
Learning of this, a beautiful woman goes off to war.
Dressed as a man, the beautiful warrior takes up her arms.
The saddle of her horse is decorated with serpents,
The harness fastened with vipers.
With one prick of the spur, her horse covers forty leagues,
With a second, she is in the thick of the battle.
Elle moves on and they get out of her way. When she recedes no one sees her.
As she turns about, the straps break
And reveal the golden apples hidden beneath the linen.

The Saracen sees her from the top of a mount.
"Do not be cowards, my gallant men,
War is feminine, the prize is a bride!"
The beauty hears him and runs to seek refuge with Ai Giorgi.
"My lord St. George, hide me, virgin that I am.
And I will build you a gold door to go in
And a silver door to go out.
The wooden roof will soon be covered in pearls."
The marble splits open and she goes in.

The Saracen comes to St. George.
"Deliver the virgin unto me, St. George the Christian.
By your grace, I will be baptised, and my son too.
They will call me Constantine, and my son Yannis."
The marble splits open and the damsel appears.

Social practices related to "shared" holy places, sacred sites where religious frontiers have been crossed, bring up one of the general questions raised by both anthropology and history: the tension between kinship and territory, two principles that organize society. Is a social group attached to a particular locality and defined in relation to a territory, or is it primarily organized around ties of kinship, descent, and alliance (Leach 1982; Goody 1990; Derouet 1995)? Is the distinction between *jus soli* and *jus sanguinis,* which operates elsewhere, still pertinent when dealing with holy places, that is, within spaces where important social activities—organized around culturally significant and specific representations of space and time—take place? And what of claims pertaining to such places in the current political context?

The ethnographic material for this chapter comes from a number of visits to the annual feast of St. George in contemporary Istanbul spanning a period of more than ten years, between 1992 and 2004.[1] It very quickly became clear that ethnographic observation in this case could not come alone, but depended upon some understanding of the sociohistorical context, and especially of "mixed" practices within the Ottoman tradition as a multicultural reality in Anatolia, a phenomenon that still remains largely undocumented.[2]

The second aspect of this study concerns the symbolic world within which cultural practices centered on St. George are inscribed. The existence of the saint is analyzed as the organizing principle behind a space-time that is bound up with the local community and that supplies a representation of the relationship between men and nature, namely the calendar of the year's local feasts. Several of these feasts mark the seasons, that is to say, the beginning and end of agricultural work, transhumance, navigation, and war. Those activities take place during the warmer months of the year in these regions, and their start and finish coincide with the cycle of the Pleiades, itself associated with a mythological set, elements of which are also found in ancient Greek traditions and in the traditions of the peoples of both Anatolia and the Middle East (Gokalp 1980).

Holy Places and Liminality

Anthropological analyses of religious rituals often make use of the concepts of *communitas* and *liminality,* which, Turner (1969) suggests, can be applied to the study of religious phenomena in an extension of Van Gennep's work on rites of passage. According to this analysis, individuals who take part in a common ritual form a *communitas* but place themselves outside society in a state of *liminality* in which the rules of everyday life are in a sense suspended or inverted. Turner also describes this state as an "antistructure." A *communitas* emerges when individuals either ignore the rules that organize their society or find themselves outside the established social structure, and organize community bonds around cultural practices. This strongly criticized theory proves to be surprisingly convincing in relation to ethnographic data on Christian places of worship in the Orient, where Christians and Muslims have coexisted for centuries.[3] Turner appears to know nothing of the practices of Eastern Christians, and still less of interconfessional situations, yet it is in such situations that the notions of *communitas* and liminality seem to take on their full meaning (Brown 1981:42; cf. Anna Poujeau's contribution to the present volume).

Turner regards religious cults as transitional phenomena characterized by a state of liminality. Because they are "betwixt and between," they mark an ambiguous period that is conducive to the formation of a *communitas,* a nonstructured community whose members all have equal status. To some extent, this analysis relates to Hasluck's "ambiguous sanctuaries"—sanctuaries of Christian origin managed by Muslim brotherhoods, and especially the Bektashis—in the Balkans and Anatolia in the 1910s (Hasluck 1929). Hasluck thought that such "shared" sanctuaries represented a transition from one "stage" to another: the transformation of a Christian holy place into a Muslim holy place was taken as a transition within a broader process of Islamization in the Ottoman world.[4]

We will see later that this hypothesis does seem to be corroborated by recent research into the period of the Ottoman conquest of, for example, Thrace; yet, it is difficult to assert that we are dealing with a place that is "in transition" whenever we encounter a "shared" holy place or a "mixed" pilgrimage. What might be called the Byzantine-Ottoman region is a vast territory in which the populations of various origins experienced many waves of Islamization over a period of more than one thousand years. The phenomenon is certainly more complex than a "moment," or a mere changing of the guard; to understand the nature of these phenomena I propose an ethnographic "zooming into" the details on one particular instance coupled with first- or secondhand historical research. My analysis is inspired by the approach adopted by Peter Brown, who has proposed a wide-ranging analysis of the cults of saints throughout the Christian world, in both the East and the West, both comparatively and also studied within their particular historical contexts (Brown 1981, 1987).

I here propose to look into the case of St. George, one of the most popular saints throughout the Christian East, from Egypt to Georgia, whose shrines in the eastern Mediterranean have traditionally attracted Muslim pilgrims (Voile

2004). My argument is based upon a series of ethnographic observations of the saint's feast in the sanctuary dedicated to him on Princes' Island (Prinkipo/ Büyükada), lying southeast of Istanbul. It is here presented in the light of archival research conducted in the Centre of Asia Minor Studies in Athens.[5]

Syngheneis and *Synchorianoi*:
The Principles of Kinship and Territoriality

My analysis of the ethnographic data on the ways St. George's Day is celebrated in the eastern Mediterranean involves two essential notions in anthropology: kinship and territory. Those notions relate to the principles and blood and soil which, while they are a priori antinomic, are associated in most societies (Kuper 1994). The complementary nature of the two principles is also evoked with reference to agrarian societies in Europe, where lineage on the one hand and residence on the other appear to determine the rights of individuals. Kinship and locality appear, in other words, to constitute the conflicting logics around which land tenure, for example, is organized (Derouet 1995). Now, as Leach demonstrates, it is not easy to maintain the distinction between the two referents when we are analyzing ethnographic data. Leach "deconstructs" the concept of kinship and suggests that this type of relationship should be examined in terms of its material context, rather than as a behavior that obeys a set of juridical rules. Kinship systems, long regarded as a basic structure of social organization in the British tradition of social anthropology, would finally "have no 'reality' at all except in relation to land and property" (Leach 1968:305). We should not, in other words, confuse kinship organizations with representations relating to them.

The same type of "deconstruction" might shed light on the study of shared or common holy places within the Ottoman world if we place the emphasis on the distinction between the analysis of social organization in relation to the religious communities (*millet*) that were established with the Ottoman juridical and administrative system and the analysis of the religious practices and representations of local communities.[6] This raises the question of the fit between juridical affiliation and religious practice, which underlies our investigation into "shared holy places." The presence of Muslin pilgrims at the shrine of a Christian saint seems to contradict a certain conception of the *millet* that sees the cultural practices of individuals as being "in phase with" their membership in a given religious community, which also determines their juridical status. We will come back to this point. Now we cannot analyze this phenomenon without calling into question our understanding of the local categories involved: practicing a "religion," belonging to a "community," "sharing" an identity or holy place, "sharing" a homeland, in the sense of a locality, are concepts that need to be contextualized within the historical and sociological space-time that concerns us here.

A study of narratives collected in the archives of Greek refugees from Anatolia reveals the presence of a strong local identity and a feeling of belonging to a village community that crossed the frontiers between religious communities in the early twentieth century. That feeling of identity and belonging is the basis for the bonds of solidarity that are forged among migrants who come from the same village, who are regarded as *synchoriani,* from the same *chorio* (village). "When a Muslim took the decision to expatriate himself, he was given protection and help by his expatriate Christian *synchorianos.*"[7] These strong ties are to be related to the local population's involvement in the annual commemorations of local saints that mark the transition from one season to the next. The fact that all locals recognize the sanctity of a holy place is one aspect of the reality of coexistence within the same territory of different religious communities, an expression of the ties between individuals and their local community.

The local Anatolian population is a social reality that is not frozen in time: whether it be monoreligious or plurireligious, it is a product of centuries of population movements and religious conversions. When we come to look at the question of "sharing" as a tradition, we will see the importance of ethnohistorical studies, and especially those of Hasluck, who observed heterodox Islamic practices in the Balkans and Anatolia in the early twentieth century. For the moment, we will simply note that Hasluck, whose analyses have inspired many recent studies of religious minorities in the Ottoman Empire, believed that heterodox religious practices should be related to the historical periods, which vary in length, over which the populations concerned converted from Christianity to Islam (Hasluck 1913–1914; Shankland 2004).

Kindred (*Synghenis*) and Blood Relations (*Omoemi*): Two Distinct Categories

In the Ottoman Empire, religious communities coexisted in the context of a juridical and administrative system that implied several levels of segregation, that found mixed marriage inconceivable, and that prescribed rights and duties that varied in accordance with the individual's ethnoreligious affiliations. According to the principles of Ottoman law, communitarian endogamy was an absolute rule, and mixed marriage resulted in the wife's conversion to her husband's religion and her exclusion from her community of origin. Under these conditions, marrying outside one's community meant defying all social logic; this could put an end to cycles of alliance, and represented a loss for both the family groups concerned. The criteria applied during the population exchanges of 1923 followed the same rules: all those inhabitants of Anatolia who were included in Greek Orthodox parish registers when they were baptized were expelled to Greece; only those Christian women who had married Muslims had the right to remain by virtue of their conversion—as they no longer belonged to the *Rum millet* or the Greek Orthodox "nation."[8]

Of course ties of biological kinship do not necessarily result in social bonds. In this case, the effect of the rule of "impossible exogamy" meant that ties of kinship were recorded in two registers with the local community. On the one hand, they left administrative traces in the parish registers of Christian churches, and in the registers of the *cadis* who represented the administration at the local level. On the other hand, they left traces in the collective memory of relations between men and women. Among Greeks, both registers were at work in the traditional distinction between the terms *synchorianos* (from the same *chorio* or village) and *synghenis* (of the same *genos* or lineage): being from the same village did not necessarily mean being of the same family. But in the case of mixed localities in Anatolia, a further distinction existed between individuals of the same parentage (*synghenis*) and individuals who shared the same blood (*omoemi*). The distinction took account of local social realities: it was possible for individuals to be biological kinsmen without necessarily being related in the social sense.[9] One example of this third referent—which appears to have been present in regions where Christians and Muslims lived side by side—can be found in Tsalikoglu's report for the Centre for Asia Minor Studies in the passage describing his visit to his village of origin in Cappadocia in 1959. The author describes how a young Muslim man addressed him by calling him a "cousin" without realizing that he was merely "of the same blood":

> He introduced himself: I am the grandson of Katir Baba, and the son of Osman Cavoul Katir. We are cousins (he meant blood relations, *omoaim-ones*). On our father's side we are descended from the Pinyatoglus, and on our mother's side from the Karakasoglus in our village. . . . Katir Baba was born in 1825, in the time of the janissaries. His tragic story is known to all Christians. [Descended from two great families], he lost his father when he was little and his mother married a Turk from our village and converted. She kept the boy with her. He grew up as a Muslim and was circumcised.

But he knew about his Christian origins. It was not possible for him to revert to Christianity on pain of death. . . . The rich Pinyatoglus regarded him as one of their own. They helped him financially. When they came back to the village from trips abroad, they remembered him. They brought him presents. . . . The Pinyatoglus had made the Muslims of the village an offer: they would keep the son of the converted mother and would buy him by paying his weight in gold. The janissary did not accept their offer, saying that when he grew up, he could earn more gold than the Pinyatoglus were offering. Young Katir (therefore) called me his cousin. We are not cousins (*Syngeneian den ehomen*). The poor boy probably meant to say that we were blood relatives (*omoaimones*) . . . blood can never, never, turn into water. Today, more than ten of the forty Muslim families in Cincidere are of Greek origin. The third generation does not hide the fact. (Tsalikoglu 1959:125–128)

Syncretic Practices in Istanbul: The Feast of St. George

April 23 has been a public holiday in Turkey since 1929. It is National Sovereignty and Children's Day (*23 Nisan Ulusal Egemenlik ve Çocuk Bayrami*), and commemorates Kemal Ataturk's seizure of power in 1920. According to the Christian calendar, this is St. George's Day, which is a traditional festival for Turkey's Rum.[10] In the countryside, it is celebrated by Masses in chapels or monasteries, followed by open-air meals or picnics. In today's Istanbul, impressive crowds of pilgrims—some one hundred thousand people—gather for the festival around the Greek Orthodox monastery at the highest point of the island of Prinkipo. Almost all the pilgrims are, in cultural terms, Muslim, and they practice a form of syncretism pretty close to what can be found in other parts of the post-Ottoman world today (see most chapters in this volume).[11] The large number of pilgrims also raises the issue of the religious nature of the event: are we talking about the emergence of a *communitas* that exists for the duration of these symbolic practices that take place in old sacred places (Hertz 1970; Turner 1969; Morinis 1992)? How do the "communities" concerned define their identity? How do tensions and passions whose roots lie in a shared history relate to contemporary issues pertaining to identity, recent modifications to representations, and national or nationalist stereotypes (Kechriotis 2002; Calotychos 2003; Papagaroufali 2005; Theodossopoulos 2006)? "Ritual time" and "sacred place" are fluid realities, and I propose to look at them by examining three calendar configurations, one corresponding to "communitarian" time, the two others to "shared," or syncretic, time.

The St. George's Day celebrations of 23 April are a well-established local tradition that goes back to the multicultural past of Ottoman society. At the beginning of the twentieth century, Christians, most of them living in Istanbul and towns on the western coast, made up 20 percent of the population. The population of the city of Istanbul has now risen to some ten million and is 99 percent Muslim. This situation contrasts sharply with the early twentieth century, when the city had a population of scarcely one million people, who spoke several languages and belonged to several religious communities. This was *la belle époque,* and it has often been described as "cosmopolitan" (Driessen 2005; Ors 2006): rich urban families of all religions shared the same way of life in a city where half the population consisted of Greek (Rum), Jewish, or Armenian "minorities" (Alexandris 1983; Berktay 1998). Princes' Island, one hour away from the center of Istanbul by steamboat, is where, among other places, the Stamboulite bourgeoisie spent their holidays in the nineteenth century.[12] Most of the inhabitants were from "minorities," and the majority were Greek Orthodox, which explains why there are two Orthodox parish churches, a cemetery, and a monastery dedicated to St. George on Prinkipo. It was already both a popular place of pilgrimage and a playground visited by wealthy people from all walks of life on Sundays. The monastery, known as St. George Koudounas ("decorated with bells") because of the little bells that adorn the armor worn by the saint depicted in the church's main icon, was both a tourist attraction and a place of pilgrimage:

> At least once a year, every family went together to the mountain to venerate the saint, to sprinkle themselves with holy water and to fill the bottles they kept for difficult moments. Whilst ordinary people went for the patronal feast, more "well to do" families often went on excursions to St. George's and held parties in the open air. On special occasions, tables were set up on the square behind the monastery, and it was the higoumene (who acted as host) who took charge of the proceedings. The society pages of the Greek newspapers of the day bear witness to the fact . . . there were always crowds at St. George's on Sundays. (Millas 1988:484)

When the Christians have left, Prinkipo is still the preserve of Istanbul's high society. This is where the rich have their villas and their local sports clubs. Here, the modern elite enjoy a way of life that is very different from that of ordinary Stamboulites. Even the pilgrims who visit the island on 23 April are townspeople who were born in Istanbul, and they do not share the same way of life as the populations from the countryside that have recently settled there.

We are in a city with an old tradition of syncretism, where the chapels and holy places of Christians have always been visited by Muslims. For the Rum, or Istanbul's Greek Orthodox Christians, this sharing is part of normal life in the capital. A woman attending Sunday Mass at the Church of the Trinity near Taksim Square in April 2004 explained how this happens: "A lot of them go to St. George's on Prinkipo because the saint gives them everything they ask for: houses, jobs, good health. He gives everything." According to her, more and more Muslims were going because the saint had a "good reputation" and because the priests were welcoming. According to the priest who was greeting the pilgrims as they came to the church when I first visited St. George's sanctuary in 1992: "The Ottomans [sic] come with faith. If I refuse to say prayers for them (for their health, houses and jobs), I would be the one who was committing a sin, a blasphemy. [. . .] They are the same prayers that we say for the *Romii* [Rum], prayers from [the book] that protects against the evil eye [Vaskania]. When they come with faith, we cannot turn them away. They [the pilgrims] have faith."

The usual visitors to these holy places are Turkish-speaking women of Muslim tradition who belong to the city's educated middle classes; they do not wear headscarves, or at least not Islamic headscarves. Having been born in Istanbul, they are familiar with the sacred geography of the city, which includes many other sanctuaries and miraculous springs. These are both Christian and Muslim holy places, and people visit them in search of a cure for their illnesses or malaise (Yerasimos 1992; Albera and Fliche in this volume). The pilgrims share this local feeling of belonging or autochthony with the Rum, who were also born and brought up in Istanbul. Syncretic practices are also part of the city's tradition of coexistence, parallel lives, and shared religious beliefs.

These traditional customs, which date back to the Ottoman era, are the symbolic basis for the syncretic practices that can still be observed today on Prinkipo. The boundaries between religions are also blurred by other "mixed" ritual practices, such as the tradition of going to St. Anthony's Catholic church in Istiklâl for midnight Mass on Christmas Eve. Once again, this is an urban tradition observed by Istanbul's Muslim bourgeoisie, along with local Catholics, and it is still very much alive (see Albera and Fliche's contribution to the present volume).

Three Ritual Temporalities

Both the Eastern and Western Christian calendars make a distinction between movable and immovable feasts. Feasts determined by the date of Easter (Shrove Tuesday, Easter, and Pentecost, for example) observe a solar-lunar calendar that changes every year, while the other feasts (such as Christmas; cf. Couderc 1946) are determined by a strictly solar calendar and do not change. St. George's Day falls between the two configurations: it is celebrated on 23 April unless that date falls during Lent or Holy Week, in which case it is moved to Easter Monday.

The specificity of the calendar gives rise to three possible configurations. According to the Church calendar, St. George's Day is celebrated on 23 April, and the pilgrims who visit the island belong, at least in theory, to both the Christian and the Muslim communities. But when St. George's Day falls before Easter, the saint's feast is not celebrated on 23 April by the Christian congregation, yet tens of thousands of pilgrims still visit the monastery because they have no "inside" knowledge of the Christian calendar. When this happens, it is not the Mass for St. George's Day that is celebrated but the Mass for the day in the church calendar (the Thursday of Holy Week, for example). As we have seen, the priests, who know that the vast majority of pilgrims are Muslim, welcome them to the monastery with their usual hospitality. "The Muslims have faith, and when they come to us we welcome them, they come with faith. And we read the prayer to them."[13]

There is, finally, a third ritual time. When St. George's Day is celebrated on Easter Monday, which by definition never falls on 23 April, it becomes a Greek Orthodox festival, and is not "mixed." When this is the case, the Rum community celebrates St. George's Day in accordance with its community tradition; after Mass, a shared meal, provided by either the monks from the monastery or the faithful, is served.

This last configuration is the festival of the Rum, a rare occurrence, providing the opportunity for a special feast. It allows the community to come together in a space-time that exists outside time, with a Mass, a meal, and singing and dancing. On one such occasion, observed in 1997, the Greek consul was the guest of honor, and most guests arrived after Mass for the agapes. That year, 23 April fell during Holy Week, and the monks and popes welcomed the pilgrims in the usual way. The Muslims come to the saint, they explained, because he has the power to cure: "Even the imam sends them to us to be cured; they [in the mosques] do not bring about cures. They also come to our churches. St. George is famous for his power to give help at home or in business. They come to make *tamata*."[14]

There is a sharp contrast between the last two configurations, the "purely Christian," or community, feast, where church ritual corresponds to devotional and festive practices, and the "syncretic festival," when church ritual and outside practices only coexist, allowing both communities to follow their traditional practices. Business as usual, though Christians now avoid going to the monastery for the pilgrimage on 23 April, which they call "the Muslims' festival." In 2004, three young women from Istanbul's Armenian community explained to me that on that day they did visit the island, but not so much for the monastery and its church: "The Muslims go on 23 April; Christians go on Sundays, when there are not so many people."

The offerings and the ritual gestures observed in these places by pilgrims evoke the most common requests. St. George cures all kinds of illnesses, but especially mental illness and misfortune.[15] He is a shepherd, and he guards his flock. In the time of the Greeks, the island's Greek Orthodox children were all dedicated to the saint and were called the "little slaves of St. George" (*ta sklavakia tou Agiou*). They wore little bells around their necks until they reached adulthood, and often until they were of an age to be married. Before they could be "set free," they had to offer the saint a candle that was as tall as they were, and have the liberation prayer read. Incubation was also practiced: the sick were brought to lie on the floor of the church for one or more nights, and had very specific thaumaturgical expectations: if the saint appeared to them in a dream, they were sure to be cured.

The Muslims who visit the saint rarely accept the bells, even though the Orthodox officiants offer them free of charge. Accepting a bell means giving something in exchange or even entering into negotiations with the saint through the intermediary of the priest: reciting a prayer, or having one recited, puts the petitioner under the saint's protection. Accepting the bell is equivalent to signing a pact with him: when the wish is granted, the bell is returned, together with a gift whose size varies depending on the donor's ability to give and whatever has been promised.[16]

It is obvious that such negotiations cannot take place between the officiant and everyone in the huge crowds that visit the sanctuary on feast days. Rather than adopting this personal approach, pilgrims perform ritual gestures outside the monastery precincts. They tie threads—preferably white threads—to trees and bushes at the bottom of the hill and unreel them as they climb the path to the top, getting as near to the shrine as they can. Strips of cloth are tied to the trees near the monastery to "tie down" the illness and make it go away.[17] They light candles outside the church and rub coins against the walls (and the frescoes, if they can get away with it): if the coins stick, their wish will be granted. Small brick, and sometime stone, edifices are built to evoke a house and marriage. Strange little constructions can be seen by the path leading to the monastery at the top of the hill. Made of precariously balanced stones, they represent houses and sometimes even a hearth, as branches are arranged on top of the stones to form a cross. These little constructions used to be built on the flat area by the monastery, on the little walls of protection overlooking the sea. It is as though the saint of the Rum could help the pilgrim emulate the stereotypical Stamboulite Rum: a well-to-do shopkeeper who owns a house and a shop.

Shared Sanctuaries

Shared sanctuaries were part of Ottoman folk culture in the Balkans and Anatolia. Those that were "claimed and frequented by both religions" are described by Hasluck as "shared sanctuaries," and in his view they represented a "transitional stage" between Christianity and Bektashism. They were found in areas where the population had been converted in the past.[18] A recent study of Bektashism in western Thrace reaches similar conclusions, and associates the formation of that religious order with the Ottoman advance across the region in the thirteenth and fourteenth centuries, and with the establishment of the corps of janissaries. These places of worship (*tekke*) were also religious centers, or "monasteries" for the holy men (*baba* or mere dervishes) who played a major role in converting the local populations to Islam en masse (Zegginis 2001). According to Zegginis, some dervishes first settled in abandoned Byzantine monasteries, sometimes living alongside heretical Christian monks. This facilitated conversion, which was a way of replacing one form of heterodoxy with another. The Bektashis prospered in the region over a long period, until they were banned in 1826, the year in which the corps of janissaries was disbanded. Some of the *tekke* that had been demolished during the crisis were later rebuilt or converted into churches after 1913, when Thrace became part of the independent Greek state. The *tekke* near the village of Potamos, now a shrine dedicated to St. George, is one example. A chapel dedicated to the Christian saints George and Constantine stands on land that once belonged to Isiklar-Nefes Baba, one of the greatest *tekke* of the Ottoman period. It is still a place of pilgrimage. Hasluck, who visited it in the 1910s, says that it was reportedly founded by the son of the king of Fez in about 1361. The monastic establishment had some fifty resident "dervishes" when the Ottoman traveler Evliya Celebi visited it as a pilgrim in 1688, and he himself carved a poem on the internal wall of the mausoleum (Zegginis 2001:199–202). Now part of Greece, western Thrace still has a sizable Muslim minority. It is surely no coincidence that it is precisely here that we find many traces of cultural practices common to the Christian and Bektashi populations, culminating in pilgrimages to the chapels and shrines of St. George on 6 May (following the old calendar), some of them involving animal sacrifice (Zegginis 2001:231–243; see also Georgoudi 1979; Tsibiridou 2000).

Black Sea Memories

Recent research carried out at the Centre for Asia Minor Studies (holding a major ethnographic archive based on interviews with Greek refugees who left Anatolia in 1924) has revealed the existence of a recurrent schema relating to St. George's Day celebrations in Turkey, and especially the Black Sea region, in the early twentieth century.[19] On the basis of this data, a distinction can be made between two situations, one inside towns, the other in the countryside. Ritual activities associated with a town or village parish reflect the organization of the *Rum millet* (Romans' nation), the official community of Orthodox Christians in the Ottoman Empire. On the saint's feast day, the parishioners gather in the church, where they are sometimes joined by Christians from neighboring villages. Traders also sometimes come to sell their wares, and mention is sometimes made of celebrations that take place after Mass, though these are unusual. People invite their family and friends into their homes, and the visitors stay for the night. The Turks sometimes go to Mass or watch the processions as the icon is carried through the region's streets. There is also mention of Turks visiting Christian homes on the day of the feast; this custom seems to be restricted to the local notables of both communities (CEAM, PO 757, PO 1–3).

In the countryside, St. George's Day is celebrated in different ways. The celebrations take place near Christian chapels or the ruins of a chapel, or in places in the wilderness where there are no buildings, and are always associated with stories about the legend of the saint, or about his apparitions. It is here, away from parishes and communitarian institutions, that the syncretic

practices can be observed. The same story is often repeated: St. George is venerated by the Turks. They call him Hidrellez and they fear him, because he is
strong and punishes those who do not respect him.[20] I identified the sites of
forty-two parishes, chapels, or monasteries dedicated to St. George in CEAM's
archives in Athens. Shared practices are recorded in five of them. All the celebrations took place in the countryside, in the presence of both Christians and
Muslims, and blood sacrifices (*kurban*) are mentioned in two cases.[21] When
these sanctuaries were no longer Christian chapels (if, that is, the building
was in ruins and had neither an altar nor a roof), a priest could not be called
in to say Mass, and only the villagers went there. But even when that was the
case, the stories in the archives tell of votive practices such as incubation, or
the custom of rubbing a coin against the wall to make it "stick." The church
in Ladik, for example, had become a *tekke* (Bektashi place of worship). The
informant's grandfather recalled:

> The Turks celebrated St. George's day too. They called him Hitirelez. [. . .]
> Both the Turks and the Greeks used to go, tear strips from their clothes
> and tied them to the branches of the trees. Then they asked the saint for a
> favour. And they took small pebbles or coins and tried to make them stick
> to stones. If they stuck, their wishes were granted. The Turks had a tomb
> inside the *tekke,* covered with a green cloth, and said that there were bones
> inside it.[22]

That there are similarities between the practices recalled by Greeks from Anatolia and those observed in Istanbul today is obvious, but the archival material
is too scant to allow further comparisons. Islam was the dominant religion in
Ottoman society, where the Christian minority lived alongside the Muslim
majority for centuries. Syncretic practices seem to be an old tradition, within
a society that has always tolerated the existence of religious minorities. For the
majority, the other was at once familiar and inferior, and there was therefore
no danger that Muslims who visited Christian sanctuaries would be polluted
(Couroucli 2003; Mayeur-Jaouen 2002). The Empire's Christian minorities,
on the other hand, were not permitted to enter the mosques that were the
majority's places of worship. They became accessible to Christian visitors after
the secular reforms of the regime of Kemal Ataturk, which designated them
as historical monuments open to visitors (Tsalikoglu 1959).

St. George and Hidrellez

St. George is often identified with legendary figures from both the Christian and Muslim worlds in the documentation on the feast of St. George in the Turko-Anatolian region: Hidr, who evokes springtime and rebirth, the prophet St. Elias, who is associated with the sun, and Hidrellez, who is present in the Turko-Anatolian region, in the stories told by Greek refugees from Anatolia, in studies of western Thrace (Zegginis 2001; Tsibiridou 2000), and in studies of Turkish folklore (Bazin 1972; Boratav 1955).

Hasluck was the first to note that Hidr was identified with both St. George and St. Elias in Anatolia as early as Byzantine times. He cites the sixteenth-century author Cantacuzinus, who mentions that Muslims venerated St. George and called him "Hetir Elias" and Frater Georgius, who was held prisoner in the Asia Minor in the early sixteenth century and who reported "the extraordinary vogue for Khidr" at that time (1929:321–322). As already mentioned, more recently, the historian Zegginis makes it quite clear that St. George is still the favorite saint of the Bektashis of western Thrace, and that they identify him with St. Elias and call him Hidrellez (2001:234–235).

Many studies of the folklore of Anatolia and the Balkans mention celebrations known as Hirdrellez, which appear to date back to pre-Islamic Turkish practices. Hidrellez is now celebrated between 2 and 6 May, and only scholars remember the link with St. George. Louis Bazin established the relation between the two feasts in his study of ancient and medieval Turkish calendars. Bazin explains that old Anatolian calendars divide the year into a cold season that begins on 26 October according to the Julian calendar (8 November according to the Gregorian calendar) and a good season beginning on 23 April (6 May Gregorian). The first date is called Kasim (the Turkish word for November) and coincides with the feast of St. Dimitrios in the Christian calendar: it marks the beginning of the winter's agricultural work, the return of the flocks from their transhumance, and the end of the fishing season. The second date is called Hidrellez (Hidir Ilyas in old Turkish) and coincides with the feast of St. George in the Christian calendar. It marks the beginning of spring and the beginning of the good season, when navigation starts again, and transhumant flocks are returned to the high pastures. The same dates coincide with the cycle of the Pleiades: the constellation is visible only during the cold season, between its acronychal rising in October and its heliacal setting in April.[23] It should be recalled that the Greek name Georgios (George) is a homonym of *georgos* (ploughman) and that St. George is regarded as the protector of shepherds. It should also be noted that St. Dimitrios is the male—and Christian—equivalent to Demeter, the Greek goddess of the earth and agriculture whose daughter Persephone spent part of the year living with her husband Hades, who was king of the underworld—the season when the Pleiades can be seen in the sky in the Mediterranean.

The name Hidir alludes to that of an Islamic prophet whose Arabic name (from the root *h-d-r*) expresses the idea of "green grass." The figure appears to be descended from a "pre-Islamic god of the rebirth of plants" that the Arab-Christian tradition identified with St. George. The term "Ilyas" is said to be the Islamic (Arabic) name for the prophet Elias (who is confused with Hidr—the Turkish Hïzïr—in Turkish folk tradition).[24] We appear to be talking about

> a Turkish folk tradition in Arabo-Islamic guise that is closely associated with a Christianized Greek tradition in which St. George plays the same role as Hïzïr-Ilyas (with St. Demetrios playing the symmetrical role). The dragon slain by the Hellenic saint . . . is probably the dragon of winter. As for St. Demetrios, whose name derives from Demeter [. . .] he probably appears here because this is the time of year when the autumn's seeds are entrusted to the earth. (Bazin 1972:721)

That the feasts of St. George and St. Dimitrios are important dates in the calendar is well documented in the ethnographic archival material on the Greeks of Asia Minor. In some places, St. George seems to be the local saint par excellence as he has two churches: a parish church inside the village and a chapel outside it, or even in the mountains. In such cases, St. George's Day was celebrated in the countryside in spring and in the village church in the autumn, and the corresponding months were known as Agiorghita.[25] The Greek Orthodox calendar also follows this chronology: the martyrdom of the saint is commemorated on 23 April, and the translation of his relics and the building of his first church on 3 November.[26]

From Myth to History

It has been emphasized that St. George is in many respects similar to the other mythological slayers of dragons and monsters. According to one version of his life, he was the son of a pagan father and was born in either Armenia or Persia. As he traveled through Cappadocia, he met a pious Christian woman and married her. There are analogies between this legend and the novel of Alexander and also the poetic cycle of Digenis Akritis, the hero of the marches of the Byzantine Empire. The theme of the *digenis* (born of two races) is very common in the legends of the Sassanid and Shiite era in Persia. The theme of the *digenis* also appears, with some variations, in the Arabic novels of Antar and Delhemma, the Turkish novel by Sayyid Battal, and Omar al-Neman's story in the *Arabian Nights*. Influenced by ancient Persian stories and legends about Alexander, the myth of the hero who is descended from two races is repeated and embellished with many hagiographic elements in the story of the Thirteenth Imam, who was born in 868. According to legend, Hasan Askarî married the granddaughter of the emperor of Byzantium, who was descended from "the apostles and Christ; their child was the Thirteenth Imam, who is the great prophet of the Shiite religion. The theme of the hero of mixed origins is common in the hagiographic literature and legends of the peoples of the medieval Middle East, including the Shiites" (Anagnostakis and Balta 1994).

We find the same motif in the legend of Sheikh Beddredin, the founder of the "Semavite" order in Andrianopolis (Edirne) in western Thrace (Zegginis 2001). The same mythological motif, which is even more similar to the legend of St. George, is associated with the figure of Sari Saltik in Albania. He was the founder of the local order of Bektashis, and large crowds of pilgrims still visit his cave on 6 May (St. George's Day). Sari Saltik is said to have been a holy man who saved the life of the daughter of a (Christian) prince and caused water to gush forth for the people of the region by killing the dragon that was terrorizing them (Clayer 1996). Another story belonging to the same cycle of legends appears in the Greek folk song about St. George.[27] The saint is described as the protector of a mixed couple (the bride was abducted), who "blesses" the only form of exogamy possible in the Ottoman world: marriage between a Muslim man and a Christian woman.

This brings us to the heart of the ambiguity surrounding the saint: whom does he protect? Or rather, what does he protect? He seems to protect neither a group insofar as it is an exclusive religious group, nor an ethnoreligious identity. He appears associated with syncretism, hybridity, and nonexclusion, with a life lived in the margins of institutions and official power. Above all, he is the protector of the local community, of all the inhabitants of a given territory; one can see a cultural continuity between him and the great Byzantine saints, also associated with local cults that made them famous, and therefore powerful (Mango 1980; Mayeur-Jaouen 2005).

Syncretism as Heritage

As we have seen, representations of a multicultural identity are associated in Turkey both with urban culture and modernity and also the heritage of the Ottoman Empire. In this context, Prinkipo's St. George might be described as a "deterritorialized" saint: the shrine gradually lost its privileged ties with its community of origin, but at the same time became part of the heritage of old Istanbul. The shared practices, or what remains of them, add substance to a contemporary story about the Ottoman past. It is the story of a multicultural society and a polyglot elite living in a cosmopolitan city. The three ritual temporalities that characterize the different lived experiences of the diverse groups of worshipers who visit the monastery of St. George symbolize modern Istanbul, which, like any megalopolis, offers an alternative to the national model of a homogeneous society. Greek and Turkish historical narratives intersect here but do not merge into one. The Greek narrative has to do with a nation-state that retains an ambiguous memory of its past as a minority religious community within the empire, and the Turkish narrative with a nation-state that increasingly looks to its imperial past as it searches for its identity.

I have here maintained that the saint's nonexclusive nature is the corollary of his local identity. This is because the two basic principles of social organization—kinship and territory—retained a relative autonomy in Ottoman society, but not in post-Ottoman nation-states that are organized around a homogeneous conception of their respective population. The tradition of hybridity and syncretism is based upon a basic opposition that, in the local context, tends to protect society from institutional interference. In that sense, the heritage of syncretism contradicts the national project that advocates ethnic, cultural, and religious homogeneity, maladapted to a narrative about the "tolerant" past of a multicultural society.

We begin here to see the outline of the vast symbolic structure that underlies the popularity of St. George as well as the shared religious practices centered on his shrines. St. George is a figure related to the legends associated with the organization of time and human labor.[28] A closer look at the historical and symbolic context of the extraordinary pilgrimage to St. George's church on Prinkipo prompts us to reexamine notions such as religious "tolerance" or "sharing" within specific situations, to be studied with the tools of ethnography and ethnohistory. This approach reveals the important role played by the notion of a local community in the construction of individual identities, the importance of mixed marriages, both real and legendary, even though they were "banned," the porosity of frontiers, and the importance of frontiers in the collective imagination. The rich symbolism of St. George flourishes in the margins of communities that are on the move; by protecting mixed marriages, the saint guarantees the symbolic survival of the local community (thanks to both mixed marriages and conversions). This local and truly chthonian spirit (specific to the earth and its [sub]soil) also intervenes in the life of the community: it establishes the agricultural calendar by helping people in their day-to-day lives and gives them succor in times of misfortune (by curing ill-nesses, or even alienation). The saint is invoked insofar as he is an all-powerful local spirit, and as part of an "ordinary" thaumaturgic quest that is at once serious and lighthearted.[29] The places inhabited by this supernatural being are sacred and inviolable, and, as we have seen, many legends refer to his ability to punish those who do not respect his dwelling or *oikos,* by bringing about accident, illness, or even death (Magdalino 1989; de Rapper in this volume). As we have also seen, the saint is polyvalent: he crosses the frontiers between religions when his churches are turned into *tekke* and, sometimes, back into churches; he is "confused" with other figures in Eastern Christianity, such as St. Dimitrios, both in legendary representations and in the calendar—all this adds to his universal character and great popularity.

St. George's shrines in the Balkans and Anatolia, which draw pilgrims from all confessions, structure the local culture's world and symbolic space-time. As we have seen, these shared sacred spaces are often found "in the wilds" and outside institutional society. They are found outside the territories of ethnore-ligious communities, in a no-man's-land that is open to all, and that allowed syncretic practices to flourish in the post-Ottoman world,[30] just as they did elsewhere.[31] While St. George, whose legend is part of a symbolic ensemble that is shared by all the peoples of the ancient East (Delehay 1909), is at home everywhere, he is still a unique figure. And his irreducible singularity is the fact that, like some permanent outsider, he is at home in frontier spaces, in the interstices. Ultimately, he represents the unity of the local community of *omo-emi* (those who share the same blood), and that unity transcends the loyalties of those religious groups that have become separate communities.

Notes

The epigraph is from Politis (1978 [1914]), *Eklogai,* "Acritic Songs," no. 72.

1. Earlier versions of this chapter were presented to the European network REMSH's conference on Networks, Exchanges, and Conflicts in the Mediterranean Area (Athens, 26–28 May 2005), to the Max Planck Institute's workshop on Eastern

Christianities in Anthropological Perspective (Halle, 23–25 September 2005), and to a workshop on shared shrines organized by the Laboratoire d'Ethnologie within the REMSH network (Nanterre, March 2006). My warmest thanks go to all those who took part for their comments and suggestions, and especially to Dionigi Albera, Jean-Pierre and Marlène Albert, Michèle Baussant, Chris Hann, Roger Just, Antoinette Molinié, and Anna Poujeau.

2. The first anthropological study of Anatolian Greeks was carried out by Renée Hirschon in 1960–1970 in a refugee district of Piraeus, near Athens (Hirschon 1989).

3. Turner's theories have recently been criticized by the many anthropologists who have been unable to confirm his theses about the liminal state or the establishment of the anti-structure (*communitas*) in the many cases of pilgrimage they have observed all over the world. Cf. Morinis (1992), who refers to his studies of Bengal, and to the work of Eickelman in Morocco, of Pruess in Thailand, of Messerschmidt and Qharma in Nepal, of van der Veer in India, of Sallnow in Peru, and of Pfaffenburg in Sri Lanka. Dubisch (1995), who has worked in Greece, is another critic who has doubts about the pertinence of the concept of *communitas*. All insist that pilgrimage is an individual affair, that it is experienced as such, and that there is no element of *communitas* in the process. In their critical introduction to theories of pilgrimage, Eade and Sallnow (1991) emphasize the anti-Durkheimian nature of Turner's theory; by placing the emphasis on the anti-structural nature of pilgrimage, they call into question the notion that its function is to reinforce social cohesion. Eade and Sallnow also stress that the phenomenon of pilgrimage is not uniform, which is why any theoretical discourse about "pilgrimage" will inevitably be incomplete: "If we can no longer take for granted the meaning of a pilgrimage for its participants, one can no longer take for granted a uniform definition of the phenomenon of 'pilgrimage' either" (1991:3). Turner himself actually thought that pilgrimages are essentially intraconfessional activities, and paid almost no attention to interconfessional pilgrimages: "With rare and interesting exceptions, the pilgrims of different religions do not visit one another's shrines, and certainly do not find salvation *extra ecclesia*" (Turner and Turner 1978:9).

4. Hasluck describes Bektashi cultural activity at these shared shrines as a "superimposition" of religions. In his view, Bektashism spread through the local populations in nonviolent ways: "Either by process analogous to that known to the ancient world as the 'reception' of the new god by the old, or simply by the identification of the two personalities. The 'ambiguous' sanctuary, claimed and frequented by both religions, seems to represent a distinct stage of development—the period of equipoise, as it were—in the transition both from Christianity to Bektashism and, in the rare cases where political and other circumstances are favourable, from Bektashism to Christianity" (Hasluck 1929:564).

5. I prefer to use the archaic "Prinkipo" rather than the more common "Büyükada" ("large island" in Turkish) when referring to the island because it is more evocative of its multicultural past. The term is part of the local vocabulary, and is understood by old Stamboulites of all confessions. In Greek, the grammatically correct term is Prinkipos, and for the islands as a whole, Prinkiponisa (Princes' Islands). The reference is to the Byzantine princes (and subsequently the sons of the sultans) who used to live there. In modern Turkish, the islands are generally referred to as "Adalar" (islands), and tourist guides use both terms. See, for example, http://www

.guideofistanbul.net/en/adalar/htlm; *Istanbul,* Guide bleu (Paris: Hachette, 2002); *Istanbul* (Paris: Guide Gallimard, 2002).

6. On Greek Orthodox *millet* see Anagnostopoulou 1997.

7. CEAM, OD, 56/1959, Rapport de mission Tsalikoglu, 79. The archives in the Centre d'Etudes d'Asie Mineure (CEAM) were collected after the exchange of populations between Greece and Turkey that followed the war between the two countries in 1919–1922, and that ended with the defeat of the Greek army. Both nation-states then pursued a policy of homogenization within their frontiers: some were "repatriated," and others were "expelled." One million two hundred thousand "Greeks," or members of the Ottoman Empire's Greek Orthodox minority, were repatriated to Greece, while 350,000 Muslims were sent to Anatolia. The departure of the Greeks marked the end of a process that began with the Armenian genocide of 1915. In 1913, one in five inhabitants of what is now Turkey was Greek; by the end of 1923, the proportion was no more than one in forty (Keyder 2002:43). The historical context was that of the end of the Ottoman Empire and the beginning of the formation of the modern Turkish nation-state. Collecting the ethnographic data that make up CEAM's archive was a scientific project carried out using the ethnographic methods of the day (1940–1970). The project was initiated by Melpo Merlier, an ethnomusicologist married to Octave Merlier, director of the Institut français d'Athènes.

8. The passports of the Rum who were "exchanged" were stamped in French: *Il ne peut retourner* (cannot return). The refugees from Anatolia reached Greece in two waves. The first wave followed the fighting between the Greek and Turkish armies. It involved coastal populations who left in a hurry and often in tragic circumstances, including those who were evacuated after the burning of Smyrna in 1922. The second, and larger, wave involved populations from the interior, who left in a more organized fashion in 1924. The Cappadocian populations mentioned in Tsalikoglu's report (see below) were part of the second wave (Anagnostakis and Balta 2004).

9. Tsalikoglu went to Turkey in 1959 on behalf of the Centre for Asia Minor Studies of Athens, where he worked as a researcher. His text refers to a village in Cappadocia. The setup he describes for the beginning of the twentieth century is comparable with the Cretan tradition in which the head of the family's religious affiliation with the "dominant religion" (the community of "Latin" Catholics during the Venetian period, and the Muslim community after the island's conquest) did not lead to the conversion of the rest of the family. According to Greene (2000:108), the Cretan system functioned because "public religion" (Catholic Christianity, Islam) transmitted through the agnatic line coexisted alongside a "private religion" transmitted by the women of the family. In this society, people who found themselves astride the two communities stood a better chance of success (Greene 2000:204). Having said that, the documents on which historians work (contemporary chronicles, local archives) tell us nothing about the cases that are of most interest to us for our present purpose. What about festive meals? Who shares which meal, and with whom? Which members of the family are invited to celebrate the head of the family's name day when the family is bireligious? But they certainly suggest that Christians and Muslims were more likely to "share"—in the broadest sense—at religious feasts (Greene 2000:106–108).

10. The term "Rum" (Turkish for "Roman") refers to Turkey's Greek Orthodox Christians, or the Christian heir to the Byzantine Empire (the Eastern Roman

Empire). They refer to themselves as Romii, which derives from Romaios ("Romans" in Greek).

11. "Syncretism" is used here to describe practices that bring together elements from several religious traditions. On the etymology and various meanings of the word see Stewart and Shaw 1994.

12. Prinkipo/Büyükada is the largest of a string of islands to the southeast of Istanbul. The others are Heybeliada (Chalki), Burgazada (Antigôni), and Kinaliada (Prôti).

13. Interview recorded on Prinkipo, 28 February 1997.

14. *Tama* (*tamata* is the plural) means both a wish or the request the pilgrim makes of the saint, and the ex-voto representing it is usually placed on the icon in the church.

15. This is one of St. George's specialties. See Hasluck, who also mentions practices of incubation in a quest for a cure for mental illness in the church of St. George in Cairo (Hasluck 1929:293, 693). See also Yannakopoulos 1995 on Anatolia (Erenköy), Bowman in the present volume, and Voile 2004:152, 255.

16. On forms of intercession in the practices of Christian pilgrims, see Brown 1981; Chélini and Branthomme 1982; and Maraval 2004.

17. The little strips of cloth that are tied to the trees correspond to a ritual gesture performed elsewhere in the Greco-Anatolian world. A piece of cloth is cut from the clothes of the person who is "carrying the illness" and hung on the saint's tree. The saint then keeps the illness away from the patient. For a detailed description of these gestures in the Black Sea region in the early twentieth century, see CEAM, PO 965. The threads are used in similar ways: the body of the patient is measured, and the thread is tied to a tree. This keeps the illness far away from its victim.

18. See the recent studies collected in Shankland 2004.

19. The choice of this region was dictated by two factors: the quality and quantity of the "village files" in CEAM's archives, and the existence of a recent bibliography on churches dedicated to St. George. This made it easier to cross-check the data in the archive, which had yet to be digitized. For a recent ethnographic study of the area, see Beller-Hann and Hann 2001.

20. The "punitive" nature of St. George's miracles and apparitions is also mentioned in several of the stories told by Egypt's Copts (Voile 2004:141–149).

21. For a detailed description of the sacrifices made to St. George in western Thrace, see Saranti-Stamouli 1931. Two animals are offered to the saint, and both are blessed by the priest. One is sacrificed and served up during the shared meal that is served after Mass; the other is given as a prize to the winner of the Turkish wrestling matches that follow the meal. All the young men in the village, both "Greek" and "Turkish," take part.

22. Centre for Asia Minor Studies, Oral Tradition Archives (CEAM, PO 965). Many documents in the archives mention that the Turks call St. George Hitirelles, Hidirelias, or similar names, and venerate him as a major and "powerful" saint. Cf. Ormonos in Pafra, PO 178; Dikencik, PO 177; Aksag, PO 16; Güluk, PO 734; Agrid, PO 757; Saraicuk, PO 41; Kayasar, PO 57; Kavelar, PO 133; Oinoi, PO 105. See also the historical and ethnographic studies of western Thrace by Saranti-Stamouli (1931) and Yannakopoulos (1995).

23. "That Hidrellez's day coincides with St. George's, that *Kasim*'s day coincides with St. Demetrios's, and that the popular festivities in which the Muslims and Christians of the Ottoman Empire (and then Turkey) coincide with St. George-Hidrellez is in itself enough to indicate that the Ottomans, whose civilization tended to be syncretic, simply took over, in their way, an earlier (Christian and probably pre-Christian) local tradition and partly Islamized it (with prophets Hïzïr and Ilyas occurring on St. George's day" (Bazin 1972:727).

24. According to Bazin, it is because of the almost perfect homonymy with the Turkish *il(k)-yaz* (early spring) that the prophet is associated with springtime, as there is no Koranic evidence to suggest that he is "the herald of summer." Bazin does not mention the Greek *hidra* and *nea hidra* (young shoots of wheat), nor does he mention the ancient Christian tradition of taking these to church to be blessed, probably at about the same time of year.

25. See Akoglou (1939:261–263); the files in CEAM's archives in Sürmeli in Pafra, CEAM, PO 186; Akdagaden and CEAM, PO 724; Adamantidis's study of Kotyora (1934), and Efpraxiadis's study of Prokopi in Cappadocia (1988). On the importance of these dates for the agricultural calendar, see also Yannakopoulos (1995) and Saranti-Stamouli (1931) on the Thrace region.

26. The reference is to the translation of the saint's relics, and the founding of the first church in Lydda.

27. Folklorists class the song as one of the frontier songs of medieval Greek literature (Politis 1978 [1914]). A distant echo of the song can be heard in the story told by a Greek refugee from the Black Sea: the Turks called him "mad [*deli*] St. George" and regarded him as their son-in-law.

28. It is not the intention of this study to take in the Christian West, but one parallel example could be mentioned. The "pagan" cult of the English Mummers, which is also bound up with the agricultural calendar, makes direct reference to the legend and imagery of St. George.

29. The labels on the ex-votos sold at the bottom of the hill the pilgrims climb on the saint's day in Istanbul are eloquent testimony to the nature of the quest. They pray for everything: for good luck (*sans*), health (*saglik*), work (*is*), a lover (*sevgili*), a good match (*kismet icin*), marriage (*evililik*), a house (*ev*), a baby (*bebek*), money (*para*), a good education (*okul*).

30. Sabbatucci (2008) dates the shift of meaning that allows the word "syncretic" (from the Greek *sygkretismos,* the association or federation of the Cretans) to go from meaning "agreement" or "concord" to meaning "mixture," as though it derived from the verb *sygkerannymi* (to mix), to the Reformation. Erasmus reportedly uses the word when he calls upon the humanists to form a confederation, as the Cretans did, in the face of Catholic reaction. He notes that the term became pejorative "because of the rigorism of both sides, and came to mean confusion or hybridity."

31. As we saw earlier, other shrines "in the wilds" in the Balkans still attract pluriconfessional crowds today, just as they did in the past.

SEVEN

A Jewish-Muslim Shrine in North Morocco: Echoes of an Ambiguous Past

HENK DRIESSEN

The first time I became aware of holy men and sacred sites shared by Jews and Muslims in North Africa was in 1984 when I was doing ethnographic field-work and archival research in the Spanish enclave of Melilla and its Moroccan surroundings. Several informants told me about a cult site in the vicinity of Nador, the major Moroccan town of the eastern Rif, where a Jewish holy man was, at least in the past, venerated not only by Jews but also by Muslims, predominantly Rif Berbers who lived in the Nador area. And, although at that time I had several other topics at hand—my main interest being processes of confrontation and accommodation among Christians, Muslims, Jews, and Hindus—in which religious identifications played a major role, in the spring of 1984 I visited the cult site and talked with the Muslim caretaker (*mqaddim*), the only person who was around at that time. Later during my fieldwork I managed to gather further oral information from Jewish as well as Muslim and Christian sources, mainly in Melilla. Unfortunately, I was never able to attend a pilgrimage to this shrine.

Muslims call the rite of visiting the shrine of a local saint *ziyara*. They make vows and leave some material object there, either money or a sacrificial animal, in exchange for the protection of the saint and his spiritual power. The Jewish counterpart called *hillula* is almost identical, including prayers, vows, offerings, and the sharing of a collective meal. Not having been present at the rites at the shrine is of course a serious handicap for an ethnographer. It was only much later that I gave the information collected in 1984 second thoughts.

What follows is a contextual reconstruction and reconsideration of what I found out about this shrine and its cult at the time of my research. With the benefit of hindsight, I will add some comparative thoughts.

Shared Local Shrines and Cults in Morocco

In precolonial and colonial Morocco the sharing of the same shrine by Jews and Muslims, mainly Berbers, and some degree of mixed or overlapping ritual activity were rather widespread. The French colonial ethnographer Voinot (1948) made an inventory of what he called "double" shrines, venerated by both Jews and Muslims. He collected approximately one hundred cases, with the highest density found in the Middle and High Atlas. For the northern part of the country, which was a Spanish Protectorate from 1912 to 1956, Voinot mentioned eleven cases. One of them, named after the Jewish saint Rabbi Saadia Datsi, is the object of this paper. His tomb is located in the area of the Spanish enclave Melilla, in the eastern foothills of the Rif mountains, which is Berber country par excellence. It is located near a hamlet in the territory of the Imazujen, who belonged to the tribal confederation of the Iqar'iyen.

Voinot's main preoccupation was classifying the collected cases. He distinguished three main categories: (1) saints claimed by Muslims and Jews alike; (2) Muslim saints worshiped by Jews; (3) Jewish saints venerated by Muslims. The instance of Rabbi Saadia fits into the third category, the largest one, which accounts for more than half of all cases. A second classificatory principle was historical origin of the saints, again with three, rather vague, categories: very ancient, old, and modern. Voinot ranked Saadia's cult as "modern," that is, its origin dates back four to five centuries. A third criterion of classification consisted of striking natural elements of the cult site: the presence of wells, rocks, caves, mountain tops, cliffs, extraordinary trees, or groups of trees. Rabbi Saadia's shrine is located not far from a cliff and marked by a huge rock and a carob tree. In accordance with the prejudices of his time, Voinot took for granted that the cult of saints was "a practice of superstitious devotion" and a "pagan survival." There is no attempt at all to contextualize the "double cult" or to consider it from a sociological perspective.

The Oral Legend of Rabbi Saadia

The legend of Rabbi Saadia belongs to the lore of the Jews of Melilla whose forebears constituted the small Jewish communities of the eastern Rif (Driessen 1992:80–82). The starting historical point of reference is the 1490s, when Jews were expelled from the Iberian Peninsula, many crossing the Mediterranean to settle in Morocco, mostly in towns. The legend narrates how a learned and pious rabbi, Saadia ed-Dati (spelled slightly differently as Datsi in Voinot's book), together with six other rabbis and their families, fled from Spain by boat. They were shipwrecked in sight of the Rifian coast but managed to get ashore. Roaming the countryside in search of a place to settle, they stopped at a Berber hamlet called Farkat, in the vicinity of present-day Nador. Rabbi Saadia went to the Jews of nearby Melilla (a few years before it was occupied by Spanish troops in 1497) to offer his spiritual services. They declined "because of internal strife." He returned to Farkat, where he and the other rabbis became the victims of an epidemic disease. After having taken a ritual bath, Rabbi Saadia wrapped himself in a funeral shroud and lay down in his tomb. He told the Berber and Jewish villagers that there would soon be a tempest and that a huge rock would cover his tomb as soon as he passed away. This happened during one of the nocturnal vigils of the villagers. Those present could not explain how the mysterious rock had fallen on the rabbi's tomb. Some of them claimed that it had been sent from heaven. The rabbi has been venerated as a holy man ever since and became the patron saint of the Jews of the eastern Rif and, since their migration to the Spanish enclave from the 1860s onward, of the Melilla Jews as well. Berber villagers also considered the rabbi a oftlineholy man, visited his shrine to pray, and asked for his help.

From a comparative point of view there are several elements in this legend that are similar to the motifs in other saint stories collected around the Mediterranean as well as in other parts of the world: forced migration as a kind of proto-pilgrimage with ordeals of all sorts (shipwreck and rejection by co-believers), wandering about before settling down, disease, anticipated and self-controlled death, a miracle as proof of the saint's closeness to God. Another common phenomenon is that there are minor variations in the legend. In the version written down by Voinot (1948:53–54) the rabbi, being persecuted in Castile, crossed the Mediterranean on a plank. There is no mention of companions at all. The Rif Berbers offered him their hospitality and a house. He refused and instead lived as a hermit on the slope of a nearby mountain. After he died, he buried himself without any help from his followers. After he finished his burial, a big stone came down to cover his tomb.

Another common characteristic of such oral legends and the pilgrimages of which they are a kind of charter is that they are being contested (cf. Coleman 2001). Voinot did not write of conflicting views at all. He suggested that all Jews had great faith in Rabbi Saadia and that he healed illnesses. The many pilgrims came, often from distant places, to put themselves under his protection. They kneeled in front of the rock, kissed it, lighted candles, read parts of the Talmud, and made gifts to the *mqaddim*. Muslim pilgrims mainly came to the shrine because of the rabbi's reputation to heal fever (including that of animals). They tied pieces of cloth to the branches of the carob tree. The Muslim *mqaddim* who acts as the servant ("slave") of the rabbi, a hereditary office that belongs to his lineage since the rabbi's miraculous death, is also the owner of the plot on which the shrine is located.

Several Jews of Melilla rejected the legend as a product of superstition on the part of their illiterate rural brothers in faith. As one of them told me: "Some of those fanatical Berber Jews [*sic*] believe that the rock was sent by God. I believe it must have rolled down from the nearby mountain during an earth-tremor." The same man, however, did not question other details in the legend. Some elderly Rifian Berbers stated that they also considered the shrine of Rabbi Saadia, whom they, however, called Sidi Yusef, after a Muslim saint, to be a sacred place. At the beginning of the twentieth century both Muslims and Jews were visiting the shrine, according to a pre-Protectorate source (Fernández de Castro y Pedrera 1911:16). For generations the shrine has been guarded by members of one Rifian lineage, who are paid for their services by the Melilla Jews. The Melilla Jews also financed the construction of a road that leads up to the shrine.

Until the 1950s Rabbi Saadia was popular among the working-class Jews of Melilla and Nador. His fame for healing barrenness also attracted Jewish women from the Oran in Algeria. Each year at the beginning of May, Jews from Melilla and the Eastern Rif gathered at his shrine to celebrate the anniversary of the rabbi's death (*hillula*). They camped nearby with relatives and friends, reciting prayers, eating commemorative meals, and celebrating the rabbi's supernatural powers. However, since the Arab-Israeli war of 1967, the Moroccan government has suppressed collective pilgrimages from Melilla. This seems to have served only to accelerate the decline of the cult, which was already going through a crisis because of large-scale Jewish emigration to Israel, Spain, France, and Latin America. While the rabbi's cult had already largely disappeared in the mid-1980s, the legend remains alive and continues to be transmitted to younger generations. It establishes a link between the Jews of the Rif and the Jewish civilization of Spain. It also validates the claim of Jews of rural origin to membership in a holy lineage founded by the rabbi through divine intervention. Finally, both the legend and cult point to the coexistence and interdependence of Jews and Berbers, and to basic similarities in their beliefs and practices.

Historical Context of the Cult Shrine

The small scattered communities of Jews lived in an area highly fragmented, in an ecological as well as a sociopolitical regard, among small groups of sedentary Berber-speaking peasants and herdsmen, who were generally poor and illiterate.[1] The fewer than one thousand rural Jews were petty artisans involved in the making of packsaddles and harnesses, silver and gold smithing, metal working, tailoring, shoemaking, ambulant trade, and magic. Since feuding was endemic in the Rif and Jews were excluded from the Rifian system of honor, they needed the protection of powerful tribal leaders. Jews found themselves at the very bottom of Berber society. They were subjected to all kinds of restrictions: for example, they had a special dress code; were forbidden to own land, possess arms, or ride horses; and were obliged to remove their footwear when passing a mosque. In other words, they were expected to show humility in public. Yet, in spite of these measures they enjoyed some freedom to move in and between tribal areas, and they played a pivotal role in trading and smuggling networks.

Jews suffered increasingly from political instability in the region, partly caused by pressures on the Rif from the main imperial powers of Europe. From the 1860s onward, Rifian Jews began to move to and settle down in Melilla, where they sought Spanish protection. To be sure, there was also discrimination and harassment of Jews by Catholic inhabitants, especially during the Holy Week processions. Waves of emigration of rural and urban Jews to mainland Spain, France, Israel, and Latin America occurred in 1945–1946 (a year of hunger in the Rif), 1948 (the foundation of the Israeli state), 1956 (independence of Morocco), and 1967 (the Six Day War). Today, there are no more Jews living in the eastern Rif, although there still is a vital Jewish community of approximately 1,100 members in Melilla.

In pre-Protectorate Morocco, the rural Jews of the Rif were in almost all respects inferior to the Berber tribesmen among whom they lived. Their occupations were generally considered infamous by, yet indispensable for, Berber society, the main reason why they were offered patronage by tribal leaders. Moreover, Jews were also "people of the Book" and in possession of ritual and magical power. To phrase their situation in sociological terms: in spite of their lowly status and meager power resources, the subordinate Jews and dominant Muslims were caught in webs of mutual dependence in Berber society. It does not come as a surprise then that the local versions of Judaism and Islam (and Catholicism for that matter, Driessen 2009)—the core of which has been and still is the veneration of holy men at shrines rooted in the landscape—reveal more similarities than differences. The commonalities include notions of sacredness; sacred topographies, or what William Christian (1989a:44) aptly called "territories of grace"; similarly structured relationships between believers and saints in terms of power and hierarchy, transaction, mediation, and reciprocity; relations in the religious domain as models of and for those in the political and kinship domains; concepts and practices of gender; and endemic conditions of insecurity for Jews and Muslims alike.

At the same time, it is also clear that there were and are contestations among and between the believers of the three religions of the Book. There is a narcissism of minor differences (cf. Blok 2001)—that is, claims about locality and authenticity—and there are small differences in belief and ritual practice. In the case of Rabbi Saadia it seems that Jews and Muslims were worshiping separately at the same shrine at least during collective pilgrimages.

Conclusion

As we all know from our own research practices, the mission of mapping and understanding cultural diversity is both a strength and a weakness of anthropology. Saint worship cum pilgrimage is a matter in point. It is an almost universal phenomenon, as is the ongoing attachment of people to specific localities as a basic source of identity, in spite of all recent rhetoric about deterritorialization, globalization, and heterotopia. At the same time, there are many different kinds of shrines, pilgrimages, beliefs, rituals, and organizational grids. How then to compare and map the differences as well as similarities? Here we may refer to an interdisciplinary research project sponsored by the Dutch Foundation for Scientific Research called "The Future of the Religious Past," which covers a broad gamut of religious topics, pilgrimage included.[2] The overall project defined four comparative domains or foci. First, *words* or narratives: discourses, key notions, sayings, and ritual formulae, oral and written. Second, *objects:* the material infrastructure of religion and the topography of divine space. Third, *gestures:* religious performances, rites, repertoires of postures, glances, and other bodily manipulations and dramatic presentations of ritual and symbolic signs. Last but not least, *powers:* forms of justification, transmission of religious authority, and the media, old and new. Let me, by way of a concluding remark, add as a fifth focus the different ways in which these overlapping domains are interrelated. This is indeed the most difficult part of comparative projects.

Notes

1. Derived from Driessen 1992, in particular the sources referred to in chapter 5 of that book.

2. See the Nijmegen subproject, "The Power of Pilgrimage: A Comparative Study," which is embedded in the "Future of the Religious Past" program of the Netherlands Organization for Scientific Research (Hermkens, Jansen, and Notermans 2009).

EIGHT

What Do Egypt's Copts and Muslims Share? The Issue of Shrines

CATHERINE MAYEUR-JAOUEN

A Tense Interconfessional Situation

Egypt is now one of the Middle Eastern countries where the interconfessional situation is most tense, and where the discourse on the other (Christian or Muslim) is most aggressive. With a few very rare exceptions, no Muslim will enter a church and no Christian will enter a mosque. Contemporary developments have seen an Egypt that was once multiconfessional become a biconfessional country divided between Copts (now less than 6% of the population[1]) and Muslims (the rest of the population). Copts are therefore very much in the minority, and have been for a long time, as Egypt appears to have become predominantly Muslim as early as the eleventh century, and increasingly so in the fourteenth and fifteen centuries (Mouton 2003). This phenomenon also explains why behaviors toward the religion of the other differ so greatly. For a Muslim, mixing with Copts, taking part in their festivals, or even, in extreme cases, attending their churches poses little threat. For Copts, the fear of conversion is a major obstacle to having any contact with the Muslim religion and means that entering a mosque is out of the question.

Since the 1970s, there has been a growing tendency for Copts to regard Muslims as a threatening other. Establishing close ties with Muslims is unthinkable. In some Sunday schools, Coptic children are taught not to make friends with Muslims; others take the precaution of never mentioning the existence of a different religion. It is increasingly rare for Copts and Muslims to watch the same television channels, and the number of militant Internet sites, many of them with links to the English-speaking Coptic diaspora, has increased. Satellite channels beamed mainly at Eastern Christians in Lebanon have recently begun to broadcast; Egyptian Copts can also receive them, and watch them when they can. The establishment of specifically Coptic channels such as Coptsat and especially the Cairo-based Aghapy in 2005 was a response to the recent increase in the number of stridently Islamist Egyptian and Arab Muslim channels. Since 2006, Coptic households in the villages of Upper Egypt have been able to listen to the Coptic monk Abûnâ Zakariyya: excommunicated by the patriarchate several years ago and officially stripped of his title, Abûnâ Zakariyya speaks on al-Hayat TV Christian Channel, from Cyprus, at eleven each evening; a lot of Copts watch him with both enthusiasm and satisfaction. With a Tafsîr and a collection of hadiths at hand, in lengthy broadcasts on his Internet site he tries to prove, point by point, that the Koran is inane. His Christian apologetics are at once defensive and aggressive.

The dominant Muslim attitude is in fact one of indifference. When they do think about Copts, Muslims do so with a mixture of respect (they are regarded as competent professionals, good doctors, and good accountants), condescension, and sometimes contempt. Copts are sometimes seen as rivals, and there is a vague feeling—which is not always expressed but which is strong among the less-educated strata of the population—that non-Muslims are destined to burn in the fires of hell and that their inferior status is basically part of the natural order of things. Some Sufis, of course, insist that all the sons of Adam are brothers, and it is becoming more common for open-minded intellectuals to give occasional talks to Coptic audiences. Copts also prove to be very useful in times of crisis when there is a need for calls for national unity. The majority of Muslims, however, simply know nothing about Copts; given that there are almost no Copts in the Delta, that is quite understandable. Even in the urban melting pot of Greater Cairo, which is home to one-third of the Coptic population, there is not much more social interaction. While the two groups used to interact in traditional neighborhoods such as Shubra, now they obviously do so less, thanks to the growing anonymity that results from the increased availability of public transport and the rise in the number of private cars. People now travel longer distances to and from work and lose their roots as they move into neighborhoods that have no past or to new towns. Marriages and deaths are now virtually the only occasions on which Coptic colleagues or neighbors come to give their Muslim neighbors their congratulations or offer their condolences (and vice versa). There has been a marked decline in the traditional exchanges of greeting between neighbors or acquaintances that once took place on the main feast days of both religions. In 2008, an Egyptian fatwa officially condemned the common practice of wishing Christians a "Happy Easter" because Islam does not recognize the resurrection of Christ. Ramadan is still the greatest feast of the year, and some Copts do join in the nightly celebrations, but it is also the period when their fear of tensions with Muslims is at its greatest. They fear that the fasting Muslims might try to demonstrate their militant piety in physical ways.

In Upper Egypt, where the percentage of Copts is higher (they are in the majority in some villages and make up almost one-third of the population in some towns), Copts know what Muslims are, and Muslims know what Copts are. They are often on good terms with their neighbors and exchange greetings on feast days. They work together on the land, and some fine examples of human fraternity can be observed among people working on shared tasks such as irrigation or harvesting. But it is also in Upper Egypt, a region famed for its vendettas and poverty, that we encounter the most violent situations: the forced conversion of a lonely Copt doing his military service, the occasional mysterious lynching that goes unpunished, the forced marriage of Coptic girls to Muslim men, and especially the riots that break out when a church is built. Everyone will say that things vary from one village to the next. The village of Al-Ghanâyim near Assiut is notorious for drug-dealing; here, Muslim children throw stones at the gate of Catholic Egyptian church schools on the eve of Ramadan. A few kilometers away in the village of Gotna, community relations are cordial. Copts and Muslims exchange greetings on their respective feast days, and sit side by side on the village council. Things can, however, quickly turn very nasty, and everyone is well aware of it. And a great deal depends on the attitude taken by the local police and administration toward the sudden and fierce outbreaks of violence that Egypt has experienced in recent years.

For a good fifteen years, the architectural landscape has been the scene of exaggerated competition between Copts and Muslims as they try to occupy visual and sonic space all over the country, in both towns and villages. Church towers are becoming higher and minarets are becoming higher. Religious institutions have developed an obsession with building, and most of the charitable funds sent from Europe and America to help the Copts have been channeled into the construction industry. As the walls grow higher, both religions' image of what the other is—as a citizen, human being, and believer—becomes more and more abstract. Muslims know little about what it means to be a Christian, and Christians know little about what it means to be a Muslim: as a rule, that is not a possible topic of conversation. Once Muslims have uttered a few pleasantries about how Islam regards Jesus as a prophet in the same way that Moses is a prophet ("Moses is your brother, Jesus is your brother, oh Mohammed" [*Mûsâ Akhûk, yâ Muhammadu, 'Isâ akhûk, yâ Muhammadu*] sing the Sufi cantors), about how all human beings are the sons of Adam and about how the peoples of the Book (who are regarded by others as pagans or *kuffâr*) are guaranteed protection, both parties keep their own counsel. Copts worry that one of their number might be converted or that one of their women might be married to a Muslim, while Muslims enjoy the tranquil self-assurance that is born of their numeric and intrinsic superiority.

Copts are almost invisible in the higher levels of government and in the mass media. There are no longer any Christians among the political elites, nor do we find Christians on football teams, in the popular soap operas on television, or in starring roles in films. It is true, it might be argued, that their diminished demographic presence (6% of the population) does nothing to encourage better representation. The fact that there were two Coptic characters in the film *L'Immeuble Yaqoubian* [The Yacoubian Building], which was released in the autumn of 2006 (they were portrayed in a very unfavorable light) was hailed for its unprecedented daring by some Copts—especially as the film was a violent denunciation of the Pharisaism of God-fearing Islamic business circles. On the rare occasions when films or soap operas make a clumsy attempt to portray Copts, they claim that they have been misrepresented, the film *Bahebb el-Sîma* [I Love Cinema] being only one example. One hears few negative comments about Copts in public: the Egyptian government's current policy, which is in fact dictated by the United States, is designed to avoid all confessional incidents (*fitna tâ'ifiyya*)—the government's nightmare—and to demonstrate its good intentions in every possible way. The Coptic Christmas (7 January) has, for instance, been a public holiday since 2003. Patriarch Shenouda III's response has been to redouble his efforts to promote an entente, at least at the official level: he wrote in person to the Muslim judge to support the demand that the Koranic exegete Nasr Hamid Abu Zayd's marriage be declared null and void on the grounds that he was an apostate, and thus lent his support to the most obscurantist fundamentalist tendencies within the Egyptian establishment.[2] American pressure and a belated recognition of the worsening situation have led the Egyptian state to mend its relationship with the Coptic Church. After the murderous incidents in Kosheh in 2000, more authorizations to build churches were granted. That same year, the bimillenary of the birth of Christ was officially celebrated. That was of course done with the tourist industry in mind, but it was also an attempt to improve Egypt's image, even though the country has become one of the main bastions of militant Islamism. A few Coptic faces are now seen in commercials on television: a television campaign to encourage rich Egyptians to pay their taxes shown in

September 2006 featured a Coptic priest exhorting his flock to do their civic duty. In the spring of 2008, a poster campaign in the metro denouncing excision showed a Muslim sheikh and a Coptic priest, surround by their respective flocks, united in their disapproval of the practice.

From Sharing to Confrontation: Developments in the Nineteenth and Twentieth Centuries

This direct and unbalanced confrontation between Copts and Muslims is, however, recent: if we look at it in historical perspective, we discover a much richer and more complex reality that has to be seen in its social, economic, and political context.

Only a few decades ago, the percentage of Copts in Egyptian society was much higher than it is today (at the beginning of the twentieth century, they still represented between 8 and 10% of the population), and the percentage of Christians in general was also higher. Their social position in trade, the administration, and political life, but also in the modern media, gave them a real visibility. It might even be said that they were overrepresented, given the proportion of Christians in the Egyptian population. Until the early 1950s, for example, many journalists, producers, and directors were Syrian Christians who had settled in Egypt, and films from the interwar period featured Christian actors or Christian roles (both Syrian and Coptic). Although everyone was very aware of their confessional identity, there was nothing obsessional about it, as there is today. Geographical or national origins and social rank were just as important, if not more important, and there was less difference between the lifestyle of a Coptic pasha and a Muslim pasha than there was between that of any pasha—Coptic or Muslim—and the lifestyle of a peasant, either Coptic or Muslim. Few Copts, especially among the elite, attended church on a regular basis, but the fact that many Muslims, including members of the elite, rarely went to the mosque helped to ensure that interfaith relations were fairly fluid. There seem to have been fewer conversions to Islam at this time, if only because there was less pressure to convert. There were no loudspeakers to call the faithful to prayer, no mosques on every street corner, and no religious signs in the workplace. There were no Koranists on television simply because there was no television, but the medium has now become a powerful agent of Islamization.

Being a Christian in Egypt did not necessarily mean being a Copt. There were Syrians (either Melkites or Greek Orthodox) in Egypt (Philipp 1985). There was a small Armenian minority who had settled there with the encouragement of Mehmet Ali, as well as a strong contingent of Greeks of Hellenic origin who arrived with the cotton boom of the 1860s. Various Levantines gravitated there from different countries, and spoke several different languages, including various Arabic dialects. The well-known case of Edward Said, who came from Palestine but lived in both Lebanon and Egypt, is quite typical.[3] In the second half of the nineteenth century, these Christians of various denominations were joined by Europeans from Italy, Malta, Austria, England, and France. Large numbers of them lived in the modern districts of the big cities, and their matrimonial alliances sometimes complicated the landscape of Egypt's Christians. These Greeks, Syrians, and Levantines—who were often obsessed with their own nationalisms—looked down on the Copts. With the exception of the few important land-owning families that emerged in Middle Egypt in the second half of the nineteenth century,[4] Copts were usually seen as social inferiors. The vast majority were peasants who bore the typical stigmata of underdevelopment: filth, superstitions, ignorance, and passivity. Muslims from the same social milieu bore the same stigmata, and the lifestyles of "native" Egyptians, be they Copts or Muslims, were in fact very similar. In about 1900, for example, Coptic women in the towns wore the face veil, as did Muslim women. Anyone seeing an unveiled woman in the street or on a tram would therefore automatically assume that she was a Christian, meaning a Syrian Christian, of course.[5]

The Levantine social and cultural elites deliberately took no notice of Egyptian shrines, which looked to the reformist Muslims of the 1880s like a classic expression of Egyptian backwardness. Egyptian pilgrimages, both Coptic and Muslim *moulids*, soon became a symbol of rural culture and the poor districts. No matter how lowly their background, both Egyptian's Syrians and the Greeks thought themselves very superior to the plebs, who were, it was said, the only people to take part in them. When Syrians and Greeks did join in, they usually did so for commercial reasons, especially at the time of the Muslim fair at Tantâ in the Nile delta. Non-Coptic Christian minorities created their own shrines, which had nothing to do with the Egyptian tradition. In the early twentieth century, the European Catholics who had arrived in the second half of the nineteenth century began, for example, to build shrines that followed the Latin model. These included the shrine of the Tree of the Virgin in Matarieh, whose cult was revived and reconstructed by French Jesuits, and the shrine of St. Theresa of Shubra in Cairo. "Lourdes grottoes" were built in the courtyards and gardens of congregational Catholic hospitals and boarding schools, and did a lot to diffuse new models of piety. In order to get an accurate picture of

the multiconfessionalism of the Egypt of the day, and of its shrines, we therefore have to talk about all those who were neither Christians nor Muslims but
who still played an important role in Egyptian society, especially in Alexandria.
They included both the long-established Egyptian-Jewish community and Italian Jews (Beinin 1998). A unique Jewish pilgrimage (*moulid*) began to be held
at Damanhûr in the Nile delta at the end of the nineteenth century, and it was
attended by large numbers of Muslims living by the river.

It would be a mistake to take an irenic view of the big Egyptian cities: this
was a world in which the Levantines' contempt for Egyptians and the sometimes militant nationalism of the Greeks and Italians were often equaled only
by the xenophobic attitude of Egyptians (both Copts and Muslims) toward
foreigners, and especially Syrians. An Egyptian nationalism was beginning
to emerge, and its attitude toward minorities who were regarded as allogenic
in both senses of the word was strongly influenced by a militant Islam that
expresses itself as early as Urabi Pasha's revolt in 1882. In the 1900s, the fervent nationalism of Mustafa Kamil turned Muslims against Egypt's Syrian
Christians. On the other hand, it has to be said that there is no record of
violent massacres or forced conversions and that Egypt has never suffered a
trauma that could be compared with the massacre of the Christians of Bilâd
al-Shâm (Syria and Lebanon) in 1860. On the contrary, Egyptian nationalism
united both Copts and Muslims against Europeans, and especially the British. The political entente between Copts and Muslims reached its apotheosis
during the revolution of 1919 and the famous episodes that saw Coptic priests
preaching at Al-Azhar and Muslim sheikhs preaching in churches. The alliance "between Cross and Crescent" was accompanied by violent outbreaks
of xenophobia directed against Egypt's Syrians (Shawâm). That xenophobia
was shared by Coptic intellectuals such as Salâma Mûsâ (1887–1958) (Monciaud 2002). The entente between Copts and Muslims—which would later
come to be surrounded by myths—continued during the interwar period
in the form of the Wafd, a nationalist political party founded by Copt and
Muslim notables, many of them from big land-owning families (Carter 1986;
Barbulesco 1985).

The Wafd and the elites did not, however, represent the whole of Egyptian society. From the 1930s onward, public opinion in general, and not only
the Muslim Brotherhood, was alarmed by reports that the congregationalist
schools were converting Muslims to Christianity. Anti-missionary campaigns
began to be organized. In 1933, activists began to target the Copts too, and the
few Copts who had converted to Islam were put on show.[6]

When the "notable" social class was removed from the political game by the Free Officers' revolution of 1952, it was replaced by an exclusively Muslim petty bourgeoisie that was intellectually close to the Muslim Brotherhood and determined to leave no political role for Christians. Nasser began his political career by driving out of Egypt the Syrians, the Greeks, and, more generally, any minority that was considered to be allogenic. The Copts were at once appreciated because they were Egyptian and relegated to the status of a "community" represented by a patriarch. The community was denied any real political rights, and even any social visibility. It was no coincidence that the charismatic Patriarch Cyril VI (1959–1971) was rewarded for his personal cooperation with Nasser: the Copts now had almost no other representatives (Voile 2004). Things got worse under Sadat (1970–1981) as the Constitution of 1980 enshrined the principle that legislation was to be based primarily on Islamic law. The religious conservatism preached by Sadat, who was trying to keep his left wing at bay, was a heavy blow to the entente between Copts and Muslims at a time when Coptic confessionalism was adopting a more fundamentalist tone under Shenouda III, who had been patriarch since 1971. The roots of the Coptic Revival that began in the 1940s have their own origins, and they probably preceded the rise of Islamism, but the hard-line communitarianism is its exact contemporary.[7]

From the 1970s onward, a hostile confrontation began to develop, with both sides displaying more and more signs of their visible differences. Coptic girls became more fashion-conscious, while almost all Muslims girls took to wearing the veil, with many of them wearing the *niqâb* from 2001 onward. Christians became increasingly circumspect in their dealings with Muslims, while Muslims paid less and less heed to their Christian neighbors—and there were proportionately fewer Christians than there had been in the past. There were more and more tales of forced or voluntary conversions, and violent, and even murderous, interfaith incidents became almost a monthly occurrence from about 2004–2005 onward.[8] There was therefore a tendency for Copts to retreat into their community (even when they were not forced to do so), while Muslims took comfort from their hegemonic claim to represent the real Egypt, and simply failed to recognize the Christian presence.[9]

As both Copts and Muslims began to place more and more emphasis on their differences, they began to forget the incredible number of things they have in common; they are compatriots, speak the same language, and have grown up with the same proverbs. Their birth and death rates are now similar. For a long time, they wore the same clothes, and they continued to do so until

Muslim women in the cities began to wear the veil from the 1970s onward. In the countryside, especially, one cannot tell the difference between a Muslim peasant and a Coptic peasant—unless one looks at the cross tattooed on the inside of the Copt's right wrist. It is no coincidence that most shared shrines are in rural areas. In the mixed villages of Upper Egypt older or illiterate Coptic and Muslim women alike still wear the veil and are draped in voluminous black *milâya,* while younger women who have been to secondary school have adopted a modern style of dress that signals their confessional differences: veils and long dresses or trousers for Muslims, and trousers or relatively short dresses, and even shorter sleeves, for Copts.

Copts and Muslims also tend to live in the same areas. It is well known that there were no ghettoes—or even specifically Christian districts—in Egypt during the medieval and Ottoman periods. The two communities—Copts and Muslims—usually lived in the same districts in the cities, and in the same villages in the countryside. While now there are districts of Cairo where one meets more Christians (Shubra, for instance), this is a fairly recent development, and there are no equivalents to the Christian districts of Aleppo or Damascus.[10] While there are still villages that are predominantly or exclusively Coptic, they are beginning to be a thing of the past. The two confessions are beginning to mix more and more, but this works to the advantage of Muslims, who are in the majority. They have the same concerns. Both Copts and Muslims find it hard to survive in a critical economic situation characterized by galloping inflation, and the shortage of bread affects them in the same way. Copts suffer neither less nor more than Muslims in a situation that is politically difficult for everyone: the police and army are all-powerful and torture is commonplace, and while the Islamist guerrilla campaign in Upper Egypt during the 1990s may have claimed some Coptic victims, its main targets were Muslim police officers, soldiers, and civil servants.

Many forms of piety, finally, are common to both groups, including contemporary exaggerations based on a shared obsession with what is and what is not permissible, as defined in the same fundamentalist terms. Sometimes, the Muslim influence is obvious: Copts from the most modest social backgrounds, such as the Cairene workers from rural Middle Egypt, regard wine and pork as forbidden (*harâm*). Sometimes the Christian influence—Coptic but also Latin Catholic—is dominant, for instance, in what Muslims say about the family and moral values, or in their use of the iconography of their sheikhs and saints. Both Copts and Muslims indulge in outbursts of ostentatious religiosity; some Muslims have the *adhân* (call to prayer) as the ring tone on their mobile phones, while some Copts have psalms, with images of Christ wearing the crown of thorns, displayed on their screens. The anxious ritualism of both Copts and Muslims is an expression of their distrust of Western modernity, which is tempting but also a source of possible corruption, and leads to assertions of values that are sometimes described as Coptic and Muslim, and sometimes as Arab and Eastern. And all use the hit songs of the moment as ringtones. When it comes to music, which is so important in Egypt, all Egyptians share the same culture. The same is true of the culture surrounding their shrines.

Coptic *Moulids* and Muslim *Moulids*: The Existence of a Shared Festive Culture

Let us go back to the end of the nineteenth century and the first half of the twentieth, as we have a number of accounts of pilgrimages in which both Copts and Muslims took part during this period. What Egyptians call a "pilgrimage" can correspond (loosely) either to a pious visit (*ziyâra*) that can be paid at any time of the year, sometimes on an individual basis but often as a member of a group, or a *moulid* (a dialectal form derived from the classical *mawlid*), or an annual saint's day celebration involving a whole neighborhood or village. The term can also refer to hybrid forms such as the religious tourism (*sihâya*) practiced by Muslims during the Mameluk and Ottoman periods, which is still popular today, especially among Copts. *Ziyâra, mawlid,* or *sihâya* . . . the three terms refer to very different realities, depending on whether one is in the city, the countryside, or the desert, or in Upper or Lower Egypt. And that diversity must always be borne in mind whenever the delicate issue of "shared" shrines is under discussion.

It should be noted, first of all, that it is almost inconceivable that pilgrims of one confession should pay pious visits (*ziyârât*) to the tomb of a saint of the other confession, first because a *ziyâra* is too individual—or reserved for family groups—to be really shared and, second, because Muslims do not pay pious visits to the tombs of Coptic saints, while Copts do not pay pious visits to the tombs of Muslim saints. Copts and Muslims venerate their own saints, or used to. It is therefore not so much during *ziyârât* as on saints' days or *moulid* (pl. *mawâlid*) that we find Christians—but very few of them—taking part in Muslim festivals and Muslims—many more of them—taking part in Christian festivals. To a visitor from outer space, *moulids* would all look much the same. The same entertainment is provided by the same fairground people: crude farces and shadow plays until the interwar period, and singers and dancing girls until the 1970s or 1980s. There are sometimes still storytellers. The same swings, shooting ranges, puppets, and galloping horses are always there. And until recently, there were alcoholic drinks and hashish for all. None of this is specifically Coptic or specifically Muslim, nor is it purely profane. This is the realm of the sacred and the festive, but not the confessional. Muslims may well have gone (and still go) to Coptic *moulids* because of the saint's *baraka*, but they went mainly to enjoy the fairground attractions, which were similar in every respect to those to be found at Muslim *moulids*. The same fairground people, who were often gypsies, went—and still go—from Coptic festivals to Muslims festivals, and took no notice of their confessional labels. The entertainment is usually provided by Muslim showmen in the case of Coptic pilgrimages; in the case of some Muslim *moulids* in Upper Egypt, it is provided by Coptic showmen, but this is more unusual.

It was Muslim tattoo artists who tattooed crosses on the inside of the right wrists of Coptic children. It was Muslim taxi drivers who took pilgrims by the hundred to the great *moulids* of the Virgin in Mustarud near Cairo, or in Dronka near Assiut. Muslim boatmen ferried pilgrims from Mît Damsîs across the Nile as they went to Sunbât, in the eastern center of the delta. In Middle Egypt, taxi drivers have both St. George stickers on their dashboards and the Muslim "travel prayer" (*du 'â' al-safar*) dangling from their rearview mirrors. The Muslim minibus drivers who ferry Coptic pilgrims from the church in Mustarud to the nearest bus station are well aware of the calendar of Coptic *moulids*, and they also carry pilgrims from the Muslim *moulids* in Tantâ or Disûq.

These pilgrimages are all characterized by the same kind of piety, and it is both demonstrative and tactile. Most Egyptian Muslims and all Copts venerate saints, believe that they can perform miracles, and attach great importance to visions and signs. The requests for miracles that are addressed to the saints are very similar, even though the vectors for the miracles themselves are different. It is the saints and the rites that differ, even at so-called shared shrines.

The Virgin, St. George, and Anonymous Saints: "Shared" Saints?

Which saints are we talking about? There are, first of all, some "saints" who look almost neutral. They are to be found mainly in the countryside, and no clear confessional affiliation can be inferred from their names. In the 1920s, the anthropologist Winifred Blackman pointed out that in the Middle East, both Muslims and Copts sometimes claimed the same saint as their own:

> In such cases, the tomb is often located on a public square, sometimes in the shade of one or more trees. Worshippers from both religions hang their votive offerings on the lowest branches. Like the Muslims, the Christians are especially fond of offering candles; when the saint is venerated by both, the candles of Muslims and Copts can be seen burning side by side. (Blackman 1948:215)

The quotation makes a significant point: it is when the cult is associated with a tree or a spring, when it has least to do with explicitly confessional forms, and when there is little clerical involvement (on the part of sheikhs, ulemas, monks, or priests) that it was most easily observed by both Copts and Muslims, and celebrated either in the village square or on the threshing floor. When it is simply a matter of joining in a procession through the streets of the village, Muslims are under no obligation to enter a church and, above all, Copts are under no obligation to enter a mosque. Saints with no particular confessional affiliation also had indeterminate names that could be either Coptic or Muslim, such as sheikh Nasr ("Victory"), sheikh Ibrâhim ("Abraham"), or sheikh Abd al-Malik ("servant of the king"). Everyone is free to imagine what they look like.

In some cases, the place was dedicated to either a Christian saint or a Muslim saint but was venerated by all. Such shared places are becoming things of the past. The Tree of the Virgin in Matarieh, which was once venerated by both Coptic and Muslim women, is probably the most famous example of how what was a multiconfessional Egyptian shrine can become a monocultural shrine. It was a sycamore tree with an impressive trunk, with a spring in the shade of its abundant foliage, in the small village of Matarieh, to the north of Cairo. It was venerated by all—and not least by the Italian Franciscans, whose presence never stopped Copts or Muslims from visiting it. But the French Jesuits began to build a nearby shrine reserved for Latin Christians alone at the beginning of the twentieth century, and Orthodox Copts fenced off the tree after the 1960s. The village of Matarieh turned into a working-class suburb, and in 2000, the conservative action of the Egyptian state finally turned the Tree of the Virgin into a purely Christian, and museum-like, shrine. In order to enter the fenced-off area, pilgrims have to buy a ticket to see a tree they can no longer touch and a spring from which they can no longer draw water.[11]

Sometimes, the name of the tree, tomb, or place is obviously Muslim. When that is the case, Copts like to suggest that the Muslim saint may well once have been a Coptic saint, and that many Muslim saints were in fact monks or martyrs from ancient Christian times who have been wrongly Islamized. In Gotna in the governorate of Sohag everyone goes to visit the caves in the desert cliff overlooking the village, which are associated with sheikh Husayn, about whom little is known in historical terms. The region's Copts think that the caves are former monastic hermitages that were—at some unspecified time—inhabited by Coptic saints. Such reminders of the past do not necessarily mean that the shrine is really shared, but they do allow Copts to claim that the place originally belonged to Copts, that the Copts were there before the Muslims, and that the shrine therefore has a certain legitimacy. The sanctity of a shrine is defined in terms of territory. Quite logically, this puts a lot of emphasis on "origins," and it should be noted that Muslims are not considered—and do not consider themselves—to be the descendants of Copts converted to Islam. They are described, and describe themselves, as always having been Muslim, and as conquerors or the descendants of conquerors.

As in the rest of the Middle East, the Virgin and St. George are especially venerated in Egypt. For a long time, they were venerated by both Christians and Muslims, but not quite in the same way. Let us begin with the Virgin, to whom so many great Egyptian shrines are dedicated. The cult of the places visited by the Holy Family during the Flight into Egypt, which developed in about the twelfth century, is the product of competition rather than entente, and its development coincided with that of the cult of the Prophet among Muslims. It was probably because of their proportional decline in the Egyptian population that the Copts developed an unassailable cult—that of the Virgin—which often replaced the cult of earlier Coptic saints. At the same time, Muslims were careful to make a cult of the indirect relics of the Prophet and his Companions and traces of their possible or hypothetical travels through Egypt. Both parties were attempting to prove that they were there first, and that their presence in Egypt is therefore legitimate. The shrines of Muslim saints were often built to compete with Christian sites. A medieval cupola was built to honor the memory of a Sufi sheikh at the entrance to the Coptic shrine in Sunbât, and the mausoleum of the telekoranist Sheikh Sharâwi (who died in 1998) was built alongside the Coptic shrine in Daqâdus. It is also possible that, in the Middle Ages, the Copts built shrines and reliquaries dedicated to the Virgin in order to checkmate sites that were already Muslim or that were in the process of being Islamized. This became much more difficult in later periods, when the reinforcement of the ban on building and restoring churches, together with the proportional fall in the number of Copts, left them little room for maneuver. The contemporary cult that has developed around the Virgin's apparitions in Zaytûn in 1968 and in Assiut in 2000 can, on the other hand, be interpreted as a reaction against the increased Muslim presence. The Zaytûn apparitions of 1968 coincided with disillusionment with Arab nationalism and its failure during the Six Day War in 1967, and marked the beginning of a religious withdrawal on the part of both Copts and Muslims. The Assiut apparitions of 2000 came after a decade of very violent clashes in Middle Egypt between the army and the civilian population, between the state and Islamists, and between Copts and Muslims. In both cases, the apparitions gave Muslims a special role: they were needed as witnesses who could confirm the sanctity of the places involved. As a rule, the Muslim who testifies that the miracle did take place has become an essential witness in Coptic accounts of miracles.[12]

As for St. George, his reputation for being an exorcist has traditionally given him a special status for Muslims. This is especially true in Mît Damsîs, where Muslims still come to consult the Coptic priests (exorcists) who officiate there during the pilgrimage. This does not imply any particular veneration for St. George: in rural Egypt, Coptic priests are traditionally regarded by Muslims as sorcerers, precisely because they are supposedly lower down the hierarchy of living beings and therefore closer to nature and more able to dominate chthonian forces. They are, in other words, usually the object of a somewhat fearful respect.

As well as exorcisms, the custom of "prophylactic baptism" is still observed at several Coptic shrines, such as the *moulid* of the Virgin in Gabal al-Tayr, where the font is filled with water that has not been blessed, so as to not confuse these ceremonies with true Christian baptisms. Should a Muslim couple see that one of the children is in danger of dying, they have no compunction about resorting to the extreme expedient of having the child baptized by a Coptic priest. This obviously does not imply conversion to Christianity: the measure is designed to protect the child from the evil eye. The magical powers of a Coptic priest, who is seen as some kind of sorcerer, are required for this ritual, just as they are required for the well-known ritual of Abû Talbo—or Tarabô—which gives protection against rabies.[13]

One final form of exchange that can still be observed is the acknowledgment of the charisma of the other religion's *living* saints. These are usually Coptic monks endowed with *baraka*, but they can, in rare instances, be Sufi sheikhs or Muslim holy women with a definite aura. As with tombs, it is more likely to be Muslims who turn to Christian saints. But for Christians and Muslims alike, these are one-off visits relating to specific problems—an autistic child, inexplicable sterility, or a serious illness—and do not involve regular attendance. Is the phenomenon of going to consult the other religion's saints bound up with a recent individuation or a quest for spiritual masters, or is it an extension of the tradition in which the priest acts as a universal sorcerer and healer? It presumably varies from one case to another. The tradition of the rural holy man is exemplified by the holy priest Yassâ (who died in 1962), who would visit both Muslims and Christians in the same spirit of charity, as the devotees—both Copts and Muslims—who venerate him in Kôm Gharîb (near Tîma in Upper Egypt) are quick to point out. The hybrid figure of Patriarch Cyril VI (who died in 1971) is another example. Even Muslims regarded him as a charismatic holy man who had thaumaturgic powers. Nasser himself acknowledged his powers, and, it is said, asked both him and the Sufi sheikh Ahmad Radwân (died 1967) to intercede on his behalf. To take a more recent example, the Coptic abbess Mother Irene (died 2006), who enjoyed a reputation for sanctity in Cairo, is no longer seen as a magician but is clearly seen as a spiritual guide, mainly by Copts but also by the many Muslim women she received.

Local Religion and Civic Religion:
From Roots to Deracination

Coptic *moulid*s are more popular with Muslims than Muslim *moulid*s are with Copts. As we have seen, this is the reflex of a minority. It is also because Coptic *moulid*s are governed by the solar calendar, which means that they follow the rhythm of the seasons and the flooding of the Nile, whereas most Muslim *moulid*s, at least in Upper Egypt, observe the lunar calendar. It is clear from the small Coptic *moulid*s in rural Upper Egypt studied by Nessiam Henein in 1971–1972, or shortly after the Aswan dam stopped the Nile from flooding, that both Muslims and Christians visit the shrine of St. George (Marî Girgis) and observe St. Michael's Day because it is an agrarian festival for both religions:

> All the inhabitants of the region, both Muslims and Christians go [to the *moulid* of Marî Girgis] on that day, bringing offerings of sheep, kids or goats. The animals are slaughtered in the courtyard of the church, in front of the door. The priest takes one quarter of the animal that has been sacrificed, and sells it to local people. The poor offer candles, curtains and mats for the church. In the evening, a service is held in the church and the martyr's praises are read aloud. After dinner, the visitors spend the night in the

church and do not leave until morning. The villagers also make cakes with wheat flour . . . and *kahk*. A special meal may also be made for the evening. [The feast of the Archangel Michael] takes place on 12 ba'ûna, the same day that they celebrate the beginning of the flood. The villagers confuse the two feasts and say that the angel Michael is giving his blessing to the water and the earth. Few of them bring offerings or attend mass in the Dêr el-Malak, which is dedicated to the saint. The feast also coincides with the end of the harvest and the threshing of the corn. On the eve of the feast, many of the villagers congratulate one another when they have finished winnowing the corn and put it into store that same evening. They make small loaves in the shape of a cross or round loafs [*bannûn*] that are left with the grain for a whole year (Henein 1988:251–252).

For a long time, large numbers of Muslims used to attend Coptic *moulids*. In the late 1920s, for example, Winifred Blackman reported that in Upper Egypt "almost as many Muslims as Christians went to the *moulid* of St. George, which was celebrated between the desert and the canal" (Blackmann 1948:223). In 1939, on the last night of the *moulid* of Barsûm El-'Aryân, to the south of Cairo, tens of thousands of Muslims mingled with the Coptic pilgrims "without the slightest friction" (McPherson 1941:15). Otto Meinardus could still write in the 1960s that many Muslims attended Coptic *moulids*, and especially the largest *moulids* in the delta: that of St. Damian, near Bilqâs, and that of St. George in Mît Damsîs (Meinardus 1970:219).

Moulids, which often involve a whole town, village, or neighborhood, are in many respects manifestations of local and of "civic" religions. Because they share the same rural or urban culture, Muslims and Copts living in the same village or neighborhood are very attached to their local patron saint. *Moulids* encourage trade, activity, and an open-minded attitude. They are part of the place's identity, and the place is sanctified by the saint's *baraka*. There is no Coptic *moulid* in Badramân, a village in the Governorate of Minyâ where three thousand Catholics and Protestants live alongside six thousand Muslims, but the Christians still join in the festival that is held in honor of Sheikh 'Abd al-Ghaffâr, a Muslim saint related to the village's mayor ('*umda*). The saint, who was famed for his generosity and piety, died in about 1970 and was buried in the center of the village. His impressive tomb is the focal point of the fair—swings, a fairground—and the Copts visit it, just as the Muslims do, but obviously do not take part in the *dhikr* that is organized by the saint's brotherhood. Conversely, Muslim neighbors can take part in Coptic *moulids* (but not the rites), even in the towns. The *moulid* of the Virgin in Zaytûn is regarded by local Muslims as "their" *moulid* (*el-mûled betâʾnâ*) because it is neighborhood-based. This does not necessarily mean that they are full participants, but it does mean that they recognize that both they and their Coptic neighbors have the same local roots. These forms of sharing are usually restricted to the "fairground" or festive aspects of the *moulid* (the meals and the swings), but they do promote an awareness of a shared local identity that finds expression in the patronal feast and that transcends the confessional divide. This is the phenomenon of the "civic religion" well-known to the specialists of medieval Western Christianity (Vauchez 1996).

The notions of a local religion or a civic religion are becoming meaningless in an era of globalization and deracination. There are now few Muslims at Copt *moulid*s, and no Copts at Muslim *moulid*s, not that there were many to begin with. Gangs of young Muslims do sometimes still go to enjoy themselves at Coptic *moulid*s in, for instance, Mustarud, but they are less fun than they used to be: thanks to the bishops' censorious attitude, there are no more dancing girls and no more wine. Muslim women (much more so than men) certainly continue to visit the tombs of Christian saints in search of a cure or support, but they do so on an individual basis and very discreetly. The church of St. Theresa in Shubra (Cairo) is a typical example: Muslim names such as that of the famous singer ʿAbd al-Halîm Hâfez (1929–1977) can be seen on the ex-votos, and veiled women still come, with their babies in their arms, to ask advice from the priest.

The days when joyous crowds of Copts and Muslims would mingle at a *moulid* are long gone. Otto Meinardus's descriptions of Coptic shrines in the 1960s could not be written today. Similarly, Nessim Henein's accounts of the small village *moulid*s of Upper Egypt describe an Egypt that no longer exists. It is mainly the archaic rural society that still existed thirty years ago that has vanished. There are probably no longer any villages in Upper Egypt, or, a fortiori, Lower Egypt where most of the villagers are peasants. Most of the people who live in the countryside no longer work on the land. The population explosion, the availability of cars, migration (either temporary or permanent), the shortage of land and the lack of work, and easier access to primary and even secondary education have resulted in the rapid erosion of rural civilization. The villagers work in the cities, leave for Cairo and the Red Sea cities, or even go abroad. Urban lifestyles are taking over the countryside. Pascal Dibie's description of Chichery in Burgundy could easily be applied to many villages in Egypt (Dibie 2006). And as rural civilization disappears, so too does the culture that allowed shared shrines to exist.

Were the shrines really shared? There are major structural differences between Coptic and Muslim *moulids*, and between Coptic and Muslim saints. Once we get away from the anonymous saints who gave a human face to holy springs and trees, the models are quite different. Coptic saints took their inspiration from monastic models or the martyrs of the Roman period, while Muslim saints are seen as the heirs to the prophets, and especially the Prophet himself, from whom they are often descended. For deeply theological reasons (or supposedly theological reasons), there are no bones or relics in Muslim shrines, while icons and direct relics are a central part of the Coptic cult of saints. Even when a Coptic shrine does not contain relics but marks a place the saint visited or a heritage site, the fact that both religions venerate it does not mean a great deal: the Virgin of the Gospels is the mother of God, and she is not the Virgin of the Koran, who is the mother of a prophet.

As for Coptic shrines, they are modeled on examples from the desert or monasteries and, by definition, do not allude to the *hajj* or the Sufi influences that are usually associated with Muslim shrines. There are, in other words, major differences between the two, and they have real practical effects. To recall a few obvious examples: there is no circumambulation of Coptic tombs; besides, their topography does not allow it. Copts have no equivalent to the Sufis' *dhikr* ceremonies, which are a classic feature of Muslim pilgrimages in Egypt. Muslims, for their part, obviously have no sacraments. These theological differences are not restricted to the details of rituals; they also explain why no one understands the other's shrine. At the church of St. Theresa in Shubra, which we have already mentioned, Muslims do process around the body of the saint, which is represented by a plaster statue. When they stand in front of icons, Muslims happily touch them, as do Copts, but they do not know which ones they should pray to because they do not understand where they stand in the iconic hierarchy: the images mean nothing to them. Both Copts and Muslims obviously light candles, but the Muslims do not always know where to put them. The idea of leaving a message for a saint seems quite incongruous to Egyptian Muslims (the letters they send to Imam Shâfiî are the exception to the rule), whereas the practice is widespread among Copts. It is therefore quite easy to identify the Muslims in the crowds of pilgrims who visit Coptic shrines, as they feel ill at ease in what is for them a very exotic environment. Copts, on the other hand, never enter mosques or even the mausoleums of Muslim saints. Those who were born in the cities make no secret of their contempt for Muslim *moulids*, and say that they are disgusted by a mechanistic and ritualistic piety that is merely for show and that has not been internalized.

*Moulid*s at a Time of Confessional Tension

The decline of rural civilization, urban norms, and reformist ideas is probably the main reason for the decline in the number of interfaith shrines. All these changes are reflected in a fundamentalist religious revival among both Copts and Muslims, and it leaves no room for exchanges and sharing. While good neighborliness still exists at the individual level, the days when Copts and Muslims venerated the same saints and rituals, and went to the same *moulid*s, are gone. Muslim reformism is the main reason for this. In the interwar period, the high priests of *salafiyya* stigmatized the shameful imitation of Christians (*tashabbuh*), and thus rejected both the Western model and the folk custom of worshiping together. In the course of the twentieth century attitudes hardened as Islamists became hostile to both Christians and the cult of saints. The Islamists pose a real threat to Coptic shrines. Coptic *moulid*s have become fortresses that are under siege and have to be closely guarded by the police. Busloads of police park outside them, and plainclothes spies or mounted police patrol the *moulid*s to ensure that no unfortunate incident disturbs the pilgrims' peace. There are two reasons for the police presence. The police are there to prevent the outbreaks of mob violence that *moulid*s, both Copt and Muslim, supposedly encourage. The police presence is also designed to protect Copts from possible attacks by Islamists, especially in Middle Egypt, where, after the incidents in Minyâ in 1990 and Sanabô, near Dayrût, in 1992, there was an intense period of guerrilla activity lasting until about 2000. Since then, there has been a steady increase in the number of confessional clashes. Police checks on places of pilgrimage reinforce the internal censorship introduced by the clergy. The closed world of the Coptic *moulid* has become more closed than ever. It is the dominant discourse of Muslim reformism rather than the radical Islamist talk of warfare and an anti-Christian jihad that explains why the overwhelming majority of Muslims now refuse to visit Coptic shrines and, more generally, to have anything at all in common with Christians.

The construction of ostentatious Islamic buildings on the sites of Coptic shrines reflects the recent and rapid rise in confessional tensions. Since the 1980s, new mosques with disproportionately tall minarets have been built alongside churches housing shrines. In Ma'sara, a minaret was built on the opposite side of the canal to the monastery of Barsûm al-'Aryan in 1990. In Mît Damsîs, an imposing mosque was hastily built to overshadow the neighboring towers of St. George's Church. There are a number of Coptic tales of miracles in which a minaret mysteriously collapsed because it offended a Coptic saint.

It is not so much the minarets, which are an inescapable part of the landscape, as the loudspeakers on the new mosques, which are beamed directly at the churches and monasteries that house shrines, that really disturb the Coptic *moulid*s at prayer time during the Friday sermon. This recent phenomenon, which is a sad reflection of the spread of Islamism, is especially obvious in Middle Egypt, which has seen so many confessional clashes. As we have seen, the Coptic reaction has been to build more and more church towers: the towers have never been so high, and the churches have never been so huge.

Militant Islamist attacks and the constraints of living in a police state are not the only things behind this irreversible process. The *moulid*s themselves have been reformed, clericalized, and brought back into line by the Coptic hierarchy. The Coptic Revival is having an effect on the Coptic community itself.[14] Coptic *moulid*s were for a long time a reflection of a common folk culture in which Copts and Muslims understood one another without having to spell things out. The world of the village was probably not idyllic, but relations between the two communities were ritualized, and each had its own role to play. The shared culture that found expression in the *moulid*s was experienced by everyone in their day-to-day lives. When they began to reform their *moulid*s, the Copts were obviously following the example set by Muslims and were trying to outdo them in their bid for respectability. They were not, however, simply imitating them: the Coptic Revival has its own dynamics. But Egyptian society has given birth to comparable phenomena in both communities: packed mosques and overcrowded parishes, inflammatory Muslim preachers and an authoritarian clergy, militant Islamists and combative monks.

The Coptic *moulid*s were one of the traditions of a community that had little dynamism. Until the 1970s, their congregations were almost exclusively rural. Neither the clergy nor the monks had any real role to play at the shrines. As a rule, the clergy came from a rural background, and their level of education was notoriously low: the priests, who were also exorcists and magicians, celebrated Mass in the *moulid*s, but they did not act as censors. Church attendance was low. The shrines, which the clergy did little to control because there were so few of them, did not bring in a lot of money, and most monasteries, which had been abandoned and stood empty, were falling into ruin.

All these monasteries, which were once isolated, are now well served by the road network. They are now the focus of regular parish pilgrimages, which, unlike *moulid*s, do not take place on specific dates and which can occur at any time of the year. Every shrine has a bookshop selling key rings, clocks with the effigies of saints on the dial, indirect relics that bring *baraka,* as well as religious pamphlets and hagiographic literature. The revival has no doubt led to the "resurrection" of monachism, but it has also brought about a revolution in the kingdom of the *moulids*. The movement to reform the shrines, and popular piety as a whole, has been under way for the last thirty years, or in other words ever since Shenouda was elected to the patriarchal throne. This religious reform movement, which often has puritanical and even fundamentalist overtones, has been facilitated by the mass recruitment of clerics and monks who were born in the towns and who have educational qualifications, and by the clericalization of the whole community. It has a lot in common with the Catholic Reformation: popular religion is being brought under control or repressed, attempts are being made to channel a new piety that is more in keeping with the customs of a police world, and a religious culture that was dominated by the lay community is being brought under clerical control. The reform of the Coptic *moulids* also represents, finally, an attempt on the part of Copts to be more reformist than the Muslims. Shenouda's version of the Coptic revival is just as fundamentalist as the Islamism of the Muslim Brotherhood, and is another illustration of how Egyptians are retreating into their religious identities. Since 1967, there has been "a rejection of 'westernized modernity,' its ideas and its practices, and a desire to go back to the authenticity of its own revitalized sources" (Martin 1997).

A new generation of saints has emerged. This is an unprecedented phenomenon, but every attempt is being made to ground it in the past, and it has launched or relaunched a new fashion for shrines. All the contemporary saints are either monks or nuns. The most important is Patriarch Cyril VI, who died in 1971 and who now ranks third in the Coptic pantheon after the Virgin Mary and St. George. Cyril was a great devotee of St. Menas, and took his name when he entered the monastery. He had a little hermitage near the ruins of the convent of St. Menas (Marî Mînâ) and regularly used it as a retreat after he became patriarch. He was buried there, and the veneration of his tomb has revived what was once the most important shrine in the Christian East. Saint Abbess Irene, who died in 2006, has brought worshipers back to Mercurios, and Abû Sayfayn. Umm Martha (died 1988) has brought them back to Tadros. The popularity of Abûnâ Fânûs (born 1931) draws crowds to St. Paul's monastery; at the rival monastery of St. Anthony, the monk Yustus (died 1976) has recently become the object of a cult. Abûnâ Yassâ, who is the last saint to have become fashionable, is buried near Tahtâ, and his cult has flourished since the early 1990s. The *moulids*' hierarchy has therefore been revolutionized by the creation of new *moulids*. Mâri Mîna (formerly known as St. Menas) in Maryût is, as we have seen, one example. The shrine was revived by the archaeological excavations that began there in 1905, but mainly by Patriarch Cyril VI, who founded a new monastery and who was buried there in 1971. Abbess Irene has made the church of Mercurios Abû Sayfayn popular once more. Local, village, neighborhood, or even regional *moulids* are no longer the most important: people travel long distances to visit Coptic *moulids*. Such shrines are venerated by the whole community, and a subtle distinction between place and feast is beginning to emerge. When the Virgin appeared in Zaytûn (Cairo) in 1968, a new and important *moulid* was created. Until 1950, Jacob Muyser could still describe the pilgrimage to the shrine of Anbâ Shenûda in Sohâg as the most important in the Nile valley, but older pilgrimages, some of which vanished centuries ago, have been revitalized and have now eclipsed it. The greatest Coptic *moulids* in the valley are now sponsored by the bishoprics and monasteries. Examples include Dronka near Assiut, Rizîqât near Armant, and the *moulid* of Abûne Yassâ near Tahtâ, which now enjoys great popularity. These are new *moulids*, and some of them were Catholic initiatives that have been taken over by the Orthodox.[15] Dronka is now the most important *moulid* on the holy mountain of Assiut, which is the Coptic capital of Middle Egypt, while farther to the north, Gabal al-Tayr is the most important near the city of Minyâ.

The *moulid* hierarchy has changed, and practices have changed too. There are now more priests and monks, and they are both educated and militant. They are not prepared to tolerate the traditional bonhomie that characterizes *moulids*. A Coptic clerical culture was slower to develop than Muslim reformism, but it is just as fervid and has declared war on the folk culture that surrounds *moulids*. From the early 1970s onward, "religious policy centred on moderating the collective ardour with which Copts express their desire for a miracle and act out their fears and frustrations. We are now seeing the emergence of a 'religious correctness' inspired by more internalized practices" (Voile 2004: Introduction). The priests emphasized the specifically religious aspect of the *moulid*, redefined the sacred, and did their best to ban anything that might be described as "profane" on the grounds that it was suspect. The very term *mûled* seemed too "popular" or even pejorative, and too Muslim. That was for etymological reasons: the literary term *mawlid* (corresponding to the dialectical *mûlid*) in fact refers to the anniversary of the Prophet's birth, to the songs and poems that were written to commemorate it, and by extension to the anniversaries of saints. It was only at the end of the Mameluk period (fifteenth century) that Copts began to use the term to describe their own shrines. The specifically Christian term *'id al-mîlâd* is used when referring to Christmas, which is the anniversary of Christ's birthday. The term *mûled* was, in a word, rejected by the priests who were arguing the case for the less popular and more respectable terms "official feast" (*ihtifâl*) or "commemoration" (*tidhkâr*). The censors' first targets were the fairs, or the one thing that Christians shared with Muslims. But the refusal to join in the festivities also has to do with the Puritanical mindset of so many Egyptians, both Christian and Muslim. The Coptic clergy obviously did not want to be outdone by the Muslim ulemas, who were criticizing Muslim *moulid*s as a result of the prevailing fundamentalism. The divorce between the religious and festive poles is a recent phenomenon, and it applies to all the great *moulid*s, both Coptic and Muslim, even though the rhythm of the reforms is not exactly the same.

The bishops' hostility toward fairground people is also an implicit, and perhaps unconscious, rejection of Islam. First, because most of the fairground people are, as we have seen, Muslims and, second, because this repressed folk culture was common to both Copts and Muslims. Over the centuries, it developed into a shared heritage in which it was impossible to distinguish between its Coptic and Muslim components. The Coptic Church is now trying to get back to its roots and to eradicate all foreign contributions: in the attempt to return to the (purely mythical) authentic tradition of a purely Egyptian Coptic Church that is descended from the pharaohs, all Greek, Roman, Arabic, and Turkish influences must be extirpated. The clergy are now exploiting the *moulid*s in order to propagate a new vulgate by handing out brief circulars summarizing the life of the saint who is being venerated and the miracles he has performed, or the history of the holy place. People from the towns and "the educated" (those who can read) provide pious biographies and cassette recordings of Masses and psalms. Everyone—both the illiterate and the educated—buys pious objects, and the increase in the amount of cheap religious junk that is on sale is a notable sign of the contemporary mutations that are taking place. Mass is now said more often, and there are more processions with crosses and icons on display, and the psalms ring out over the fairgrounds and are retransmitted over loudspeakers. When the *ziyâra* is steeped in a specifically Christian religiosity, there is no room for Muslims.

The Coptic Church itself is becoming increasingly opposed to such exchanges, even when they are fictional and especially when there is an element of magic involved. The local bishop has, for example, banned Muslims from having their children baptized at Abûnâ Yassâ's shrine on pain of fatal illness. He has also banned them from taking communion at the shrine: the practice may have developed for magical reasons, though that may be a Coptic fantasy.[16] The days when half of the crowds that flocked to Coptic *moulids* were Muslims are long gone. Neither Muslims nor Copts want to mix. While a few veiled Muslim women—mostly mothers who are worried about their children or women suffering from depression—still go to shrines because of the *baraka* of Coptic saints, they are a tiny minority among the crowds of Christian pilgrims.

Conclusion: A Shared Heritage?

Shrines are no longer meeting places because both Copts and Muslims are trying to define their own culture and identity, and to reject any shared past. For the most part, Coptic *moulids* are now the exclusive property of Copts, and Muslim *moulids* are still the sole property of Muslims. Now that the clergy have taken control of their rites, there is no room left for the Other. The Copts are trying to reconstruct a Coptic Egypt that is mythically complete and intact. Inside the walls of their churches and within their monastery precincts, the faithful can at last sing psalms at the top of their voices. Microphones amplify the prayers and litanies, and carrying icons in processions is a demonstration of their religious affiliation. For once, the Coptic Church can make an ostentatious and public demonstration of its fervor and religiosity. A church is also a space where Copts are free to express their faith and piety without being afraid.

For Copts—much more so than for Muslims—their shrines are ways of asserting their prior claim to the land of Egypt. For Muslims—much more so than for Copts—they are a way of recalling the legitimacy of a land that was converted long ago—and that has connections with the Prophet and his Companions—and where pre-Islamic prophets such as Joseph and Jesus simply foretold the coming of the Sufi saints who lie in Egypt's Muslim mausoleums. For both Copts and Muslims, the *moulids* are proof that Egypt was a country that was chosen by God: it is mentioned in both the Bible and the Koran.

These protestations of identity are, perhaps, more strident at the main regional and national shrines, where the influence of the bishoprics and monasteries is strongest. Not all Egypt's shrines are on this scale, and it is really at small shrines that do not attract pilgrims from afar and at village patronal feasts that it is still possible to find Copts and Muslims joining in the same processions, or dancing together around a "shared" shrine. A shared heritage in which dancing, music, colors, cooking, and smells promote a physical sense of belonging to a place cannot vanish too rapidly.

Belonging, election, and heritage: an awareness that Copts and Muslims do share something more important than shrines underpins recent clumsy attempts on the part of a few intellectuals and artists from Cairo to treat their *moulids* as folklore. The operettas that use a *moulid* as a theme, and the books with photographs comparing Coptic and Muslim *moulids*, are all reminders—which take little heed of the need for scientific rigor—that Copts and Muslims do have a shared culture, and that it finds expressions in their *moulids*. And ultimately, what do Egypt's Copts and Muslims have in common? The fact that they are all Egyptians.

Notes

1. For the percentage, see Courbage and Fargues 1992. The 1996 census confirmed that the percentage of Copts in the Egyptian population had fallen. Until recently, there were, proportionately, many more Christians in Bilâd al-Shâm (including Syria-Lebanon).

2. In May 1992, Dr. Nasr Hamid Abu Zayd, who taught at the University of Cairo, submitted a list of his publications to the Standing Committee of Academic Tenure and Promotion in an application for advancement. One member of the university accused Abu Zayd of "affronts to the Muslim faith" because of his work on a liberal exegesis of the Koran. The committee, and then the Council of the University of Cairo, refused to grant him promotion. A jurist then lodged a complaint with the Personal Status Court in Giza, demanding that Abu Zayd be divorced from his wife, Dr. Ibtihal Younes. The request was based upon the claim that Dr. Abu Zayd was an apostate: a Muslim woman cannot be married to an apostate. The request was initially rejected, but was then accepted by the Cairo Court of Appeal, which annulled the marriage between Abu Zayd and Ibtihal Younes in 1995. Having received death threats, the couple had to flee Egypt for the Netherlands.

3. See his memoir *Out of Place* (Said 1999). Cf. Ilbert and Yannakis 1992. See also Kirou 2003.

4. Such as the Wissas and the Faltas. See Wissa 2000.

5. As can be seen from a significant passage in the memoirs of the Egyptian feminist Nabawiyya Mûsâ, *Târîkhî bi qalamî,* rev. ed. (Cairo: Matba'at al-mar'a wa l-dhâkira, 1992), 81.

6. The ongoing work of Francine Costet-Tardieu clearly demonstrates the essentially political aspect of these reports, which were manipulated by Sheikh Al-Marâghî, who was Sheikh of Al-Azar in 1932–1933 (Costet-Tardieu 2005). An article in the missionary journal *The Muslim World* reports the worries of some Coptic clerics at this time (Rev. Sergius, "When Copts Becomes Muslims," *Muslim World* 26, no. 4 [1936]: 372–379).

7. This is the convincing thesis put forward by Dina el-Khawaga in her doctoral dissertation *Le Renouveau copte: La communauté comme acteur politique* (Paris: IEP, 1993).

8. On these conversions to Islam, see Guirguis 2008.

9. It should, however, be noted that when Copts emigrated, they usually did so for economic reasons; large numbers of Egyptian Muslims also emigrated for similar reasons. On the position of Copts today, see el-Khawaga, *Le Renouveau copte*; Masson 2001a, 2001b. The reports written for *Proche-Orient Chrétien* by Father Jacques Masson, S.J., are the best source of documentation on the Copt question in today's Egypt.

10. The tiny, museographic district of Old Cairo is in no sense an equivalent to the Christian districts of towns in Syria. Cf. Vivier 2005, 2006.

11. See Jullien 1886; Mayeur-Jaouen 1992; Meinardus 1987. For a recent description of the site, see Keriakos 2008.

12. A parallel between the apparitions in Zaytûn and Assiut is drawn by Sandrine Keriakos in her *Saintetés en partage* (Keriakos 2008). Cf. her contribution to the present volume.

13. On these practices, see Viaud 1978.

14. On the Coptic revival, see Sidarouss 1980. The recent collaborative collective study is van Doorn-Harder and Vogt 1997. The most complete account is el-Khawaga; see note 7.

15. Cf. Viaud 1978: 56. For a general account of both Coptic and Muslim shrines, see Mayeur-Jaouen 2005.

16. The feast of Abûna Yassâ often occasions rivalry with the relatively high number of Catholic Copts in the Tîma and Tahtâ regions. Cf. Mayeur-Jaouen 2008.

NINE

Apparitions of the Virgin in Egypt: Improving Relations between Copts and Muslims?

SANDRINE KERIAKOS
Translated by David Macey

Devotional practices centered on saints in contemporary Egypt are often seen as an essentially, or primarily, communitarian phenomenon. We therefore study Coptic practices on the one hand, and Muslim rites on the other. When it comes to saints, religions never mix, or so it is said, rather as though similar practices existed in parallel but never came into contact. Yet if we divorce Christians and Muslims in this way and establish a watertight frontier between their respective practices, we overlook one phenomenon that is at work in contemporary Egypt: the existence of practices common to both. Copts and Muslims are sometimes observed gathering around holy figures, who may or may not be "shared," and giving their piety free rein without any religious distinctions. They do meet and mingle in holy places. We therefore simply cannot study Egypt's religious dimension by restricting devotional practices relating to the sacred to either the Christian or the Muslim community. There are overlaps, and there are places that encourage worshipers of both religions to come together, and there are events and saintly figures that encourage them to do so. Two figures stand out: St. Georges, who is often identified with Al-Khidr by Muslims, and the Virgin Mary, who is mentioned in both the Bible and the Koran. This study will concentrate on the latter by looking at an unusual phenomenon. Egypt seems in fact to be something of a special place, as Mary has often appeared there since the 1960s. In most cases, her apparitions have given rise to some form of encounter between Christians and Muslims. This chapter looks at how such encounters are structured, at what makes them possible, at the way they are reported in the press, both communitarian and governmental, and at the extent to which they have survived the changes that have taken place in Egyptian society, where the religious divide is now more pronounced than ever. Written sources (articles in the press and Coptic hagiography) and interviews, some of them with Orthodox Coptic priests, will be used to evoke the memory of these encounters and to look at their contemporary relevance.

The Phenomenon of Marian Apparitions in Egypt

Maryam is very dear to the believers who have built so many shrines to her in Egypt and who go on pilgrimages to them as different times throughout the year. Al-ʿAdhraʾ *moulid*s take place at the various sites that the saint reportedly visited during the flight into Egypt. The Virgin herself also appears to have a special fondness for the Egyptian people, and often visits them in her own way. The Nile Valley is in fact the site of a remarkable phenomenon: the Virgin continually appears there at irregular intervals and in different forms, but with a frequency that demands attention. She sometimes appears more than once in the same place, appearing in places that she reportedly visited to protect the baby Jesus two thousand years ago. The most striking modern examples are Zeitun and Asiut, where she appeared in 1968 and 2000 respectively. As Henri Holstein remarks (2002:101) of contemporary Christianity: "Apparitions play a major role . . . and help to give piety a particular character. In the Middle Ages, pilgrims were motivated by a desire to visit places associated with the memory of Jesus or his Apostles and which Christianity therefore held dear, such as Jerusalem, Rome or Santiago de Compostello. Pilgrims are now more interested in going to shrines built in places where the Virgin has appeared." Examples include La Salette, Lourdes, Fatima, and, more recently, Medjugorje, all of which have been visited by the Virgin. Their fame is such that they attract millions of pilgrims every year. The phenomenon of Marian apparitions is not specific to Egypt and can be observed throughout Christendom, both Catholic and Orthodox. It does, however, take on a particular significance in the Nile valley, where Christians like to think that they are privileged witnesses to apparitions of saints in general and of the Virgin in particular. The Egyptian people like to think that Mary has a very special affection for the Egypt that gave her shelter, and that she is only too happy to give them the occasional reminder of that by appearing to them.

All the sources that mention the Virgin's apparitions and transfigurations in Egypt insist that they have happened so often that it seems impossible to count them. The many eyewitness accounts that have been passed on by the oral tradition report that thousands of the faithful have had personal encounters with the Virgin, who appeared to them in a dream or vision, usually at night. The Coptic tradition, on the other hand, reports a series of apparitions from late antiquity to the present day. They were seen mainly by Orthodox Coptic patriarchs and (neo-)martyrs. I will list them in chronological order.

1. The Virgin is reported to have appeared to Pope Dimitri I at the beginning of the third century. He was reputed to be one of the less well educated patriarchs, and she appeared to impart a knowledge that was more in keeping with his rank.

2. In 380, Pope Theophilus (384–412), the twenty-second pope of Alexandria, was about to go to the Al-Muharraq monastery to consecrate a church. At this point, the Virgin appeared to him and explained that the church had already been consecrated by Christ himself when he came to Egypt in order to flee Herod. She also took the opportunity to tell him the whole story of the Holy Family's travels. This apparition gave birth to the apocryphal text known as *The Vision of Theophilus* (see Valensi 2002)

3. At the beginning of the fifth century, she appeared to resolve a theological dispute between St. John Chrysostom and Pope Theophilus, and took the side of the latter.

4. The Abassid caliph Al-Ma'mun (813–833) had ordered the destruction of all the churches in Egypt, and especially the church in Atrib, near what is now the town of Benha. The priest in charge asked for a stay of execution of four days. During that period, the Virgin appeared to the caliph and softened his heart. All the churches in the country were spared.

5. In 978 the Fatimid caliph Al-Mu'izz li-Din Allah was inspired by one of his ministers, a former Jew who had converted to Islam, to put the faith of Christians to the test. In order to do so, he challenged the sixty-first patriarch, Abraham I (976–979), to move Mount Muqattam, and reminded him of Jesus' words: "Because of your unbelief . . . verily I say unto you . . . If ye have faith as a grain of mustard seed, ye shall say unto this mountain, Remove yourself to yonder place and it shall remove" (Mt 17:20).

   Not knowing what to do, the pope prayed before the icon of the Virgin for three days. She then spoke to him, telling him not to worry and that she was by his side. And the mountain did move, plunging both Muslims and Christians into great fear.

6. In 1047, she appeared while Christodoulos (1047–1078), the sixty-fifth primate to lead the Coptic Church, was celebrating Mass.

7. In 1624, she appeared to Pope John XV (1621–1631). He is said to have always spoken to the Virgin, who advised him on all matters through her icon.

8. On 25 April 1844, she appeared to Sidhom Bishay. He was in the process of being martyred by representatives of the government, and implored her to relieve his pain and put an end to his suffering; she eventually granted his wish. Sidhom Bishay is now recognized as a saint by the Orthodox Coptic Church, and large numbers of pilgrims visit Damietta to see the reliquary in which his body is preserved intact. It is said that after his martyrdom, Copts were allowed to carry the cross in their funeral processions. Until then, that practice had been forbidden.

This brings us to the era of Marian apparitions in the twentieth century, when we find that the phenomenon changes. In this period, the Virgin always appears not to one individual or one member of the clergy, but to the whole people, and often to Muslims as well as Christians, to followers of confessions other than Coptic orthodoxy, and even to atheists. This tells us a lot about the changes that have taken place. Marian apparitions are no longer associated with any form of elitism. The saint no longer appears only to those who are high up in the religious hierarchy, but to specific religious communities or to individuals who have dedicated their lives to God. She no longer appears to just one person, as had previously been the case both in Egypt and elsewhere (as in Lourdes, where she appeared only to Bernadette, and Fatima, where she appeared to three children), but to everyone.

The first of these "collective" apparitions took place on 14 June 1954 in the Coptic Patriarchate of Jerusalem. On several different occasions, pupils at St. Anthony's school—most of them were Christian, but there was one Muslim girl—saw her in various classrooms. We have here, I think, the first indications of a phenomenon that was to become more pronounced: the saint begins to appear to the people, and is no longer revealed solely within the patriarchate, or only to clerics or pious men. In contemporary Egypt, the apparitions are meant to be inclusive and nonsectarian: anyone can witness them. There has therefore clearly been a change in the relationship with the saint, or even with sainthood in general. The laity can now apprehend it on a personal basis, without the help of the clergy. The apparition in Jerusalem clearly signals this change: the Virgin appears in the patriarchate, not to the clergy but to a mixed class in which Christians rub shoulders with Muslims. At this stage, the phenomenon exists in an embryonic state, as though it were a trial run for a second apparition that would reveal its full extent a few years later. The timid presence of a Muslim child would soon become a truly mixed phenomenon concerning both the followers of Christ and the followers of Mohammed. When the Virgin appears in Egypt in the twentieth century, she does so in a collective context, appearing to thousands of people and on several occasions, with some apparitions going on for months. The most striking example is still the apparitions of the Virgin that occurred in Zeitun from April 1968 onward. Brigitte Voile devotes one chapter of her book on the Copts under Nasser to them (Voile 2004). But when Voile talks specifically about sainthood among Egypt's Christians, she turns it into a phenomenon that is essentially communitarian. It is true, and this should not be forgotten, that this apparition occurred at a time when the Copts had embarked upon a "spiritual renaissance" designed to reorganize the community around its saints. The saints were everywhere. More and more images of saints were appearing in homes, and they could be seen in the churches and monasteries that housed their relics. The saints themselves were constantly appearing. The Marian apparitions in Zeitun are obviously part of this continuum. If, however, we restrict them to the Coptic sphere, we fail to see the phenomenon in all its complexity. For our purposes, the interesting thing about these apparitions it that they were not just for the benefit of the Coptic community. Muslims saw them in the same way that Christians saw them, and this allowed the emergence of a shared place of worship.

Apparitions of the Virgin in Zeitun

While the striking thing about the Egyptian apparitions is that they happened more than once, those that occurred in Zeitun are the most impressive, and they are the ones that have caused most ink to the spilled. It is not only that they are the most spectacular apparitions to have occurred in the Christian world—no other apparition in two thousand years of Christianity has ever attracted so many devotees and curious spectators. They also occurred in places of worship that are used by both Christians and Muslims.

Egyptians remember the Virgin's apparitions in this little suburb in north-eastern Cairo as an unprecedented event: they occurred more than once over an extended period of time and were extraordinarily powerful. Beginning on 2 April 1968, the Virgin appeared several times on the five domes of the church in Zeitun, which is dedicated to her. This ensured that the repercussions of this manifestation of her sainthood were felt far beyond Egypt's frontiers, and that both the national and the international press took an interest in it. The apparitions led to an unprecedented display of devotion on the part of both Christians and Muslims. A number of factors explain what they converged on Zeitun.

The Scriptural Concordance

It should be noted that neither Christians nor Muslims were indifferent to the fact that it was the Virgin herself who appeared to them, as she is an emblematic figure in both Islam and Christianity. Many of them think that it is important to emphasize that God did not cause Jesus or some other saint to appear, but Mary, who is seen in similar ways by both communities. Mary is mentioned several times in the Koran.[1] As in the Gospel, she is the mother of Jesus, and it is her virginity that marks her out from other women. In the Muslim religion, Mary is venerated mainly for her virtues: her virginal purity, humility, and piety make her a model for believers. According to Islam, she is also one of the four perfect women in the world, the others being Asiya (Pharaoh's wife), Khadija (the wife of the Prophet), and Fatima (daughter of the Prophet and wife of ʿAli).

For their part, Egypt's Christians have a particular affection for the woman they call "the queen of saints" (*malikat al-qiddisin*) or "mother of light" (*umm al-nur*). Like Islam, Orthodox Christianity sees her as a woman who has undoubtedly been chosen by God, as we can see from the biblical verse: "Hail, thou who art highly favoured, the Lord is with thee: blessed art though amongst women" (Lk 1:28). The Coptic Church's cult of Mary is certainly one of the most important, and it makes her the saint par excellence. In addition to the month of *kyahk* (December/January), which is completely dedicated to her, the Synaxarion contains no fewer than thirty-two commemorations of her. One falls in 2 April (24 *baramhat*), which is the date of the saint's first apparition in Zeitun.[2]

Marian Piety in Egypt

The similarity between the Mary of the New Testament and the Mary of the Koran inevitably has its effects on the way religion is experienced in everyday life. Egyptians have adopted the custom of gathering at the Marian sites that are now found throughout Egypt. These include Daqadus, Samannud, Musturud, the Al-Muharraq monastery, and the Gabal al-Tayr monastery near Asiut, to mention only the most famous.[3] These Marian shrines are real crossroads for the followers of the two religions, who like to demonstrate their devotion to Mary by going to the places she visited during the flight into Egypt because they are convinced that they have been blessed: "All places of pilgrimage have one thing in common: it is believed that miracles once happened in these places, that they still happen, and that they might happen again" (Valensi 2002:221). There is nothing new about these overlaps; on the contrary, they have a long history, demonstrating that the Marian cult has always facilitated exchanges between individuals of the two religions. As early as the late fifteenth century, Felix Fabri, who spent several weeks in Egypt, said that in Cairo he saw "a very old tree that both Christians and Muslims venerated because it had afforded shade to the Virgin and the baby Jesus" (Valensi 2002:124). He also describes the garden in Matariah, where these shared beliefs overlap and intersect.

The Flight into Egypt: A Shared Tradition

Most of these sites are associated with the places in the Nile valley where the Holy Family stayed during their flight into Egypt. In the Christian tradition most of these stories come from apocryphal accounts such as the *Gospel of Pseudo-Matthew* (also known as the *Infancy Gospel*) and the *Childhood of Jesus* (or the *Childhood of Jesus in Arabic*). There is also a variant known as the Armenian *Gospel of the Infancy*. There are also two other traditions that are mainly reported by the Eastern churches, the *Story of Joseph the Carpenter* and the *Vision of Theophilus*. While this is, a priori, a Christian tradition, it is not unknown in Islam. Like the Bible itself, the Koran obviously does not mention it in so many words. It does make a minor allusion to it when it says of Mary and Joseph that "we . . . gave them shelter on a peaceful hill-side watered by a fresh spring" (XXIII, 50). Similarly, the Gospel of St. Matthew is the only one to mention it, and it does so very briefly, as only their departure and return are mentioned (Mt 2:13–15, 19–21). Religions, however, are not based on sacred texts and divine revelations alone. Tradition also has a major part to play. Like the

Christian apocryphal texts, Islam's historic-religious stories (*hadith, sira, Qisas al-Anbiya'*) have more to say on this subject. The story of the Holy Family's journey through Egypt, as recounted by the Christian tradition, seems to have been in circulation in the peninsula that gave birth to Islam at a very early date. It is mentioned by Wahb b. Munabbih (654–655/728–732), who wrote in the first half of the seventh century and who is regarded as the first person to write *Qisas*. His followers Al-Farisi (eighth century), Al-Tha'labi (eleventh century), and Ibn Kathir (fourteenth century) also mention it.[4]

As Lucette Valensi remarks (2002:55) in her detailed study of the resonances of these well-known stories for the Muslim religion and the ways in which it is has (re-)appropriated them, it usually attempts to find traces of Christianity and Judaism in Islam: "Given that they came first in historical terms, this is quite legitimate. But when Islam and Arabic became the dominant religion and the dominant language, it is possible that they in their turn influenced traditions that already existed in what were now Islamic societies. . . . The exchanges are therefore not one-way, or between the older religions and the latest monotheism." The reworkings of this tradition and the probable interaction between the two religions concerned have generated a religious episode that now seems to be a point of reference for both Christians and Muslims. Egyptian Christianity certainly attached some importance to it at a very early date as, according to the ancient texts mentioned by Valensi, "The Holy Family's flight into Egypt was being commemorated as early as the fourth and fifth centuries."[5] But Egyptian Islam also appropriated it, and made this "historical" sequence part of the common heritage of both Christians and non-Christians with such a degree of compatibility that it is, it might be said, common to all Egyptians (Valensi 2002:91). There is in fact nothing specifically Christian about Marian topography in Egypt.

Stories and Attitudes

There are therefore scriptural, traditional, and practical reasons why both Christians and Muslims should converge on Zeitun. But let us now look at what happens when they meet at the spot where the actual apparitions occurred.

All the eyewitness accounts of the 1968 apparitions insist on making the same point: both Christians and Muslims were present in the church in Zeitun, and there were no differences between them. No one took much notice of their neighbor's religion: the pilgrims were interested only in seeing the Marian apparition and receiving the saint's blessing. The contemporary reports published in the press make the same point. While *Al-Ahram* and other government newspapers all gave the apparitions in Zeitun some coverage, it was the Copt weekly *Watani* that spoke about them at greatest length as it covered the event throughout its duration, or in other words until 1971, it seems. The articles devoted to it are a real gold mine, as they include over 2,400 eyewitness accounts. They come from very different sources: in some cases, the articles simply mention the names of those who saw the Virgin, or who told journalists that they had done so, but others tell real stories in which both Christians and Muslims explain what they saw in detail. Still others tell stories of actual cures, and not just of visions. In that sense, the sample provided by *Watani* is highly revelatory. Of the 2,430 accounts I have been able to trace, 2,157 (89.76%) are attributable to Christians and 188 (7.83%) to Muslims, while 58 (2.41%) could not be placed in either category, either because the names of the witnesses could be either Christian or Muslim or simply because they were not given. While the percentage of Muslims is tiny compared with that of Christians, it is interesting to note that Muslims took the trouble to write to the editor of *Watani* to describe the miracle they had been vouchsafed. On reading these stories, we find that there is no significant difference between those told by Christians and those told by Muslims. Muslims appear to have been able to enter the church perimeter without too much difficulty, and began their vigil alongside the Christians who were present. When the Virgin appeared, both Christians and Muslims raised their hands, and asked her to intercede on their behalf, to grant them a cure or to relieve their sufferings. We sometimes find touching accounts in which Muslims went to the church without knowing how they should behave; they watched their neighbors, and began to chant the same litanies and say the same words. Other accounts are still more astonishing in that they could come from either Muslims or Christians. On 1 March 1970, a Muslim women called Nagat Hashim Hasan told the paper:

> I had not been feeling well for some months, but the doctors did not know what was wrong with me. So my family took me to Zeitun and the priests who were there immediately understood that I had been possessed. They prayed until the spirit left my body. When I went home with my sister, I went into the bathroom and found that my body was covered in crosses. So I went back to Zeitun, and asked the priests to say prayers to glorify and thank God.[6]

Others, in contrast, place greater emphasis on their religious affiliations. Making the sign of the cross, describing the Virgin as a saint (*al-qiddisa Maryam*), or saying a Hail Mary indicates that the witness was a Christian, while reciting the Exordium or verses relating to Mary (from the "Al-Imran" and "Maryam" suras) or pronouncing the famous formula *Allah akbar* are indications of his or her Islamic affiliation.[7] In some cases it is also possible to identify members of the Muslim community in the crowd, especially during the period of Ramadan. Once again, the reports give eloquent accounts of the climate that prevailed at Zeitun: every morning, the priests in the church took it upon themselves to let the Muslims present known when it was time for *suhur* so that they could eat before beginning their daily fast.[8] Some Muslims, on the other hand, sometimes felt obliged to state their religion because they feared that if they were carried away by the emotions of the crowd, they would seem "too Christian." When, for instance, Michel Nil interviewed Zaynab Tahir, who lived in Zeitun at this time, she told him (Nil 2000:52–53):

> So the apparitions had been going on since the beginning of the month. No, I didn't really believe there would be an apparition this century. Although I live so near by . . . I had never thought of going there. Mainly because, I have to tell you, I am of the Muslim religion and I know that the Virgin had appeared in Lourdes . . . to some Catholic girl. Given my religion and the fact that she was appearing on the roof of a church, I said to myself: "I won't see her, not me." She wasn't going to appear to me, was she? And I also said to myself: "Even if it is true, I don't need . . ." And I also know that when the Holy Virgin appears to someone, it is to give them a message. So I said: "She's probably chosen who to appear to, so even if I go there—this was at night—I won't see anything . . . I was in a little alleyway. I said: "These children are having me on: it's pitch dark! . . . And why are all these people screaming like hysterics?" I didn't understand. And then one of my son's friends said "Madame, when I say 'one, two, three . . .' run, so that you don't get trampled underfoot." That's what I did, because there was a crowd and you couldn't get near. I caught up with one of them and I ran. . . . The sky was completely dark. I said to myself: "Oh come on, where is this apparition?" And then suddenly, between two of the church's cupolas, I saw! . . . I began to scream as though I was hysterical, like the rest of the crowd. To tell you the truth, I was frightened to make the sign of the cross, or whatever. So I said, in Arabic, "There is no other God but God" What do you expect? (she laughs, as though she were embarrassed).

Ritual differences therefore become blurred at Zeitun, and even when they were observed, no one took any notice of them. The new Marian site thus became an enormous number of identical pilgrims praying in the same way: there was no way of telling them apart.

We find the same lack of differentiation when we look at the many miracles that occurred there. The devotees went there primarily because they were hoping for a cure. Seventy-nine (11.5%) of the 708 miracles recorded by the Copt weekly were performed for the benefit of Muslims, and 600 (84.74%) for Christians.[9] Once again, there are few perceptible differences between Christians and Muslims in this brief examination of the eyewitness accounts—which looks, of course, at only a sample. As they were all equal in the face of illness, they all benefited from the Virgin's intercession, and bore witness in exactly the same way. The eyewitness accounts show that Christians and Muslims had a very similar perception of miracles, that they were all eager to see one, and that they were happy to talk about them. The miracles, the stories, and the ways in which they addressed themselves to the Virgin were the same: both Christians and Muslims asked her to intercede on their behalf in the same way. This practice shows that an intercessor-intercesee relationship exists in Islam as well as in Christianity. *Watani* gives many examples, including that of ʿUkasha Zaki Muhammad. His three children had a constant fever caused by an internal illness. After a long stay in hospital, they had been forced to return home, but their state of health was getting worse. Not knowing what to do, their father began to pray, and asked the Virgin to intercede on their behalf and to make them better. He prayed to her directly, just as a Christian would have done. He then went so far as to ask the saint to appear to him. When they saw him praying, his wife and aunt laughed at him. But when he went to bed, he did indeed see the Virgin, who granted him his request. Being unaccustomed to this kind of manifestation, he woke up with a start and told his wife what had happened. Once again, she refused to believe him. The next day, the three children knocked on the bedroom door: they were in perfect health. A bewildered Muhammad asked his wife what had happened. She explained that she too had received a visitation from the Virgin, who had told her to drink a glass of water and to give some to her children. She did what she was asked. Although he was relieved, the husband could not stop himself from criticizing his wife for her refusal to believe him. The Virgin had therefore appeared to his wife in order to convince her too.[10]

Muslims are also quite happy to appeal to the Virgin's "intermediaries," or senior members of the Coptic clergy. The stories show that priests and monks often step in to help Christians and Muslims alike, which only goes to show that at Zeitun, the cure is more important than the actor . . .

Ramadan ʿAli Husayn tells the story of his wife Fatima Zaki Rida:

Fatima had been suffering from parotitis for four and a half years. The treatment she was receiving could not cure her. One day, she wanted to go to Zeitun, but she could not go on her own and leave our little girl at home. So I told her that I would go and pray to God for a cure. But the Virgin did not appear that evening. But as she slept, Fatima saw white-robed nuns operating on her. The next day, she went to the hospital for her monthly check-up and to see if the illness was spreading. The doctor found nothing. He asked her to come back the following Saturday, but the illness had gone. When she came home, she saw the nuns again, and she smelled the scent of incense in her room during the night. Then the Virgin appeared to her, and said "Congratulations!" Fatima asked to meet Pope Cyril VI to tell him about the miracle.[11]

It transpires from these stories that Muslims behave in very Christian ways, and it might even be said that custom requires certain practices to lose their primarily Christian connotations. In this case, the priest is not a member of the Coptic clergy: it is one of the saint's auxiliaries who helps to complete the cure. Priests and nuns are agents of the Virgin rather than of the Church. Fatima Ahmad's story makes this point by telling how the Virgin appeared to her to ask her to go to Zeitun and to meet a priest there: he would pray over her son, who was suffering from a muscular complaint. She went to Zeitun the next day. The priest prayed over the child and gave him a cross and some oil, telling him to anoint himself with it as soon as he got home. He did so. When he got up the next day, he was in perfect health.[12]

Other members of the Muslim community ask Mary to intercede in more "orthodox" ways. Reciting a verse from the Koran when she appears, or reciting it with her, seems to be as effective a way of obtaining a cure as asking her to intercede. According to this conception, pious acts, including reciting the Koran, will be rewarded. In such cases, it is the Koran, rather than the saint, that acts as the intercessor (cf. Wensick and Schimmel:183–185). We can see this principle at work in the story Nayruz Banub tells about his work colleague Muhammad Zaki:

He was suffering from angina, and went to Zeitun to pray to God to cure him. But when he got home, he had another attack and, while he was in bed, he again asked God to cure him. At that point, he heard the door of his bedroom open, and saw a woman who was surrounded with light. She came up to him and reassured him. He began to recite the verses from the Koran that mention how Mary was chosen by God. The next day, he was better.[13]

Others address their prayers to the Virgin indirectly. Fayiza 'Ali Hasan, for instance, recited the "Maryam" sura three times every morning. The subterfuge of asking the Virgin to intercede while reciting the Koran obviously works, as the Virgin finally appeared to her and told her she was cured after a few weeks.[14]

These stories are revelatory in a number of ways. The coming together of Christians and Muslims is not just a physical event that takes place in a specific place, such as Zeitun in this case. It also happens at the level of practice, as the followers of one religion imitate the attitudes of the other. If need be, they are quite prepared to appropriate the methods adopted by others in order to obtain a cure. The practice of intercession is of course banned by Sunni orthodoxy. But in this case, as with all *walis*, the precepts imposed by official Islam suddenly cease to have any effect, as these miracles are neither controlled nor encouraged by religious leaders. It has much more to do with a private initiative. When it is a matter of satisfying needs or relieving suffering, all the constraints or norms that are imposed by official religions are ignored and give way to what might be called "folk" customs. The explanation lies in an old familiarity with them on the part of Christians and Muslims alike. The devotee is alone with the saint, out of scriptural legality and the patronage of the clergy and the ulemas.

Muslims as Guarantors

The reason why so much emphasis is placed on eyewitness accounts from Muslims is that Muslims play a special role in these apparitions, and that (Christian) journalists always do all they can to emphasize their importance. The sources describing the Virgin's various apparitions in Zeitun mention an impressive number of eyewitnesses. Forty million people from different countries and of different nationalities and religions are reported to have witnessed them.[15] The Virgin's first apparition in the inner suburbs of Cairo occurred at 3:30 on the morning of Tuesday, 2 April 1968. The first to see her were workers at the bus depot opposite the church. They were standing outside the door to the garage when their attention was caught by a beam of light coming from the church's cupola. They watched carefully and saw a girl in a white dress. She had prostrated herself before the cross on top of the church's central dome. At first, they thought that she was a woman who was trying to commit suicide. One of the workers ran to stop her from throwing herself off the roof, and shouted to her to be careful. The fire brigade had been called, and a crowd had gathered in front of the church. The young woman then stood up on the roof and turned to face the crowd, with an olive branch in her hand. The peace symbol did not escape the notice of the watching crowd. The halo of light around her then became brighter, and allowed the first spectators to gradually make out her features and to realize that she was Mary. Intrigued by all the shouting, crowds of Christians and Muslims quickly began to gather in the church courtyard, all spellbound and caught up in the same religious fervor. This was the first instance of an act of faith that was to be repeated over a period of almost three years. From that day onward, thousands of people—Egyptians and foreigners, Christians and Muslims—came from the four corners of the earth to witness the miracle and to strengthen their faith.

The important thing about this initial apparition is that the first witnesses were all Muslims. This is highly significant: the miracle is witnessed by some-one of a different religion. Unless such a witness is present, there can be no shared place of worship. The fact that it is a Muslim who witnesses a phe-nomenon that occurs in a Christian building guarantees its authenticity. As Catherine Mayeur-Jaouen (2005:348) puts it: "There could not be better proof that this was a real miracle." If the first witness had been a Christian, he would obviously have been dismissed as a liar; Muslims, who are assumed to be either more incredulous or neutral, make much better witnesses.

The miraculous dimension of Zeitun was demonstrated in the same way. The first person to see the Virgin was a Muslim, and one of his coreligionists was the first beneficiary of her intercession. We are told that Faruq Muhummad Atwa, who was one of the first witnesses, was the beneficiary of the saint's heal-ing powers. He had injured a finger. Unable to find a suitable way of treating the wound, the doctors had told him that they were going to amputate. When he saw the young woman on the roof, he thought that she was trying to commit suicide, and pointed at her with his finger as he warned her to be careful. When he went to see the surgeon next day, the surgeon took off the bandage on his finger and was amazed to see that the wound had healed perfectly. The miracle is mentioned in all the sources and all the descriptions of the apparitions.[16] There is an obvious desire to foreground this miracle because the beneficiary was a Muslim. The journalists give the stories of Muslims their rightful due, and sometimes prioritize those stories in which a certain incredulity turns into a form of repentance. There are many such accounts, including that given by Husayn Husayn Muhammad Musa:

> On 15 October, I went to the moulid of Sittina Zaynab and prayed in the
> mosque. On my way back, I met Makram Nagib Musa, a Christian friend.
> I wanted to tell him about the apparitions of the Virgin but refrained from

doing so, telling myself that it was none of his business. When I got home, I had a vision. I was in a holy place, in front of the church of the Virgin, in the middle of a crowd that was looking at the sky. The people were shouting that *Umm al-Nur* was about to appear. I went into the church to see if anyone was shining a light to give the impression that an apparition was taking place. I went back outside, and the light was still there. So I prayed to the Virgin to beg her forgiveness, and assured her that I now believed in her apparition. . . . The light remained until I woke up.

I wanted to write about my experience for the benefit of anyone who had doubts about these apparitions. God has showered with us with his blessing and those of all the prophets and saints.[17]

The astonishing thing about the metamorphosis is often just how radical it is. In one incident, a foreign journalist who was visiting the suburb of Zeitun with the minister for labor and an Egyptian television executive was accosted by a local who insisted on telling his story. This is the journalist's version (Brune 2004:4–41):

At first, he was violently hostile and insulted the pilgrims who passed his house on their way to the church.

He used to throw stones at them, and called the police to have them arrested. But the Virgin appeared to him and asked him why he was behaving in this way. She begged him to change his ways, and suggested that he should paint a cross on his house.

Although he remained a Muslim, he was so convinced that the apparitions were authentic that he painted forty large crosses on all the walls of his house.

There is also a common tendency to rely upon the stories of Muslims in high places. We are, for instance, told that Kamal Hamida, the deputy governor of Cairo, and Faruq Ghallab, the parliamentary leader of the independent group, saw the Virgin on 1 June. No full account of their Marian experience is given, and their names are simply included alongside others in the list of eyewitnesses, but the articles do point out that they are famous.[18] And contemporary Egyptian accounts are not the only ones to adopt this approach. In 1969, J. Palmer, a Benedictine from St. Meinard's Archabbey, made a special journey from the United States to gather material on the Zeitun apparitions for a book that was later published under the title *Our Lady Returns to Egypt*. He included eyewitness accounts from non-Christians (most of them Muslims in high places) because he too realized that they had to be included in any coverage of such a sensitive issue as an apparition in a context where Christians and Muslims lived side by side: if Muslims believed it was authentic, everyone would believe it.

The invocation of Nasser as a guarantor is also interesting. Some sources (but not the majority) make a point of telling their readers that Nasser went to Zeitun in person to witness the apparitions. His presence went unnoticed because he did not mingle with the crowd and reportedly saw the apparition from inside a private house:

> Every evening, the crowd gathered in the church and looked to the sky in the hope of seeing the Virgin. The scene was repeated several times over the next few days. This inspired President Nasser to go there with the Secretary of the Islamic Council Husayn al-Shafi'i. They went to the house of Ahmad Zaydan, a fruit vendor, which was opposite the church. Nasser waited there until the Virgin appeared at 5 in the morning. (cited in Johnston 1980:23)

There are those who point out that this is in fact a "posthumous account," given that the sources that refer to the presence of Nasser date from after 1972, and that earlier accounts make no mention of it. It is therefore likely to be a Christian construct designed to give the apparitions greater credibility and legitimacy, but also to demonstrate that Nasser was sympathetic to the Coptic community. What could be more convincing than the story of a president who did not mingle with the crowd, and whom no one could have seen? There are other traces of the president's furtive visit. Father Constantine, who was one of the priests in charge interviewed by Brune, stated that the church in Zeitun had a visitors' book. Nasser reportedly signed and dated a message confirming that he had seen the Virgin in Zeitun (Brune 2004:9). It is impossible to verify this story because the book has, unsurprisingly, disappeared, and no one knows where it is!

Even though it is never spelled out in so many words, there is a real awareness that Muslims were being used as "guarantors." They both confirm that the apparition was real and reinforce the self-image Egypt has always tried to project: it is a tolerant nation where Christians and Muslims live side by side in perfect harmony.

The Attitude of the Coptic Clergy

Neither the attitude of the pilgrims, their devotion, nor the miracles they were vouchsafed can provide a full explanation for the process that allowed Muslims and Copts to meet in Zeitun. The attitude of the Coptic hierarchy, and even of those at its highest level—Patriarch Cyril VI set the example—was also very important.

It is noteworthy that little or no importance is given to the theological explanations one might have expected to find in the various commentaries on Zeitun. The first thing we should note is the disconcerting ease with which the Coptic clergy abandons one of the Church's notions, namely the belief that Mary is the mother of God. For while the Virgin of the New Testament does share many of the same attributes as the Koranic Mary, she is fundamentally different. For Christians, Mary is the mother of God; for Muslims, she is the mother of a prophet. The Syrian writer Sadiq Jalal al-'Azm was the first to raise this fundamental issue.[19] The reason why he finds it so difficult to understand the attitude of the Coptic authorities is that he fails to see the phenomenon of the apparitions from an interfaith perspective: the implications of the public events that took place at Zeitun are political and national rather than religious. All the explanations that are given for the apparitions are based on the same model: they erase any distinctive signs that might offend anyone, and find many signs that can be used to invoke Egypt's special role and national unity. For similar reasons, no source ever dares to give an explanation as to why the Virgin appeared on the roof of a church rather than a mosque or somewhere else. Because they are controversial, such issues were discussed in private, and remained within the Copt community. The official sources—both written and oral—never raise the issue of where the apparitions took place.

In the case of Zeitun, religious, eschatological, and theological explanations are avoided in favor of the contextual and political justifications that further encourage the rapprochement between Christians and Muslims.

The Silence of the Virgin

If I may be so bold as to give my own interpretation, the significant thing about the apparitions in Zeitun—as opposed to those in Lourdes or Fatima— is that the Virgin does not speak. She does not deliver any specific message. Many thought that "her silence [was] in itself an important message" (Brune 2004:195). The "absence of any message" was often seen as an appeal for peace and an invitation to both Christians of different confessions and individuals following different religions to unite. That is why she appeared with an olive branch in her hand—the classic symbol of peace for Christians—and that is why she appeared in Zeitun, which, as everyone was quick to point out, means "olive tree." The apparitions were steeped in the themes of pacifism and tolerance. She did not come to give Christianity precedence, or to condemn Muslims:

> The Virgin still maintained her prodigious silence. . . . The absence of any spoken sign was interpreted as a sign of her maternal tact and tenderness for all her children, no matter what their religion. If, for example, she had declared herself to be the mother of Christ, the Muslims, who do not recognize the divinity of Christ, would have rebelled and tried to pick a fight with the Christians. If she had identified herself as the Virgin of the Immaculate Conception, the Copts, who believe that it was only at the time of the Annunciation that she was made a saint, would have found it difficult to accept her fully. The Madonna therefore simply adopted the stance of a woman saying her prayers, as though she was inviting all present to come together in God through their prayers, irrespective of their beliefs. (Johnston 1980:19)

Her presence was the only message she brought, and by remaining silent she allowed everyone to project their own relation with God and, more specifically, to identify with her. Indeed, it was her silence that brought Christians and Muslims together: the saint's silence made it perfectly clear that she had appeared to everyone. Had she spoken, that would not have been the case. Her silence allowed everyone to interpret the apparition as they thought fit. While the devout saw it simply as a sign that the Virgin was lending individuals her support, the journalists and the Coptic clergy took it as a sign that the whole nation enjoyed her support. We therefore have to look at the historico-political context.

The Historico-political Dimension

No book published before 1968 makes the claim that Zeitun was one of the places visited by the Holy Family on their journey through Egypt. It is now officially described as such by both Coptic hagiographic booklets about the Holy Family and Muslim *Qisas* about Jesus and His Mother.[20] One typical feature of all these sources is that they locate the saint's apparition in a historico-political context. Cyril was the first to do so, in his initial statement to the press: he specifically said that the Virgin had begun to appear on 2 April, and that this was quite credible because the *historical* evidence proved that the Virgin had come this way as the church in Zeitun was on the road to Matariah; it is now claimed that this was the road taken by the Holy Family in its journey across Egypt. The historicity of the event is obviously open to challenge, as it is well known that the foundations of Coptic history are strangely weak. But the Church constantly resorts to the tactic of superimposing the history of the nation on its religious tradition, and interprets Egypt's contemporary history in the light of its past history. We have here an unusual phenomenon: while contemporary events are usually interpreted in the light of the past, the opposite happens where the Virgin is concerned. The meaning of her contemporary apparitions is interpreted in the light of the political dimensions that are taken on by the earlier apparitions. What is much more significant is that this makes contemporary events a continuation of the sacred history of Egypt and demonstrates that the country has not lost pride of place in the divine plan. This also suggests that the figure of Mary has a lot to do with the nation's history. She can become a sign in her own right, without any help from Christ, even though he was the central figure in the original epic. In his commentary on the Zeitun apparitions, Milad Hanna explains why the figure of a woman figures so prominently in Egyptian beliefs, and why both Christians and Muslims are so eager to welcome such figures:[21]

> The really surprising thing is that the apparitions of the Virgin sent both Muslims and Christians into raptures. This Egyptian phenomenon has nothing to do with the Virgin herself or with fact that Islam has great respect for the Virgin. It relates to an old Egyptian heritage: the legend of Isis. For the Ancient Egyptians, Isis was a goddess. The Trinity is a notion that dates back to the time of the Pharaohs: Osiris was the father, Isis was the mother, and Horus was the son. Egyptians have therefore always paid homage to a female figure.[22]

The explanation for the similarity between Christian and Muslim practices therefore lies, it is claimed, in the existence of a common heritage that distinct religious affiliations leave unchanged.[23]

As we have seen, the figure of Mary shows Christians and Muslims that they share the same values, and that those values are ultimately based upon the many similarities between the Koran and the New Testament: the Virgin is therefore the one figure to appeal to both communities.

The fact that Christians and Muslims share almost the same conception of the Virgin was not the only reason for the shared devotions that were seen in Zeitun. Another factor—and it is certainly more powerful than any religious awareness that Islam and Christianity share the same values—might explain the presence, not of members of different religious communities, but of Egyptians in general: the defeat in the Six Day War with Israel. At the time of the

Zeitun apparitions, the devout were not the only ones who needed a saint. Losing the war had left a bitter taste in the mouths of all Egyptians. In the press reports, the believers (*mu'minun*) who went to Zeitun suddenly became citizens (*muwatinun*). In this context, there was a desire to see the Virgin as a source of unexpected help, and she was accorded a quasi-political status. Zeitun was not just a place where someone sent by God could encounter believers with a heightened sense of religiosity. It was also a fortified town (*place forte*) where hope could be reborn and where the possibility of victory over the enemy could be envisaged once more. This was not the first time that an apparition of the Virgin had been bound up with the fate of the nation. When the miracle at Muqattam occurred, the saint herself allowed the Copts to find their place in Egyptian society by sparing them from a new period of discrimination.[24] What was new was that her field of action was no longer restricted to the Coptic community but was extended to include all Egyptians—Christian and Muslim.

The apparitions had two effects. On the one hand, they gave the people as a whole the feeling that they were under the protection of the Virgin; on the other, they gave new hope to desperate believers who thought that the Virgin's implicit message was the victory over the Zionists that they had been promised. *Al-Ahram* put it very clearly in its issue of 5 May 1968: "The apparition of the Virgin shows that God will grant us victory and that heaven will not abandon us."[25] For his part, *Watani's* Antun Nagib Matar places the Virgin's apparitions at the heart of the Arab-Israeli conflict. It also succeeded in establishing a link between the saint's first visit during the flight into Egypt and her apparition at the church in Zeitun: according to the journalist, the saint had gone into exile for a second time, and this was a "repeat of the flight into Egypt" (Voile 2004:224). As she had said nothing, these words were put into her mouth: "I come in peace, as I came before, and I will go home to Palestine when the storm has passed, and when it has been cleansed of those who are killing my family and turning my loved ones into vagabonds."[26]

The rapprochement between Christians and Muslims is good for the fatherland. And it is essential. To that extent, the ecumenical rapprochement at Zeitun becomes a patriotic act. The saint's apparitions also provide, finally, a pretext or a framework for talking about the war, but also about the coming victory that the saint's visit seemed to guarantee. "United in their faith, Christians and Muslims will be united in battle and in victory."[27]

Apparitions of the Virgin: An Egyptian Phenomenon

At the time of Zeitun, public opinion was already attempting to argue that Egypt played a special role in the apparition phenomenon. Attempts were made to argue that the apparitions that had occurred elsewhere in the world—meaning, effectively, Lourdes and Fatima, as Egyptians speak only in elliptical terms of those that have occurred in the East and the rest of the world—were nothing compared to those in Egypt because, unlike the Zeitun apparitions, they were one-off events, short-lived and, more importantly, witnessed by only a few people.

In Egypt, this sense of privilege was later reinforced as believers claimed to be in almost permanent contact with the Virgin. And indeed, the phenomenon of the apparitions at Zeitun was not a one-off phenomenon. It happened again in Edfu in 1982, in Shubra in 1986, at the Monastery of the Virgin in Dronka in 1990, in Shantana al-Hagar in 1997, and in Asiut in 2000, to mention only the most "renowned" examples. The Virgin appeared, that is, on many occasions. Public opinion viewed the Zeitun apparitions as a prototypical phenomenon that was destined to be repeated: the later apparitions were no more than a repetition of those at Zeitun, which were still very much alive in everyone's memory. The features noted in the analysis of the Zeitun apparitions were also present in later apparitions. The image of the Virgin that emerged was specific not to Zeitun, but to Egypt: the new apparitions were replicas of those of 1968. Everyone could see the silent Virgin who appeared on the roof of a Coptic church over a period of days or even months,[28] and at irregular and unpredictable intervals, whereas the other apparitions had taken place on specific dates and at specific times, as in Fatima and Medjugorje. She appeared in different forms (the sad Virgin, the Virgin and Child, the Virgin wearing a crown, and so on). The same hybrid, and very dense, crowd gathered inside and outside the church.[29] The preliminary signs (the play of the light, the doves, the incense . . .) and the miracles that usually accompanied the apparitions continued to affect everyone, irrespective of their religion. Whatever the context, the Virgin or her apparition always represented a symbol of unity, and never of tension. Most of the apparitions were therefore collective. There was no notion of having been chosen: when the Virgin appeared, everyone could see her, not just a few children or seers.[30] The apparitions brought Christians and Muslims together, and were sometimes seen as highly patriotic events.

From an Egyptian Virgin to a Coptic Version: The Phenomenon Evolves

The hagiographic sources describe the phenomenon as something that is quite static and repetitive. If, however, we look at the media coverage and the political context of all the apparitions, we find that it changes. During the 1968 apparitions at Zeitun both the communitarian press and the government press echoed Egyptians' enthusiasm.

Hundred of articles were published describing both the popular fervor expressed in Zeitun and the political context, which had a considerable influence on the rapprochement between Christians and Muslims. One thinks, for instance, of the attitude of the country's political and religious readers (and especially of the legendary friendship between Cyril VI and Nasser), and of the country's defeat at the hands of Israel in the Six Day War. The Nasser period was marked by the emergence of more shared places of worship. But, as we have seen, the apparitions in Zeitun were not a one-off phenomenon. Other apparitions occurred later. One cannot help but note that there were none between 1971 (the apparitions in Zeitun went on until 1971) and 1982 (the date of the Edfu apparition), and that this period coincides, curiously enough, with the Sadat presidency. This is probably an indication that under the *Raïs's* regime, the concern for the nation's cohesion and the interest in the Coptic question did not take the form that they had taken under Nasser. In this context, saintly interventions were doomed to failure, or at least had a more limited influence on the impulse to worship together. The Sadat era brought about a rupture between Christians and Muslims, who retreated back into their own churches and mosques. This allowed them very few opportunities to mix. The usual explanation for the change is the rise of fundamentalist currents, and Sadat's desire to be closer to them than his predecessor. Then there were the open enmity and disagreements, and sometimes the open conflict, between the head of state and the head of the church, Shenouda III. That, perhaps, is why the Virgin chose not to appear while Sadat was in power. That she was, on the other hand, quite ready to appear when Mubarak took power was a sign that Egypt was about to revert to the model advocated by Nasser, in which Christians and Muslims could envisage coming together to venerate a holy figure with the backing of the state. The rapprochement could not, however, take quite the same form, precisely because in Egypt the Marian phenomenon reflects the influence of the political context. To put it in very schematic terms, the changing political context suggests a transition from a Virgin who urges unity to a Virgin who reveals the existence of conflict, or from an Egyptian Virgin to a Coptic Virgin. From the 1980s onward, we find that the Marian apparitions do not occur in the climate of complete entente that was reported in 1968. Zeitun may well have served its purpose in that it promoted national unity in 1968, but the formula no longer works in contemporary Egypt. And while there was some talk of an entente between Christians and Muslims during recent apparitions, it does not seem to have the same intensity. We do, however, find that there was also talk—both sophisticated and naïve—of how "national unity" was preserved at the Marian sites. This is an indication that there is a discrepancy between the behaviors and the commentaries on them, as we can see from the way in which the sources' descriptions of the apparitions change. We have now reached the point where one wonders if we really are talking about shared places of worship and a Christian-Muslim entente. If it does still exist, it is no longer as widespread as it once was. Most Muslims have now ceased to go to Christian *moulids*, and fewer of them go to the sites of the apparitions. Conversely, the Coptic clergy goes there en masse to oversee the phenomenon and to make it semi-official or lend it a certain credibility—but only in the eyes of the Church.

It is also interesting to note that Virgin chooses conflict-ridden places for her later apparitions. Shubra, Shantana al-Hagar, and the Islamist fief of Asiut were all the scenes of clashes between Copts and Muslim fundamentalists. One journalist wrote about Shubra: "The story of the Virgin's apparitions has begun once more. . . . Once again, the story takes place in a poor district with a Christian majority that has been badly hit by the economic crisis and the problems caused by fundamentalist religious movements. The people therefore have faith and expect miracles."[31] As a journalist on the *New York Times* reminds us:

> It was in Shubra at another church nearby that a bomb exploded during a wedding in August 1981, killing five people. The bombing was only one of many incidents in two years of almost continuous religious strife. . . . Religious tensions appeared to ease in the years after President Sadat was assassinated in October 1981. But last summer [1985] demands by Moslem fundamentalists for a total imposition of Sharia law led to confrontations with the government, and religious extremism is again very much a concern in Egypt.[32]

The level of tension between Christians and Islamic fundamentalists subsequently rose in Shantana al-Hagar. When I was there, we were advised not be alarmed by the armed and suspicious villagers, who kept their distance from the movement. Few Muslims took part in this display of devotion in the way that they had in Zeitun. As a rule, the only justification for their presence was the fear that things would get out of hand. The police quickly made the decision to block all access to the church—as they had already done in Shubra—"to prevent fundamentalist outrages."[33] It is said that when the village's Muslims saw thousands of Christians pouring into the village and trampling their fields, they began to stone them. The Christians, for their part, saw this as an expression of their social status: their self-esteem improved because they had met a representative of God who supported a Christian minority that was being persecuted by the Muslim majority. Shantana al-Hagar was a sort of *mise en abime* of Egyptian Christians' perception of their fate: "chosen" and "persecuted" are now the key words in any description of their condition.[34]

During the Asiut apparitions of 2000, the police once more tried from the outset to prevent people from entering the perimeter of the church. While no one really knows when the phenomenon began on the night of 17 August, one Usama Gamil explains that the police arrived at about 1:30 A M and were deployed to block access to the sector, and even to clear it.[35] The bishop of Assiut later explained that the police and government services had had to carry out a search to make sure that the apparition was not a trick, which was why they had initially prevented people from getting near the church. While we do not know how they carried out their search, it does seem that they realized that this really was a supernatural phenomenon. There was nothing unusual about the police intervention and investigation. An investigation had already been carried out in Zeitun, and no one had objected. The forces deployed on this occasion seemed to have used such violence that many worshipers were unhappy, and access to the church was restricted for the duration of the apparitions, and not just for the time required to carry out the investigation. The intervention of the security forces is proof that such gatherings were seen as potentially disorderly mobs rather than as crowds of worshipers. Yet if Ra'uf Tawfiq, a journalist on *Sabah al-Khayr* who visited Asiut in October 2000, is to be believed, there had never been a more peaceful interfaith gathering, and there was no sign of any police presence inside the perimeter of St. Mark's church:

> I am astonished by the climate of understanding and love that prevails here. No one is shouting or insulting anyone. If someone is thirsty, tens of hands reach out to give him water. If someone is tired, they make room for him to sit down. When I got here, I could see no police officers. Everyone here feels that he has a duty to promote this image of entente, and there is no sign of any violence. . . . But we know that things always get out of hand at these

gatherings and that there are always minor problems. But this is different: the people here have gathered to pray as they wait for signs from heaven.[36]

Press reports should obviously be taken with a pinch of salt. Marian apparitions are certainly shared experiences, but their degree of intensity appears to vary, depending on which source we read. It is because it can (no longer) be taken for granted that the two communities will mix that perceptions of just what is being shared and of what is at stake are so contradictory. Both the Christian and Muslim religious revivals of the second half of the twentieth century led to a new emphasis on identity. In some cases, this resulted in a complete rejection of anything that was "other" or that went against a strict interpretation of the texts, in an isolationism that is not dissimilar to the religious fundamentalism that appears to separate or drive apart religious groups that were once able to coexist. Marian apparitions do not completely escape this reality. Fear of reprisals on the part of the fundamentalists goes some way toward explaining this change. In 2000, the norms imposed by the radicalization of Egyptian society were, as it happens, very recognizable: society was divided into sectors, some reserved for women and children, and others for men.[37] This segregation now applies in most public places in Egypt, where every possible attempt is being made to prevent the sexes from mixing. Religious fundamentalism, which is considered to be an expression of the fear of provocation for some and the explanation for the apparitions according to others, is a central feature of the apparitions. Tensions between the two communities have replaced what was once described as an eminently interfaith phenomenon. Indeed, the sources suggest that there is some justification for seeing it as a Coptic phenomenon rather than a shared one.

Marian apparitions are so frequent in contemporary Egypt that the newspaper *Al-'Arabi* describes them as an Egyptian phenomenon in an article published in 1997 under the title "The Virgin Has Appeared Four Times in the Second Half of the Twentieth Century: Why Does She Choose to Appear in Egypt?"[38] One feels entitled to ask: "Why does she choose to appear to the Copts?" In the contemporary context, the Virgin usually appears when the Copts need her. And Copts do see the apparitions as an eminently Christian phenomenon, and make the Virgin an advocate of their cause. When, for instance, Michel Nil asked an Orthodox Copt called Victor Fakhri what the apparitions mean to him, he replied: "I think that she has come especially to tell the other religions that are present in Egypt not to do our Church any harm" (Nil 2000:86–87). In this context, the tone is not virulent, but witnessing Marian apparitions is viewed as one of the Orthodox Coptic Church's privileges. Its effects on Christian-Muslim relations in Egypt are a secondary consideration. Marian apparitions have done little to prevent the rise of fundamentalism in Egypt, or to reduce political tensions between Christians and Muslims. While manifestations of the sacred were once greeted with the same enthusiasm on the part of both Christians and Muslims and led them all to converge on Zeitun, such gatherings are now less likely to occur. Christians and Muslims still mingle at Marian sites, but the intensity of the gatherings is not what it once was. It is hard to be convinced by the media's attempts to cultivate the myth of how the Virgin's apparitions can promote better relations between the two communities.

Notes

1. Sura XIX is titled "Maryam," but there are many other reference to her in the Koran. They can be found at II, 87, 253; IV, 156–157; V, 17, 75; XIX, 16–34; XXIII, 50; LXVI, 12. Her birth is described (III, 35–36) She is referred to as "daughter of Imran" (III, 35; LXVI, 12). She is also described as "Sister of Aaron" (XIX, 28). Her presence in the shrine is recorded (III, 37). The Annunciation is invoked (III, 42–47; XIX, 16–22; XXI, 91; LXVI, 12). Michel Dousse (2005:14) has identified thirty-four mentions of Mary in the Koran. The formula *'Isa ibn Maryam* ("Jesus son of Mary") that means so much in Islam is used thirty-two times.

2. Cf. Al-Anba Butrus al-Gamil, Al-Anba Mikha'il and Al-Anba Yuhanna, *Al-Sinksar al-gami' li-akhbar al-qiddisin al-musta'mal fi kana'is al kiraza al-murqusiyya fi ayyam wa ahad al-sana al-tutiyya,* vol. 2 (Cairo: Maktabat al-Mahabba, 1972), 56–57.

3. A full list can be found in Meinardus, 2003:70–71.

4. For a more detailed account of these authors and their writings, see Valensi 2002:68–69.

5. Ibid., 91.

6. 'Izzat Sami, "Indama tagalla nur al-'Adhra' 11 marra fi layla wahida; Zahara al-nur masa' al-gum'a wa ada'a al qubba al-sharqiyya," *Watani,* 1 March 1970, 2.

7. Cf. notamment Mus'ad Sadiq, "Mu'gizat shifa' gadida bi-kanisat al-Zeitun," *Watani,* 12 May 1968, 2–3.

8. 'Izzat Sami, "Layla fi rihab al-'Adhra'," *Watani,* 7 December 1969, 2.

9. Twenty-nine (4.11%) could not be classified in this way.

10. Mus'ad Sadiq, "Al-gumu' shahadat al-'Adhra' fagr al-ithnayn al-madi," *Watani,* 18 August 1968, 2, 5.

11. Mus'ad Sadiq, "Dala'il al-zahira al-ruhiyya: Risalat al-sama' ila sukkan al-ard," *Watani,* 16 June 1968, 2, 5.

12. Cf. 'Izzat Sami, "Indama tagalla nur al-'Adhra'."

13. Mus'ad Sadiq, "Shahadu al-tagalli fi al-lahza allati sawarthum fiha al-shukuk," *Watani,* 6 July 1969, 2.

14. Mus'ad Sadiq, "Bidaya tayyiba lil-'am al-gadid fi kanisat al-'Adhra' bil-Zeitun," *Watani,* 4 January 1970, 2.

15. The sources obviously overestimate the number of people who visited the site during the apparitions. While it is conceivable that Egyptians went there in their millions, the figure of forty million is obviously an exaggeration and reveals a desire to make the phenomenon look more important and to emphasize its popular appeal.

16. For the Arabic sources, see in particular the issues of *Watani* dated 21 April and 5 May 1968, and 'Abd Al-Masih Basit Abu Al-Khayr 1998, 78.

17. Mus'ad Sadiq, "Al-uluf yushahidun al-'Adhra' tatagalla bi-wuduh masa' al-sabt," *Watani*, 3 November 1968, 2.

18. See Mus'ad Sadiq, "Dala'il al-zahira al-ruhiyya."

19. Sadiq Jalal al-'Azm, *Naqd al-fikr al-dini* (Beirut: Dar al-tali'a lil-tiba'a wa al-nashr, 1968). In his critique, the Syrian intellectual adopts a scientific point of view, and on this basis his primary target is the Egyptian press, and especially *Al-Ahram*. In his view, it is unfortunate that such an influential paper, which is read throughout the Arab world, should have reported the supposed apparition. Such phenomena have to do with popular beliefs, and it is certainly not the job of a government newspaper to report them. In his view, this is all the more so in that the context does not allow it. He deplores the strategy of using Egyptians' religious fervor to distract their attention from the repercussions of the Arab defeat in the 1967 war against Israel. And he has no hesitations about attacking the Coptic clergy. Sadiq Jalal al-'Azm's detailed analysis demonstrates the invalidity of the arguments used by Egyptian bishops and priests, especially when they evoke the Muqattam miracle (see above) or St. Luke's description of the Virgin, which appears to have become the model for all subsequent descriptions. The religious and the miraculous are not, in his view, an adequate response to the harsh realities the Arab world and Egypt have to face up to.

20. See, inter alia, al-Badrawi 2001.

21. Milad Hanna is an engineer, professor, and Coptic intellectual. He is also one of the few Christians in Egypt to have held ministerial office (as minister for housing).

22. Interview recorded on 8 September 2005. Although he restricts the argument to the Virgin's role in Egyptian Christianity, a Catholic bishop who prefers to remain anonymous argues along similar lines: "The Virgin plays a very important role in Coptic rites. Why? Because Egyptians have always been quick to beatify women ever since the time of the Pharaohs, since the time of Isis and Osiris. Women could become Pharaohs (remember Hatchepsout, amongst others), and women could play important roles at state level. For similar reasons, women play an important role for Copts. They accepted the Virgin because they were already prepared to sanctify women. They do not share the Arab mentality. That is why they had no difficulty in beginning to venerate the Virgin Mary" (interview recorded on 5 September 2005). It should be noted that every reference to a Pharaonic tradition is used to explain the fact that Muslims have adopted practices that appear to be purely Christian.

23. This thesis is harshly criticized by Catherine Mayeur-Jaouen (*Pèlerinages d'Egypte*, 14): "As a rule, it is claimed that the moulids are still the same; it would be the place of a religious syncretism in which both Copts and Muslims are expressions of the soul of an eternal Egypt whose origins to back to ancient times [. . .] The moulids have the reputation of preserving the image of an Egypt in which the religious phenomenon will always show the influence of the Pharaohs of old."

24. See above.

25. Sadiq ʿAziz, "Amama 150 sahafiyyan ʿalamiyyan uʿlina bayan al-baba Kirollos sihhat zuhur al-sayyida al-ʿAdhraʾ fi al-Zeitun," *Al-Ahram*, 5 May 1968.

26. Antun Nagib Matar, "Ayy hadaf lil-samaʾ min haza al-fayd al-mubarab? Wa ayy risala turidu an tiballighuha lana," *Watani*, 16 June 1968, 5.

27. Antun Nagib Matar, "ʿAla maratib al-insaniyya wa al-wataniyya," *Watani*, 12 January 1969, 2.

28. It is interesting to note that, while the Virgin always appears on an orthodox Coptic church, the church is not always dedicated to her, even though that was the case in Zeitun, Edfu, and Shantana al-Hagar. She also appeared at St. Dimyanaʾs church in Shubra and at St. Markʾs in Asiut.

29. I personally experienced this at Shantana al-Hagar in 1997. In his account of the Asiut apparitions of 2000, the journalist Raʾuf Tawfiq gives a detailed description of the difficulties the pilgrims had in getting to the site of the apparitions and, in some cases, staying there. Cf. Raʾuf Tawfiq, "Tagruba la tunsa: Anwar al-ʿAdhraʾ fi samaʾ Asiut," *Sabah al-Khayr*, 3 October 2000.

30. During the classical period of the Coptic Churchʾs history, an apparition was a form of election: only the patriarchs could see it. In the contemporary period, everyone has the opportunity to do so. For similar reasons, when a prophet—and especially Muhammad—or a Sufi sheikh appears to a believer in a dream, it is once more a sign that he had been chosen—at least to the Muslim imagination. The apparition brings a message and is therefore part of a revelation that is not accessible to all. With the recent Marian apparitions, the notion of election disappears completely, both in the Christian sphere and in the Muslim sphere.

31. Mustafa al-Saʿid, "Qissat zuhur al-ʿAdhraʾ," *Al-Ahali*, 16 April 1986.

32. Roberto Suro, "Coptic Dusk in Cairo: The Faithful and the Wary," *New York Times*, 26 April 1986, 2.

33. Hamdi al-Husayni and ʿAtif Hilmi, "Irhamuha; Muharriran li-Ruz al-Yusuf tabaʿa al mawqif fi al-layl wa al-nahar," *Ruz al-Yusuf*, 1 September 1997.

34. Many take the view that the two things go together. The Copts believe that they have always been oppressed in order to reveal that they are Godʾs chosen people. Folk beliefs are invoked to justify that claim. Egyptians believe that anyone who is physically disabled (blind, deaf . . .) has in fact been chosen. God is omnipotent. When He brings disabled people into the world, it is so that they can bring a message. Copts tend to apply this belief to their community. They suffer because suffering reveals their special destiny. If they were not persecuted, there would be no proof of their chosen status.

35. ʿAbd al-Masih Basit Abu al-Khayr, 1998, 9.

36. Tawfiq, "Tagruba la tunsa."

37. Basima William, "Min barakat al-tagaliyyat al-nuraniyya bi-kanisat Mar Murqus bi-Asyiut: ʿawdat al-miʾat min al-usar al-qibtiyya al-muhagira ila ahdan al-saʿid baʿda quraba rubʿ qarn," *Watani*, 22 October 2000, 5.

38. "Zaharat arbaʿ marrat khilala al-nisf qarn al-akhir: li-madha tufaddil al-ʿAdhraʾ al-zuhur fi Misr," *Al-ʿArabi*, 19 May 1997.

TEN

Sharing the *Baraka* of the Saints: Pluridenominational Visits to the Christian Monasteries in Syria

ANNA POUJEAU

Places of Worship to Visit

Since the 1980s, numerous Christian monasteries have been founded or rebuilt in Syria.[1] These places of worship are always geographically remote from the largest cities and sparsely distributed throughout the country. However, the majority of them are situated in the Qalamun, a mountainous region north of Damascus spanning approximately sixty miles, and are of the Greek Orthodox faith.[2] Thus, there are no less than eight monasteries in the village of Saydnaya and its surrounding countryside.[3] For Damascenes, the name of this sizable market town in the mountains—around twenty miles from the Syrian capital—is directly associated with the many places of worship to be found there, and more specifically with the Greek Orthodox monastery dedicated to the Virgin, built in AD 547 (Deir Sayda Saydnaya).[4] This monastery is a place of benediction housing a miraculous icon of the Virgin (a reproduction of one of the four icons painted by St. Luke, according to local history). Every year, thousands of Christian and Muslim *zûar*[5] (visitors) from all denominations enter the *shaghûla*,[6] a tiny room at the heart of the monastery, to bow before the urn that houses and protects the icon of the Virgin, reputed to have the power to resolve problems of female sterility.

Twenty miles from there, in the village of Ma'lula, one can visit two more of the region's famous monasteries: the St. Thecla monastery (Deir Mar Taqla) and the monastery of Sts. Serge and Bacchus (Deir Mar Sarkis wa Bakhos). Further north, on the road to the city of Homs, the monasteries of St. Moses the Ethiopian (Deir Mar Musa al-Habashi) and St. Elias (Deir Mar Elias), the St. George monastery of Homeyra (Deir Mar Jirjis min Homeyra), and a few others dot the Syrian landscape. All of these places of worship are equipped with an infrastructure capable of accommodating large scout groups and numerous other visitors, who might stay anywhere from a few hours to several days.

Some monasteries house exclusively male or female communities. Exceptions are St. Moses the Ethiopian and St. Ephrem, which are home to both monks and nuns. Each of the remaining places of worship is inhabited by a lay caretaker or solitary monk responsible for looking after daily maintenance, receiving visitors, and collecting donations. Some of the monasteries stand alongside the ruins of Byzantine churches or ancient monasteries dating back hundreds of years. A few other places of worship were built on completely unused sites; these are visited only by Christians.[7] Most monasteries are built near a water source said to be miraculous, or around places where saints have left their mark (such as the site of an apparition), or near a saint's tomb.[8]

The latter are visited by Christians of all denominations,[9] but also by Druze, Alaouites, Sunnis from the country or the region, and, finally, large groups of Shiite pilgrims, often from Iraq or Iran. They come to visit the tomb,[10] or the site of a saint's apparition,[11] or the monastery founded by a saint,[12] with the very pragmatic aim of making a vow and benefiting from the saint's *baraka*. The monasteries are places where anyone can come to perform certain rituals and receive graces: the healing of a sickness, the birth of a child, a successful marriage, and so on. These rites might be held directly in front of the saint's tomb—as in the monastery of St. Thecla—or in front of an icon reputed to be miraculous, such as in the *shaghûla* at the St. George monastery, or in that of the monastery of Our Lady in the village of Saydnaya.

Every year the monasteries also hold celebrations in honor of the saints to whom the places of worship are dedicated. During these festivities, which often last several days, Syrian Christians of all denominations travel to the various places of worship, where they build a homogeneous religious group through certain rituals and practices. However, far from being set up, in this sense, as the premises of an exclusive community, the Christian monasteries in Syria divide into several differentiated spaces where believers of all origins can express their faith. These different constitutive levels in the monastery reveal symbolically complex places. They are flexible denominational and communal spaces where the barriers between denominations and religious communities can be crossed. In these places, in the heart of which visitors come to prostrate themselves, worship follows certain clearly established procedures from which, to some extent, the denominational membership of the faithful has been erased. For Christians and Muslims of all denominations, monasteries are places for practices that, though they may not be entirely communal, are at least distinctive, not ordinary, and are also in some cases prohibited.

Here we will be showing how these diverse, sometimes ambivalent cultural places are constructed. With this in mind, we will see how a particular elaboration of sanctity is integral to these spaces, which are in fact erected around a saintly figure, where individuals from several denominations can come together and worship.

The Saint, a Figure of Opposition

Sanctity is the bedrock upon with these monasteries are founded. Consequently, its particular elaboration, through various hagiographies and local lore, defines the symbolic structure of these places of worship. In Syria, monasteries are on the margins of society, exempt from a number of its rules. In this chapter we will present and analyze some ethnographic elements collected since 2004 in the Greek Orthodox monastery of St. Thecla, in the village of Maʿlula (in the region of the Qalamun, forty miles from Damascus), home to a religious community comprising fifteen cloistered nuns of all ages from different social strata.

This large, multistory place of worship is built against a cliff at the northern edge of the village. A hundred-stair ascent inside the monastery leads visitors to the *shaghûla* containing the saint's tomb. The history of the founding of the monastery, as it is disseminated to visitors through booklets handed out by the nuns, recounts that St. Thecla, daughter of the governor of the city of Konya,[13] took refuge in a cave in the mountain bordering Maʿlula in the year AD 45. The saint was escaping soldiers her father had sent to hunt her down and kill her because of her recent conversion to Christianity by the sermons of St. Paul (who was passing through the city at the time) and her refusal to marry a young pagan man to whom she had been promised by her parents. After having crossed most of (modern-day) Turkey and Syria, the saint arrived in the Qalamun region, where two consecutive miracles occurred, enabling her to finally escape her father's grip.

The first miracle takes place not far from the village of Maʿlula. The scene is a field, where the saint encounters peasants busily sowing the wheat. By looking at the sky and speaking the words "Let your wheat become ears, at once," the saint makes the wheat instantly ready for harvest. This saves her from the persecution of her father because, when his men arrive in the area and ask the peasants if they have seen the saint, the peasants say they met her at the time of sowing. Seeing the height of the wheat ears, the soldiers are discouraged and decide to turn back.

The second miracle takes place just as the soldiers are questioning the peasants. This time St. Thecla is at the end of her strength, facing one of the highest summits of the Qalamun mountain chain. After she pleads for God's help in surmounting it, the mountain divides in two with a great crash, opening a rift that allows the saint to reach the other side effortlessly.

On the other side of the mountain, she takes up residence in a cave, where she lives as a hermit until the end of her life, feeding on grass and quenching her thirst with the drops of water falling one by one from the walls of her shelter.

Some archaeological studies attest to the fact that from the fourth century AD, there were men living alone in caves near the one that is supposed to have sheltered St. Thecla. In the seventeenth century, the Greek Orthodox church of Antioch built a monastery, dedicated to this saint, around the cave containing her tomb.[14]

It is therefore a figure notable for her faith in Christianity, but also for her resistance to both paternal and political authority, who founded the place where the faithful would later come to worship her.

The saint's local hagiography[15] also tells that it was Thecla who evangelized the inhabitants of the village of Ma'lula. From her place of seclusion, the saint continued to challenge authority and combat paganism. She even converted the remaining pagan population in the surrounding area. This extraordinary figure also performed many miracles for the faithful who came asking for mercies and healings. From the time of her conversion by St. Paul until her death as an ascetic in a Syrian mountain cave, the saint's entire life illustrated opposition. Her choice to live ascetically and her evangelistic deeds expressed opposition to pagan beliefs and the power that supported them. In a sense, her struggle is the foundation of her sanctity. The battle she waged against power created her own power, that of her *baraka*. Consequently, when visitors of all denominations worship the saint today, they are also recognizing her opposition to the established order of her time.

Furthermore, observation and analysis of the day-to-day existence of the monastery's nuns reveal that "opposition," in various forms, organizes and structures their lives in a wholly particular manner. Although tasks and responsibilities are, to an extent, divided between the superior, the nuns, the novices, and the postulants, this is not done according to a strict, clearly established hierarchical order. And while sometimes the division of different monastery duties can tend toward a communal organizational style, this is always resisted by the saint through apparitions, dreams, or even miraculous acts. A number of stories collected at the monastery show the saint's ceaseless opposition to the monastery's superior and the order she is attempting to establish there. The nuns and some regular visitors recount how the saint discredits the abbess's superiority through extraordinary acts, thus positioning herself as the monastery's supreme authority figure.

In fact, in this place of worship, everything is conceived as the fruit of the saint's desire. Her inexhaustible organizational will is conveyed perfectly in a story about a nun taking the novitiate habit three years earlier:

> When she entered the monastery as a postulant at the age of twenty-nine, Wadad was obeying a desire she said she had felt since childhood. However, after three years as a postulant, the superior still had not offered to allow her to wear the novitiate habit, her most cherished wish. She ultimately decided to leave the monastery, thinking she no longer really wanted to enter religion. She returned to her family sixty miles away in the city of Homs. Fifteen days later, she received a summons from the superior, who asked her to return to the monastery without explanation. Upon Wadad's return, the superior told her that she should go into seclusion for three days and fast so that she could receive the novitiate habit. Wadad immediately complied, and at the end of a long ritual, she became a novice at the Saint Thecla monastery.
>
> A few weeks after the ceremony, the superior told Wadad of the events that had precipitated her receiving the novitiate habit. A few days after the young woman left the monastery, the superior received a telephone call from a Lebanese monk she had never met. After asking the superior if a young woman by the name of Wadad was a postulant at the monastery, he described a dream from the previous night that had deeply troubled him. In the dream he saw the Saint Thecla monastery, which he had never visited, with this young woman washing the cave containing the saint's tomb. According to the oneiric vision, there were also numerous icons of the saint; Saint Thecla herself suddenly "came out" of one of these and started questioning the young woman. She asked her name, and then said she was astonished not to see her dressed in a nun's habit. The young woman replied that she was only a postulant. The saint then began dressing her in the novitiate habit, telling her she must now be a nun in her monastery.

The message of the dream was very clear. The superior was quick to understand the urgency of the situation and call the young woman back to the monastery. According to the Lebanese monk, through his dream, the saint wanted to let the superior know that she should prepare the young woman's novitiate. The nun said that after hearing this story, in spite of her past doubts, she decided to submit to the saint's will, as expressed through the voice of the Lebanese monk. She no longer had any doubts and now asserts that "the saint really does want to make a daughter of her."

Through the Lebanese monk's dream, the saint asserted her superiority and her position as the master and guardian of the monastery and its nuns. In this case, her power was manifested well beyond the monastery's walls and Syria's borders, but it is more often in or around the monastery that her apparitions take place. Through dreams, apparitions, and more striking events, the saint not only strongly establishes her presence in her place of worship, she also creates a dialogue with the nuns she "visits"—as the nuns themselves say—with the goal of readjusting the superior's decisions when she regards them as unjust or wrong, and establishing her own order in the monastery.

The fact that these sorts of events could be the result of manipulation or invention does not in any way depreciate the interpretation that can be made of them. They provide invaluable information about the nature of the relationships uniting the saint, the nuns, and the superior, as well as the role the figure of the saint plays in the monastic institution. She is without question its leader, and although the superior says her choices are guided by the saint, under no circumstances can she substitute for her. With her ability to manifest her desires in a multitude of forms, St. Thecla can always make her will known and regularly oppose the authority of the superior and any hierarchical order.

Thus, the monastic community's organizational principle is based on opposition to power in all its forms. As a consequence, no clear hierarchy can be durably established in the monastery. The nuns of St. Thecla monastery make up an almost egalitarian community; it is an exceptional "religious order" within the denomination to which they belong. In fact, it is markedly different from the clearly hierarchical order constituted by the ecclesiastics who play the power game. Priests, bishops, and patriarchs establish relationships with the country's politicians and make their religious vocation part of a "world order."[16] For example, they place themselves at the center of political debates; like the Syrian government, the patriarchs of the various denominational churches have long declared their support for the Palestinian struggle against Israel. More recently, the Greek Orthodox Church actively campaigned for the presence of Syrian troops in Lebanon, placing themselves in opposition to some other large churches in the region (particularly the Maronite Church), but garnering even more support from the Syrian government.

The monasteries, with their monastic communities built around a saintly figure, make the principle of opposition to power an important foundation of their symbolic constructions and forms of organization. Thus, they create spaces on the margins of society. However, "on the margins of"—and not "marginal to"—society, they can occupy an important place in the constitution of Christendom in Syria.

A World on the Margins

The monastery eludes a number of conventions. The rule prohibiting Christians from converting from one church to another does not apply to monks and nuns, who can freely enter the monastery of their choice, whatever its rite. At the St. Thecla monastery, there are nuns from both the Greek Orthodox and Greek Catholic denominations.

A few monks and nuns shared stories about monastic revelations with me, and in most of them, the saints are attributed a decisive role. Saints often appear in the dreams of future monks. The saints send them a clear message, calling on them to come and serve them in the monastery dedicated to them. So any rule that excluded one of these places of worship would be calling into question the saints' authority and their ability to make their will known. Monks sometimes say that the monastery itself appeared to them in a dream. When they do the rounds of the monasteries in the region and find themselves standing in front of the one in their dream, they do not hesitate to choose it as their place of worship, no matter what rite it belongs to.

Here we see that in monasteries, an individual's denominational membership is not an exclusion factor, whereas in parishes it is, in a strict sense. These particular places of worship are spaces where individual personality takes precedence over adherence to the denominational groups that determine collective identities elsewhere. In fact, in the Oriental Christian world, where everyone strictly inherits their father's denomination, the child is baptized in the father's rite, and it is impossible to abandon it for another.[17] Marriages are consecrated in the husband's church, although the wife still keeps the denomination she inherited from her father. Funerals are always held in the rite of the deceased, and in Damascus every denominational church has its own cemetery.

However, at the monastery, it is possible to go against the current in some areas. This considerably broadens each monastery's sphere of activity. In fact, under the leadership of the saint, interdicts cease to exist and the prerogatives of individual churches are erased. For example, spouses of the Maronite denomination can marry in the church of a Greek Orthodox monastery, but also spouses not sharing the same denomination can marry in a monastery of a third rite. Similarly, a Greek Orthodox child can be baptized in a Syriac Catholic monastery. People wishing to do so simply have to inform their home parish, which cannot oppose their choice and must register the sacrament. The spouses or parents involved speak the vows (*nazûr*) they would have made to the saint in exchange for which they would have promised a marriage or a baptism in the saint's monastery. Thus, every year, a number of children are baptized at the St. Elias monastery, near the city of Homs, during the week of the saint's celebrations from 21 to 28 July.

Therefore, monasteries are never places of exclusion or banishment. In the context of their position as religious institutions on the margins, monasteries can also be places where delicate everyday matters can be resolved. When mourning obligations prevent a marriage from being celebrated in the town or city parish—since neighbors and family members would consider this shameful (*'îb*)—the rite can be held in the monastery without any problem. It is not shameful to seal the union there; the memory of the deceased will not be tarnished. A marriage that would have been seen as a shameful act in the parish becomes a blessed (*mubârak*) act in the monastery, since it is placed under the protection, or blessing (*baraka*), of the saint. However, there is no large celebration with chanting, ululation (*zaghârîd*), music, and dancing. But a meal is still offered to guests, and the atmosphere is fairly festive.

Similarly, throughout the year, monasteries are the scene of amorous meetings between young people. For many Christian girls, visits to the monastery are their only authorized unaccompanied outings. Preventing a visit to the saint is in fact a delicate matter, and parents will even assign their daughters a few pious tasks, like bringing back cotton soaked in oil or making a particular vow. The point is of course for boys and girls to meet there; alongside the religious rituals, an important game of seduction is established between them. The monastery and its surroundings, the desert or the mountain, are transformed into a vast pickup joint.

Just as mourning interdictions relating to marriage can be lifted in the shelter of the monastery, the interdiction[18] (*harâm*) against association between girls and boys ceases to exist. Not only can delicate matters be resolved there, but a reversal occurs as well. Under the protection of the saint, there is a drastic turnaround. The monastery's walls keep the rules of the outside world at bay. They are effectively kept in check by the saint's all-powerful *baraka*. Activities curbed in the name of social order lose their element of impurity and even become blessed. Things that are elsewhere considered ʿaib or harâm become mubârak on the holy ground.

This reversal, made possible by sanctity that has been constructed at the heart of the monasteries, offers members of various Christian denominations the chance to come to a liminal, eminently public monastic space and form a truly homogeneous Christian group.

Thus, once each year, on the occasion of the monasteries' patron saint celebrations, large festivities are organized, and Christians from all over the country attend. People come to perform pious acts and try to benefit from the blessing of the saint, who is extolled for his or her many amazing revelations during this festive period. At the festivities of the St. Elias monastery near Homs, believers crowd around an elderly woman who claims she can hear the saint speak. It is also during these celebrations that believers sacrifice sheep at the monastery as a way of thanking the saint for graces received. All of this takes place in a very festive atmosphere, especially when some elderly women offer the saint their chants and praises, which the rest of the assembled women welcome and encourage with loud ululations. However, the most impassioned aspect of the celebration is certainly the work of the young men (shabâb). They take charge of a significant portion of the festivities and conduct the main events, such as the procession of the saint's icon, the lighting of the abuleh (fires) and the setting off of firecrackers and fireworks. The behavior they display has an exuberance that is not tolerated in day-to-day life. For the duration of the celebration, and even a few days before and after, they make it a point of honor to get drunk, sing at the top of their lungs, boast, and dance the dabka (a traditional dance)[19] for hours on end, demonstrating their virility to the whole community.

Ultimately this crowd of several thousand people, who have traveled from all over the country to take part in the celebration and stay at the monastery, drastically transforms this place for a time. There is a good deal of promiscuity between men and women, and no segregated spaces, not even when the believers rest. The celebrations transform the monastery—normally a place of reserve and silence—into a place where it is acceptable to transgress all kinds of everyday rules. They say that the wilder, the larger, and the more beautiful the celebration, the greater will be the saint's baraka.

By virtue of the monasteries' geographical location, their communities' internal organization, and the relationship they establish with the world— ordinarily and during the annual saint celebrations—they are spaces on the margins of society. As much as possible, the earthly hierarchy is strongly defied.

However, monasteries are at the same time spaces where particular social relationships can be established, and this helps sustain a certain social balance. They are not only symbolically an element central to the group's composition, but they enable this group to be created as such. We have observed that activities that could disturb order in an everyday context may take place at the monastery. In the liminal space the saint has created there, these activities lose their transgressive aspect and even assume a sacred character.

Therefore, the monastic space helps maintain a social order that might otherwise be under threat. This place of liminality is a space where a *communitas* (Turner 1974) can truly emerge. In the works of this author, *communitas* can be generally defined in opposition to structure, or as an anti-structure. Therefore, *communitas* and structure make reference to two distinct forms of society. *Communitas* appears when there is no social structure composed of status hierarchies. At the liminal stage of the ritual, or in the spaces of liminality represented by places of pilgrimage (Turner and Turner, 1978), one finds none of the characteristics of social structure. And *communitas* evokes, among other things, the notion of equality. During this phase of temporal or spatial liminality, individuals are "neither here nor there" and are treated as equals. According to Turner, this is when a feeling of "cohesion" is created between them. Here we find a fundamental feature of what is created in the Syrian Christian monasteries we have just described.

Pluridenominational Spaces

In places like these, symbolically constructed on the margins of society, individuals from different religious denominations can jointly worship the saint, whereas in day-to-day life, in the town and city parishes, these same cultural practices draw boundaries between denominations.

Unlike churches, monasteries are spaces Muslims can visit without restriction. In Damascus, a group of Muslims clearly identifiable by the women's clothing (veils and long robes) could not enter a church without being immediately ejected. This is also the case in a number of monastery churches, which are not really the place of worship to visit. However, in the space properly marked by the saint's *baraka* (tomb, apparition site, icon . . .), no one—neither monks, nuns, nor simple lay guards—can prevent visits, regardless of whether the visitors are Christian or Muslim. In fact, everyone who passes through the monastery entrance is considered to be under the saint's protection. Moreover, it is said that these people come to the monastery because the saint has brought them there. Following this reasoning, the main task of the nuns at St. Thecla monastery—who say they are devoted to serving the saint—is to guide all visitors, whatever their denominational membership, to her tomb at any time, day or night. With this in mind, there is a specific nun responsible for keeping vigil over the saint's tomb. She is never separated from the key that opens the saint's cave, and she is always standing by, prepared to enable access—even late in the evening, even during Mass. Her day is entirely dictated by the visits to the saint.

Nevertheless, in the place of worship, the nuns can sometimes try to restrain or channel the circulation of non-Christian visitors, or "Muslims," as they are all designated without distinction. For example, they will refuse entry to the monastery church, particularly when they see large groups of Iranian or Iraqi Shiite pilgrims entering through the different monastery terraces overlooking the village. As soon as these dozens of women, all wearing black veils, descend from the buses that bring them to the monastery from Damascus,[20] the nuns give the signal to the one in charge of supervising the church to close it. From the moment they arrive at the place of worship, the Shiite pilgrims are guided directly to the saint's cave.

However, sometimes the nuns allow a limited group of Muslims[21] to enter the monastery church, while strictly prohibiting photography. According to the nuns, the Muslims could tear the photos in the future, thus committing an act of desecration. Very often, they are also not allowed to get close to the iconostasis, and they must keep to the back, near the door.

Muslims are not really sure how to behave in the church. They often stay close to the door. Sometimes they carefully move toward the church's interior. Every now and then, whether voluntarily or not, they display behavior that the nuns interpret as offensive. Some of them refer to Jesus as Issa,[22] and sometimes there are men who do not hesitate to ask young nuns the reasons for their monastic vocation. These nuns take this as an attack. No Christian would dare ask this question in this way. For the nuns, this is a very private subject. They place it on the same level as a romantic encounter, and in principle, they would speak about it only with the monastery's superior. During my fieldwork, the nuns revealed the story of their monastic vocation only quite late, and always in a tone of confidence. They never offered it spontaneously; I always had to ask them. When they had made up their minds, they would invite me to spend an evening alone in their cell. After having spoken about many other subjects, they would begin recounting their story late at night. Some of them were quite uncomfortable at first. Others could not tolerate being disturbed in the middle of their story, and this is why they shut themselves up with me in their cell. A number of them told me I was the only one (aside from the superior of the convent) to hear the story of their monastic revelation. So it is easy to understand their discomfort when Muslim strangers ask to know the reason for their way of life.

Another reason why the nuns hesitate to admit non-Christians to the church is that it is a place where ecclesiastics perform rituals, around which, to a certain extent, the Christian community is formed. Obviously Muslims cannot find their place in these settings since their adherence to another religion bars them from participating in rituals designed to aggregate the group's participants. Hence, when Muslims enter the church during Mass, they are unceremoniously—even aggressively—ejected by the nuns. However, some veiled Muslims wearing long robes are eager to cover the same itinerary inside the monastery as that of most Christian visitors, so when Mass is not in progress, they also enter the church. They cross the threshold with caution. Like the Christians entering, they keep their voices low, kiss the door, and, in exchange for a cash donation placed in a wooden urn, light thin orange candles made available by the nuns. Then they put them inside a large, rectangular, leather receptacle containing sand. Sometimes they also slide prayers into the urn, and even bury them in the sand that holds the candles, lighting one above them. In this sense, they have adopted the Christians' behavior perfectly.

Muslims rarely go any further into the church. The Christians continue with their visits and also kiss the icons arranged on the church walls.

The holy place itself and the rest of the monastery (made up of the church and the residents' living quarters) are two noticeably different religious spaces. Moreover, they are located on different levels. To reach the saint's cave from the monastery entrance, visitors must climb a number of fairly high stairs, so although this holy place is located in the monastery, it constitutes a distinct second space within it. Believers who go there are separated even more from the outside world. In fact, the monastery's high outer walls create a clear separation from the rest of the village. The second phase of separation from the outside is accomplished by way of the long, narrow stairway—built onto a cliffside—that each visitor must climb to reach the saint's tomb.

In the cave, religious practices are highly regimented in some respects. Recommendations placed at the monastery entrance and all along the route inside call on visitors to assume a respectful attitude, thus regulating the basic framework of their behavior. On the gate separating the saint's cave from the rest of the monastery, there is a notice reminding visitors that they are entering a holy place and should therefore respect the silence and behave appropriately.

Here they find themselves facing an empty space, and although the small cave containing the saint's tomb is clearly visible, there are more arrows indicating the path visitors must follow.

At the entrance to the *shagûla,* there is a sign instructing visitors to remove their shoes. And then—more effective than a written instruction—the low door itself forces visitors to bow when entering the cave. At that moment they are all compelled to adopt the same physical posture. In this small place, measuring about seven square meters, a nun sits to the left of the entrance close to the door. She supervises visitors. There is an exact route every visitor must follow. In any case, the place is so small that there are no other possibilities. A large tray of candles placed at the center of the semicircular cave forces visitors to go around it and walk along the walls, on which are hung several icons of the saint, left by believers in thanks for graces received. There are also two urns for collecting offerings from visitors, one at the cave's entrance and one at the exit (which are two different doors). Thus everyone entering the cave passes a first urn, into which they must deposit money if they wish to light candles. Visitors then pass in front of the tray of candles. At the halfway point, the faithful find themselves in front of the saint's tomb, but the cave is often invaded by crowds, forcing visitors to wait their turn before kneeling.

In the cave, some people remain standing, others kneel, and some prostrate themselves with their forehead to the ground. Believers make every effort to visibly manifest their faith and their submission to the saint. Everyone adopts the physical posture that best suits them. As long as it is pious, it can assume a variety of forms. Believers can walk on their knees, murmuring prayers with their head down, or they can kiss every icon on the cave walls as they advance toward the tomb. They can also simply wait their turn to kneel before the tomb.

Muslims are not embarrassed by their gestures here. Overall, they respect the basic behavioral guidelines provided at the cave entrance: respectful behavior and silence. Inside, they say their prayers, whatever form they might take. The saint's tomb is located below, embedded in the wall of the cave. At the very least, everyone is forced to kneel. Some of the faithful press their head or their body against the railings sheltering the tomb while articulating their prayers. Others crouch down completely in front of the tomb and keep their forehead on the ground. Anyone can attach religious offerings (*nuzûr*[23]) to the railings protecting the tomb, in thanks for graces received or even as a testament to one's faith in the saint. There are all kinds: simple banknotes (one can distinguish Turkish, Lebanese, Iranian, and Jordanian banknotes) or more personal objects such as jewels—often watches, but also bracelets, necklaces, and rings, *'in zarqa* (blue eyes said to protect against misfortune).

Despite the crowd, visitors spend at least a few minutes before the tomb. Directly in front of the cave's exit, they can take cotton soaked in oil or a few white strings woven by the nun in charge of supervising the cave. The exit door is located in front of the water source from which the saint would have drunk during her lifetime. Here there is another sign in several languages, once again regulating everyone's practices. Among other things, it asks visitors not to immerse their hands in the water source and not to allow drops to fall on the ground. The railings on this, as well as the chain securing the metal cup, force believers to lean over the source in order to drink. On busy days, another nun stands nearby to supervise visitors and, if necessary, help them fill bottles they take home with them.

One can find similar constraints in almost all holy places. Their visitors' behavior is partly regimented, limiting the range of expression in observance.

The visits, controlled from beginning to end, involve homogeneous but diverse practices, and they can all coexist. Christians and Muslims of all denominations often come here to visit the saint for similar reasons, and the saint does not discriminate when granting graces. Everyone can benefit, and the stories circulating in the country about miracles granted by saints involve more Muslims than Christians. In this context, the monastic communities guarantee an appropriate relationship with the saint, establishing a general code of contact between the saints and their visitors.

The nuns told me of a rich Saudi Arabian family that came to visit St. Thecla and received a miracle for their mute granddaughter through the nun in charge of supervising the cave. To intercede with St. Thecla on their behalf, she prayed and immersed the cave key in a small dish containing oil of unction near the lighted candles, then held the key in front of the mouth of the girl to be cured and turned it as if she were unlocking a door. Everyone considered St. Thecla to have performed the miracle. However, it should be noted that in her story, the nun specified that she had performed the miraculous gestures herself.

The superior offered me another version of the miracle. She claimed that when she met the Saudi Arabian family in the reception area before they made their way to St. Thecla's cave, she told them that the saint might perform a miracle for their mute granddaughter, who had already seen several doctors in Europe and the United States. She advised them to go to the *shagûla* and ask the nun stationed there to perform the gestures described above. We see that, in their descriptions of the event, the nun and the mother superior place themselves in competition with one another. Even if they do not claim the ability to perform the miracles alone, they still claim an intermediary position between the saint and the Muslim pilgrims. They can transmit the saint's *baraka* to secure the little girl's recovery. The mother superior made it quite clear that the girl did not start speaking until she and her family had returned to the reception area. When the superior stroked her hair, the little girl spoke her first words.

Conclusion

Monasteries built around sites marked by saints describe spaces on the margins. They are places that assemble Christians around certain rituals, and where everyone, whether Christian or not, can come to request graces from the saints to whom the monasteries are dedicated. The monasteries are therefore particular places of worship for the country's Christians and for Muslims of all denominations, from Syria and beyond. The walls of these monasteries—which are becoming increasingly numerous in Syria—draw a clear line of demarcation with the outside world. The borders between denominations and religious communities can be crossed in these flexible religious spaces.

However, we saw that the place of worship itself was a space where ritual practices can be shared as long as these are expressed within a precise framework. As a space on the margins, the monastery views and offers itself as a place where denominational membership is erased and irrelevant. This is especially true for the Christians, whereas the relationship Muslims have with the monastic institution as a broader ritual space is more qualified. The distinctions between Christians, Druze, Alaouites, Sunnis, and Shiites are only erased in the cave, at the heart of the holy place.

In fact, as we have seen, when it comes to the ritual modalities involved in relating with the saint, religious membership is never decisive. It is precisely the nonexistence of all denominational claims that is relevant in one's relationship with the saint. Unlike other places of worship, it is not the community that is expressing itself. The individuality of each person's relationship with the saint takes precedence, whatever one's denominational membership. Thus, from an essentially pragmatic perspective, at the monastery, it is really only the saint's *baraka* that can be shared.

Notes

1. The country has a plural population: a Sunni Muslim majority and several minority groups stemming from dissident Islamic sects: Shiites, Druze, Alaouites and Ismailis. There is also a significant Christian group, around 5 percent of the population according to estimates (Courbage 2007).

2. For more details on the Greek Orthodox monastic revival in Syria, see Poujeau 2009.

3. An important village in the region. Until a few decades ago, this village and the surrounding area had an almost homogeneous Christian population.

4. According to the history of the foundation of the monastery conveyed by nuns, it was the Roman Emperor Justinian who founded the monastery, with the goal of honoring a vow to the Virgin Mary, who appeared to him in the form of a gazelle while he was camping in the area with his army.

5. They come to pay *ziyârât* (visits) to the saint.

6. This is an Aramean term that literally means the "famous, very renowned icon." In the region, *shaghula* designates the cave or small room containing the saint's icon or tomb where visitors go to worship the saint.

7. For example, the Greek Orthodox Blemana monastery near the city of Latakia, the Syriac Orthodox St. Ephrem monastery (near the city of Saydnaya), and St. Mary's Monastery near the city of Hassake and the Iraq border.

8. For more details on how these places of worship are founded in Syria, see Poujeau 2010.

9. The Syrian Christian population is divided into several denominations. The majority is Greek Orthodox, but there are also Greek Catholics; Syriac Orthodox; Syriac Catholics; Apostolic, Catholic, and Protestant Armenians; Assyrians; Chaldeans; Maronites; Roman Catholics; and finally a mixture of all Protestant sects.

10. Such as in the Greek Orthodox St. Thecla monastery, located in the village of Ma'lula.

11. For example, this is the case at the monastery dedicated to St. Elias near Homs, as well as the monastery of Our Lady in the village of Saydnaya.

12. Here I am referring to the monastery of St. Moses the Ethiopian near the city of Nabk.

13. Turkish city.

14. The Greek Orthodox Church itself dates the beginning of construction at around the seventeenth century. At that time it consisted of monastic cells built by the monks themselves, distributed around the saint's cave. It was only at the beginning of the twentieth century that the monastery's current church was built, and, from year to year, different structures were erected, eventually forming the building we know today.

15. There exists another St. Thecla hagiography—more widespread in the Christian world—recounting that the saint took refuge in Seleucia, Turkey, where her tomb is a similarly important place of pilgrimage. This second hagiography is little known in Syria, even among the nuns of the St. Thecla Monastery.

16. This idea of world order and religious order was developed by Isabelle Rivoal (2000) in the context of her research on the Druze community in Israel.

17. There are, however, a few cases of moving from a Catholic rite church to an Orthodox rite church when divorcing, something that can be authorized and decreed only by patriarchal Orthodox tribunals. In these cases, the Catholic spouse wishing to end the marriage barters his divorce to the Orthodox church in exchange for becoming a member. The Orthodox church provides a divorce certificate, and this allows the spouse to remarry in his new church. This practice is neither openly acknowledged by the Orthodox churches nor recognized by the Catholics.

18. In this context, I have translated *harâm* as "interdiction." It comes from the verb *harrama:* to forbid.

19. A farandole dance: each dancer has to tap his feet and hop to the rhythm of the music of the *darabukka* (tambourine) and the *nayé* (oriental recorder). The first dancer performs acrobatic figures to lead the rest of the dancers.

20. In fact, Damascus is a pilgrimage city for Twelver Shiites. They mainly come to visit the tomb of Sayyida Zaynab (granddaughter of the Prophet and daughter of Imam Ali) in the southern outskirts of the city, the tomb of Sayyida Ruqqaya (sister of Imam Ali) in the Al-Amara quarter of the Old City, and the head of Husayn Mashad al-Husayn (the prophet's grandson) located in the Old City at the Umayyad Mosque. For more details on the subject of these pilgrimages, see Mervin 1996.

21. The women's clothing (scarf and robe) make it possible to see that they are not Shiites on a pilgrimage to Damascus, but rather Muslims from nearby villages and cities.

22. This is how he is designated in the Koran.

23. In Arabic, *nazr* (plural *nuzûr*) designates both vows and thanksgiving, the offering to the saint.

Crossing the Frontiers between the Monotheistic Religions, an Anthropological Approach

DIONIGI ALBERA

Translated by David Macey

The phenomena examined in this book are at odds with the very widespread view that religious identities in the Mediterranean area are divided by the fault line of the clash between "the West" and "Islam." Relations between these two blocs appear to be heading in the direction of complete incompatibility, or even some form of war. The only bulwark against this massive and inevitable mutual repulsion—and it is weak and often no more than a pretense—is supposedly the desire to promote a semblance of entente through rhetorical statements and declarations of good intent on the part of political and religious leaders, or through learned debates between scholars—the classic example being the Islamic-Christian dialogue (which now seems to be running out of steam).

It would of course be absurd to deny that the history of the monotheisms in the Mediterranean has been influenced by powerfully exclusivist tendencies or that those tendencies are still very much at work. It is, however, also possible to observe the effect of the overcrowding that results from the presence within the same space of the three monotheisms and their countless followers. This context gives us an opportunity to examine how ordinary behaviors can deviate from institutionalized religions. If we look at the religious in terms of lived experience and in terms of everyday practices, we find that traditions and forms of worship sometimes overlap as the "guardians of the temples" look on, sometimes benevolently and sometimes vindictively. The studies collected here take a different look at the religious behaviors of Mediterranean populations and reveal one of the most interesting (and least known) phenomena to be observed in the region: the permeability of the frontiers that divide its religious communities.

How are we to define the ways in which religious frontiers can be crossed? The present volume refers to a host of concepts that, to a certain extent, overlap: mixed worship, sharing, hybridity, intersection. The emphasis is on the contributions of what is primarily an anthropological approach, but no attempt has been made to invoke a conceptual standardization that might prematurely force the analyses into a ready-made classificatory carapace. Terminological issues are, however, important—and some contributors (Baskar, Bowman, Couroucli) do address them. All the notions used here are open to criticism, and are not without a certain vagueness, referring as they do to different aspects (places, people, practices, beliefs) with varying degrees of precision. At this stage, they do nonetheless appear to be complementary in many ways, and they shed some light on several facets of complex phenomena that are difficult to grasp.

Can we apply the notion of syncretism—which has a long history and which is still surrounded by controversy (Stewart and Shaw 1994)—to the contexts studied in this book? The answer appears to be "yes," provided that we use the term in a "weak" sense to denote the circulation and intermingling of heteroclite practices and beliefs. The porosity discussed here shows that even self-confident religions with intransigent tendencies are affected by cross-border practices. And yet these overflows do not lead to a fusion of religious forms, or to a complete and recognizable "syncretism" in the strong sense of the term. We are, in other words, a long way from Brazil's *candomblé* and *macumba*. The situations described in the previous chapters have more to do with the way people who circulate between different and competing religions cobble together ad hoc arrangements from disparate elements. These cross-border explorations "make do" with elements derived from two or more structured religious ensembles, but do not result in the construction of new syncretic entities, nor do they appear, for that matter, to be associated with any significant incidence of conversion.

Religious Mixing in the Eastern Mediterranean: The *Longue Durée*

The eastern Mediterranean, from Egypt to the Balkans and from the Middle East to Turkey, is now the main center of shared worship. Until recently, similar phenomena were observable in the Maghreb, but they have almost completely died out in recent decades. In Europe, in contrast, religious mixing is a recent phenomenon, and still a limited one, even some Marian shrines are also visited by what is admittedly a very small minority of Muslims (Albera 2005b).

As Maria Couroucli emphasizes in her introduction to this book, the current situation is the product of a long history. Displays of mixed worship are both well established and recurrent in the eastern Mediterranean (and, to a lesser extent, North Africa). The eastern Mediterranean differs from the sea's European shores in that the human landscape has long been a religious patchwork that made possible religious overlaps. The Byzantine Empire never displayed any desire to fight a crusade against Islam, and the dismantling of its eastern frontiers was for a long time characterized by a certain intermingling with Muslim populations. The various Muslim dynasties that ruled the territories they had seized from the Empire—the Umayyads, the Abassids, the Fatimids, the Ayyubdis, the Mameluks, the Seljuks, the Ottomans—did not try to make them religiously homogenous. There were of course periods of repression and forced conversions, but on the whole Christian and Jewish minorities (*dhimmi*) living under Muslim rule were for centuries granted protected status.

In the land of Islam, religious overlaps have often occurred. The phenomenon that saw Muslims praying in churches and other Christian places of worship was, for instance, widespread under the Umayyads (Bashear 1991). Other sources, and especially the "monastery books" compiled by Muslim authors, are testimony to the fact that Christian monasteries played an important role in Abbasid society—in Iraq, Egypt, and Syria—and show that large numbers of Muslims visited them. Just like the Christians, Muslims went there for votive reasons, and some monasteries were especially famous for their healing powers (Landron 1994:31–35). Over the following centuries, there are more and more references to interfaith crossovers. References to such phenomena appear here and there in travelers' tales, chronicles, hagiographies, and polemics both in the Middle Ages and in the modern period.

The research carried out in the first decades of the twentieth century by the English scholar Frederick Hasluck (1929) on relations between Christians and Muslims in the Ottoman Empire makes a major contribution to our understanding of these phenomena, as several chapters are explicitly devoted to them. With great erudition, Hasluck collected hundreds of examples of how religions can overlap from a period spanning several centuries. His fieldwork and the information provided by his correspondents about the situation in his day added to this storehouse of knowledge. Both his historical and contemporary sources appeared to show that relations between religious groups in the Ottoman Empire tended to be symbiotic. Both Christians and Muslims were happy to address their requests to shrines administered by the other religion, provided that they had a reputation for being efficacious (Hasluck 1929:100). Indeed, these crossovers were, according to Hasluck, a "common," almost banal phenomenon (Hasluck 1929:97). This interreligious circulation was sometimes used by the clergy and some mystical orders as part of a strategy to strengthen their control over holy places. From that point of view, Hasluck pays particular attention to the activities of the Bektashis (1929:405–477).

Hasluck's research was carried out in a period when the Ottoman regime's end was approaching. The clash of bellicose nationalisms was changing the ethnic and religious profile of broad sectors of the eastern and southern Mediterranean. A process of homogenization was putting an end to centuries of coexistence. The human landscape was profoundly modified by the two Balkan wars (1912 and 1913), the First World War, the war between Greece and Turkey (1919–1923), and a series of killings, deportations, and forced departures. The creation of the state of Israel (1948) also had a major impact in the ethnoreligious homogenization of the region and its polarization around religious identities. The decolonization process in the Arab countries—which won their independence from the European powers that had, in most cases, taken the place of the Ottoman Empire—in its turn simplified the framework. The construction of a religious-based nationalism and the incorporation of Islam into the state led to a new rigidity and a loss of pluralism, even within Islam itself. Then there was the exodus of almost all Jews and most of the European population from North Africa. In the 1970s, the fighting in Cyprus led to a divorce between Muslim and Christian populations that had previously lived side by side. A few years later, the war in Lebanon exacerbated the differences between the many confessions that lived in the country. And the wars that raged in the former Yugoslavia throughout the 1990s led, finally, to more forced displacements and to ethnic and religious "cleansing" on a huge scale.

The practices studied in this book occur in this difficult context. In addition to the factors already mentioned, an additional point is the rise to power of strictly fundamentalist tendencies within the Muslim camp, influenced by the reformism of *salafiyya* and by Wahhabism. The minority Christian communities in the Arab countries often felt threatened, and reacted by emphasizing their difference. The Coptic Revival of recent decades is an obvious example of this phenomenon. Everything, in short, seems to lead to the closure of religious frontiers, to a narrowly defined identity politics, and to a strict policing of devotional practices. Where and how, one might ask, can we look for signs of porosity in such a climate? And yet, as the data presented here demonstrates, they are still there—and in some cases even more pronounced than ever—even though they are often hampered by the generally hostile sociopolitical environment.

This book reconstructs an overall picture of a transitional phases characterized by the gradual dissolution of an old Mediterranean order based on enclaves and connections (Horden and Purcell 2000), of a patchwork of territories, peoples and religious forms (Hauschild, Kottman, and Zillinger 2005:139–174) in which religious mixing was often socially acceptable. The powerful drive to homogenize both territories and identities has not completely destroyed local specificities. The ebb and flow of religious monism and pluralism—to borrow the notions Ernest Gellner derives from a stimulating rereading of David Hume's "sociology of religions"—still went on—to some extent—throughout this phase, and paved the way for new hybridizations as a result of the transnational currents that wash through a globalized world.

While mixed worship is still very much part of the religious landscape of the eastern Mediterranean, it is also by definition a relatively unstructured phenomenon. Hence the changeable and sometimes unpredictable nature of its manifestations. If we wish to arrive at a better understanding of these phenomena, it seems important look at in-depth research into a number of specific contexts, and to pay great attention to the specific features of each of them. As Galia Valtchinova suggests in her contribution, we have to look at the interplay between structures of worship and agency, and identify the "elementary structures" of religious sharing by looking carefully at gestures, attitudes, and words. The case studies in the various chapters make no claim to being statistically representative of the contemporary phenomena of religious overlapping in the Mediterranean area. They are, on the other hand, sufficiently varied to reveal more general tendencies. Without wishing (or being able) to take account of the full wealth of the suggestions made in the contributions collected here, the following pages do attempt to summarize the collective contribution they make and to relate it to a number of problematic issues.

Crossing the Frontier

The mixing analyzed in these contributions mainly concerns the two biggest groups in the region: Muslims (as represented by the Sunni, Shiite, Druze, and Alawi branches of Islam) and Eastern Christians. In most cases, mixed practices imply a one-way crossing of the religious frontier: it is Muslims who go to Christian shrines. The same applies to Catholic shrines in Muslim countries. These one-way crossings are the most widespread configuration in Turkey and in the Balkans, Egypt, and Syria. There seem, on the other hand, to be fewer contemporary examples of Christians visiting Muslim sites, though they have been mentioned in some contexts (de Rapper, Bowman, Mayeur-Jaouen, and Baskar).

There are historical precedents for the trends that emerge from these contemporary examples. Ever since it appeared, Islam has always played the more active role in this kind of exchange. Islam's partners in these overlappings have usually been the various confessions of the Christian world. The way Muslims behave obviously reflects a fairly open-minded attitude toward the monotheisms that came before Islam, but, given that most shared places of worship are in territories under Islamic control, it also reflects the dominant position of a group that often feels that it has the right to enter the holy places of religious minorities while preventing others from visiting its own holy places. What is more, the inferiority of the minority could also be associated with its possession of "magical" powers that the majority group may need to call upon. This applies both to the situation of Copts in Egypt (Mayeur-Jaouen) and that of Jews in Morocco (Driessen).

It has to be added that Islamo-Christian crossovers once worked in both directions. For several centuries, large numbers of Christians used to visit Muslim places of worship in Anatolia and the Balkans, and their presence in shrines controlled by the mystical orders was tolerated and even encouraged.[1] These were not purely rural or peripheral practices. Sixteenth- and seventeenth-century sources describe Christians visiting the Eyyub mosque in Istanbul (Hasluck 1929:108–109), and Christian women used to visit the tomb of Zumbal Efendi in the same city in the nineteenth century (Albera and Fliche).

Some forms of joint attendance at the same shrines concern only Jews and Muslims. Henk Driessen's chapter is devoted to one such example, and shows that the tomb of a Jewish saint in the north of Morocco was until recently also venerated by Muslims. Judeo-Muslim cults were especially common in the Maghreb. Until the Jewish population left en masse, such cults were especially important in Morocco, where a whole range of shrines were venerated by both Jews and Muslims.[2] In his updated version of the inventory drawn up by Louis Voinot in 1948, Issachar ben Ami lists 140 saints who are the objects of common cults and divides them into three categories: Jewish saints who are also venerated by Muslims (90); saints claimed by both Jews and Muslims (36); Muslim saints who are also venerated by Jews (14).[3] Other examples of mixed Judeo-Muslim veneration have been recorded in Algeria (Dermenghem

1954:125–126) and Tunisia (M'Halla 1998:121–131), where the crossovers once more go in both directions.

One further characteristic to emerge from the contemporary examples examined in these chapters is the absence of purely Judeo-Christian devotional crossovers. Once again, this is part of a long-term trend: Jews and Christians (both Eastern and Western) rarely mix in the same places of worship. The now fashionable category of "Judeo-Christian" seems to be of little use where these phenomena of mixed worship are concerned. There are, on the other hand, some records of holy places being visited by followers of all three monotheisms in the past. During the Ottoman period, Muslim, Jewish, and Christian women used to visit the tomb of Helvaci Baba in the Shehzade mosque (Istanbul) to ask for the saint's help (Mansell 1997 [1995]:55). Similar cases have been reported in Algeria where, even in the 1950s, the appeal of some Islamic saints was not restricted to Muslims alone. Dermenghem observes that at this time "it was common for afflicted Jewish and Christian to visit Muslim marabouts" (Dermenghem 1954:126n1). These crossovers appear to have almost died out; no cases of this kind are discussed in this book.

The Topography of Religious Mixing

Several contributions to the present volume deal with locally based phenomena of mixed worship. They occur in villages, small country towns, and the surrounding territory. These mixed shrines are often to be found in rural areas, and they are part of a shared sacred geography that transcends religious diversity. The fact that the whole population sets aside its religious differences to take part in commemorating local saints on important dates in the year's calendar is an indication of its awareness of living in a "territory of grace," and of its gratitude to the supernatural beings whose benevolent power guarantees that the group's vital activities will be crowned with success.[4] It is not just religion that is shared: food, music and, dancing all help to reinforce what Catherine Mayeur-Jaouen calls "a physical sense of belonging."

Maria Couroucli demonstrates how, in the Anatolia of the early twentieth century, the territorial feeling of belonging to a village resulted in the crossing of religious frontiers as whole villages joined in the other's festivals, especially on St. George's Day. In village and town parishes, Muslims sometimes attended Mass, joined in as the icon was processed through the streets, or were invited into the homes of Christians. The celebrations that took place in the countryside were even more mixed, with common votive practices. On the fringes of institutions and the periphery of village territories, confessional frontiers became blurred and allowed the emergence of a human community sharing a common knowledge on its ancestral lands.

Gilles de Rapper's chapter describes the local reorganization of a sacred topography in which, in a context of weak ecclesiastical organization, religious frontiers became somewhat blurred after the fall of the dictatorship. In postcommunist Albania, the Ottoman term *vakëf* refers to a holy place of unknown or uncertain religious connection that is normally visited by different religious groups. Most of these places are ruins, tombs, or monasteries that are peripheral to the village's main place of worship (the mosque or church). We find echoes of this topography in other places where the institutional net is loosely knit, as in Rhodopes (Bulgaria) in the first part of the nineteenth century (Valtchinova).

Bojan Baskar's chapter looks at practices of interreligious cooperation, such as helping neighbors who follow a different religion to build a shrine or looking after it when they are away. This is in keeping with the rules of good neighborliness or *komsiluk,* a set of implicit rules and ritual mechanisms designed to ensure that *millet* could live together at a local level under the Ottoman Empire (Baskar, Valtchinova). Despite the fact that the informal codes of *komsiluk* were powerless to resist the nationalist pressures of the wars of the 1990s, these forms of sociability have not, according to Baskar, completely disappeared, especially in certain places in today's Bosnia, where they still give rise to a desire to learn to "live together" once again.[5]

The cases analyzed by Glenn Bowman also look at religion at the local level. The Muslims and their Christian neighbors who, in the 1980s, gathered at the Palestinian monastery of Mar Elyas to celebrate the feast of the prophet Elias were united by ties of friendship and neighborliness that transcended religious boundaries. Following a miraculous apparition of the Virgin in the little town of Beit Sahour at this time, the council decided to establish a commission made up of representatives of the town's main religious communities (Orthodox Christians, Muslims, Catholics, and Greek Catholics) to build a shrine that could be used by both Christians and Muslims. In both these cases, local or "civic" solidarities were subsumed into a more general nationalist discourse in which a shared Palestinian identity that transcended religious differences became the basis for opposition to the dominance of the state of Israel. The examples from Macedonia studied by Bowman demonstrate in similar fashion that interfaith crossovers still occur in small towns, and can involve either a Christian church that is also attended by Muslims, a mixed shrine with objects worshiped by both Christians and Muslims, or a Muslim place of worship that is used once a year by Christians.

The *moulids* of rural Egypt evoked by Catherine Mayeur-Jaouen also pertain to a local level. Until recently, these festivals, in which the religious dimension merges into the festive and commercial dimension, often attracted both Muslims and Christians. This celebratory mixing, which in some cases can still be seen today, reflects a local patriotism that finds tangible expression in an attachment to a local patron saint. The festive dimension, which is an essential part of any *moulid,* is also present in other examples where mixed worship goes hand in hand with an enjoyment of a pleasant spot or a relaxed space—often in the countryside—where people can share a moment of relaxation, have a hearty meal, and savor the pleasures of being together (de Rapper, Valtchinova, Bowman, Couroucli).

In a number of the cases examined here, the phenomenon of mixing occurs in a decidedly urban context. There is still a local dimension to most of Egypt's urban *moulids*, which have become an expression of the identity of a neighborhood or a common urban culture (Mayeur-Jaouen). In a megalopolis such as Istanbul, one can still observe large numbers of Christians and Muslims visiting the same places of worship and reviving the city's old tradition of syncretism. Every year, St. George's monastery on the island of Büyükada attracts tens of thousands of Stamboulite Muslims (Couroucli), as do the Orthodox church of Ayın Biri and the Catholic church of St. Anthony of Padua in the city center (Albera and Fliche).

Some travel much farther to go to visit shared shrines. The tomb of Rabbi Saadia Datsi in the Spanish enclave of Melilla was very much part of the local topography of the sacred, but in the first half of the twentieth century it was also visited by Jewish and Muslim pilgrims from afar (Driessen). Some Christian monasteries in Syria that are famous for their *baraka* attract not only locals, but also pilgrims from the rest of the country, and even from abroad. Christians of different denominations are joined by large number of Muslims from Syria, Iraq, and Iran. In such case, several dimensions coexist and overlap. Although such monasteries are the focus of local solidarities, they have also become catalysts for long-distance pilgrimages (Poujeau).

In all the cases mentioned so far, the spiritual power of the shrine is usually well established and part of a recognized tradition. Mixed worship can, however, also be observed in new sites where supernatural grace suddenly manifests itself in spectacular ways. The Bulgarian cult of the True Cross is one example. It emerged in the 1930s, after a wandering preacher had mystical visions. After a period of success, the pilgrimage was banned between 1960 and 1980. It was revived toward the end of that period on the initiative of the parish priest of the nearest town, who reportedly received a message from God in a dream. In the effervescent atmosphere of the postcommunist period, more and more pilgrims began to have visionary experiences. The site acquired a certain fame and, by the 1990s, was attracting not only Orthodox Christians, but also Muslim Pomaks from the region, Protestant Rom, and practitioners of yoga and New Age religions (Valtchinova).

While the apparitions of the Virgin that occurred in the West Bank town of Beit Sahour in 1983 appear to have been subsumed into a local devotional dimension, those that occurred in Egypt from the 1960s onward had a much wider impact. In these cases, we see large-scale devotional phenomena converging on the churches where the Virgin manifested herself to the faithful, without making any distinction as to their religion. Several of these sites were capable of drawing huge crowds where Copts mingled with Muslims. These phenomena attracted the attention of the press, mobilized the ecclesiastical hierarchy, and were exploited by the strategies of politicians (Keriakos).

On the whole, there exists a wide range of places that encourage mixed worship. Their peripheral location—the fact that they are beyond the reach of the authorities and that there is little clerical presence—presumably makes them conducive to interfaith crossovers. But this is far from being an exclusive situation. Places that have a larger attendance and that are under a stronger surveillance by the clerical apparatus of supervision can, however, also be conducive to mixed worship. Local solidarity networks seem to generate significant bonds that encourage people to cross the religious divide, but once again this is far from being an absolute rule, and mixing can also be observed in long-distance pilgrimages and in the context of large, anonymous gatherings.

Hybrid Saints

Who are the holy figures who give shrines a spiritual aura that can attract worshipers of a different religion? Can we identify them on the basis of their specific features? It has to be said, first of all, that in some cases this dimension is almost absent or at least not very pronounced. We are talking about local figures whose profile is indeterminate and who have no more than a schematic hagiography. Mixed attendance therefore tends to focus on very small rural shrines that are deep in the countryside and associated with rituals based on the farming calendar. The spiritual magnetism of such places is in itself enough to attract people of a different religion. In such cases, we are close to what Jacques Berque (Berque 1955:256) has defined as "the anonymous sacred." This situation was probably more widespread in the past, when the vast majority of the population lived in the countryside. We find echoes of this in Anatolia at the beginning of the twentieth century (Couroucli), and in contemporary Albania (de Rapper). In the recent past, Egypt too abounded in almost neutral saints whose cult was often associated with elements of the mineral or vegetable kingdom (a spring, a tree . . .). Their names were indeterminate and could belong to either Copts or Muslims: "sheik Nasr ('Victory'), sheik Ibrâhim ('Abraham') or sheik Abd al-Malik ('servant of the king')" (Mayeur-Jaouen, this volume). Speaking of the Judeo-Muslim saints of Morocco, Louis Voinot remarked that "despite the legends, which are used to try to establish their identity, nothing is known about many of the figures with double cults, and some are simply mythical" (Voinot 1948:126).

In other cases, mixed worship has, in varying degrees, been displaced onto what Jacques Berque calls the "figurative sacred," which is associated with figures with a definite identity. (Berque 1955:256). From that point of view, some of the figures who appear in several chapters of this book appear to be intermediaries who encourage interfaith gatherings. Their theoretical or legendary background means that they are effective go-betweens who facilitate religious crossovers.

Of all these figures, it is probably Mary who does most to encourage a devotional rapprochement between Christians and Muslims (see Keriakos, Mayeur-Jaouen, Bowman, Poujeau, Albera and Fliche). Although there is an element of doctrinal discontinuity where the Virgin is concerned, there is some theological continuity between Christianity and Islam. The Virgin is a central figure in two suras of the Koran, and she is the only female figure to be mentioned there by name. Because of this textual background, the Marian cult has attracted Muslims who go to Christian shrines to say prayers to her. While the Egyptian apparitions were a particularly significant moment in the development of a religious mixing focused on the Virgin, it should not be forgotten that Muslims hold many Marian shrines dear. The list should also include Bethlehem, Ephesus, and Harissa (Lebanon), to mention only the main shrines attended by both Muslims and Christians, but it would take several pages just to list them all (Albera 2005a).

Saint George is another figure who appears again and again in significant fashion in this book. He should in fact be described not as one figure, but as a conglomerate of transreligious figures who are effectively interchangeable.

Saint George is often identified with the Koranic figure of Al-Khadir, or "the green man," who is also known as Khidr, Khader, Hadir, Hizir. This *wali* is not mentioned by name in the Koran, but he is identified with the Servant of God who accompanies Moses in Sura XVIII 59–63. Although the Koran says little about him, Al-Khadir enjoys great popularity. This proteiform figure has often been identified with various Jewish and Christian saints, and especially with St. Elias and St. George. In Anatolia, the major festival known as Hidrellez identifies Al-Khadir with Elias. As a general rule, shrines dedicated to St. Elias and St. George are often visited by Muslims, while Christians visit those dedicated to Al-Khadir, whom they identify with one of St. George's avatars (Augustinović 1972).

The stories that are told about certain "transitional" figures sometimes become a narrative equivalent to the devotional ambivalence that surrounds them. The hagiographic tradition relating to Jewish Moroccan saints who are also venerated by Muslims, for instance, often gives the saint a Muslim companion who "accompanies his master on all his travels, caters for his needs and shows undying loyalty to him" (Ben Ami 1990:114–115). In many cases, the saint first reveals his supernatural qualities to a Muslim in an oneiric vision or through some other prodigious sign. As in the case examined here by Driessen, when the Jewish population left Morocco en masse, the job of guarding the sanctuaries of Jewish saints was often given to a Muslim. In some versions of the legendary St. George cycle, he is the son of a pagan father and a Christian mother, and is described as protecting a mixed couple (a Muslim man and a Christian woman). This relates him to the motif of the *digenis* ("born of two races"), which is very widespread in both Muslim and Christian traditions in the East. Even though the connection is vague, the saint's hagiography takes us back to the theme of interfaith crossovers, but also to the distant ties of kinship that form the basis for the local community of *omoemi* (those who share the same blood), which transcends the divide between distinct religious groups (Couroucli). A similar logic, which once more corresponds to the idea of a vague kinship—which is at the origins of the good neighborliness of mixed villages and guarantees the complementarity of religious communities within the framework of *komşuluk*—seems to be at work in the legends of the Bulgarian Pomaks in the Krastova Gora region, who claim that the patron saints of the main *tekkes* in the area were the brothers of Jesus (Valtchinova).

The links between legendary stories and religious crossovers are still more obvious in the case of other transreligious saints such as Sarı Saltık, Barak Baba, and Hadji Bektâch, who have been widely venerated since the Middle Ages, especially in Anatolia and the Balkans (Balivet 1999:255–270). The Muslim orthodoxy of these figures is somewhat dubious, and their religious affiliations are often rather vague. Their cycles sometimes describe them as Muslim mystics, and sometimes as Christian monks. They adopt different guises, undergo metamorphosis after metamorphosis, perform miracles, and are always on the move. The disguise motif also appears in the case of the Orthodox church of Sveti Nikola in the Macedonian town of Makedonski Brod, which is described by Glenn Bowman. Inside the church, there is the tomb of a saint that is venerated by both Christians and Muslims. The saint himself is not easily identifiable. According to local Christians, he is an old man with a beard—Sveti Nikola-who once performed ritual acts to ensure that the plague spared the town. Muslims tell the same story, but say that the old man was Hadir Baba, a Bektashi saint who disguised himself as a Christian.

As with the spatial dimension, there is once more no simple or univocal explanation for the spread of these mixed cults. Crossovers occur even when there are no links, either explicit or implicit, between the saint who "inhabits" the site and the crossing of religious frontiers. Some religious overlaps occur, for instance, under the patronage of holy figures who unequivocally belong to one religion. In Istanbul, the eminently Catholic figure of St. Anthony of Padua also attracts an orthodox Christian "clientele" and Muslim devotees (Albera and Flichte). The shrine in Laç in northern Albania provides a further example of mixed worship at the church of St. Anthony of Padua (de Rapper). The cult of St. Thecla in the Qalamun region of Syria is a further example of how Muslims can venerate an exclusively Christian saint: the monastery in Maʿlula is a well-established center for interfaith crossovers, and is still very influential today (Poujeau). In Cairo, Muslim women attend the church of St. Theresa of Avila (Mayeur-Jaouen). Some chapters of this book describe how Christians visit sites associated with figures who are clearly Muslim. The Egyptian village of Badramân is one example. Here, Christians take part in the festivals held in honor of Sheik ʿAbd al-Ghaffâr, a local Muslim saint who died in 1970 and who is buried in the middle of the village (Mayeur-Jaouen). It would not be difficult to find other examples. In the first decades of the twentieth century, Palestinian Christians from Bêt Djâlâ and Bethlehem used to take offerings of candles to the mausoleum of el-Badrîyeh in Sarâfat and prayed to the Muslim saint (Canaan 1927:146). In Ramleh, a Catholic Palestinian recently paid for the restoration of the maqâm of the Koranic figure of Nabî Sâlih. Every year, he supplies the candles and oils need for devotional practices when he visits it in the saint's feast day (Aubin-Boltanski 2007:57–58).

We can therefore conclude that, while it is inevitably heterodox, the crossing of religious frontiers can be made easier by narrative constructs that somehow cross the religious divide; some worshipers succeed in overcoming what appear to be insurmountable theological and doctrinal barriers in their quest for the salvation and well-being they expect to find thanks to the mediation of another religion's "pantheon," either because they admire a certain saint, because they are merely curious, or simply because they want to join in the festival.

The effects of the supernatural presence that is attributed to certain sites are multifarious. The sacred power of the site, which is bound up with the power of its saint, does not simply capture the attention of the faithful despite their denominational differences. It also makes the religious specialists who are in charge of the sanctuary more willing to accept the transversal demand for religious goods. In her contribution, Anna Poujeau points out, for example, that the staff of Syrian monasteries that have *baraka* are more welcoming to pious Muslim visitors than the staff of churches in the towns. All who cross the threshold of the monastery—Muslim or Christian—must be given hospitality because they are considered to be under the protection of the saint who is venerated there, and the saint does not discriminate on religious grounds.

Recognition of the charisma of the other religion's *living* saints is a further example of contemporary interfaith exchange (to which Catherine Mayeur-Jaouen draws our attention). In Egypt, for example, Coptic monks who have *baraka* are visited by Muslims who want their help in dealing with serious problems, most of them related to their health. In a few cases Sufi sheiks or Muslim holy women attract Christian worshipers for similar reasons, though this is more unusual.

Mixed Worship: Actors and Structures

The chapters of this book analyze in detail some of the contexts in which mixed worship takes place. Who are its protagonists? Can we draw up a typical profile of the people who cross religious foundations and who look elsewhere—in the holy dwelling place of another confession—as they pursue their pious quest? The cases examined in this book suggest that those who visit shared places of worship come both from the lower classes (in the country and the town) and from sections of the urban middle classes. The shrines of other religions seem to attract more women than men because women are less involved in more "official" forms of worship, but men do often cross religious frontiers.

The structures in which devotional crossovers occur are often controlled by religious institutions. Several of the Albanian *vakëf* studied by Gilles de Rapper are, on the other hand, exceptions to the rule. Glenn Bowman gives an interesting example of a mixed place of worship under secular control. The case of Beit Sahour, a small town in the Bethlehem area, has already been mentioned. In 1983, some of the villagers were reported to have seen apparitions of the Virgin Mary in an underground water tank. Shortly afterward, the council decided to build a shrine where both Christians and Muslims could worship. The building's dome makes it look like a Muslim *maqâm,* but it is surmounted by a cross. Inside, there are devotional objects with both Christian and Muslim connotations. The various religious communities booked access to the shrine for their ceremonies through the council, but sometimes came together for shared ceremonies. Everyone drew water from the tank below the shrine, which is said to have healing powers. As Glenn Bowman remarks, "The shared character of the shrine of Bir es-Saiyideh both reflected the common everyday experience of a mixed community with shared traditions and expressed the political program of a local leadership committed to defeating sectarian fragmentation." This situation was, however, short-lived. The Orthodox Church quickly took control of the shrine—but that did not stop pious Muslims from visiting it or from contributing to its upkeep.

Another case analyzed by Bowman—this time from Macedonia—demonstrates how the management of shared shrines can change hands. The current layout of the church of Sveti Nikola—which contains a tomb covered in carpets and representations with Muslim motifs—seems to be the result of the recent appropriation of a Bektashi *tekke* by Orthodox Christians. During the period that followed the Balkan wars and then under communism, the place was probably disused but still visited by the two communities. The fact that the saint is so difficult to identify—some say that he was a Christian, others that he was a Muslim—meant that both Christians and Muslims could visit it, and may also have made it easier for the Orthodox Church to take it over.

This process has to do with the well-known mechanisms linked to the transfer of a place of worship from one religion to another. In his pioneering work, Frederick Hasluck puts them into three categories: conversion, intrusion, and identification (Hasluck 1929:457–458). The circulation of a series of legends may indicate that the saint venerated in a particular place was secretly converted, that his mausoleum also houses the tomb of a holy figure of another religion, or even that the saint was in reality the transfiguration or a misrepresentation of someone of a different religion. These mechanisms were very visible in the syncretic missionary work of the Mevlivis and the Bektashis, who played a major role in the transfer of many shrines, and especially rural shrines, from Christianity to Islam in Anatolia and the Balkans. Although less spectacular than violent conquest, these practices helped to reshape the religious landscape over a period of hundreds of years. And, as we can see from the example of Sveti Nikola, they allow mixed worship to continue after the transfer takes place because they exploit a certain indeterminacy or "ambiguity," which may, should the context change, allow the shrine to be returned to its original owners.

Even though it is sometimes the result of prolonged negotiations and transitions, and even though it may not be permanent, the management of shared sanctuaries usually does seem, at any given moment, to be "monopolistic." Worshipers of other religions can perform their devotions inside the shrine, and elements of another cult may be tolerated inside its sacred space (as in the Macedonian case of Sveti Nikola), though this is more unusual. But there is usually no joint institutional management.

"Interfaith in the Making"

In most of the cases examined in detail in this book, our observations concern Muslims who visit Christian sites. We therefore have a large enough corpus of data to be able to put forward a number of general remarks about the division of sacred space, about practices and sociability, and about the interaction between the actors and the structures that are devoted to the cult.

So far as the use of space is concerned, there is, first of all, a minimal level of sharing, as at some Egyptian *moulids*, where the intermingling is usually restricted to the fair and the entertainment, activities that are held outside the place of worship itself (Mayeur-Jaouen). Similar remarks apply to the feast of Alidun or Ilindan (St. Elias), which used to be held at the *türbe* in Gerozo in northern Bosnia, where Orthodox Christians joined in the afternoon feast with the Muslims (Baskar). In the examples taken into consideration in different chapters, it is, however, more usual for Muslim worshipers to enter the religious space itself (a chapel, church, or monastery). They are sometimes preferentially channeled to one specific place. In the case of the monastery at Ma'lula in Syria, they are allowed to visit the cave where St. Thecla is said to be buried, but are sometimes discouraged from entering the church itself, especially when they come in very large groups (Poujeau). Elsewhere, they have easy and immediate access to the church, but even when this is the case, the allocation of space is a subject for subtle negotiations (Bowman, Albera and Fliche, de Rapper). The distinction between internal and external space tends to disappear when crowds are present, as ecstatic attitudes are adopted in the expectation of apparitions or other visionary manifestations (Keriakos, Valtchinova).

When we look at the mixed congregations that gather in the same places of worship, the question of the visibility of confessional affiliations immediately arises: to what extent are they displayed or concealed when visiting the sacred dwelling place of the other? From this point of view, the main variable has to do with vestimentary markers, which are usually more visible in the case of women, as at the church of St. Theresa in Cairo, which is visited by veiled Muslim women. The same phenomenon can be observed when Christian monasteries in Syria are visited by groups of Shiite pilgrims from Iran or Iraq, as all the women wear black veils (Poujeau). The examples taken from Istanbul reveal some variations: some Muslim women adopt an "Islamic" vestimentary semiotics (a headscarf covering the neck; long, flowing coats), while others dress in European style (Albera and Fliche, Couroucli). In shared places of worship in Albania, this vestimentary coding is less obvious, and it is difficult to tell Muslims and Christians apart, not only on the basis of what they are wearing, but also on the basis of which religious objects they display, as Christians do not have a monopoly on the cross here (de Rapper). The general variability that emerges from these chapters suggests that vestimentary attitudes depend on a variety of factors that go beyond the issue of joint worship. Deciding what to wear when visiting a Christian site is a matter of individual choice, but the decisions may also be influenced by the political context, or the individual's social environment and personal history, and so on. Individuals enter the sacred places of the other religion wearing the clothes they wear in everyday life: they enter this "other" space with symbols of a religious identity that may or may not be on display, or on the contrary wearing more neutral clothes.

In several cases, the devotional gestures performed by Muslims in Christian spaces derive from a shared repertoire of demonstrative and tactile piety (Mayeur-Jaouen). This may involve using candles, incubation, making offerings of money or in kind, tying ribbons or strips of cloth to the branches or trees or to the grills protecting the tomb of a saint, leaving prayer intentions near holy places, rubbing coins against walls or touching objects that have healing powers (such as the tomb of a saint), slipping through chains, taking home some pieces of cotton soaked in oil, touching or drinking the water of holy springs. Muslims do not even have a monopoly on blood sacrifices. The practice was still observed by Christians in the Black Sea region and in western

Thrace in the early twentieth century (Couroucli), and is still observed today in Albania (de Rapper) and in Bulgaria (Givre 2006).

The boundaries between devotional habits sometimes vary from one place to another. According to Catherine Mayeur-Jaouen, "Egyptian Muslims do not leave written messages for a saint, whereas the practice is widespread amongst Copts." In Turkey, in contrast, the gesture is part of a repertoire common to both religions (Albera and Fliche). We can also identify local variations, rather as though both Christians and Muslims were experimenting with elements from the same devotional lexicon. Examples include the little stone structures that are erected in the surroundings of the monastery of St. George on Bükükada island (Couroucli), or, to stay in Istanbul, the keys that are handed out at Ayın Biri Kiliesi or the altar gates that are opened and closed in the church of St. Anthony of Padua (Albera and Fliche).

We also find examples of what might be called distortion: gestures that are borrowed from the Muslim repertoire and adapted to a different context. As a result, a "foreign" devotional structure can be creatively appropriated. We might cite, for example, the circumambulation around the statue of St. Theresa in Cairo (Mayeur-Jaouen), the way Muslims take off their shoes in Albanian churches (de Rapper), the recitation of Muslim prayers in Christian churches (and sometimes the quiet reading of suras from the Koran), praying with open hands raised to heaven (Albera and Fliche, Bowman), using water from the stoup in St. Anthony's church in Istanbul to perform "ablutions" (Albera and Fliche), or the way some Muslims prostrate themselves on the floor in St. Thecla's cave in the monastery in Ma'lula (Poujeau).

A second set of practices reveals how Muslims have adopted the gestures and symbols of the "Other" by respecting Christian devotional modus operandi. In the late 1960s, Muslims made the same gestures as the Christians with whom they mingled as they waited for the Virgin to appear to them in the church in Zeitun (Egypt). Keriakos cites examples of "Muslims [going to] the church without knowing how they should behave; they watched their neighbors, and began to chant the same litanies and say the same words." The imitation of specifically Christian practices obviously raises the problem of the transgression of the limits of one's own religion in a particularly acute way. The response to that problem seems to vary from one context to another (and depends, naturally, on individual choices that are difficult to evaluate). In that respect, the story told by the Muslim woman who went to Zeitun is significant. When she felt that she was seeing the Virgin, she began to cry out, just like the crowd around here, but, suddenly afraid that she might transgress a boundary (by, for instance, inadvertently making the sign of the cross), began to recite the Islamic creed (Keriakos).

Although Islam prohibits the worship of images, it is commonplace for Muslims visiting the shrines discussed here to venerate icons. They are quite happy to touch them (Mayeur-Jaouen) but find it harder to imitate the Orthodox habit of kissing them—at least in Macedonia (Bowman), as Muslims who visit churches in Albania do touch and kiss the icons (de Rapper). Muslims do much the same to the statues in Catholic churches in Turkey and Egypt (Albera and Fliche, Mayeur-Jaouen).

For Muslims, the cross is probably the most pronounced mark of difference, and it is at this point that most Muslims begin to refuse to imitate Christians. Yet some Muslims have adopted the practice of making the sign of the cross in Albania (de Rapper). Moreover, Muslims have also been known to visit sites that are dedicated to the cult of the cross, such as Krastova in Bulgaria. Valtchinova describes the exceptional, and very revealing, case of "an instance . . . observed in May 1994, when, after the sacrifice of a lamb (the *kurban*), a Pomak woman dipped her hands into the blood and then embraced the cross, leaving bloody marks on it. . . . Its sense was immediately accessible to the Orthodox, and those passing by or watching did not seem surprised or offended." References to the magical functions of the cross can also be found in eyewitness account of the phenomena that occurred in Zeitun (Egypt). In 1970, a Muslim woman who had been exorcised by Coptic priests felt herself being freed from the spirit that had possessed her. When she got home, she found that her body was covered in crosses. In another case, the priest who prayed over the son of a Muslim woman, who was suffering from a muscular complaint, gave her a cross and some oil to anoint him (Keriakos).

In Egypt, the Christian symbol of baptism is imitated by some Muslims who, especially during certain *moulids*, ask the Coptic clergy to baptize their children if they are seriously ill. This is a prophylactic form of baptism, and the priests are careful not to confuse it with Christian baptism. At the *moulid* of the Virgin in Gabal al-Tayr, for example, an enormous font is filled with unblessed water for prophylactic baptisms (Mayeur-Jaouen). The same phenomenon has been observed elsewhere, as in Syria and Bosnia in the first decades of the twentieth century (Thoumin 1929; Vucinic 2002).

Taking part in Mass is another frontier that is difficult to cross. At the Ma'lula monastery in Syria, Muslims are denied access to the church while Mass is being celebrated (Poujeau). Even in the region of Albania studied by de Rapper, Muslims do not take part in Mass, even though religious boundaries are here often unclear. In Istanbul, in contrast, this hurdle is easily overcome. In the Catholic church of St. Anthony of Padua, for example, Muslims can be seen almost every day, sitting in the pews as Mass is being said. Some of them even go up to the altar rail as Communion is being given. This has become so frequent that the priest always announces in advance that Communion is reserved for those who have been baptized, to stop them from doing so (Albera and Fliche).

The interaction between the followers of different religions inside these shrines is complex. Most of the time, the interaction is minimal and episodic, and moments of communion are rare. The way in which the various parties behave is influenced by the structure of the places of worship in question, and by the actions of those in charge of them (such as the nuns at the Ma'lula monastery or the attendants in the church of St. Anthony of Padua in Istanbul). The structure of worship is often elastic enough to allow "others" to join in. A subtle management of space preserves invisible boundaries and ensures that some spaces remain inviolable. There is, however, still some intrusion. How do those whose presence there is more "legitimate" react? The situations analyzed in this book suggest that Christian attitudes toward the presence of Muslims within a sacred space can be schematized as indifference, condescension, or acceptance. At all events, the various ethnographic studies that have been carried out do not reveal any overt conflicts or aggressive displays of rejection. This objective tolerance appears to be bound up with a tacit recognition that the existential condition of Christians and Muslims is the same: given life's difficulties and the threat of illness, they all need supernatural help. It also reflects the fact that both parties are discreet, and respect the unspoken rule of noninterference (Valtchinova, Albera and Fliche). Silence appears to be almost a precondition for mixed worship. It helps to create what Victor Turner calls an existential *communitas,* but it is a *communitas* that is diluted, silent, and fragmented.

The presence of non-Christians often involves interaction with those specialists in the other religion who run the shrine, and who may perform the ritual acts. The attitude of the clergy is a crucial influence on how mixed congregations behave. While they do not all take the same stance by any means, most of the priests who control shrines appear to be open-minded and to respond positively to the "transversal" demand for religious goods (de Rapper, Valtchinova, Albera and Fliche, Keriakos, Bowman, Mayeur-Jaouen). They are quite willing to perform rites and to bless Muslims who ask them to do so (Couroucli, Mayeur-Jaouen, Albera and Fliche). They may carry out exorcisms

(Mayeur-Jaouen), perform prophylactic baptisms (Mayeur-Jaouen, Keriakos), or simply listen and offer spiritual help (Albera and Fiche, Mayeur-Jaouen).

"Grassroots" religious specialists seem, judging from the cases under examination, to be fairly tolerant (and often much more so than might be expected). The attitude of the institutions to which they are, in one way or another, answerable is more complex. On the one hand, from the point of view of the religious apparatus, the detour via the "other" can of course confirm the power (and therefore the superiority) of its doctrine. The miracles Christian saints perform for Muslims are one example. In Egypt, Muslim eyewitnesses have become the essential guarantors of the authenticity of the Virgin's apparitions (Keriakos, Mayeur-Jaouen); in Syria, there are many stories about how Christian saints have granted Muslims favors (Poujeau). And while Christian communities do not, in the present context, openly proselytize (with, of course, the exception of some Protestant groups), the possibility that some Muslims may convert is welcomed. Some highly placed figures in the Catholic hierarchy do take a favorable view of the mixed congregations that attend Catholic places of worship because they are sympathetic to the Islamic-Christian dialogue. Yet, on the other hand, the type of religiosity that characterizes mixed worship is not designed to please the guardians of orthodoxy, and the religious indeterminacy that may result is in sharp contrast with the demand for a clear definition of religions' respective territories. The example of Egypt is highly significant in this respect. The reawakening of fundamentalist religions is leading to increased mutual distrust on the part of both Muslim reformists and Coptic revivalists. It is driving Muslims and Copts further apart and into their own respective spaces because it is based upon a shared obsession with what is licit and what is illicit. In this competitive atmosphere, which can result in physical violence, the growing clerical control over Coptic *moulids* and the demonstrations of piety associated with Marian apparitions has coincided with a decline in Muslim involvement in recent years, which had already been discouraged by injunctions from the Islamic authorities and the violent threats issued by Islamists (Mayeur-Jaouen, Keriakos).

A Lingua Franca

Although summary, the above comments give some idea of the richness of the contributions collected here. They demonstrate the polyphonic nature of religious mixing, and take into account a multiplicity of contexts, forms, and protagonists. This general survey, which is the first of its kind, makes no claim to being exhaustive. It is inevitably a preliminary account. Further research is needed to define a more coherent and complete framework at both the descriptive and the interpretative level. It is hoped that the range of cases and approaches presented here will act as stimuli to further work.[6]

Having said that, it is already possible to see what the ethnographic studies collected here might contribute to contemporary debates, and first of all to the debate about the clash of civilizations that has had so much media coverage and that has so many political implications. The "clash of civilizations" is often seen as synonymous with a clash of religions, and is usually reduced to meaning the clash between the Christian West and Islam. These examples of mixed worship give the lie to the widespread view that, in the Mediterranean area, the barriers between the monotheisms are insurmountable, and refute the gloomy scenario of an inevitable clash of civilizations (which cannot, in any case, be reduced to the ideologies that claim to represent them). They also offer a perspective on interreligious relations that goes beyond the doxa that has it that "churches" and states have initiated a dialogue between cultures and religions. Although they examine a variety of situations, the various chapters all exemplify much the same principle: even in the exclusivist context of the monotheisms, religious identities can be composite, and exchanges and experiments are possible. Competition and mutual hatred are not, in other words, part of the DNA of Mediterranean religious "cultures"; when it is possible, people can cross the frontiers that divide them in peace.

Their ability to refute some of the metaphysical propositions of a pessimistic philosophy of history is not, however, the only merit of these grassroots observations. Their findings are part of a historical process and they help, in their turn, to shed light on that process. We are talking about a transition characterized, in the eastern Mediterranean, by the decline of the rural world, the assertion of nationalisms—especially through processes of religious homogenization—and the rise of religious reformisms with rigorist and scriptuary overtones. Over the last few decades, there appears to have been a decline in religious mixing as a result of the combined aggressiveness of these nationalisms and fundamentalisms. It would be surprising if that were not the case. And yet the extent of the resistance should not be underestimated. In some cases, religious pluralism is actually becoming more common, as, for example, in some postsocialist countries. The church in Béchouate, in the Bekka Valley in Lebanon, was recently the site of a miraculous event concerning a statue of the Virgin. The first witness was a Muslim child on 21 August 2004. The shrine suddenly became the epicenter of a huge pilgrimage that attracted pilgrims of all denominations. In the following months hundreds of thousands of pilgrims representing all the denominations present in Lebanon visited it (Aubin-Boltanski 2008).

It is therefore difficult to give a diagnosis, or to provide a prognosis. Although they can still be observed everywhere, phenomena of mixing are affected by random factors that influence their concrete manifestations because they have no institutional basis. In that respect, one episode mentioned by Glenn Bowman is significant: the symbolic contribution made by the emigrant who goes back to his village in Macedonia with a view to giving the village church a larger cross can upset the delicate equilibrium that allows Muslims access to that space. Religious crossovers also seem to react quickly to their sociopolitical context, to the events that punctuate the life of a town, region, or state (Albera and Fliche). It is therefore difficult for an ethnographer to distinguish between the rapid pulse of the events and the slower rhythms of historical transitions. Much will depend, in any case, on how the political situation in the Mediterranean as a whole develops.

In more general terms, the contributions collected here may help to further advance the anthropology of pilgrimage. This center of interest, which is still relatively new, has developed as a result of a number of major contributions (Turner 1974b; Turner and Turner 1978; Eade and Sallnow 1991; Morinis 1992). With some exceptions, the anthropological studies concentrated on monodenominational situations. According to Victor and Edith Turner, who are the authors of the most influential book on the subject, this is in fact an intrinsic feature of the phenomenon: they suggest that pilgrims of different historical religions do not visit the shrines of others. The data presented here disavow that thesis.

It is possible to identify three main approaches to the anthropological study of pilgrimage. The first, which takes its inspiration from Durkheim's perspectives on religion, sees the phenomenon as an element in the social cohesion that helps to construct and preserve wider collective identities (either territorial, political, or religious). The second approach is associated with the name of Victor Turner who, taking his inspiration from Arnold Van Gennep's work on rites of passage, identifies an element of *communitas* (characterized by the spontaneity of relationships and the abolition of distinctions) in the ritual phenomenon, and contrasts it with the rigidity of roles in ordinary social structures. From this perspective, pilgrimage is one manifestation of what Turner defines as an anti-structure. It corresponds to a quest for the universal, in which people are, to some extent, set free from the constraints inherent in the social roles of everyday life, and experiment with egalitarian relationships with other pilgrims. The third approach is inspired mainly by the contributions of John Eade and Michael Sallnow, who view the pilgrimage as a mosaic of heteroclite actors and different points of view, in which egalitarianism can coexist alongside nepotism, and fraternity alongside conflict, and in which heterogeneous practices and distinct discourses could coexist or compete. While other visions emphasize the "full" nature of shrines, which are supposedly saturated with the symbols found inside them, this approach insists that, on the contrary, such places are "empty," and can therefore accommodate a plurality of meanings and practices.

Without going into these debates in greater detail, it should be noted that these points of view can be seen as not so much competing paradigms as complementary interpretations that draw our attention to various facets of a polymorphous phenomenon that is not easily reducible to one general model.[7] The examples of mixed worship examined in this book are testimony to this pluralism. In several cases, they are expressions of local or national solidarities that make it possible to overcome the religious divide. The *communitas* dimension does emerge in a certain number of situations, but it is not conspicuous. Above all these ethnographic studies do seem to allow us to enter into a dialogue with the approach that insists that, even in the case of monoreligious and monoconfessional pilgrimages, shrines are multiform places where various practices and interpretations can overlap and compete.

The anthropological interest, which is even more recent, in the theme of shared sanctuaries was stimulated by discussions of an article by Robert Hayden, which is based on an analysis of a number of shared sanctuaries in India and the Balkans (Hayden 2002a). Hayden proposes, in order to describe such situations, the notions of "competitive sharing" and "antagonistic tolerance." He recommends the adoption of a process-based approach in which syncretism is regarded as a historical materialization of the state of relations between religious communities. According to this perspective, mixed worship is nothing more than a moment within a process in which each group tries to monopolize the shrine. Hayden therefore attempts to demonstrate that, even when people of different religions mix and tolerate one another's devotional practices, the tolerance is illusory and represents, at best, a pragmatic adaptation to circumstance in which it is not possible to repress the other group's practices. Some chapters (Bowman, Baskar) of this book propose a direct and critical discussion of this position. It should, moreover, be noted that, on the whole, the ethnographic and historical data presented here cannot be reconciled with Hayden's schema, which appears to hypostasize the postulates of religious nationalism by turning them into the premises for a comparative argument. The range of attitudes and behaviors described here is infinitely richer and infinitely more varied. In a field in which there is a temptation to develop "grand" theories, based on a rapid examination of a limited number of cases, it seems to me to be important to bring together thick ethnographic descriptions. Having said that, I am not suggesting that we react to the "gloomy" side of interpretations such as Hayden's by falling back on an irenic view of interreligious relations. We must never forget that—as many of the elements discussed here suggest—especially when it comes to the monotheistic religions, coexistence, mixing, and sharing are never completely divorced from elements that are potentially competitive and conflict-ridden.

In general terms, we are dealing with a complex interplay between practices and identities that are usually shrouded in secrecy. In some cases, permeability at the devotional level does, however, seem to coexist with an insistence on the "strong" identities preached by the great religions of the Book. While the violations of the exclusivism basic to all the monotheisms are flagrant and while the hybrid practices are striking, mixing with individuals of a different religion does not result, so to speak, in any evident damage to existing religious identities. Indeed, these "transgressions" usually appear to be associated with the preservation of the initial religious polarization. The adoption of highly heterodox practices can, in other words, be reconciled with respect for at least the basis principles of one's own religion (ritualism, ethics, dogma, and so on). Keriakos gives a significant example of this hybrid situation when she describes the Egyptian Muslims who, having held a night-long vigil in the church in Zeitun in the hope of seeing the apparition of the Virgin during the month of Ramadan, regularly begin their day-long fast (and are even told by the priests when it is time for *suhûr*). It is only in situations where there is little clerical influence, as in the postcommunist Albania described by de Rapper, that religious identities appear to give way to a degree of indeterminacy.

The phenomena described in these chapters are fragile and clandestine. Discretion and opacity appear to be preconditions for their survival. They are tactical compromises (Certeau 1990), and they can be observed wherever religious and political apparatuses leave them some room for maneuver. They take their inspiration from an eclectic pragmatism, both when they ask for supernatural intercession and when they search for new ritual forms. Efficacy is all that matters. This religiosity is focused on concrete manifestations of the sacred and on the engineering of rituals. Hence the importance of those mediator-saints who are accessible to the faithful because there are images of them and records of their time on earth. Yet this religiosity is unlikely to result in the emergence of a new and clearly identifiable religious idiom. It is, rather, a transreligious *koine* that resists historical changes, even though it is dominated, subaltern, and implicit. Its basic vocabulary, which is made up of ritual gestures, thaumaturgical hopes, and objects that have supernatural powers, is a sort of *lingua franca* that is spoken in whispers and still circulates almost silently from one religion to another.

Notes

1. See the many sources examined in Hasluck 1929:109–118.

2. See, inter alia, Voinot 1948, and Ben Ami 1990. On the way these pilgrimages continued after the Jewish population left en masse, see Lakhassi 2002.

3. I use the figures established by Ben Ami 1990:112–114. There are some discrepancies between his figures and those given by Voinot.

4. On the notion of the "territory of grace," see Christian 1989:44.

5. From that point of view, Baskar's contribution echoes Aïda Kanafani-Zahar's work on the post-war period in Lebanese society. See especially Kanafani-Zahar 2004.

6. For recent comparative perspectives on religious mixing in the Mediterranean, see Ayoub 1999; Balivet 1999; Cuffel 2003; 2005; Albera 2005a; 2005b; 2008.

7. For the argument that pilgrimage should be interpreted with a certain eclecticism, see Dubisch 1995:44–45.

REFERENCES

ʿAbd Al-Masih Basit Abu Al-Khayr. 1998. *Zuhurat al-ʿAdhraʾ hawla al-ʿalam*. 4th ed. Cairo: Matbaʿat al-Misriyyin.

Abinun, M. 1988. *Les lumières de Sarajevo: Histoire d'une famille juive d'Europe centrale*. Paris: Jean-Claude Lattès Editions.

Abu Al-Khayr, B. 2000. *Zuhur al-ʿAdhraʾ wa al-tagaliyyat al-ruhiyya fi Asiut*. Cairo: Matbaʿat al-Misriyyin.

Adamantidis, T. 1934. "Comment on fêtait la Saint-Georges dans la Mer Noire." *Messaionika Grammata* B: 236–240 (in Greek).

Akoglu, X. 1939. *The Folklore of Kotyora*. Vol. A. Athens: Editions Xenou (in Greek).

Al-Badrawi, R. 2001. *Qisas al-Anbibaʾ; ʿIsa ibn Maryam, Zakariyya wa Yihya, ʿalayhim al-salam*. Cairo: Al-Gazira International.

Albera, D. 2005a. "La Vierge et l'islam: Mélanges de civilisations en Méditerranée." *Le Débat* no. 37 (November–December): 134–144.

———. 2005b. "Pèlerinages mixtes et sanctuaires 'ambigus' en Méditerranée." In *Les Pèlerinages en Moyen-Orient: Espaces publics, espaces du public*, S. Chiffoleau and A. Madoeuf, eds., 347–378. Beirut: Institut Français du Proche-Orient.

———. 2008. "'Why Are You Mixing What Cannot Be Mixed?' Shared Devotions in the Monotheisms." *History and Anthropology* 19, no. 1: 37–59.

Albert, J-P. 1997. *Le sang et le ciel: Les saintes mystiques dans le monde chrétien*. Coll. "Historique." Paris: Aubier.

———. 2000. "Les lieux où souffle l'esprit." *Archives de Sciences Sociales des Religions* 111 (July–September): 111–123.

Alexandris, A. 1983. *The Greek Minority of Istanbul and Greek-Turkish Relations, 1918–1974*. Athens: Center for Asia Minor Studies.

Anagnostakis, I., and E. Balta. 1994. *La découverte de la Cappadoce au XIXe siècle*. Istanbul: Eren.

Anagnostopoulou, S. 1997. *Mikra Asia, 190s aionas—1919, I ellinorthodoxes kinotites, apo to millet ton Romion sto Elliniko Ethnos* [Asia Minor, 19th Century—1919, The Greek Orthodox Communities, from the *Millet* of the *Rum* to the Greek Nation]. Athens: Ellinika Grammata.

Anba Butrus Al-Gamil al-, Al-Anba Mikha'il and Al-Anba Yuhanna. 1972. *Al-Sinksar al-gamiʿ li-akhbar al-qiddisin al-mustaʿmal fi kanaʾis al-kiraza al-murqusiyya fi ayyam wa ahad al-sana al-tutiyya.* Cairo: Maktabat al-Mahabba.

Anonymous. 1994. *Krastova Gora: Alleluyah on the Hill.* Asenovgrad, Bulgaria: Reghion Press (in Bulgarian).

Anonymous. 1996. *Rhodopian Jerusalem: Krastova Gora.* Asenovgrad, Bulgaria: Reghion Press (in Bulgarian).

Arininski, V. 2000. *The Miracles on Krastova Gora.* Plovdiv, Bulgaria: Prizma (in Bulgarian).

Arutjunova-Fidanjan, A. 1978. *Tipik Gregoria Pakuriana* [The Typicon of Gergorios Pakriani]. Erevan: Armenian Academy of Sciences.

Asdracha, C. 1976. *La région des Rhodopes aux XIIIe et XIVe siècles: Etude de géographie historique.* Athens: Texte und Forschungen zur byzantinish-negriechische Philologie.

Aubin-Boltanski, E. 2003. "La réinvention du mawsim de Nabî Sâlih. Les territoires palestiniens (1997–2000)." *Archives de Sciences Sociales des Religions* 123: 103–120.

———. 2007. *Pèlerinages et nationalisme en Palestine: Prophètes, héros et ancêtres.* Paris: Editions de l'EHESS.

———. 2008. "La Vierge et la nation" (Liban, 2004–2007). *Terrain,* no. 50: 82–99.

Augustinovich, A. 1972. *"El-Khadr" and the Prophet Elijah.* Jerusalem: Franciscan Printing Press.

Ayoub, M. 1999. "Cult and Culture: Common Saints and Shrines in Middle Eastern Popular Piety." In *Religion and Culture in Medieval Islam,* ed. R. G. Havannisian and G. Sabagh, 103–115. Cambridge: Cambridge University Press.

Aziz, Sadiq. 1994. "Al-baba Kirollos yuʿlin: Zuhur al-ʿAdhra' haqiqa: Bayan rasmi lil-baba yuʾakkid zuhuraha ʿiddat marrat fi kanisat al-Zeitun." *Al-Ahram,* 5 May (1968).

Badir, Najla. 2000. "Mata satazhar al-ʿAdhra' marratan ukhra." *Sabah al-Khayr,* 22 August.

Baer, M. 2004. "The Conversion of Christian and Jewish Souls and Space during the 'Anti-Dervish' Movement of 1656–76." In *Archaeology, Anthropology and Heritage in the Balkans and Anatolia: The Life and Times of F. W. Hasluck, 1878–1920,* ed. D. Shankland, 2:183–200. Istanbul: Isis.

Baeva, V., and G. Valtchinova. 2009. "A Women's Religious Organization in Southern Bulgaria: From Miracle Stories to History." *History and Anthropology* 20, no. 3 (September): 317–338.

Bakaršić, K. 2001. "The Never-Ending Story of C-4336 AKA Sarajevo's Haggada Codex." *Wiener slawistische Almanach* (Vienna and Munich), *Bosnien-Herzegowina: Interkultureller Synkretismus,* special issue, 52: 267–289.

Balivet, M. 1999. *Byzantins et Ottomans: Relations, interactions, succession.* Istanbul: Isis.

Balta, E. 1995. *Les Vakifs de Serrès et de sa région (XVe et XVIe s.).* Athens: Institute for Neohellenic Research, National Hellenic Research Foundation.

Barbulesco, Luc. 1985. "La communauté copte d'Egypte 1881–1981." Doctoral thesis. Reprinted in *Les Chrétiens égyptiens aujourd'hui: Eléments de discours.* Cairo: Dossiers du CEDEJ.

Bashear, S. 1991. "Qibla Musharriqa and Early Muslim Prayer in Churches." *Muslim World* 81, no. 3–4: 266–282.

Bausinger, H. 1971. *Volkskunde: Von der Altertumsforschung zur Kulturanalyse.* Tübingen: Tübinger Vereinigung für Volkskunde.

Bax, M. 2000. "Planned Policy or Primitive Balkanism? A Local Contribution to the Ethnography of War in Bosnia-Herzegovina." *Ethos* 65, no. 2: 317–340.

Bazin, L. 1972. "Les calendriers turcs anciens et médiévaux." Thesis, Paris III, université de Lille III.

Bazin, M. 2005. "Diversité ethnique et disparités régionales." In *La Turquie,* ed. Semih Vaner, 389–428. Paris: Fayard-CERI.

Beinin, J. 1998. *The Dispersion of Egyptian Jewry: Culture, Politics and the Formation of a Modern Diaspora.* Berkeley: University of California Press.

Bell, J. 1999. "The Revival Process: The Turkish and Pomak Minorities in Bulgarian Politics." In *Ethnicity and Nationalism in East Central Europe and the Balkans,* ed. T. Sfikas and C. Williams, 237–268. Brookfield, Vt.: Ashgate.

Beller-Hann, I., and C. Hann. 2001. *Turkish Region: State, Market and Social Identities on the Black Sea Coast.* Oxford: James Currey.

Ben Ami, I. 1990. *Culte des saints et pèlerinages judéo-musulmans au Maroc.* Paris: Maisonneuve et Larose.

Benovska, M. 2006. "Friendship Groups in Leisure Time in Bulgaria: Examples from the Socialist and Postsocialist Period." Working Paper 86, Max Planck Institute for Social Anthropology, Halle, Germany.

Bensa, A., and E. Fassin. 2002. "Les sciences sociales face à l'événement." *Terrain* 38: 5–20.

Berque, J. 1955. *Structures sociales du Haut-Atlas.* Paris: PUF.

Blackman, W. 1948. *Les Fellahs de la Haute-Egypte.* Paris: Payot.

Blok, A. 2001. *Honour and Violence.* Cambridge: Polity.

Boratav, P. N. 1955. *Contes turcs.* Paris: Erasme.

Borromeo, Elisabetta. 2005. "Les catholiques à Constantinople: Galata et les églises de rite Latin au XVIIᵉ siècle." *Revue des mondes musulmans et de la Méditerranée,* nos. 107–110: 227–243.

Bougarel, X. 1996. *Bosnie: anatomie d'un conflit.* Paris: La Découverte.

Bourcart, J. 1922. *Les confins albanais administrés par la France (1916–1920): Contribution à la géographie et à la géologie de l'Albanie moyenne.* Paris: Delagrave.

Bowman, G. 1990. "Religion and Political Identity in Beit Sahour." *Middle East Report* 20, nos. 3–4: 50–53.

———. 1993. "Nationalizing the Sacred: Shrines and Shifting Identities in the Israeli-Occupied Territories." *Man: The Journal of the Royal Anthropological Institute* 28, no. 3: 431–460.

———. 2001. "The Two Deaths of Basem Rishmawi: Identity Constructions and Reconstructions in a Muslim-Christian Palestinian Community." *Identities: Global Studies in Culture and Power* 8, no. 1: 1–35.

———. 2007. "Nationalizing and Denationalizing the Sacred: Shrines and Shifting Identities in the Israeli-Occupied Territories." *Chronos: Revue d'histoire de l'Université de Balamand* 16: 151–207 (in Arabic).

Bozarslan, H. 2004. "Islam, laïcité et la question d'autorité dans l'Empire ottoman et en Turquie kémaliste." *Archives de Sciences Sociales des religions* 125: 99–113.

———. 2004. *Histoire de la Turquie contemporaine.* Paris: La Découverte.

Bringa, T. 1995. *Being Muslim the Bosnian Way: Identity and Community in a Central Bosnian Village.* Princeton N.J.: Princeton University Press.

———. 2002. "Averted Gaze: Genocide in Bosnia-Herzegovina, 1992–1995." In *Annihilating Difference: The Anthropology of Genocide,* ed. A. L. Hinton, 194–225. Berkeley: University of California Press.

Broun, J. 1993. "The Schism in the Bulgarian Orthodox Church." *Religion, State and Society* 21, no. 2: 202–220.

———. 2000. "The Schism in the Bulgarian Orthodox Church, Part 2: Under the Socialist Government, 1993–1997." *Religion, State and Society* 28, no. 3: 263–289.

Brown, P. 1971. "The Rise and Function of the Holy Man in Late Antiquity." *Journal of Roman Studies,* no. 61: 81–101.

———. 1981. *The Cult of the Saints: Its Rise and Function in Latin Christianity.* Chicago: University of Chicago Press.

———. 1987. "The Saint as Exemplar in Late Antiquity." In *Saints and Virtues,* ed. J. Stratford Hawley, 3–14. Berkeley: University of California Press.

Broz, S. 1999. *Dobri ljudi u vremenu zla: Sudionic i svedoci.* Banja Luka, Bosnia and Herzegovina: Prelom.

———. 2004. *Good People in an Evil Time: Portraits of Complicity and Resistance in the Bosnian War.* Ed. Laurie Kain Hart. New York: Other Press.

Brubaker, R. 1996. *Nationalism Reframed: Nationhood and the National Question in the New Europe.* Cambridge: Cambridge University Press.

Brune, F. 2004. *La Vierge de l'Egypte.* Paris: Le Jardin des livres.

Brunnbauer, U. 2004. *Gebirgsgellschafter auf dem Balkan. Wirtschaft und Familienstrukturen im Rhodopengebirge, 19.20. Jahrhundert.* Vienna: Bhöhlau.

Bryer, A. 1979. *The Late Byzantine Monastery in Town and Countryside.* Oxford: Basil Blackwell.

Buda, A. 1985. *Fjalor enciklopedik shqiptar* [Albanian Encyclopaedic Dictionary]. Tirana, Albania: Akademia e Shkencave e RPS të Shqipërisë.

Bulut, A. 2005. *Çift başli Yilan: Karadeniz'de yüzyılın ikinci rumlaştırma opersyonu.* Ankara: Uc Ock Yayıncılık.

Calotychos, V. 2003. *Modern Greece: A Cultural Poetics.* Oxford: Berg.

Campbell, D. 2003. *Nacionalna dekonstruckcija: Nasilje, identitet i pravda u Bosni.* Sarajevo: Forum Bosnae 21.

Canaan, T. 1927. *Mohammedan Saints and Sanctuaries in Palestine.* London: Luzac.

Carmichael, C. 2002. *Ethnic Cleansing in the Balkans: Nationalism and the Destruction of Tradition.* London: Routledge.

Carnoy, H., and J. Nicolaïdes. 1893. *Le folklore de Constantinople.* Paris: E. Lechevalier.

Carter, B. L. 1986. *The Copts in Egyptian Politics.* London: Croom Helm.

Ćeman, M. H. 2006. "Povijest, tipologija, struktura, funkcije i topografija grada u bosanskom ejaletu od 15. do 19. stoljeća." PhD thesis. ISH-Postgraduate School of the Humanities, Ljubljana, Slovenia.

Certeau, M. de. 1990. *L'invention du quotidien.* Tome 1: *Arts de faire.* Paris: Folio.

Chélini, J., and H. Branthomme. 1982. *Les chemins de Dieu: Histoire des pèlerinages des origines à nos jours.* Paris: Hachette.

Chiffoleau, S. 2006. "Fêtes et processions de Maaloula: Une mise en scène des identités dans l'espace d'un village chrétien." *Revue des mondes musulmans et de la
Méditerranée,* nos. 115–116: 173–189.

Christian, W. A. 1989a. *Person and God in a Spanish Valley.* 2nd rev. ed. Princeton, N.J.:
Princeton University Press.

———. 1989b. *Local Religion in Sixteenth-Century Spain.* Princeton, N.J.: Princeton
University Press.

Claverie, E. 1991. "Voir apparaître: Les 'événements' de Medjugorje." In *L'Evénement en
perspective,* special issue, *Raisons pratiques* 2: 157–176.

———. 2003. *Les guerres de la vierge.* Paris: Gallimard.

Clayer, N. 1990. *L'Albanie, pays des derviches: Les ordres mystiques musulmans
en Albanie à l'époque post-ottomane (1912–1967).* Wiesbaden, Germany: Otto
Harrassowitz.

———. 1996. "Les hauts lieux du bektachisme albanais." In *Lieux d'Islam,* ed. M. A.
Amir-Moezzi, 168–183. Paris: Autrement.

Clayer, N., and A. Popovic. 1995. "Balkans." In *Le Culte des saints dans le monde
musulman,* ed. H. Chambert-Loir and L. Guillot, 338–358. Paris: Ecole Française
d'Extrême-Orient.

Coleman, S. 2001. "Pilgrimage." In *International Encyclopedia of the Social and
Behavioural Sciences,* 11445–11448. London: Elsevier.

———. 2002. "Do You Believe in Pilgrimage? Communitas, Contestation and
Beyond." *Anthropological Theory* 2, no. 3: 355–368.

Comidas de Carbognano, C. 1992. *Descrizione topografica dello Stato Presente di
Constantinopoli arricchita di figure* (a cura di Vincenzo Ruggeri). Rome: Pontificio
Instituto Orientale.

Costert-Tardieu, F. 2005. *Un Réformiste à l'Université Al-Azhar: Oeuvre et pensée de
Mustafâ al-Marâghî (1881–1945).* Paris: Karthala; Cairo: CEDEJ.

Couderc, P. 1946. *Le calendrier.* Paris: Presses Universitaires de France.

Courbage, Y. 2007. "La Population de la Syrie." In *La Syrie au présent: Reflets d'une
société.* Coll. "Sindbad." Arles: Actes Sud.

Courbage, Y., and P. Fargues. 1992. *Chrétiens et juifs dans l'islam arabe et turc.* Paris:
Fayard.

Couroucli, M. 1992. "Le *lalein* et le *graphein,* parler et écrire en grec." *Revue des
mondes musulmans et de la Méditerranée* 75/76, nos. 1–2: 257–271.

———. 2002. "Le nationalisme d'Etat en Grèce. Les enjeux de l'identité dans la politique nationale, XIXᵉ–XXᵉ siècle." In *Nationalismes en mutation en Méditerrané
orientale,* ed. A. Dieckhoff and R. Kastoriano, 41–59. Paris: CNRS editions.

———. 2003. "Genos, ethnos, nation et Etat-nation." *Identités, Nations, Globalisation,
Ateliers,* no. 26: 287–299 http://ateliers.reunes.org/8737.

Crampton, R. J. 1997. *A Concise History of Bulgaria.* Cambridge: Cambridge
University Press.

Cuffel, A. 2003. "'Henceforth All Generations Will Call Me Blessed': Medieval Tales of
Non-Christian Marian Veneration." *Mediterranean Studies,* no. 12: 37–60.

———. 2005. "From Practice to Polemic: Shared Saints and Festivals as 'Women's
Religion' in the Medieval Mediterranean." *Bulletin of SOAS* 68, no. 3: 401–419.

Cushman, T. 2004. "Anthropology and Genocide in the Balkans: An Analysis of
Tradition." *Anthropological Theory* 4, no. 1: 5–28.

Deguilhem, R. 2003. "Le *wakf* dans l'Empire ottoman jusqu'en 1914." In *Encyclopédie de l'Islam,* 11:95–101. Leiden, The Netherlands: E. J. Brill.

Delaperriere, N., B. Lory, and A. Mares, A., eds. 2005. *Europe médiane: Aux sources des identities nationals.* Paris: Institut d'études slaves.

Delehay, H. 1909. *Les légendes grecques des saints militaires.* Paris: Picard.

Dermenghem, E. 1954. *Le culte des saints dans l'islam maghrébin.* Paris: Gallimard.

Derouet, B. 1995. "Territoire et parenté. Pour une mise en perspective de la communauté rurale et des formes de reproduction familiale." *Annales,* Edition de l'EHESS, no. 3: 645–686.

Dhima, A. 1989. "Vështrim antropologjik për zonën e Vakëfeve (Korçë)." *Etnografia shqiptare,* no. 16: 247–275.

Dibie, P. 2006. *Le village métamorphosé: Révolution dans la France rurale.* Coll. "Terre humaine." Paris: Plon.

Dizdari, T. 2005. *Fjalor i Orientalizmave në gjuhën shqipe.* Tirana, Albania: AIITC.

Dobreva, D. 2005. "Die Geistermesse in Stanimaka. Politische Implikationen eines interntionalen Erzählstoffes." *Bayerische Jahrbuch für Volskunde* (Munich): 93–101.

Donia, R. J. 2006. *Sarajevo: A Biography.* Ann Arbor: University of Michigan Press.

Doorn-Harder, N. van, and K. Vogt, eds. 1997. *Between Desert and City: The Coptic Orthodox Church Today.* Oslo: Novus Forlag, Institute for Comparative Research in Human Culture.

Doubt, K. 2000. "O latentnoj funkciji etničkog čišćenja u Bosni." *Forum Bosnae* 7–8: 44–54.

Douglas, M. 1966. *Purity and Danger.* London: Routledge.

Dousse, M. 2005. *Marie la musulmane.* Paris: Albin Michel.

Driessen, H. 1992. *On the Spanish-Moroccan Frontier: A Study in Ritual, Power and Ethnicity.* Oxford: Berg.

———. 2005. "Mediterranean Port Cities: Cosmopolitanism Reconsidered." *History and Anthropology* 1: 129–141.

———. 2009. "Local Religion Revisited: Mediterranean Cases." *History and Anthropology* 20, no. 3: 281–288.

Dubisch, J. 1995. *In a Different Place: Pilgrimage, Gender and Politics at a Greek Island Shrine.* Princeton, N.J.: Princeton University Press.

Duijzings, G. 2000. *Religion and the Politics of Identity in Kosovo.* London: Hurst.

Dundar, F. 1999. *Türkiye Nüfus Sayımlarında Azınlıklar* [Minorities in Turkish Censuses]. Istanbul: Doz Yaylınları.

Dupront, A. 1987. *Du sacré: Croisades et pèlerinages, images et langages.* Paris: Gallimard.

Durić, R. 1983. *Pjesme o Budalini Tali.* Banja Luka, Bosnia and Herzegovina: Glas.

Eade, J., and M. Sallnow. 1991. *Contesting the Sacred: The Anthropology of Christian Pilgrimage.* London: Routledge.

Efpraxiadis, L. 1988. "Prokopi Kappadokias, Thessalonica" (in Greek). Privately published by author.

Eldarov, S. 2004. *Orthodoxy on War: The Bulgarian Orthodox Church and Bulgaria's Wars, 1877–1945.* Sofia: Voenno Izdatelstvo (in Bulgarian).

Eliseu, Frei. 2007. "'Sent Antuan': uma igreja entre minaretes. Istambul: a terra onde S. Francisco lançou a semente de 'Paz e Bem.'" *Mensageiro de Santo António,* no. 2 (February).

El-Leithy, Tamer. 2006. " Sufi, Copts and the Politics of Piety: Moral Regulation in Fourteenth-Century Upper Egypt." In *Le développement du soufisme en Égypte à l'époque mamelouke*, ed. Richard Mc Gregor and Adam Sabra, 75–119. Le Caire, France: Institut français d'archéologie orientale.

Elsie, R. 2001. *A Dictionary of Albanian Religion, Mythology and Folk Culture.* London: Hurst.

Erlich, V. S. 1996. *Family in Transition: A Study of 300 Yugoslav Villages.* Princeton, N.J.: Princeton University Press.

Falo, D. 2003. *Tragjedia e Voskopojës.* Tirana, Albania: Shoqata kulturore Arumunët e Shqipërise.

Fernandez de Castro y Pedrera, R. 1991. *El Rif: Los territorios de Guelaia y Quabdana.* Málaga, Spain: Zambrano Hermanos.

Filipov, N. 1996. *Voden through the Centuries.* Assenovgrad, Bulgaria: Ecobelan (in Bulgarian).

Filipović-Fabijanić, R. 1978. "Verovanje u kurativnu moć kultnih grobova Srba i Hrvata u Bosni I Herceogovini." *Glasnik zemaljskog muzeja Bosne i Hercegovine u Sarajevu*, Etnologija, new series, 33: 57–84.

Foss, C. 2002. "Pilgrimage in Medieval Asia Minor." *Dumbarton Oaks Papers* 56: 129–151

Fotev, G. ed. 2000. *Neighbourhood of Religious Communities in Bulgaria.* Sofia: Institute of Sociology, Bulgarian Academy of Sciences (in Bulgarian and English).

Gellner, E. 1983. *Muslim Society,* Cambridge: Cambridge University Press, 1981.

———. 1983. *Nations and Nationalism.* Oxford: Blackwell.

Georgieva, T. 1995. "Coexistence as a System in the Everyday Life of Christians and Muslims in Bulgaria." In *Relations of Compatibility and Incompatibility between Christians and Muslims in Bulgaria,* ed. Zhel Yazkov, 151–178. Sofia: IMIR.

Georgoudi, S. 1979. "L'égorgement sanctifié en Grèce moderne: les 'Kourbania' des saints." In *La Cuisine du sacrifice en pays grec,* ed. M. Detienne and J. P. Vernant, 271–307. Paris: Gallimard.

Ghodsee, K. 2009. *Muslim Lives in Eastern Europe. Gender, Ethnicity and the Transformation of Islam in Postcolonial Bulgaria.* Princeton NJ: Princeton University Press.

Givre, O. 2006. *Un rituel "balkanique" ou un rituel dans les Balkans? Approche anthropoloqie du kourban en Bulgarie et en Grèce du Nord.* Doctoral thesis, Université Lumière-Lyon-II.

Gokalp, A. 1980. *Têtes rouges et bouches noires: Une confrérie tribale de l'Ouest Anatolien.* Paris: Société d'Ethnographie.

———. 1992. "Le règne de l'écriture pour oreilles averties." *Revue des mondes musulmans et de la Méditerranée* 75/76, nos. 1–2: 19–28.

Goody, J. 1990. *The Oriental, the Ancient and the Primitive: Systems of Marriage and the Family in the Pre-industrial Societies of Eurasia.* Cambridge: Cambridge University Press.

Greene, M. 2000. *A Shared World: Christians and Muslims in the Early Modern Mediterranean.* Princeton, N.J.: Princeton University Press.

Grigorov, V. 1998. "*Turbes* Venerated by the Bulgarian Muslims in the Central Rhodopes." In *The Muslim Culture in the Bulgarian Lands*, ed. R. Gradeva and S. Ivanova, 553–567. Sofia: IMIR.

Gruev, M. 2000. "On the Spread of Heterodox Islam among the Bulgarian Muslims." *Minalo* [The Past, Sofia] 2: 23–30 (in Bulgarian).

———. 2003. *Between the Red Star and the Crescent: Bulgarian Muslims and the Political Regime (1944–1959).* Sofia: IK Kota/IMIR (in Bulgarian).

Guirguis, L. ed. 2008. *Conversions religieuses et mutations politiques en Egypte: Tares et avatars du communautarisme égyptien.* Paris: Non-Lieu.

Habib Al-Misri, I. 2003. *Tarikh al-kanisa.* Cairo: Maktabat al-Mahabba.

Hadžijahić, M., M. Traljić, and N. Šukrić. 1977. *Islam i muslimani u Bosni i Hercegovini.* Sarajevo: Starješinstvo Islamske zajednice.

———. 1978–1979. "Sinkretistički elementi u islamu u Bosni i Hercegovini." *Prilozi za orijentalnu filologiju* 28–29: 301–328.

Hahn, J. G. von. 1854. *Albanesische Studien.* Jena, Germany: Fredrich Mauke.

Hart, L. K. 1992. *Time, Religion and Social Experience in Rural Greece.* Lanham, Md.: Rowman and Littlefield.

Hasluck, F. W. 1913–1914. "Ambiguous Sanctuaries and Bektashi Propaganda." *Annual of the British School at Athens* 20: 55–68.

———. 2000 (1929). *Christianity and Islam under the Sultans.* Vol. 1. Istanbul: Isis Press.

———. (1929). *Christianity and Islam under the Sultans.* Vol. 2. Oxford: Clarendon Press.

Hauschild, T., S. L. Kottman, and M. Zillinger. 2005. "Les syncrétismes en Méditerranée." In *Paix et guerres entre les cultures: Entre Europe et Méditerrané,* ed. E. La Parra and T. Fabre, 139–174. Arles: Actes Sud/MMSH.

Hayden, R. M. 2002a. "Antagonistic Tolerance: Competitive Sharing of Religious Sites in South Asia and the Balkans." *Current Anthropology* 43, no. 2 (April): 205–231.

———. 2002b. "Intolerant Sovereignties and 'Multi-Multi' Protectorates: Competition over Religious Sites and (In)tolerance in the Balkans." In *Postsocialism: Ideals, Ideologies and Practices in Eurasia,* ed. C. M. Hann, 159–179. London: Routledge.

———. 2005. "Inaccurate Data, Spurious Issues and Editorial Failure in Cushman's 'Anthropology and Genocide in the Balkans.'" *Anthropological Theory* 5, no. 4: 545–554.

Henein, N. H. 1988. *Marî Girgîs, village de Haute-Egypte.* Cairo: IFAO.

Hermkens, A. K., W. Jansen, and C. Notermans, eds. 2009. *Moved by Mary: The Power of Pilgrimage in the Modern World.* Abingdon, UK: Ashgate.

Herskovits, M. 1941. *The Myth of the Negro Past.* New York: Harper and Brothers.

Hertz, R. 1970 (1928). *Sociologie religieuse et folklore.* Paris: Presses Universitaires de France.

Hervieu-Leger, D. 2000 (1993). *Religion as a Chain of Memory.* New Brunswick, N.J.: Rutgers University Press.

Heyberger, B. 2001. *Hindyya: Mystique et criminelle 1720–1728.* Coll. "Historique." Paris: Aubier,.

Hirschon, R. 1989. *Heirs of the Greek Catastrophe: The Social Life of Asia Minor Refugees in Piraeus.* Oxford: Oxford University Press.

———, ed. 2003. *Crossing the Aegean: An Appraisal of the 1923 Compulsory Population Exchange between Greece and Turkey.* Oxford: Berghahn Books.

Holstein, H. 2002. "Etude: les apparitions mariales." *Cedrus Libani* (Dossier: *Le Mystère de Marie*), no. 65: 101–107.

Horden, P., and N. Purcell. 2000. *The Corrupting Sea: A Study of Mediterranean History.* Oxford: Blackwell.

Hörmann, K. 1888. *Narodne pjesne muhamedovaca u Bosni i Hercegovini.* Vol 1. Sarajevo: Zemaljska štamparija.

Hornby, L. G. 1927. *Balkan Sketches.* London: Brentano's.

Hoxha, G., and E. Hobdari. 2005. "Rapport préliminaire sur les fouilles archéologiques dans l'église Saint-Pierre (Shën Pjetri) à Voskopojë." In *Patrimoines des Balkans. Voskopojë sans frontières 2004,* ed. M. Durand, 121–129. Coll. Patrimoine sans frontières. Paris: Somogy Editions d'art.

Hristemova, M. 2005. "Un Registre obituaire du Monastère de Backovo du XVIIIe siècle." *Etudes Balkaniques* (Sofia: Institute for Balkan Studies) 4: 3–20.

Huntington, S. 1993. "The Clash of Civilisations?" *Foreign Affairs* 72, no. 3: 22–49.

Ilbert, R., and I. Yannakis. 1992. *Alexandrie 1860–1960: Un modèle éphémère de convivialité.* Paris: Autrement.

Ippen, T. 2002 (1908). *Shqipëria e vjetër.* Tirana, Albania: K & B.

Ivanova, S., ed. 2000. *Krastova Gora—The Useful Miracle: An Ethnosociological Study of the Sacred Center Krastova Gora.* Sofia: East-European Institute of Humanities (in Bulgarian).

———. 2001. "Holy Men and Utility: The *Turbe* of Sari Baba at Momchilovsti near Smolian." In *Ethnology of Sufi Orders: Theory and Practice,* ed. A. Zhalyazkova and J. Nielsen, 432–547. Fate of Muslim Communities in the Balkans 8. Sofia: IMIR.

———. 2005. "Muslim Charity Foundations (*Vakf*) and the Models of Religious Behaviour of Ottoman Social Estates in Roumeli (late15th to 19th centuries)." *Islam am Balkan,* special issue, *Wiener Zeitschrift zur Gesischte der Newzeit* 5, no. 2: 44–68.

Jalal Al-Azm, S. 1968. *Naqd al-fikr al-dini.* Beirut: Dar al-taliʿa lil-tibaʿa wa al-nashr.

Jezernik, B. 1998. *Dežela, kjer je vse narobe: Prispevki k etnologiji Balkana.* Ljubljana: ZPS.

Johler, R. 1999. "A Local Construction, or: What Have the Alps to do with a Global Reading of the Mediterranean?" *Narodna umjetnost: Hrvatski časopis za etnologiju i folkloristiku* (Zagreb) 36, no. 1: 87–102.

Johnston, F. 1980. *When Millions Saw Mary.* Tiverton, UK: Augustine Publishing.

Jullien, M. 1886. *L'arbre de la Vierge à Matarieh.* In *L'Egypte: Souvenirs bibliques et chrétiens.* Lille: Desclée de Brouwer.

Kanafani-Zahar, A. 2004a. "La réconciliation des druzes et des chrétiens du mont Liban ou le retour à un code coutumier." *Critique internationale,* no. 23: 55–57.

———. 2004b. *Liban: Le vivre ensemble. Hsoun, 1994–2000.* Paris: Geuthner.

Kanev, K. 1975. *The Past of the Village of Momchilovsti: A Contribution to the History of the Central Rhodopes.* Sofia: Oteestven Front (in Bulgarian).

Karamihova, M., and G. Valtchinova. 2009. "Talking War, 'Seeing' Peace: Approaching the Pilgrimage of Krastova Gora (Bulgaria)." *History and Anthropology,* 20, no. 3: 339–362.

Kechriotis, V. 2002. "From Trauma to Self-Reflection: Greek Historiography Meets the Young Turks' 'Bizarre Revolution.'" In *Clio in the Balkans,* ed. A. Christina, 91–108. Thessalonika: CDRSEE.

Keriakos, S. 2008. "Saintetés en partage: Mythes et enjeux du rapprochement entre chrétiens et musulmans autour des reliques et des apparitions de saints dans l'Egyzpte contemporaine (1968–2006)." Doctoral thesis, Aix-en-Provence/Geneva.

Keyder, C. 2002. "The Consequences of the Exchange of Populations for Turkey." In Hirschon, ed., *Crossing the Aegean,* 39–52.

Khawage, D. el-. 2001. *Le renouveau copte: La Communauté comme acteur politique.* Paris: IEP.

Kieser, Hans-Lukas. 1999. "Missions chrétiennes et identité ottomane." In *Figures anonymes, figures d'élite: pour une anatomie de l' "Homo ottomanicus,"* ed. M. Anastassiadou and B. Heyberger, 165–176. Istanbul: Isis.

Kirou, Trimi. 2003. "Quel cosmopolitisme à l'ère des nationalismes? La colonie grecque alexandrine (1882–1922)." *Cahiers de la Méditerranée* 67 (December): 177–199.

Konstantinov, Y. 1992. "An Account of Pomak Conversions in Bulgaria (1912–1990)." In *Minderheitenfragen in Südosteuropa,* ed. G. Seewan, 343–357. Sudest Institut München: R. Oldenbourg Verlag.

———. 1997. "Strategies for Sustaining a Vulnerable Identity: The Case of the Bulgarian Pomaks." In *Muslim Identity and the Balkan State,* ed. H. Poulton and S. Taji-Farouki, 33–53. New York: New York University Press.

Kostallari, A. 1980. *Fjalor i gjuhës së sotme shqipe.* Tirana, Albania: Akademia e Shkencave e RPS të Shqipërisë.

Kotzageorgi, X. 1999. *Oi Ellines tis Voulgarias. Ena istoriko tmima tou peripheriakou Ellinismou* [The Greeks of Bulgaria. A Historical Parcel of Peripheral Hellenism]. Thessalonika: IMHA.

Krämer, G. 1989. *The Jews in Modern Egypt, 1914–1952.* Seattle: University of Washington Press.

Kuper, A. 1994. *The Chosen Primate: Human Nature and Cultural Diversity.* Cambridge, Mass.: Harvard University Press.

Ladas, S. 1932. *The Exchange of Minorities: Bulgaria, Greece and Turkey.* New York: McMillan.

Lakhassi, A. 2002. *Ziyara to a Pilgrimage Center in Morocco: The Case of Sidi Hmad U-Musa (SHM).* Tokyo: Islamic Area Studies Project.

Landron, B. 1994. *Chrétiens et musulmans en Irak: Attitudes nestoriennes vis-à-vis de l'islam.* Paris: Cariscript.

Lane, E. W. 1904. *The Manners and Customs of the Modern Egyptians.* 2 vols. 5th ed. London: East-West Editions.

Leach, A. 1968. *Pul Eliya: A Village in Ceylon.* Cambridge: Cambridge University Press.

———. 1982. *Social Anthropology.* Glasgow: Fontana.

Lederman, R. 2005. "Unchosen Grounds: Cultivating Cross-Subfield Accents for a Public Voice." In *Unwrapping the Sacred Bundle: Reflections on the Discipline of Anthropology,* ed. D. Segal and S. Yanagisako, 49–77 Durham, N.C.: Duke University Press.

Lemerle, P. 1977. "Le Typikon de Grégoire Pakourianos." In *Cinq Etudes sur le XIe siècle byzantin.* Paris: Editions du CNRS.

Lockwood, W. G. 1975. *European Moslems: Economy and Ethnicity in Western Bosnia.* New York: Academic Press.

Lomouri, N. 1981. *Kistorii gruzinskogo Petritzongosko monastirja* [Contribution to the History of the Georgian Monastery of Petritzon]. Tbilissi, Georgia.

Lory, B. 1985. *Le sort de l'héritage ottoman en Bulgarie: l'exemple des villes bulgares, 1878–1900.* Istanbul: Institut français d'études anatoliennes and Association pour le développement des études turques.

———. 1989. "Ahmed Aga Tamraslijata: The Last Derebey of the Rhodopes." *International Journal of Turkish Studies* 4, no. 2 (Fall–Winter): 179–202.

———. 1993. "Strates historiques des relations bulgaro-turques." *Cahiers d'Etudes sur la Méditerrannée Orientale et le Monde Turco-Iranien* [CEMOTI, Paris], 15: 147–157.

Lovrenović, I. 2000. "Paradoxi bosanskoga konfesionalizma." *Forum Bosnae* 7–8: 112–120.

———. 2002a. *Bosanski Hrvati: Esej o agoniji jedne europsko-orijentalne mikrokulture.* Zagreb: Durieux.

———. 2002b. "The Voices of Sarajevo's Night." *Forum Bosnae* 15: 303–312.

Maček, I. 2000. *War Within: Everyday Life in Sarajevo under Siege.* Uppsala, Sweden: Acta Universitatis Upsaliensis.

Magdalino, P. 1989. "Honour among the Romanoi: The Framework of Social Values in the World of Digenis Akrites and Kekaumenos." *Byzantine and Modern Greek Studies* 13: 183–218.

Mango, C. 1980. *Byzantium: The Empire of New Rome.* London: Weidenfeld and Nicolson.

Mansell, P. 1997 (1995). *Constantinople: City of the World's Desire.* London: Penguin.

Maraval, P. 2004. *Lieux saints et pèlerinages d'Orient: Histoire et géographie des origines à la conquête arabe.* Paris: Cerf.

Martin, M. 1997. "Le renouveau dans son contexte." In Van Doorn-Harder and Vogt, eds., *Between Desert and City.*

Massicard, E. 2004. "L'Islam en Turquie, pays 'musulman et laïc.'" In O. Roy, *La Turquie aujourd'hui,* 55–67. Paris: Universalis.

Masson, J. 2001a. "Les coptes entre tradition et modernité." *Proche-Orient Chrétien* 51: 121–136.

———. 2001b. "Trente ans de règne de Shenouda III, pape d'Alexandrie et de toute l'Afrique." *Proche-Orient Chrétien* 51: 317–332.

Mayeur-Jaouen, C. 1992. "Un Jésuite français en Egypte, le R. P. Julien." In *Itinéraires d'Egypte: Mélanges offerts au père Martin.* Cairo: IGAO.

———. 2002. *Saints et héros du Moyen-Orient contemporain.* Paris: Maisonneuve et Larose.

———. 2005. *Pèlerinages d'Egypte: Histoire de la piété copte et musulmane, XVe–XXe siècle.* Paris: Editions de l'EHESS.

———. 2008. "Abûnâ Yassà: un pèlerinage copte orthodoxe de Haute-Egypte face aux coptes catholiques et musulmans." In *Pèlerinages et coexistences interconfessionnelles,* ed. Anne-Sophie Vivier-Muresan, special issue, *Chronos: Revue d'histoire de l'Université de Balamand* 18: 109–128.

McPherson, J. W. 1941. *The Moulids of Egypt: Egyptian Saint-Days.* Cairo: Nile Mission Press.

Meinardus, O. 1970. *Christian Egypt, Faith and Life.* Cairo: American University in Cairo Press.

———. 1987 (1963). *The Holy Family in Egypt.* Cairo: American University in Cairo Press.

Menarios, H. D. S. 1993. "Les apparitions de la Vierge à Jérusalem en 1954." *Le Monde copte,* no. 23: 83–84.

Mervin, S. 1996. "Sayyida Zaynub, banlieue de Damas ou nouvelle ville sainte chiite?" *Cahiers d'études sur la Méditerranée orientale et le monde turco-iranien,* no. 22 (July–December): 149–162.

M'halla, M. 1998. "Culte des saints et culte extatique en islam maghrébin." In *L'Authorité des saints: Perspectives historiques et socio-anthropologiques en Méditerranée occidentale,* ed. M. Kerrou, 121–131. Paris: IRMC-MAE.

Mile, L. K. 1984. *Çështje të historisë agrare shqiptare (fundi i skek. XVIII—vitet '70 të shek). XIX.* Tirana, Albania: Akademia e Shkencave e RPS të Shqipërisë.

Millas, H. 1988. *Prinkipos.* Athens: Melissa (in Greek).

Monciaud, Didier. 2002. "'Egyptien pour l'Egypte (1930–1931)', campagne nationaliste économique et controverses sur l'identité." In *Débats intellectuels au Moyen-Orient dans l'entre-deux-guerres,* special issue, *Revue des mondes musulmans et de la Méditerranée,* no. 95–98, March: 355–380.

Moranjak-Bamburać, N. 2001. "On the Problem of Cultural Syncretism in Bosnia and Herzegovina." *Wiener slawistische Almanach* (Vienna and Munich), *Bosnien-Herzegowina: Interkultureller Synkretismus,* special issue, 52: 5–42.

Morinis, A. E., ed. 1992. *Sacred Journeys: The Anthropology of Pilgrimage.* Westport, Conn.: Greenwood Press.

Mouton, J.-M. 2003. "L'islamisation de l'Egypte au Moyen Age." In *Chrétiens du monde arabe,* ed. B. Heyberger, 110–126. Paris: Autrement.

Mujačić, M. 1972. "Međunacionalni odnosi u jednom gradu: Primer Dervente." *Gledišta* 11: 39–53.

———. 1973. "Susjedni odnosi u jednoj lokalnoj zajednici." *Sociologija sela* 11, no. 1: 39–53.

Murko, M. 1951. *Tragom srpsko-hrvatske narodne epike.* Vol. 1. Zagreb: JAZU.

Musa, Nabawiyya. 1999. *Târîkhî bi qalamî.* New ed. Cairo: Matba'aat al-mar'a wa l-dhâkira.

Neuberger, M. 2004. *The Orient Within: Muslim Minorities and the Negotiation of Nationhood in Modern Bulgaria.* Ithaca, N.Y.: Cornell University Press.

Nikočević, L. 2006. "State Culture and the Laboratory of Peoples: Istrian Ethnography during the Austro-Hungarian Monarchy." *Narodna umjetnost* 43, no. 1: 41–57.

Nil, M. 2000. *Les Apparitions de la Vierge en Egypte, 1968–1969.* 3rd ed. Paris: Téqui.

Niškanović, M. 1978. "Ilindanski dernek kod turbeta Đerzelez Alije u Gerzovu." *Novopazarski zbornik* 2: 163–168.

———. 1985. "Stanovništvo sela Gerzova u Bosanskoj Krajini." *Glasnik zemaljskog muzeja Bosne i Hercegovine u Sarajevu,* Etnologija, new series, 33: 131–160.

O'Leary, De Lacy. 1937. *The Saints of Egypt.* London: Society for Promoting Christian Knowledge.

Ors, I. R. 2006. "Beyond the Greek and Turkish Dichotomy: The Rum Polites of Istanbul and Athens." *South European Society and Politics* 1: 79–94.

Papagaroufali, E. 2005. "Town-Twinning in Greece: Reconstructing Local Histories through Translocal Sensory-Affective Performance." *History and Anthropology* 3: 335–347.

Peri, E. 2001. *Zagoria dhe traditat e saj. Monografi.* Tirana, Albania: Albin.

Pérouse, Jean-François. 2004. *La Turquie en marche: Les grandes mutations depuis 1980.* Paris: La Martinière.

———. 2005. "'Les non-musulmans' à Istanbul aujourd'hui: une présence en creux? Le cas de l'arrondissement de Fatih." *Revue des mondes musulmans et de la Méditerranée,* no. 107–110: 261–295.

Philipp, Thomas. 1985. *The Syrians in Egypt 1725–1975.* Stuttgart: Steiner.

Politis, N. 1978 (1914). *Eklogai* [Selected Greek Popular Songs]. Athens: Bayonakis.

Port, M. van de 1998. *Gypsies, Wars, and Other Instances of the Wild: Civilization and Its Discontent in a Serbian Town.* Amsterdam: Amsterdam University Press

Poujeau, A. 2007. "Les Monastères de Syrie: Ancrage sacré des Eglises et inscription politique dans le territoire national." *Théologiques* (Montréal) 15, no. 1: 95–112.

———. 2010. "Monasteries, Politics and Social Memory: The Revival of the Greek Orthodox Church of Antioch in Syria during the Twentieth Century." In *Eastern Christians in Anthropological Perspective,* ed. C. Hann and H. Goltz, 177–192. Berkeley: University of California Press.

Poulton, H. 1991. *The Balkans: Minorities and States in Conflict.* London: Minority Rights Publication.

Preston, J. J. 1992. "Spiritual Magnetism: An Organizing Principle for the Study of Pilgrimage." In *Sacred Journeys: The Anthropology of Pilgrimage,* ed. A. Morinis, 31–46. Westport, Conn.: Greenwood Press.

Rihtman-Auguštin, D. 1984. *Struktura tradicijskog mišljenja.* Zagreb: Školska knjiga.

———. 2000. *Ulice moga grada: Antropologija domaćeg terena.* Belgrade: Biblioteka XX vek.

Rivoal, I. 2000. *Les maîtres du secret: Ordre mondain et ordre religieux dans la communauté druze en Israël.* Paris: Editions de l'EHESS.

———. 2002. "Penser l'identité communautaire et les frontières sociales." *Lucette Valensi à l'oeuvre: Une histoire anthropologique de l'islam méditerranéen.* Paris: Bouchène.

Rizvić, M. 1980. *Bosanskohercegovačke književne studije.* Sarajevo: Svjetlost.

———. 1994. *Panorama bošnjačke književnosti.* Sarajevo: Ljiljan.

Roksandić, D. 2003. *Triplex confinium: ili o granicama i regijama hrvatske povijesti, 1500–1800.* Zagreb: Barbat.

Sabbatucci, D. 2008. "Syncrétisme." *Encyclopaedia Universalis.* Encyclopaedia Britannica.

Sahlins, M. 1985. *Islands of History.* Chicago: University of Chicago Press.

Said, E. W. 1999. *Out of Place: A Memoir.* London: Granta.

Said, M. al-. 1986. "Qissat zuhu>r al-'Adhra'." *Al-Ahali,* 16 April.

Saint-Pierre, Ph. De. 2006a. "Rencontre avec le père Alphonse Sammut, prêtre en Turquie." *Le Messager de saint Antoine,* no. 1234 (November).

———. 2006b. "Saint Antoine à Istanbul." *Le Messager de saint Antoine,* no. 1234 (November).

Salama, U. 2000. "Marratan faqat aqarrathuma al-kanisa al-qibtiyya: usturat zuhur al-'Adhra' fi Misr." *Ruz al-Yusuf,* 15 September.

Sammut, Alfonso. 2006. "La Chiesa di Sant'Antonio di Istanbul." *Il Missionario Francescano,* no. 7.

Saranti-Stamouli, E. 1931. "O Agios Georgios is tin Thrakin." *Mesaionika Grammata* 20: 146–169.

Sikimić, B., and P. Hristov. 2007. "Introduction." In *Kurban in the Balkans,* ed. B. Sikimić and P. Hristov, 9–14. Belgrade: Institute for Balkan Studies.

Sémelin, J. 2005. *Purifier et détruire: Usages politiques des massacres et des génocides.* Paris: Seuil.

Shankland, D., ed. 2004. *Archaeology, Anthropology and Heritage in the Balkans and Anatolia: The Life and Times of F. W. Hasluck 1878–1920.* 2 vols. Istanbul: Isis.

Shaw, S., and E. K. Shaw. 1977. *History of the Ottoman Empire and Modern Turkey.* Cambridge: Cambridge University Press.

Sidarouss, F. 1980. "Eglise copte et monde moderne." *Proche-Orient Chrétien* 30: 211–265.

Simić, A. 2000. "Nationalism as a Folk Ideology: The Case of Former Yugoslavia." In *Neighbors at War: Anthropological Perspective on Yugoslav Ethnicity, Culture and History,* ed. J. Halpern and D. Kideckel, 103–115. University Park: Pennsylvania State University Press.

Skendi, S. 1967. "Crypto-Christianity in the Balkan Area under the Ottomans." *Slavic Review* 26, no. 2: 227–246.

Sorabji, C. 2006. "Managing Memories in Post-War Sarajevo: Individuals, Bad Memories and New Wars." *Journal of the Royal Anthropological Institute* 12: 1–18.

———. 2007. "A Bosnian Neighbourhood Revisited: Tolerance, Commitment and *Komsiluk* in Sarajevo." In *On the Margins of Religion,* ed. J. de Pina-Cabral and F. Pine, 97–112. London: Bergahn.

Stahl, P. 1986. *Household, Village and Village Confederation in Southeastern Europe.* Trans. Linda Scales Alcott. East European Monographs. New York: Columbia University Press.

Stewart, C. 1994. "Syncretism as a Dimension of Nationalist Discourse in Modern Greece." In Stewart and Shaw, *Syncretism/Anti-Syncretism,* 127–144.

———. 1999. "Syncretism and Its Synonyms: Reflections on Cultural Mixture." *Diacritics* 3: 40–62.

Stewart, C., and R. Shaw, eds. 1994. *Syncretism/Anti-Syncretism: The Politics of Religious Synthesis.* New York: Routledge.

Stojanovski, A. 1979. "One Legend Affirmed." *Newsletter of the History Museum of Macedonia* 4: 53–57.

Sulo, A. 1997. *Qyteti muze i Beratit Popullsia.* Berat, Albania: UEGEN.

Sulo, B. 1999. "Deri kur me ulërimin e Balilit?" *Diaspora shqiptare,* no. 5: 29–31.

Tapova-Zaimova, V. 1989. "La Vie quotidienne d'après le *Typicon* du monastère be Backovo (1083)." In *I katheimerini zoi sto Vizantio* [Everyday Life in Byzantium]. Athens: Centre for Byzantine Studies.

Taussig, M. 1987. *Shamanism, Colonialism and the Wild Man: A Study in Terror and Healing.* Chicago: University of Chicago Press.

Theodossopoulos, D. 2006. "Introduction: The 'Turks' in the Imagination of the 'Greeks.'" *South European Society and Politics* 1: 1–32.

Thoumin, R. 1929. "Le culte de sainte Thècle dans le Jebel Qalamûn." In *Mélanges de l'Institut français de Damas,* 1:161–180. Beirut: Imprimerie catholique.

Tirtja, M. 1976. "Survivances religieuses du passé dans la vie du peuple (objets et lieux de culte)." Édition spéciale à l'occasion de la Conférence nationale des études ethnographiques en Albanie, *Ethnographie albanaise* (June): 49–69.

———. 2004. *Mitologjia ndër shqiptarë.* Tirana, Albania: Shkenca.

Todorova, M. 2004. "Conversion to Islam as a Trope in Bulgarian Historiography, Fiction and Film." In *Balkan Identities. Nation and Memory*, ed. M. Todorova. New York: New York University Press.

Torre, Angelo. 1995. *Il consumo di devozioni. Religione et comunità nelle campagne dell'Ancien régime.* Venice: Marsilio.

Troeva-Grigorova, E. 2010. "Biographies of a Saint: Memory and Identity of Muslim Bulgarians." *Ethnoscripts* 12, no. 1: 63–76.

Tsalikoglu, E. 1959. "My Expedition to Asia Minor in the Summer of 1959." Athens: Centre for Asia Minor Studies, File no. OD 56 (typed ms., in Greek).

Tsibiridou, F. 2000. *Les Pomaks dans la Thrace grecque: Discours ethnique et pratiques socioculturelles.* Paris: L'Harmattan.

Turner, V. W. 1969. *The Ritual Process: Structure and Anti-Structure.* London: Routledge and Kegan Paul.

———. 1974a. *Dramas, Fields and Metaphors: Symbolic Action in Human Society.* Ithaca: Cornell University Press.

———. 1974b. "Pilgrimages as Social Processes." In Turner 1974a, 166–230.

———. 1982. *From Ritual to Theatre: The Human Seriousness of Human Play.* New York: Performing Arts Journal.

Turner, V. W., and E. Turner. 1978. *Image and Pilgrimage in Christian Culture: Anthropological Perspectives.* Oxford: Basil Blackwell.

Valensi, L . 1986. "La Tour de Babel: Groupes et relations ethniques au Moyen-Orient et en Afrique du Nord." *Annales*, no. 4: 817–838.

———. 2002. *La Fuite en Egypte: Histoires d'Orient at d'Occident.* Paris: Seuil.

Valter, S. 2002. *La Construction nationale syrienne: Légitimation de la nature communautaire du pouvoir par le discours historique.* Coll. Moyen-Orient. Paris: CNRS Editions.

Valtchinova, G. 2000. "Entre mythe et histoire: Symbolisme de la Ville et de la Croix dans le pèlerinage de Krastova, en Bulgarie." *Revue des Etudes slaves* 72, nos. 1–2: 119–128.

———. 2005. "Krastova Gora et les réseaux de dévotion populaire orthodoxe dans les Rhodopes (Idée nationale, Orthodoxie et grécité au XXᵉ siècle)." *Etudes balkaniques*, no. 2: 45–67.

———. 2009. "Visionaries and the National Idea in Interwar Bulgaria: The Circle of the Orthodox Association *The Good Samaritan*." *Acta Ethnographica Hungarica* 54, no. 2: 265–285.

Vauchez, M. A., ed. 1996. *La Religion civique à l'époque médiévale et moderne (Chrétienté et Islam).* Actes du Colloque de Nanterre, 21–23 June 1993. Collection de l'Ecole française de Rome, no. 213. Rome: Ecole française de Rome.

Veer, P. van der. 1988. *Gods on Earth: The Management of Religious Experience and Identity in a North Indian Pilgrimage Centre.* LSE Monographs of Social Anthropology 60. London: Athlone Press.

———. 1994. "Syncretism, Multiculturalism and the Discourse of Tolerance." In Stewart and Shaw, *Syncretism/Anti-Syncretism*, 196–211.

Veličković, N. 2005 (1995). *Lodgers.* Evanston, Ill.: Northwestern University Press.

Viaud, G. 1978. *Magie et coutumes populaires chez les coptes d'Egypte.* Paris: Présence.

Vivier, A. S. 2005. "Quand le Caire se révèle copte: Traits et enjeux des pratiques de sociabilité des coptes orthodoxes dans Le Caire contemporain." *Revue des mondes musulmans et de la Méditerranée,* nos. 107–110 (September): 205–227.

———. 2006. "Chrétiens d'Orient entre intégration urbaine et ghetto: coptes du Caire et Arméniens d'Isfahan." *Proche-Orient Chrétien* 56: 66–96.

———, ed. 2008. *Pèlerinages et coexistences interconfessionnelles,* special issue, *Chronos: Revue d'histoire de l'Université de Balamand.*

Voile, B. 2004. *Les Coptes d'Egypte sous Nasser: Sainteté, miracles, apparitions.* Paris: CNRS Editions.

Voinot, L. 1948. *Pèlerinages judéo-musumans du Maroc.* Paris: Larose.

Vucinic, V. 2002. "CA Comment." *Current Anthropology* 43, no. 2 (April): 225–226.

Wensick, A. J., and A. Schimmel. "Shafâ'a." In *Encyclopédie de l 'islam.* Leiden, the Netherlands: Maisonneuve et Larose.

Weyl Carr, A. 2002. "Icons and the Object of Pilgrimage in Middle Byzantine Constantinople." In *Dumbarton Oaks Papers,* 56:75–92.

Wissa, Hanna. 2000 (1994). *Assiout: The Sage of an Egyptian Family.* Rev. ed. Sussex: Book Guild.

Yannakopoulos, G. 1995. *O teleutaios Ellinismos tou Renkioi* [The Last Hellenes of Renköy]. Asprovalta: Cultural Association of Asprovalta.

Yerasimos, S., ed. 1992. *Istanbul 1914–1923: Capitale d'un monde illusoire ou l'agonie des vieux empires.* Paris: Autrement.

Žanić, I. 1998. *Prevarena povijest: Guslarska estrada, kult hajduka i rat u Hrvatskoj i Bosni i Hercegovini 1990–1995. godine.* Zagreb: Durieux.

Zegginis, E. 2001 (1996). *O bektassismos sti Ditiki Thraki* [Bektashism in Western Thrace]. Thessalonica, Greece: Pournaras Press.

Zhelyazkova, A. ed. 1995. *Relations of Compatibility and Incompatibility between Christians and Muslims in Bulgaria.* Sofia: IMIR.

Žunić, D. 1998. "Neighbour and Fellow Citizen." In *Rasizam i ksenofobija: Prilozi za međunarodni skup "Interkulturalnost versus rasizem i ksenofobija,"* Beograd, 17.–19. *maj 1997,* ed. B. Jakšić. Belgrade: Forum za etničke odnose.

CONTRIBUTORS

DIONIGI ALBERA is Senior Researcher at the CNRS and director of the Institut d'Ethnologie Méditerranéenne, Européenne et Comparative (MMSH, University of Aix-en-Provence).

BOJAN BASKAR is Professor of Social Anthropology and Mediterranean Studies at the Ethnology and Cultural Anthropology Department of the University of Ljubljana.

GLENN BOWMAN is Senior Lecturer in Anthropology in the School of Anthropology and Conservation at the University of Kent, Canterbury, UK.

MARIA COUROUCLI is Senior Researcher at the CNRS (Laboratoire d'Ethnologie et Sociologie Comparative, Université Paris Ouest Nanterre-la-Défense) and Director of Greek and Balkan Studies at the Ecole Française d'Athènes (Greece).

GILLES DE RAPPER is a social anthropologist at the CNRS (Institut d'Ethnologie Méditerranéenne, Européenne et Comparative—MMSH, University of Aix-en-Provence).

HENK DRIESSEN is a cultural anthropologist and Professor of Mediterranean Studies at the Radboud University of Nijmegen, the Netherlands.

BENOÎT FLICHE is Researcher at the CNRS, Centre for Turkish and Ottoman Studies, at the École des hautes études en sciences socials (EHESS) in Paris.

SANDRINE KERIAKOS is Assistant Professor at the University of Geneva (Unit of Muslim Civilization and Arabic Language—Faculty of Arts).

CATHERINE MAYEUR-JAOUEN is Professor at l'Institut national des Langues et Civilisations Orientales (Paris).

ANNA POUJEAU is postdoctoral researcher at the University of Liège (Laboratoire d'anthropologie sociale et culturelle).

GALIA VALTCHINOVA, Ph.D. in History (Sofia, 1988) and D.Sc. in Ethnology (Sofia, 2005), is a senior researcher at the Bulgarian Academy of Sciences, Institute of Balkan Studies, Sofia.

INDEX

Abbasid dynasty, 221
'Abd al-Ghaffar, Sheikh, 163, 231
Abraham I, Patriarch, 176
Abu Zayd, Nasr Hamid, 151, 172n2
accommodation, 8
agency, 12, 60–61, 70, 223
Ahmeti Baba, 42
Al-Ahram (Egyptian newspaper), 182, 193, 200n19
Alaouite (Alawi) Muslims, 203, 216, 217n1, 223
Al-'Arabi (Egyptian newspaper), 198
Albania, 2, 7, 29–30, 115, 134, 229; clerical influence minimized in, 243; Greek border with, 39; Muslims in churches, 236, 237; sacrifices practiced by Christians in, 235–236; vestimentary coding in, 235. *See also* *vakëf* (shared holy place in Albania)
Albanian language, 23, 32, 36, 48n4
Albera, Dionigi, 7, 70
Alevi Muslims, 86, 90n27, 101
Alexander, legends of, 133, 134
Alexis I Comnenus, Emperor, 89n19
Algeria, 4, 224, 225
Ali (Prophet's son-in-law), 20, 54, 60, 179, 218n20
Alidun/Ilindan festival, 54, 55, 60, 234. *See also* Elias, St.
Anatolia, 94, 99, 224, 225, 229, 234; Anatolian calendars, ancient and medieval, 132; Greek refugees from,

122, 138nn7,8; mixed holy places, 6, 7; in Ottoman period, 2; religious mixing in, 119; shared sanctuaries in, 129; transreligious saints venerated in, 230–231. *See also* Turkey
animals, 42
"antagonistic tolerance," 17, 26
Antar, novel of, 134
anthropology, 54, 67, 119; comparative, 1, 4; Croatian, 62; cultural diversity and, 146; kinship and territory as essential notions in, 121
anti-Semitism, 52
"Anti-Semitism Is Foreign to the Muslims of Bosnia and Herzegovina" (Korkut), 52
anti-syncretism, 8, 11–13, 27n1
appropriation, 8
Arabian Nights, 134
Arabic language, 8, 30, 153, 181
Arab-Israeli war of 1967 (Six-Day War), 144, 145, 161, 192–193, 195, 200n19
Arabs, Christian, 96
Aramaic language, 101
Armenian Church of the Archangels (Istanbul), 98
Armenian genocide (1915), 2, 138n7
Armenians, 94, 96, 97; in Egypt, 152–153; Monophysite, 71, 89n19; in Ottoman Turkey, 125; at St. Anthony of Padua (Istanbul), 100, 101, 107; in Syria, 217n9

national unity and, 196; silence of the Virgin, 190–191

Zeneli Baba, 37, 41

ziyâra (pious visit), 8, 141, 157, 170

Zümbül Effendi, tomb of, 94–95, 224

www.ingramcontent.com/pod-product-compliance
Ingram Content Group UK Ltd.
Pitfield, Milton Keynes, MK11 3LW, UK
UKHW020003310125
454458UK00010B/603